THE
NEW BOOK
OF
KNOWLEDGE
ANNUAL

THE
NEW BOOK
OF
KNOWLEDGE
ANNUAL
2008

HIGHLIGHTING EVENTS OF 2007

⟿The Young People's Book of the Year⟾

Scholastic Library Publishing, Inc.
Danbury, Connecticut

ISBN-13: 978-0-545-03757-0
ISBN-10: 0-545-03757-3

ISSN: 0196-0148

The Library of Congress Catalog Card Number: 79-26807

STAFF

FERN L. MAMBERG
EDITORIAL DIRECTOR

DEBBIE A. LOFASO
CREATIVE DIRECTOR

JOHN PERRITANO
SENIOR EDITOR

SUSAN PETRUZZI
PHOTO RESEARCHER

LIGHTHOUSE INDEXING PLUS
INDEXER

FRANCINE O'BUM
PRODUCTION MANAGER

YOUNG PEOPLE'S PUBLICATIONS

VIRGINIA QUINN MCCARTHY
EDITOR IN CHIEF

EDITORIAL STAFF
ELAINE HENDERSON
Executive Editor

MICHAEL JIMENEZ
Senior Art Director

SARA A. BOAK
MATTHEW ZIEM
KEVIN M. MAYER
EVELYN SAMORÉ
PATRICIA A. BEHAN
PATRICIA RAETHER
ROSEMARIE KENT

CONTENTS

10 In the Pages of This Book. . .

12 THE WORLD IN 2007
14 The Year at a Glance
18 January
20 February
22 March
24 April
26 May
28 June
30 July
32 August
34 September
36 October
38 November
40 December
42 Militants on the Rise
48 The War in Iraq
52 The Web Explosion
58 Cuba: Looking Ahead
62 Around the World
68 Newsmakers

74 ANIMALS
76 Animal Antics
84 Where Have All the Honeybees Gone?
86 Mythical Creatures: Animals
      That Never Were
92 What's in a Name?
94 Koalas: Living Teddy Bears
98 Animals in the News

104 SCIENCE
106 Climate Chaos!
112 Full Steam Ahead!
116 The Inside Scoop on Ice Cream
122 Water Lilies—Floating Gardens
128 Light for Health
132 Fossils: Records of Earth's Past
138 Space Briefs

144 MAKE AND DO
146 Inviting Birds to Your Backyard
152 It's Game Time. . .
154 Paper Stained Glass
156 Stamp Collecting
160 A Root in Your Soup
162 Crafty Characters
166 Many Friends Cooking
168 Coin Collecting

170 SPORTS
172 Baseball
175 Little League Baseball
176 Basketball
179 Football
182 Golf
183 Hockey
186 Ice Skating
186 Skiing
187 Swimming
188 Tennis
190 Sports Briefs

196 LIVING HISTORY
198 The 400th Anniversary of Jamestown, America's First Colony
204 Are You Superstitious?
208 Amelia Earhart—Pioneer Pilot
212 The New Seven Wonders of the World
216 The Ins and Outs of Fads
222 Franklin Delano Roosevelt: A Remarkable Leader
226 Portrait of a Pirate

230 SPOTLIGHT ON YOUTH
232 Careers With Plants
240 2007 Kids' Choice Awards
242 Kid Stuff
248 WWW.Coolsites
250 Circus Smirkus

254 CREATIVITY
256 The Magic of Harry
260 2007 Academy Awards
262 It's Movie Time!
268 Louis Comfort Tiffany: Master Designer
274 2007 Emmy Awards
276 The Music Scene
282 People, Places, Events

288 FUN TO READ
290 The Plot to Kill Hitler
302 Best Books, 2007
304 Aladdin and the Wonderful Lamp
312 Poetry
314 Robin Hood and the Shooting Match

323 THE NEW BOOK OF KNOWLEDGE—2008
324 Penguins
329 Egypt
336 Ferdinand and Isabella
337 Handball
339 Feet and Hands
345 Disarmament
347 Gerbils
348 Germany
365 Guinea Pigs
366 Berlin
370 Hamsters
371 Fruits and Fruit Growing
376 Orangutans

377 SUPPLEMENT
378 Deaths
384 Independent Nations of the World
390 The United States
394 Canada

396 INDEX

414 ILLUSTRATION CREDITS AND ACKNOWLEDGMENTS

CONTRIBUTORS

deNAPOLI, Dyan
Former Senior Penguin Aquarist, New England Aquarium; Founder, THE PENGUIN LADY Educational Programming, including Penguin Rescue!; Penguins! Fascinating Facts and Tantalizing Trivia; Global Warming: A Problem for Penguins; Penguin Parade
PENGUINS

FOSTER, William C.
Former Director, United States Arms Control and Disarmament Agency
DISARMAMENT

GISHLICK, Alan D.
Visiting Professor of Geology, Gustavus Adolphus College
FEET AND HANDS

HUGHES, Meredith Sayles
Cofounder, The Food Museum at *foodmuseum.com;* Author, *Plants We Eat* series
(REVIEWER) FRUITS AND FRUIT GROWING

KORB, Lawrence
Former U.S. Assistant Secretary of Defense; Senior Fellow, Center for American Progress; Author, *A New National Security Strategy in an Age of Terrorism, Tyrants, and Weapons of Mass Destruction; Reshaping America's Military*
(REVIEWER) DISARMAMENT

KURTZ, Henry I.
Author, *The Art of the Toy Soldier; John and Sebastian Cabot*
THE PLOT TO KILL HITLER

MARIS, Gary L.
Senior Professor of Political Science, Stetson University; Author, *International Law: An Introduction*
BERLIN; GERMANY

MIKHAIL, MONA N.
Hagop Kevorkian Center for Near Eastern Studies, New York University; Author, *Seen and Heard: A Century of Arab Women in Literature and Culture; Images of Arab Women: Fact and Fiction*
(REVIEWER) EGYPT

O'CONNELL, Charles J.
Former Chairman, National Handball Committee of the Amateur Athletic Union (AAU)
HANDBALL

PASCOE, Elaine
Author, *South Africa: Troubled Land; Neighbors at Odds: U.S. Policy in Latin America; Racial Prejudice; Fooled You! Fakes and Hoaxes Through the Years; Freedom of Expression: The Right to Speak Out in America*
AROUND THE WORLD

PATENT, Dorothy Hinshaw
Faculty Affiliate, University of Montana; Author, *The Buffalo and the Indians: A Shared Destiny; Big Cats; White-Tailed Deer; Garden of the Spirit Bear; Animals on the Trail with Lewis and Clark; Biodiversity; Gray Wolf, Red Wolf; Prairie Dogs*
GERBILS; GUINEA PIGS; HAMSTERS

PHILLIPS, William D., Jr.
Professor of History and Director of the Center for Early Modern History, University of Minnesota; Coauthor, *The World of Christopher Columbus*
FERDINAND AND ISABELLA

SHUMAKER, Robert
Director of Orangutan Research, Great Ape Trust of Iowa; Member of the Advisory Board, Orangutan Conservancy; Author, *Primates in Question: The Smithsonian Answer Book*
ORANGUTANS

TESAR, Jenny
Author, *Science on the Edge: Stem Cells; Endangered Habitats; Global Warming; Scientific Crime Investigation; The Waste Crisis; Shrinking Forests; What on Earth Is a Meerkat?;* Coauthor, *Discover Science Almanac*
SPACE BRIEFS

VAN RYZIN, Robert
Editor, *Coins* magazine; Author, *Striking Impressions: A Visual Guide to Collecting U.S. Coins*
COIN COLLECTING

WARREN, Ruth
Author, *First Book of the Arab World*
EGYPT

IN THE PAGES OF THIS BOOK . . .

How closely did you follow the events of 2007? Do you remember the people who made news during the year? What about the trends—what was in and what was out? Who won in sports? What were the top songs, films, and television shows? What important anniversaries were celebrated? All these helped to make up your world in 2007—a year that was like no other.

Here's a quiz that will tell you how much you know about your world—about what took place during the past year and about other things, as well. If you're stumped by a question, don't worry. You'll find all the answers in the pages of this book. (The page numbers after the questions will tell you where to look.)

On January 1, 2007, Ban Ki-moon of (North Korea/South Korea/Central African Republic) took office as the eighth Secretary-General of the United Nations. (*18*)

In August, the team from _____ won the 2007 Little League World Series. (*175*)

Which TV stars won Emmy Awards in 2007 for best actor and actress in a comedy series? (*274*)

The crew of a New Zealand fishing boat in the waters near Antarctica captured the world's largest (colossal squid/giant tortoise/woolly mammoth) in February. (*20*)

In April, a high-speed train in the country of _____ traveled at 357 miles (575 kilometers) per hour, setting a speed record for railed vehicles. (*24*)

Which National League baseball team won its seventh World Series in October? (*172*)

The 400th anniversary of (Plymouth/Massachusetts Bay/Jamestown), England's first permanent colony in America, was celebrated in May. (*198*)

The year 2007 marked the 200th anniversary of the launch of Robert Fulton's successful steamboat up the Hudson River. The steamboat's name was _____ . (*112*)

How many times has ice-skater Kimmie Meissner won the gold medal at the U.S. Figure Skating Championships? (*186*)

James, an English (foxhound/springer spaniel/setter), was named America's top dog at the Westminster Kennel Club dog show in February. (*101*)

In the summer, the famous English soccer star David Beckham moved to the United States and joined the Los Angeles _____ . (*190*)

In 2007, a series of reports from a United Nations panel of 2,000 scientists confirmed that people are responsible for what major problem confronting Earth? (*106*)

(*Flotsam/The Higher Power of Lucky/Penny From Heaven*), the story of a 10-year-old girl, won the 2007 Newbery Medal as the best American literary work for children. (*302*)

In 2007, wildfires caused great destruction in California and in the European country of _____ . (*33, 38*)

In May, 13-year-old Evan O'Dorney won the 2007 Scripps National Spelling Bee by spelling the word "serrefine." What does the word mean? (*247*)

The United States removed the (bald eagle/hairy woodpecker/naked mole rat) from its list of endangered and threatened species in 2007. (*98*)

The San Antonio _____ defeated the Cleveland Cavaliers to win the 2007 National Basketball Association title. (176)

One of the most enduring fads celebrated its 50th anniversary in 2007. What fad was it? (216)

At the 2007 Grammy Awards, (Chris Brown/Carrie Underwood/Imogen Heap) was named Best New Artist of the Year. (281)

In January, Democratic Representative Nancy Pelosi became the first woman to hold the position of Speaker of the U.S. _____ . (69)

The 10th anniversary of the death of Diana, Princess of Wales, was marked during 2007. Where was a huge celebratory rock concert held for her? (73)

The seventh and final Harry Potter book was published in 2007. Its title is *Harry Potter and the Deathly (Gallows/ Wallows/Hallows)*. (254, 256)

The 2007 Academy Award for Best Motion Picture went to _____ . (260)

A former vice president of the United States won the 2007 Nobel Peace Prize. Name him. (69)

In July, the Great (Hall/Mall/Wall) of China was named one of the New Seven Wonders of the World. (213)

In 2007, millions of _____ , the most helpful and useful insects in the world, were mysteriously disappearing in North America. (84)

A Disney Channel made-for-TV musical—a sequel to the 2006 megahit—drew the largest audience in cable TV history in August. Name the movie. (283)

Golfer (Michelle Wie/Morgan Pressel/ Suzann Pettersen) became the youngest golfer to win a Ladies Professional Golf Association major tournament, on April Fools' Day. (182)

The main groups in war-torn Iraq are the Sunni Muslims, the Shi'ite Muslims, and the _____ . (48)

At the 2007 Kids' Choice Awards, which TV show did 40 million kids select as their favorite? (241)

The Labrador retriever is the most popular dog in the United States. The second most popular is the tiny (Yorkshire terrier/Chihuahua/Boston terrier). (101)

Roger Federer, the top-ranked male tennis player, won three Grand Slam events in 2007: the Australian Open, Wimbledon, and _____ . (188)

In November, oil spills fouled the waters of San Francisco Bay and the waters of what country 6,000 miles away? (39)

The 25th anniversary of the (Statue of Liberty/Vietnam Veterans Memorial/ Korean War Memorial) was marked in 2007. (284)

In 2007, Raúl _____ continued to lead Cuba, because his famous 81-year-old brother Fidel was still too ill to lead the country. (58)

In which country were Taliban fighters still attacking U.S. forces? (43)

The number of Web sites on the Internet was estimated to be (7/70/700) million. (52)

On December 2, 2007, President Hugo Chávez of _____ lost a vote that would have allowed him to serve an unlimited number of terms. (61)

THE WORLD IN 2007

An Iraqi child peeks out from a doorway as a U.S. soldier searches his family's home for weapons. The search was part of a neighborhood sweep in Baghdad, Iraq's capital. The number of U.S. troops stationed in Baghdad increased in 2007, the fifth year of the Iraq war. The increase was part of a larger "surge" that brought the number of U.S. troops in Iraq to more than 160,000. It was hoped that the additional troops would end fighting between rival Iraqi groups and bring order to the city and the country.

THE YEAR AT A GLANCE

The threat posed by global climate change took center stage in 2007. The U.S. war in Iraq and the rise of Islamic extremism were among other top concerns. But as always, the year brought lighter moments, too.

A WARMER WORLD

The Earth is growing warmer, and it will grow still warmer in the years ahead—unless people take action now. That was the conclusion of a series of reports issued in 2007 by a United Nations panel, of international scientists, the Intergovernmental Panel on Climate Change (IPCC).

For years, many scientists have been warning of climate change and pointing to the basic cause— the release of carbon dioxide and other heat-trapping gases, mainly through the burning of gasoline, oil, coal, and other fossil fuels. The IPCC confirmed that these "greenhouse" gases are building up in the atmosphere, trapping heat and causing the climate to warm. The effects are already being seen worldwide, but especially near the poles. There, the melting ice is threatening both polar bears (above) and penguins. And the effects are likely to get worse—causing rising sea levels, increased droughts, and powerful storms, and harming delicate ecosystems. The panel warned that these changes could have an impact on everything from crop production to public health.

The reports were meant to serve as a call to action, and the IPCC set out some of what needs to be done. To stop global warming— or at least reduce it—people will need to use energy much more efficiently. Power plants and factories will need to stop relying on fuels such as coal, which emit tons of carbon dioxide. People will need to turn to cleaner fuels, to renewable energy sources such as wind and solar power, and to new technologies such as hydrogen fuel cells.

New targets for cutting greenhouse-gas emissions were the focus of an international climate summit meeting in December 2007 in Bali, Indonesia. Despite the urgency, some nations—including the United States—weren't ready to agree to cuts. But Americans were taking action to reduce greenhouse gases individually and on state and local levels. And the IPCC shared the 2007 Nobel Peace Prize with former U.S. Vice President Al Gore (right), a leader on this issue, for their efforts to spread knowledge about the climate crisis.

IRAQ AND TERRORISM

The spread of radical Islam, the threat of terrorism, and the U.S. war in Iraq were interwoven threads in world events in 2007. The Iraq war, which began in March 2003 with a U.S.-led invasion that overthrew Iraqi dictator Saddam Hussein, entered its fifth year. U.S. troops fought Islamic terrorists, including members of Al Qaeda, the group that staged the September 11, 2001, attacks in the United States. And they tried to control fighting between Iraq's ethnic and religious factions.

Despite the soldiers' efforts, violence continued (left). In early 2007, U.S. President George W. Bush ordered a "surge" in U.S. troop levels, increasing the total to more than 160,000. The extra troops succeeded in improving security in some of the areas where violence was worst. But the increase in security wasn't matched by an increase in national unity, as had been hoped. The Iraqi government, elected in 2006, failed to pass legislation and take other steps to bring the warring factions together. Meanwhile, daily life was a struggle for Iraqis. And growing numbers of Americans were against the war, which was sure to be an issue in the upcoming 2008 U.S. presidential election.

In the Muslim world, anger over the U.S.-led war in Iraq was thought to be one of several factors fueling a spread of extreme forms of Islam. Al Qaeda appeared to be building a stronger following, and the threat of terrorist attacks by this and similar groups continued.

After the September 11 attacks, the United States had driven Al Qaeda from its bases in Afghanistan and overthrown the Taliban, the extremist Muslim militia that then ruled most of that country. But in 2007 Taliban fighters were on the attack in Afghanistan. And Al Qaeda was said to be operating from new bases just over the border, in Pakistan.

Iran, which is ruled by fundamentalist Muslim clerics, was another source of concern. Many people believed that Iran was seeking nuclear weapons. And this country has supported radical and terrorist groups in the Middle East. Among them is the Palestinian group Hamas (right), which has violently opposed Israel. This has stalled efforts to end the long conflict between the Palestinians and Israel and set up an independent Palestinian state. In 2007, in a violent split between the two major Palestinian factions, Hamas seized control of the Gaza Strip, one of two territories where the Palestinians have limited self-rule. The other territory, the West Bank, was under the control of the Fatah faction.

OTHER WORLD EVENTS

Years of diplomacy paid off when North Korea agreed to disable its nuclear facilities in 2007. North Korea had used the facilities to produce fuel for nuclear weapons, and there was hope that this Asian nation might now give up those weapons. But North Korea is ruled by a secretive dictatorship, and some experts warned that its leaders might plan to continue the weapons program under cover.

In several countries, powerful rulers took steps to consolidate their control during the year. Russia has had a democratic constitution since the early 1990's, when Communism collapsed and the old Soviet Union broke apart. But since taking office in 2000, Russian president Vladimir Putin (left) has gradually extended his control over the government, business, and the media. In 2007, Putin was in the last year of his second term. The constitution barred him from seeking a third term, but he seemed likely to keep power. In early December, he led his United Russia Party to overwhelming victory in parliamentary elections. Outside observers said the elections were unfair.

Like Putin, Venezuelan president Hugo Chávez has steadily gathered power over government and society. Chávez was first elected in 1998 with strong support from Venezuela's poor and has steered the country toward socialism. In 2007 he proposed changing the constitution to give the president sweeping new powers and allow him to stay in office for life. But in a December vote, Venezuelans rejected the changes by a narrow margin.

Cuba, one of the few remaining Communist countries, was on the brink of a new era. Fidel Castro, Cuba's longtime leader, turned 81 in 2007. Too ill to govern, he had turned over the job of running the government to his younger brother, Raúl. People were looking ahead and wondering what changes might come to Cuba after Fidel Castro's death.

New leaders took office in two important Western European countries. In May, Nicolas Sarkozy was elected president of France, succeeding Jacques Chirac. And in June, Gordon Brown replaced Tony Blair as Britain's prime minister and head of the Labour Party.

IN THE UNITED STATES

In the United States, a new Congress began work in January. Democrats were in control of both houses for the first time since 1994. And Representative Nancy Pelosi, a Democrat from California, became the new Speaker of the U.S. House of Representatives—the first woman ever to hold that position.

The focus turned to product safety in March, when many pet foods were recalled (right). The foods contained a chemical that sickened and killed cats and dogs throughout the United States. The problem was

16

traced to contaminated ingredients imported from China. Later in the year a number of other products from China, including toys and toothpaste, were recalled when they were found to contain harmful substances. Demands were made for higher standards and better oversight for imports.

An exceptionally long and severe drought spread across Alabama and into Mississippi, Tennessee, Georgia, and the Carolinas. Crops withered, pastures dried up, and cities such as Atlanta, Georgia, faced water shortages. The drought persisted through the fall, and climate scientists couldn't say when it would end.

Work continued on the *International Space Station,* with U.S. space shuttles once again delivering key equipment. One of the missions, in October-November, was extended to fifteen days so that astronauts could repair a torn solar wing on the *ISS* (right). The solar wings provide electric power on board the station. The repair was accomplished in a difficult spacewalk.

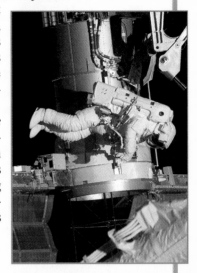

ON THE BRIGHT SIDE

Back on Earth, people could get reports on the shuttle missions—and just about anything else—by turning on their computers and logging on to the Internet. Through the service called the World Wide Web, the Internet had grown into a basic tool of everyday life. Millions of people were using it to work, learn, shop, play, share information, stay in touch with friends, meet new people, and much more.

New technology was also shaping the music world in 2007. CD sales were in a slump as fans continued to download their favorite tunes from the Internet. Listeners were also finding out about new artists and new releases online, and that helped singers and musicians find new audiences for their work.

Amazing computerized special effects and digital animation brought moviegoers to theaters. Among the summer's most popular films were sequels to hits of past years. *Harry Potter and the Order of the Phoenix,* the fifth movie in the Harry Potter series, was one of those. But an even bigger event for Harry Potter fans was the release of the seventh and final book in the series, *Harry Potter and the Deathly Hallows* (right), in July.

On television, *High School Musical 2* set a cable-TV audience record in August. A sequel to the 2006 made-for-TV movie *High School Musical,* it featured Zac Efron and other young stars of the first production. Another young star was 15-year-old Miley Cyrus. With the lead role in the popular cable-TV series *Hannah Montana,* a couple of albums on the music charts, and a sold-out concert tour, 2007 was definitely her year.

In sports, the Boston Red Sox swept the World Series, defeating the Colorado Rockies in four games. It was the second World Series championship in four years for the Red Sox, who until 2004 had failed to win baseball's top prize for 86 years. Their success was proof of the power of persistence.

JANUARY

1 South Korean statesman Ban Ki-moon became the eighth Secretary-General of the United Nations. He succeeded Kofi Annan of Ghana, who had served since 1997.

1 The former Communist countries of Bulgaria and Romania became the 26th and 27th members of the European Union (EU). Founded in 1957 as the six-member European Economic Community (EEC), the EU promotes political, economic, and social cooperation among its member states. (In March, the EU celebrated the 50th anniversary of its founding.)

5 The American Dialect Society voted "plutoed" the 2006 word of the year. "To pluto" something is to demote or devalue it. This is what happened to the planet Pluto in 2006, when the International Astronomical Union downgraded it from a true, or classic, planet to a "dwarf planet."

10 President George W. Bush announced that he would send more than 20,000 additional U.S. troops to Iraq in an effort to halt the violence there. The troop "surge" would bring the total number of U.S. troops in the country to about 160,000.

Government change in January: Following the formation of a coalition government in **Austria,** Alfred Gusenbauer became chancellor of the country. He replaced Wolfgang Schüssel, who had been chancellor since 2000.

For five days during mid-January, California suffered its worst freeze since 1947. Many crops were damaged when temperatures plunged to the 20's and teens. Hardest hit were the state's citrus crops, and the orange harvest was 39 percent below the previous year. Because California grows about 95 percent of the nation's navel oranges during the winter, prices rose nationwide.

President George W. Bush delivers his sixth State of the Union address to Congress. Behind him are Vice President Dick Cheney and Speaker of the House Nancy Pelosi—the first woman ever to hold that position.

President George W. Bush's State of the Union Address

"We've been through a lot together. We've met challenges and faced dangers, and we know that more lie ahead. Yet we can go forward with confidence—because the State of our Union is strong, our cause in the world is right, and tonight that cause goes on."

That was the message President George W. Bush brought to the U.S. Congress on January 23, in his 2007 State of the Union address. The State of the Union address, which is given every year to Congress, is a chance for the president to outline his plans for the year ahead. Here are some highlights of Bush's address:

Domestic affairs: The president proposed changes in health care and energy policies. He said he would submit a budget that would eliminate the nation's budget deficit in five years. And he said the government should cut spending instead of borrowing money without raising taxes. Bush also called for immigration reform, improvements in education, and strengthening the military.

Foreign affairs: Much of Bush's speech had to do with the Iraq war and the war on terrorism. He called on Americans to support his sending more U.S. troops to Iraq, and he called on Iraq's leaders to begin taking responsibility for security in every Iraqi province. "Our country is pursuing a new strategy in Iraq," Bush said, "and I ask you to give it a chance to work."

Democratic response: After a president gives a State of the Union address, a member of the opposing political party responds. In 2007, Virginia Senator Jim Webb gave the Democratic Party response. He said that sending more troops to Iraq wasn't the right answer. Webb called on Bush to withdraw troops, not increase their numbers.

FEBRUARY

2 Tornadoes spawned by fierce thunderstorms struck central Florida, north and west of Orlando. Because the storms struck around 3:00 A.M., when TV's and radios were off and most people were asleep, few people heard the warning. At least 20 people were killed, and some 1,500 homes, many of them trailers, were destroyed or severely damaged. Governor Charlie Crist declared a state of emergency in four counties, and President George W. Bush promised federal aid. Weather experts blamed the tornadoes on El Niño, a natural phenomenon that disrupts normal weather patterns around the world.

22 It was announced that a New Zealand fishing boat had caught a rare colossal squid in the frigid waters of Antarctica. The squid weighed 1,089 pounds (494 kilograms) and was 33 feet (10 meters) long. Scientists believe it was the largest colossal squid ever landed. The crew had to battle with the squid for two hours before it could be hauled onto the ship. It was then frozen and taken to New Zealand, where it was delivered to New Zealand's national museum. Marine biologists at the museum planned to defrost and study the colossal squid, whose scientific name is *Mesonychoteuthis hamiltoni.*

Government change in February: In national elections in **Turkmenistan,** Kurbanguly Berdymukhamedov was elected president. He replaced Saparmurat Niyazov, who had been president from 1992 until his death in December 2006.

The world's largest colossal squid is brought aboard a New Zealand fishing boat in the Ross Sea, near Antarctica. The gigantic sea creature was dining on a hooked toothfish when it was hauled from the deep.

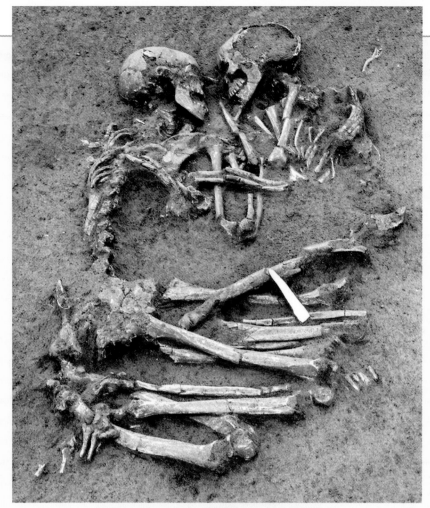

A Stone Age hug: These fossils of an embracing prehistoric couple were found in northern Italy.

A Prehistoric Hug

In early February, Italian archaeologists unearthed the skeletons of a young couple who had lived 5,000 to 6,000 years ago, in the late Neolithic period. The man and woman were found with their arms wrapped around each other—the first known Stone Age couple to be buried together, hugging.

"It was a very emotional discovery," said archaeologist Elena Menotti, who had led the dig. "From thousands of years ago, we feel the strength of this love," she said.

That thousands-of-years-old love reminded people of another Italian love story: William Shakespeare's *Romeo and Juliet.* The skeletons were found outside of the city of Mantua, which isn't far from Verona—the city in northern Italy that was the setting for *Romeo and Juliet.*

Experts have determined that the prehistoric couple were probably young when they died, because their teeth were in good shape. And the fact that they were found together indicated that they had probably died a sudden death.

In addition to the skeletons, the archaeologists uncovered arrowheads, a knife, and other flint tools. The skeletons and the other artifacts will be studied to determine their exact age. Then they will be put on display at the Mantua Archaeological Museum. The display will show the skeletons just as they were found—together.

MARCH

14 U.S. President George W. Bush, with First Lady Laura Bush, ended a five-nation, weeklong trip to Latin America. Bush visited Brazil, Uruguay, Colombia, and Guatemala. His final stop was in Mexico, where he met with Felipe Calderón, that nation's new president. Their main topic of discussion was about the millions of illegal Mexican immigrants living in the United States.

26 In a historic meeting, Roman Catholic leader Gerry Adams and Protestant leader Ian Paisley met face-to-face for the first time ever and agreed to form a joint administration in Northern Ireland, which is part of the United Kingdom. (Paisley and Catholic political leader Martin McGuinness were sworn in on May 8—each with equal power in the new government.) It was hoped that the alliance would finally end decades of Catholic-Protestant violence and thousands of deaths in Northern Ireland.

Government change in March: In national elections in **Mauritania,** Sidi Ould Cheikh Abdallahi was elected president. He replaced Ely Ould Mohamed Vall, who had led the country since 2005.

The Grand Canyon Skywalk in Arizona was dedicated on March 20 and opened to the public a week later. The horseshoe-shaped, glass-bottomed walkway juts out 70 feet (21 meters) from the Canyon's West Rim, some 4,000 feet (1,220 meters) above the Colorado River. It was built by the Hualapai Indians, who own the land. Visitors who took part in the ceremonial "first steps" on the Skywalk included former astronaut Buzz Aldrin, who walked on the moon in 1969.

Which pet food should I buy? This question was on the minds of pet-owning consumers after the recall of more than 100 brands of tainted cat and dog food.

A Massive Pet-Food Recall

A nationwide recall of pet foods began in the United States on March 16, when it was learned that certain foods were sickening and killing cats and dogs. In the following weeks, manufacturers voluntarily recalled more than 100 brands of dog and cat foods. Most were canned or pouch-type products made by Menu Foods, Inc., and sold under different brand names.

The U.S. Food and Drug Administration (FDA) launched an investigation. FDA scientists tested pet-food samples and found that two vegetable proteins in the foods—wheat gluten and rice protein concentrate—had been contaminated. They contained melamine, a material used in plastics. Melamine isn't highly toxic, but little is known about its effects on dogs and cats. Initially, just 16 food-related deaths of cats and dogs were confirmed. But the FDA received thousands of reports of pets suffering kidney damage from eating the tainted foods.

The contaminated ingredients in the recalled pet foods were traced to specific companies in China. It was thought that these companies had added ground-up melamine scrap to wheat gluten and similar products. Thus, when the products were tested for protein levels, the melamine made the products seem higher in protein than they actually were. The FDA barred imports from these companies. It also began to test all wheat gluten and similar products imported from China.

In the following months, other products from China were found to be unsafe. Among them were toothpaste containing a toxic chemical, toys containing lead, seafood containing banned substances, and a snack food contaminated with salmonella bacteria. This led to demands for more testing and stricter safety standards for Chinese manufacturers.

APRIL

3 A French high-speed bullet train, the V150, traveled at a speed of 357 miles (575 kilometers) an hour, setting a new world record for railed vehicles. The previous record, 320 miles (515 kilometers) an hour, had been set by another French high-speed train in 1990. The V150 came close to breaking the speed record for any train, which was set by Japan's magnetically levitated (maglev) train in 2003. The maglev, which doesn't touch its rails, traveled at a speed of 361 miles (581 kilometers) an hour.

17 Zalmay Khalilzad became U.S. Ambassador to the United Nations. He succeeded John Bolton, who had held the position for 16 months. Khalilzad was nominated by President George W. Bush in February 2007 and was unanimously confirmed by the U.S. Senate. He became the highest-ranking Muslim in the U.S. government. Previously, Khalilzad had served as U.S. Ambassador to Afghanistan (2003–05) and to Iraq (2005–07).

Government changes in April: In national elections in **Nigeria,** Umaru Musa Yar'Adua was elected president. He succeeded Olusegun Obasanjo, who had been president since 1999. . . .In **North Korea,** Kim Yong Il was appointed premier. He replaced Pak Pong Chu, who had served in that position since 2003. . . . .In **South Korea,** Han Duck Soo was named premier. He replaced Han Myeong Sook, who had been premier since 2006.

France's V150 bullet train set a world speed record in April, traveling 357 miles (575 kilometers) an hour. France, along with Germany and Japan, is a leader in high-speed trains, and has 400 such trains in service. They operate on about 1,100 miles (1,770 kilometers) of special track.

Mourners gather at a makeshift memorial on the Virginia Tech campus to pay tribute to the 32 victims of the mass shooting there.

Mass Shooting at Virginia Tech

The worst mass shooting in U.S. history took place on April 16, at Virginia Polytechnic Institute and State University (Virginia Tech) in Blacksburg, Virginia. A student, Cho Seung-Hui, opened fire in a dormitory and a classroom building, killing 27 students and five teachers. Then he turned the gun on himself.

Like others who have carried out mass shootings, Cho, 23, was said to be a loner. A South Korean, he had immigrated to the United States when he was 8, with his family. His former high-school classmates in Centreville, Virginia, said he sometimes had been teased and bullied. Few people at Virginia Tech knew him. Those who did sensed that he was deeply troubled. He seldom spoke. For creative-writing classes he wrote stories, poems, and plays filled with anger and violence. In late 2005, a Virginia court ordered him to get psychiatric treatment. But no one followed up, and he didn't get treatment.

The shooting raised many questions. What could have been done to prevent Cho from being a danger? Could the campus have been made more secure? And why was Cho able to buy the guns he used? Under federal law, a person ordered by a court to get psychiatric treatment may not buy a gun. But in 2006, Cho bought two guns legally under Virginia law. After the shooting, Virginia quickly closed the loophole that allowed those sales.

Virginia Tech wasn't the first U.S. school to be the scene of a mass shooting. One of the most shocking such events took place in 1999 at Columbine High School in Jefferson County, Colorado. Twelve students and a teacher were killed there. Since then, officials had worked hard to prevent similar events and to identify signs that a troubled student might turn to violence.

MAY

4 A mile-wide tornado with winds exceeding 205 miles (330 kilometers) an hour leveled the town of Greensburg in southwestern Kansas. About 95 percent of the town was destroyed, and at least ten people were killed. The tornado was an F-5, the highest possible rating, on the scale that measures the strength of tornadoes according to the damage they cause. Greensburg's Kiowa County was declared a disaster area by the federal government.

25 President George W. Bush signed into law a bill raising the federal minimum wage from $5.15 per hour to $7.25 per hour. In a three-stage increase, the minimum wage would go to $5.85 per hour on July 24, 2007; to $6.55 per hour on July 24, 2008; and to $7.25 per hour on July 24, 2009. It was the first time in ten years that the federal minimum wage had been increased.

Government changes in May: In **East Timor,** José Ramos-Horta won the runoff presidential election. He replaced Kay Rala Xanana Gusmao, who had been president since 2002. . . .In presidential elections in **France,** Nicolas Sarkozy was elected president; he succeeded Jacques Chirac, who had been president since 1995.

On May 8, an Israeli archaeologist announced the discovery of the tomb of King Herod (the Great). Herod was king of Judea from 37 to 4 B.C., when it and the rest of the Holy Land were ruled by the Romans. Herod built a hilltop palace fortress called Herodium, 7 miles (12 kilometers) south of Jerusalem. It was at Herodium (below) that the archaeologists, who had been digging there for 35 years, found Herod's gravesite.

Queen Elizabeth II visited Jamestown, Virginia, during her royal trip to the United States. (She is shown here accompanied by Vice President Dick Cheney.)

A Royal Visit to America

Great Britain's Queen Elizabeth II, accompanied by her husband Prince Philip, the Duke of Edinburgh, paid a six-day (May 3-8) state visit to the United States. This was the royal couple's fourth state visit to the United States; the last one was in 1991, when George H. W. Bush, the father of President George W. Bush, was president.

Here are some of the highlights of the 81-year-old monarch's visit:

■ On May 4, the Queen visited Jamestown, the site of England's first permanent American settlement. Jamestown, founded in 1607, was celebrating its 400th anniversary. The Queen had also visited Jamestown 50 years earlier, in 1957, to celebrate its 350th anniversary.

■ Two days later, the Queen watched the 133rd running of the Kentucky Derby, at Churchill Downs in Louisville, Kentucky. Queen Elizabeth is an avid horse enthusiast, and the Kentucky Derby is the most famous horse race in the United States.

■ Queen Elizabeth and Prince Philip—along with 130 other guests—attended a formal dinner at the White House, in Washington, D.C., on May 7. President George W. Bush and First Lady Laura Bush hosted the lavish affair. Both the Queen and President Bush remarked on the close ties between their countries. On the last night of her visit, the Queen hosted a dinner at the British embassy for President Bush and other Washington dignitaries.

Sarkozy named François Fillon premier; he replaced Dominique de Villepin, who had been premier since 2005. . . .In **Latvia,** Valdis Zatlers was named president by the nation's parliament. He succeeded Vaira Vike-Freiberga, who had been president since 1999. . . .Chang Chun-hsiung was named premier of **Taiwan.** He replaced Su Tseng-chang, who had held that position since 2006.

JUNE

15 The world's longest rail tunnel on land opened in the Bernese Alps in southern Switzerland. Called the Lötschberg Base Tunnel, it is 21.5 miles (34.6 kilometers) long. The length surpasses that of Japan's Hakkoda Tunnel, the previous record holder at 16.4 miles (26.5 kilometers). But Japan's undersea Seikan Tunnel, which is 33.5 miles (53.9 kilometers) long, remains the longest railway tunnel in the world.

22 The space shuttle *Atlantis* ended a two-week trip to the *International Space Station (ISS)*. The *Atlantis* crew consisted of Commander Frederick Sturckow; pilot Lee Archambault; and mission specialists Patrick Forrester, Steven Swanson, John Olivas, James Reilly, and Clayton Anderson. Anderson stayed on the *ISS,* replacing Sunita Williams, who returned to Earth aboard the *Atlantis.* Williams had been in space for 194 days, 18 hours, and 58 minutes—a record for female astronauts and cosmonauts.

Government changes in June: Tony Blair, prime minister of **Great Britain** since 1997, resigned. He was succeeded by Gordon Brown, Chancellor of the Exchequer. . . .In **Israel,** the parliament elected former prime minister Shimon Peres president. He replaced Moshe Katsav, who had been president since 2000. . . . In **Samoa,** Tupuolo Taisi Tufuga Efi was named head of state by the nation's parliament. He replaced Malietoa Tanumafili II, head of state from 1962 until his death in May 2007.

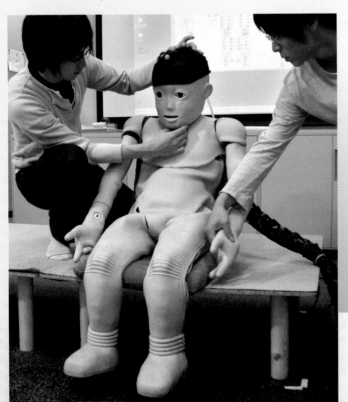

Japanese scientists developed a robot that acts like a real child. The Child Robot with Biomimetic Body, or CB2, is 4.3 feet (1.3 meters) tall and weighs 73 pounds (33 kilograms). It has 56 pneumatic muscles, 197 sensors for touch, cameras for eyes, and an artificial vocal cord. The robot toddler changes facial expressions, crawls, speaks, and wobbles like a 1- or 2-year-old. The researchers, who are studying child development, are trying to raise CB2's "intelligence" level to that of a 3-year-old.

Chatting in a giant beach chair at the G-8 meeting in Germany: Japanese Premier Shinzo Abe, Canadian Prime Minister Stephen Harper, French President Nicolas Sarkozy, Russian President Vladimir Putin, German Chancellor Angela Merkel, U.S. President George W. Bush, British Prime Minister Tony Blair, Italian Premier Romano Prodi, and EU Commission President José Manuel Barroso.

President Bush Meets With World Leaders

President George W. Bush visited six European nations between June 5 and June 11. The main purpose of his trip was to attend the summit meeting in Germany of the leaders of the major industrialized nations, known as the Group of Eight (G-8). On his way to Germany, Bush stopped in the Czech Republic; he spoke about locating part of a U.S. missile-defense system in that country—a move strongly opposed by President Vladimir Putin of Russia.

Bush then traveled to the G-8 meeting, which was held at Heiligendamm, a resort town in Germany. The G-8 consists of Canada, France, Germany, Great Britain, Italy, Japan, Russia, and the United States.

The two major topics discussed at the G-8 meeting were global warming and aid to Africa. The nations said they would aim to cut carbon-dioxide emissions by 50 percent by the year 2050. But the United States wouldn't agree to mandatory limits on the emissions. The G-8 leaders promised to provide Africa—the poorest continent—with debt relief and other aid; as well as $60 billion to fight AIDS, tuberculosis, and malaria.

During the meeting, Bush met with Russian President Putin to further discuss the U.S. plan for a missile-defense system in Eastern Europe. Following the G-8 meeting, Bush traveled to Poland, Italy, Albania, and Bulgaria.

(In July, Putin traveled to the Bush family home in Kennebunkport, Maine, for additional discussions on the missile-defense system and the generally strained U.S.-Russian relations.)

JULY

1   British police completed a roundup of suspected terrorists after two car bombs were found and defused in London, England, on June 29; and a Jeep was rammed into an entrance of the Glasgow (Scotland) International Airport and set ablaze on June 30. Two men living in England—a British-born Iraqi Muslim and an Indian-born Muslim—were captured at the Glasgow airport. Police suspected that the two, a doctor and an engineer, were also responsible for the London incident. Others were also charged in the case.

14   Russian President Vladimir Putin suspended Russia's participation in the Treaty on Conventional Armed Forces in Europe. The treaty was conceived during the Cold War and ratified in 1992, a year after the Soviet Union collapsed. It limited the number of troops, heavy artillery, and combat aircraft in Europe. It applied to the United States and its North Atlantic Treaty Organization (NATO) allies; and to Russia and its former Soviet republics, as well as to the former Warsaw Pact nations. Putin's actions came amid worsening U.S.-Russian relations. Russia resented that its former allies were joining NATO. And Putin attacked U.S. plans to build a missile-defense system in Poland and the Czech Republic.

Government changes in July: In **Albania**, the parliament elected Bamir Topi as president. He succeeded Alfred Moisiu, who had been president since 2002. . . .In **India**, Pratibha Patil was elected the country's first female president. She succeeded A.P.J. Abdul Kalam, who had held the office since 2002.

Russian scientists announced that the frozen carcass of a 10,000-year-old baby mammoth had been discovered in Siberia by a reindeer herder. The carcass was 4 feet (1.2 meters) long, and was thought to be a 6-month-old female. It was so well preserved that the trunk and eyes were nearly intact, and there was even some fur remaining. Mammoths are prehistoric elephants that lived from 4.8 million to 4,000 years ago. Climate change or over-hunting by humans probably brought about their extinction.

The 82nd annual Wild Pony Swim was held on July 25, 2007—and more than 40,000 people cheered the ponies on!

A Wild Pony Swim

The Chincoteague Wild Pony Swim, held annually since 1925, takes only about three minutes, but it's a world-famous event. Every July, dozens of wild ponies swim across the narrow channel between Assateague and Chincoteague islands, on the Eastern Shore of Virginia. Some 40,000 spectators were on hand to watch the 2007 swim on July 25, and millions more watched on television.

Assateague is mostly wild, and wild ponies have been there for 300 years. The first ponies may have swum ashore from a ship that ran aground. Today there are two herds on Assateague, which is divided between Maryland and Virginia. In the northern part of the island, the Maryland part, the National Park Service watches over one herd. In the southern part of Assateague, the Virginia herd belongs to the Chincoteague Volunteer Fire Company.

The pony swim is a fund-raiser for the Chincoteague Volunteer Fire Company. Each year on the last Wednesday in July, Chincoteague "saltwater cowboys" separate young horses from the herd and swim them across to Chincoteague. There, the ponies are auctioned off. Those that aren't sold swim back to Assateague. The pony swim and auction help the wild ponies. By keeping the number of ponies on Assateague under 150, it prevents the herd from overgrazing that island and damaging its sensitive habitat.

The event was made famous by Marguerite Henry's *Misty of Chincoteague*, a 1947 children's book. Based on a true story, it's about a brother and sister growing up on Chincoteague. They raise money harvesting clams so they can buy a wild pony they name Misty.

AUGUST

1 An eight-lane interstate highway bridge across the Mississippi River in Minneapolis, Minnesota, collapsed during the evening rush hour. About 50 vehicles fell into the river or onto its banks, killing 13 people and injuring about 100. Its supporting structure was found to be in poor condition in 2006, and it was undergoing repairs when it fell. The federal Transportation Department said it had notified all U.S. states to inspect bridges similar in design and construction to the steel truss-arch bridge.

15 An 8.2-magnitude earthquake struck the southern coast of Peru, killing about 540 people and injuring hundreds more. At least 17,000 people were left homeless. Several strong aftershocks caused further damage.

20–21 President George W. Bush met with Canadian Prime Minister Stephen Harper and Mexican President Felipe Calderón in Montebello, a resort town in Quebec, Canada. The discussions covered trade issues and security along the countries' borders.

21 A 12-day mission to the *International Space Station* (*ISS*) ended when the space shuttle *Endeavour* returned to Kennedy Space Center. The purpose of the mission was to bring supplies to the *ISS* crew and new components for the space station's completion. The *Endeavour* crew consisted of Commander Scott Kelly, pilot Charles Hobaugh, and mission specialists Tracy Caldwell, Richard Mastracchio, Barbara Morgan, Benjamin Drew, Jr., and Canadian astronaut Dafydd Williams.

One of Minnesota's most heavily traveled bridges collapsed in August, plunging cars and drivers 60 feet (18 meters) below. There are about 750 similar bridges throughout the United States.

Deadly wildfires ravaged Greece in one of the country's worst disasters. Greece's ancient temples and statues, including the winged statue of victory (right), barely escaped destruction.

Wildfires Devastate Greece

Dozens of wildfires raged across parts of Greece in late August, tearing through forests and engulfing entire villages. About 65 people were killed, and 4,000 homes were destroyed. More than 500,000 acres (200,000 hectares) of farmland and forests were devastated.

Some of the fires were in the northwest part of the country, near the Albanian border, and on an island north of Athens, the capital. But hardest hit was the Peloponnese, a wide peninsula that makes up the southern end of Greece. The fires burned right up to the edge of ancient Olympia, the historic site where the Olympic Games had been founded 2,800 years ago. The flames were brought to a halt before the winged statue of victory, ancient temples, and other antiquities were destroyed.

The wildfires were fanned by strong winds across parched, bone-dry land. They were finally brought under control on August 29, five days after they had started. There were some reports that the fires had been caused by arson, and a number of people were arrested.

Some 20 countries, including the United States, rushed firefighters and other aid to help Greece battle the blazes. Many countries also pledged to send money for humanitarian assistance.

Government changes in August: In **Turkey,** the parliament elected Abdullah Gul president. He succeeded Ahmet Necdet Sezer, who had held that position since 2000.

SEPTEMBER

5 German law-enforcement officials arrested three Islamic terror suspects and seized large amounts of explosives. The officials said that the three militants had been planning to attack Frankfurt International Airport and Ramstein Air Base, a huge U.S. military base in southwestern Germany.

9 President George W. Bush returned to the United States after attending the 21-nation Asia-Pacific Economic Cooperation (APEC) summit in Sydney, Australia. The president met with Australian Prime Minister John Howard, Russian President Vladimir Putin, Chinese President Hu Jintao, and other APEC leaders. At the end of the meeting, the leaders issued the Sydney Declaration on Climate Change, a nonbinding commitment to work toward energy efficiency. Prior to arriving in Australia, President Bush made a surprise stop at a U.S. military base in Anwar Province, Iraq, where he praised the U.S. troops.

17 President George W. Bush named retired federal judge Michael B. Mukasey as U.S. Attorney General. He replaced Alberto Gonzales, who had resigned. (Mukasey was confirmed by the U.S. Senate on November 8.)

Happy Birthday, :-) The "smiley face" emoticon celebrated its 25th anniversary on September 19. On that date in 1982, Scott Fahlman, a computer professor at Carnegie Mellon University, said he had made up and used the emoticon for the first time in a message to an online electronic bulletin board. Today, the computer "smiley face"—a colon followed by a hyphen and a parenthesis—is used a billion times a year in e-mails around the world.

A September Spiderfest!

"Come into my web," said the spider to the fly, "and bring all your relatives!" Were those the words of a boastful spider? No! This web was truly humongous (above), and it was woven together by thousands of cooperative spiders. And on Labor Day weekend, people flocked to Lake Tawakoni State Park in Wills Point, Texas, to see it. So many people showed up that park officials dubbed the holiday "Spiderfest."

The enormous web stretched 200 yards (183 meters)—making it twice the size of a football field. It covered seven large juniper and oak trees, as well as the nearby trail and lake. A ranger had found the huge web in early August, and it continued to grow throughout the month.

An entomologist identified a dozen different spider families in the web. But he believed that long-jawed orb weavers had made most of it. Spiders, unlike ants and bees, aren't known for their cooperative behavior. So scientists were surprised that thousands of them had acted as a social group.

The web may have developed into monster proportions because of weather conditions and its location: There was a lot of rain, and a nearby pond provided the spiders with an ample supply of mosquitoes. When the web was partially damaged by wind and rain, the spiders rebuilt it. But the web's days were numbered—the life cycle of spiders comes to an end in the fall.

Government changes in September: Yasuo Fukuda was named premier of **Japan.** He succeeded Shinzo Abe, who had been premier from 2006 until his resignation on September 26. . . .Following parliamentary elections in **Morocco,** Abbas el Fassi was named premier. He succeeded Driss Jettou, who had been premier since 2002. . . .In national elections in **Sierra Leone,** Ernest Bai Koroma was elected president. He succeeded Ahmad Tejan Kabbah, who had been president for all but one year between 1996 and 2007.

OCTOBER

20 As a result of a devastating 14-month-long drought, Georgia Governor Sonny Perdue declared a state of emergency for much of the state. Other parts of the Southeast—including Alabama, North Carolina, South Carolina, and Tennessee—were also hard hit by the drought, which was described as the worst on record in the Southeast. Rain totals were at least 10 inches (25 centimeters) below normal. Lakes were shrinking, well levels were falling, and crops were dying. In many areas, severe restrictions were placed on water use.

30 President George W. Bush nominated James Peake, a former U.S. Army Surgeon General and decorated Vietnam War veteran, to be U.S. Secretary of Veterans Affairs. He replaced Jim Nicholson, who had served since 2005. (The U.S. Senate confirmed the appointment on December 14.)

31 President George W. Bush nominated Edward Schafer, a former governor of North Dakota, to be U.S. Secretary of Agriculture. He replaced Mike Johanns, who had served since 2005. (The U.S. Senate had not confirmed the appointment by the end of December 2007.)

Government changes in October: In general elections in **Argentina,** Cristina Fernández de Kirchner was elected president. She succeeded her husband, Nestor Kirchner, who had been president since 2003. In **Poland,** following parliamentary elections, Donald Tusk became premier. He succeeded Jaroslaw Kaczynski, who had been premier since 2006.

Drought in almost one-third of the Southeast caused severe water shortages. Below: The water level in Georgia's Lake Lanier, which supplies drinking water for most of the residents of Atlanta, fell to historically low levels, exposing some of the lake bottom.

The 2007 Nobel Prizes

Chemistry: Gerhard Ertl of Germany "for his studies of chemical processes on solid surfaces." Through painstaking research, Ertl unlocked the secrets of some widely used but little understood chemical interactions. His methods laid the foundation of modern surface chemistry, which has helped explain why iron rusts, how fuel cells work, and how catalytic converters clean up car exhaust. The award was announced on his 71st birthday.

Economics: Leonid Hurwicz, Eric Maskin, and Roger Myerson of the United States, for laying the foundations of mechanism design theory. The theory is a tool that economists and others use to analyze group decision-making. It helps distinguish situations in which markets work well from those in which they do not. Hurwicz, 90, was born in Russia. He was the oldest person ever to receive a Nobel Prize. Maskin and Myerson, both 56, expanded Hurwicz's original theory to a variety of situations.

Literature: Doris Lessing of Britain for her novels, stories, and other works. Lessing, 87, grew up in Southern Rhodesia (now Zimbabwe) and moved to London, England, in 1949. Her best-known novel is *The Golden Notebook*. Like many of her works, it deals with the experiences of women. The Nobel committee praised her "fire and visionary power."

British author Doris Lessing won the Nobel Prize for Literature.

Peace: The Intergovernmental Panel on Climate Change (IPCC) and Albert Gore, Jr., for efforts to spread knowledge about the threat of global warming. The IPCC is a United Nations network of scientists formed to assess and report on the impact of climate change. Gore, 59, is a former U.S. vice president (1993–2001) and presidential candidate (2000) who has become a world leader on this issue. His award-winning 2006 documentary film *An Inconvenient Truth* showed how the use of fossil fuels is spurring global warming.

Physics: Albert Fert of France and Peter Grünberg of Germany, for the discovery of a physical effect called "giant magnetoresistance" (GMR). Technology based on GMR is widely used today to read data on computer hard disks. Its discovery made possible the miniaturization of hard disks for use in laptop computers, music players, and other devices. Fert, 69, and Grünberg, 68, discovered GMR independently in 1988.

Physiology or Medicine: Mario R. Capecchi, 70, and Oliver Smithies, 82, of the United States; and Martin J. Evans, 66, of Britain (all working independently), for discovering ways to precisely modify the genes of mice. Their work has allowed scientists to raise mice with specific genetic changes for use in research. Such mice have helped show how certain genes work. And they have served as models for human diseases in which genes play a role, including cancer, heart disease, Alzheimer's disease, and cystic fibrosis.

NOVEMBER

6   California Governor Arnold Schwarzenegger reported that the wildfires that had devastated the southern part of the state were "firmly under our control." The fires, which began on October 21, killed 10 people and destroyed more than 2,000 homes and other buildings in an area that stretched from the Mexican border to north of Los Angeles. More than 500,000 acres (200,000 hectares) of land were burned, and about 500,000 people were evacuated from the area.

7   The space shuttle *Discovery* ended a 15-day mission to the *International Space Station (ISS)*. The purpose of the mission was to add the Harmony module to the *ISS*. The *Discovery* crew consisted of Commander Pamela Melroy; pilot George Zamka; and mission specialists Scott Parazynski, Daniel Tani, Stephanie Wilson, Douglas Wheelock, and European Space Agency astronaut Paolo Nespoli of Italy. Tani remained on the *ISS,* replacing Clayton Anderson, who returned to Earth aboard *Discovery*. With Pamela Melroy at the helm of *Discovery* and Peggy Whitson commanding the *ISS,* it marked the first time that two women were in charge of two spacecraft at the same time.

15   A devastating cyclone ravaged southern Bangladesh. About 3,500 people were killed, and more than a million were left homeless.

27   A one-day Middle East peace conference was held in Annapolis, Maryland. Representatives from 45 countries, 16 of them Arab, and seven inter-

British scientists announced on November 20 that they had found the fossilized claw of an ancient sea scorpion in Germany. The claw was 18 inches (46 centimeters) long, making the 390-million-year-old scorpion a monstrous 8 feet (2.5 meters) long. Scientists have found fossils of other big bugs, including mammoth millipedes and colossal cockroaches, but the sea scorpion was the biggest bug ever.

50 cm

Above: Russian soldiers clean up oil-fouled shores near the site of the massive oil spill. Left: An oil-soaked bird is treated by workers in California. More than 50,000 seabirds died in the two oil spills.

Two Oil Spills: 6,000 Miles Apart

In November, two severe oil spills—one in California and the other in a waterway between Russia and Ukraine—caused grave environmental damage.

On November 7, a container ship sideswiped the San Francisco-Oakland Bay Bridge, releasing 58,000 gallons (220,000 liters) of oil into San Francisco Bay. The oil quickly spread to a large part of California's northern coast, killing more than 20,000 seabirds.

On November 11, a fierce storm hit the Strait of Kerch, a short waterway that links the Black Sea and the Sea of Azov. Ten Russian ships sank or ran aground. One of them, an oil tanker, spilled 560,000 gallons (2.1 million liters) of fuel oil into the waterway. The oil killed about 30,000 seabirds.

national organizations attended the meeting, hosted by U.S. President George W. Bush. Israeli Prime Minister Ehud Olmert and Palestinian President Mahmoud Abbas agreed to negotiate a peace treaty by the end of 2008. Such a treaty could bring an end to sixty years of violent conflict between Israel and the Palestinians and lead to the establishment of a Palestinian state.

Government changes in November: Following parliamentary elections in **Australia,** Kevin Rudd became prime minister. He replaced John Howard, who had been prime minister since 1996. . . .In presidential elections in **Guatemala,** Alvaro Colom Caballeros was elected president, effective January 2008. He succeeds Oscar Berger Perdomo, who had been president since 2004. . . .Following parliamentary elections in **Jordan,** Nader al-Dahabi became prime minister. He replaced Marouf al-Bakhit, who had held the position since 2005. . . .In **Slovenia,** Danilo Türk was elected president. He replaced Janez Drnovsek, who had been president since 2002.

DECEMBER

2 Russian President Vladimir Putin's United Russia Party won a resounding victory in parliamentary elections. Putin, who must step down when his second term as president runs out in May 2008, later named long-time ally Dmitri Medvedev as his preferred successor to compete in the March 2008 presidential elections. Should Medvedev win, as is expected, he would name Putin premier. With control of parliament, and an ally in the presidency, Putin would thus remain the most powerful person in Russia.

13 U.S. underwater archaeologists announced they had discovered the remains of a ship they believe was once commanded by Captain William Kidd, one of the most famous pirates of the late 1600's. The ship was found in 10 feet (3 meters) of water near Catalina Island on the southeastern coast of the Dominican Republic. Kidd abandoned the ship, the *Quedagh Merchant,* in 1699 and it sank soon after. The wreckage yielded cannons and anchors.

Government change in December: In South Korea, Lee Myung Bak was elected president, effective February 2008. He succeeded Roh Moo Hyun, who had been president since 2003.

From December 3–15, more than 185 countries attended a conference on global warming—the United Nations Framework Convention on Climate Change—in Bali, Indonesia. The countries, including the United States, agreed to a timeline to come up with a plan to substantially reduce the emissions of heat-trapping gases. The plan would replace the 10-year-old Kyoto Protocol, which will expire in 2012. Below, a demonstrator at the conference is dressed as a polar bear—whose survival is threatened by global warming.

. . .and Looking Ahead to 2008

Here are a few anniversaries that will be noted in 2008:

• The 150th anniversary of the birth of Theodore Roosevelt, the 26th president of the United States and a world-renowned conservationist, on October 27, 1858.

• The 125th anniversary of the opening of the Brooklyn Bridge, on May 24, 1883. The bridge spans the East River, connecting Brooklyn and Manhattan, two of New York City's five boroughs.

• The 125th anniversary of the eruptions of Krakatoa, an island-volcano between the islands of Java and Sumatra in Indonesia. The eruptions were the most violent explosions on Earth in modern times. They blew away two-thirds of the island and could be heard 3,000 miles (4,800 kilometers) away.

• The 100th anniversary of the establishment of the Grand Canyon National Monument, on January 11, 1908. It became a U.S. national park in 1919. The Grand Canyon, in northern Arizona, is 280 miles (450 kilometers) long and about 1 mile (2 kilometers) deep.

• The 75th anniversary of the opening of the film classic *King Kong* in New York City, on March 2, 1933. The 50-foot (15-meter) ape is considered by many to be the best screen beast in history.

• The 50th anniversary of the founding of the National Aeronautics and Space Agency (NASA), on October 1, 1958. NASA was designed to develop space-exploration systems and to demonstrate those systems in flight.

Terrorist acts by radical Muslim groups were on the rise in 2007. In Afghanistan, Taliban fighters staged killings, kidnappings, and suicide car bombings (above, in Kabul).

MILITANTS ON THE RISE

The threat of terrorism inspired by extreme forms of Islam was a worldwide concern in 2007. Six years had passed since terrorists attacked the United States on September 11, 2001, starting what U.S. leaders have called a "war on terror." But Al Qaeda, the group that carried out that attack, was still operating. There were signs that the group was building a stronger following as its ideology spread—and planning new attacks.

Al Qaeda claims to act in the name of Islam, which is the world's second largest religion. Most of the world's Muslims (followers of Islam) don't accept its extreme view of their faith. Al Qaeda's supporters are Islamic fundamentalists. Islamic fundamentalists want to restore a pure form of Islam that they think existed in the A.D. 600's. They want religion to govern everything in life, from politics to dress. Western culture and values, they say, corrupt the Islamic world.

However, fundamentalists don't all agree on what the ideal Islamic society would be or how to create it. And only a small group of fundamentalists support Al Qaeda's violent goals: to drive Westerners out of Muslim nations, overthrow Muslim governments "corrupted" by Western influences, and unite all Muslims in a single Islamic nation. But these extreme views and terrorist acts have spread in recent years, partly due to anger over the U.S.-led war in Iraq. The spread affected Muslim and Western countries alike in 2007.

IN AFGHANISTAN

In October 2001, the United States struck back at Al Qaeda in Afghanistan, where the terrorist group was then based. U.S. and allied troops overthrew the Taliban, an Islamic militia that ruled most of the country and had sheltered Al Qaeda. Taliban and Al Qaeda fighters fled to the wild mountains along

Afghanistan's border with Pakistan. A new government was elected, putting the country on the path to democracy. Afghanistan seemed to have a promising future.

Then, in 2003, the United States began the war in Iraq. About 20,000 U.S. troops stayed in Afghanistan, some under the command of the North Atlantic Treaty Organization (NATO). But many more troops and other resources were sent to Iraq. The Taliban saw an opening. Its fighters began to creep back over the border and attack villages in southern Afghanistan. Afghan forces weren't strong enough to get the upper hand. NATO and American troops took up the fight, but they were spread thin.

That pattern continued in 2007. The Western forces kept control of large towns and cities, but the Taliban fighters operated freely in the southern countryside. They staged suicide attacks, roadside bombings, kidnappings, and killings. Many such acts were aimed at Westerners and other foreigners, but most of the victims were Afghan civilians. Western troops were able to drive the Taliban fighters out of some areas but couldn't stay to keep them out—and the Afghan security forces were too weak to do so.

A policeman destroys opium poppies in Afghanistan. The Taliban uses drug profits to buy weapons.

The violence claimed a growing number of lives. The Taliban also encouraged farmers to grow opium poppies, the source of heroin and opium. Western governments and Afghan leaders had tried to stamp out this practice, but the illegal drug trade flourished. In 2007 the poppy crop increased by 17 percent. Afghanistan accounted for 93 percent of the world's opium.

For many farmers, opium poppies were simply the best way to make a living. The country remained desperately poor. Ongoing violence and widespread corruption hampered development. A government survey showed that only 31 percent of the people had safe drinking water, and just 7 percent had sanitary toilets.

IN PAKISTAN

Just over Afghanistan's eastern border is a region of Pakistan called the tribal belt. The Pakistani government has little control in this area. Tribal leaders make the law. Al Qaeda and the Taliban found a safe haven there after they were driven from Afghanistan in 2002.

In November 2007, Pakistanis protested against President Musharraf's declaration of a state of emergency and the suspension of the constitution. He said his actions were intended to counter terrorism. But he arrested his political opponents, adding to the nation's political unrest and turmoil.

In a November ceremony, Musharraf (right) transferred his powerful post as military commander to a successor. The following day he was sworn in as president for another term.

The United States has viewed Pakistan as an important ally in the fight against terrorism. It has pressured Pakistan's president, General Pervez Musharraf, to root out the extremists. But that hasn't happened. In fact, radical Islamist organizations have flourished even outside the tribal belt, and Pakistan has seen a wave of terrorist bombings. And Musharraf faced growing political problems in 2007.

Musharraf was head of the Pakistani army as well as president of the country. He took over the government in 1999, ousting Prime Minister Nawaz Sharif, who had led the country for five years. Sharif and other rivals were forced into exile. Musharraf appointed himself president in 2001 and was then elected in a referendum in 2002. His term was set to end in 2007, and elections were set for October. But Pakistanis were increasingly unhappy with his rule. In March, Musharraf suspended one of his main critics, Iftikhar Muhammad Chaudhry, from his post as chief justice of the Supreme Court. Lawyers and opposition parties took to the streets in violent protests.

The government's next problem centered on the Red Mosque, in the capital city of Islamabad. The mosque had become a center for Islamist radicals. They pressured the government to impose Islamic law, or *sharia,* on Pakistan. Students from the mosque began to patrol Islamabad as self-appointed vice squads. In late June, they kidnapped seven Chinese nationals. And they threatened to carry out suicide attacks if the government took action against them. After trying to work out a settlement, government troops stormed the mosque in July. More than 50 militants were killed. Critics blamed the government for allowing extremism to take hold.

Also in July, Pakistan's Supreme Court ruled that Chaudhry's dismissal was illegal, and he returned to his post. The court soon ruled that former Prime Minister Sharif, who planned to run in the upcoming election, could return to the country. But Musharraf defied the court and deported Sharif as soon as he arrived in the country, in September.

The United States was working behind the scenes to find a path to democracy. It hoped for a power-sharing deal between Musharraf and Benazir Bhutto, another former prime minister. Bhutto had been the first woman leader of an Islamic country when she became prime minister of Pakistan in 1988. She had left office in 1996 amid charges of corruption and had lived abroad since then. Bhutto returned to Pakistan in mid-October. Cheering supporters lined the streets of Karachi, her home city. But the celebration was marred by two explosions, which killed 134 people. Islamic militants were blamed.

More violence lay ahead. But meanwhile, Musharraf had been re-elected president by the national and provincial legislatures, which choose the president in Pakistan. Opposition parties had challenged the election. The Supreme Court was to decide if he was eligible for another term—and it was likely to rule against him.

Before that could happen, Musharraf declared a state of emergency and suspended the constitution. The general said he took action to defend the country from Islamic militants. But he promptly arrested his political opponents, not militants. He dismissed the Supreme Court and appointed judges who would support him. He then stepped down as army chief and was sworn in as president on November 29.

Musharraf ended the state of emergency in mid-December, although curbs on the press and other restrictions remained. Meanwhile, former Prime Minister Sharif was allowed to return. Sharif and Bhutto both began to campaign for parliamentary elections, which were scheduled for January 2008. But on December 27, Bhutto was assassinated at a campaign rally. The outlook for elections—and the country—was suddenly in doubt.

The violence and political unrest in Pakistan caused great concern in the West. Pakistan has nuclear weapons, and a stable government is important there. And the West needs Pakistan's cooperation in the fight against Al Qaeda.

IN THE WEST

Al Qaeda has met with setbacks in some parts of the world. In Europe, for example, attacks by terrorists linked to the group were thwarted in several countries.

In June, British police found two car bombs in London before they detonated. The next day two men rammed a Jeep into an entrance to Glasgow International Airport in Scotland. The Jeep exploded in flames, and one of the men died of burns. Three other suspects, all Muslim doctors, were charged. Several others, also in the medical profession, were arrested. Most were later released without being charged.

On September 4, eight men were arrested in Copenhagen, Denmark, on suspicion of plotting a bomb attack. Authorities said that the arrests resulted from an international investigation, and that some of the suspects had links to high-ranking members of Al Qaeda. Six of the eight were later released.

A day later, German police arrested three men suspected of planning attacks against sites frequented by Americans. The targets included the U.S. air base at Ramstein, the largest such base in Germany; and Frankfurt International Airport, one of the busiest in Europe. The suspects were a Turkish resident of Germany and two German citizens, converts to Islam who had trained in terrorist camps in Pakistan. They had amassed huge amounts of explosive chemicals.

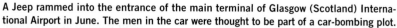

A Jeep rammed into the entrance of the main terminal of Glasgow (Scotland) International Airport in June. The men in the car were thought to be part of a car-bombing plot.

Turkey: Between Two Worlds

Turkey straddles two continents, with territory in Asia and Europe. Turkish society straddles two worlds, too, blending aspects of Western and Muslim culture. Most Turks are Muslims. But the constitution bars any role for religion in government. Religion has been kept out of public life ever since Mustafa Kemal Ataturk established modern Turkey as a secular (nonreligious) state in 1923. But in 2007, some people wondered if that was changing.

Turkish Prime Minister Recep Tayyip Erdogan had started his career as an Islamist. But as Turkey's leader since 2003, he had defended secular traditions. Turkey had stayed a strong ally of the West and a member of NATO. Erdogan has even been campaigning for Turkey to join the European Union. However, his critics said that religion had begun to creep into politics nevertheless.

In 2007 a dispute over the Turkish presidency put a spotlight on the issue. Parliament chooses the president in Turkey, and Erdogan nominated Abdullah Gül, a devout Muslim with a background in political Islam. Secular politicians in parliament, backed by the Turkish military, objected. Erdogan then called for new elections in July. And his AK Party won a resounding victory. The party increased its seats from 34 percent to 47 percent in parliament. Erdogan thus continued as prime minister with stronger support. And parliament elected Gül as president in August.

For the first time in modern Turkey's history, leaders with strong religious ties controlled parliament and the presidency. Even so, Gül promised to support the secular tradition.

The AK Party's support is strongest in rural areas. The secular tradition is strongest in the cities. Only time will tell if the division between them will grow, or if Turkey can continue to bridge two worlds.

In 2007, for the first time in modern Turkey's history, leaders with strong ties to Islam (Islamists) held the presidency and the prime ministership. Secular Turks—those who want to keep religion separate from government—held a number of rallies in protest.

The arrests kept people in the West on edge. They knew that in 2004, bombs placed on commuter trains in Madrid, Spain, had killed 191 people; and in 2005, suicide bombers killed at least 52 people on the London transport system. While there had been no attack on U.S. soil since 2001, several plots had been uncovered.

Terrorists had clearly not stopped trying. Most of the attacks and plots could be traced back to Al Qaeda leaders in Pakistan. But there was also concern about "home-grown" terrorists who were inspired by extremist ideology, spread by the Internet as well as by fundamentalist religious leaders.

IN IRAN

A strict Islamic government has controlled Iran since 1979. Iran's leaders haven't been linked to Al Qaeda. They follow a different branch of Islam, Shi'ism. Most Muslims follow Sunnism, and there is a long history of division between the branches. But Iran's leaders are fundamentalists. They see the West as their enemy, and they have supported terrorism. Iran's extremist positions have hardened since 2005, under Iranian President Mahmoud Ahmadinejad.

Iran's influence has grown in the Middle East in recent years. It's the world's fourth largest exporter of oil, and oil prices have soared. And in 2003 the United States overthrew Iran's biggest rival in the region—the government of Saddam Hussein, in neighboring Iraq.

Tensions between Iran and the West have also risen. Since 2003, there have been growing concerns that Iran is trying to develop nuclear weapons. In that year, inspectors from the U.N. International Atomic Energy Agency (IAEA) found that the Iranians were secretly enriching uranium, a key step in making nuclear fuel. Such fuel could be used in nuclear weapons or in a nuclear power plant. Iranian President Ahmadinejad insists that Iran wants nuclear power, but Western countries believe weapons are the goal. Western diplomats have tried to get Iran to give up its nuclear program without success. In 2006 the U.N. Security Council demanded a halt to the program and, when Ahmadinejad refused, imposed limited sanctions (restrictions) on trade with Iran.

The standoff continued in 2007. Sanctions were renewed and tightened, but Iran defied them and limited the IAEA's freedom to make inspections. The sanctions hurt Iran's economy, which was already shaky. But oil income helped Iran weather the problems.

The United States pressed for stronger sanctions. Iran's past support of terrorism made its nuclear ambitions especially worrisome. U.S. officials also accused Iran of supplying weapons used to attack U.S. troops in Iraq. They were open about wanting a change of leadership in Iran. Some talked of possible military action against Iran.

Growing friction with the West gave Ahmadinejad an excuse to crack down on dissent at home. Labor leaders, students, and advocates for human and women's rights were arrested. More than 150,000 people were picked up for "un-Islamic" dress, including men with Western haircuts and women who allowed some of their hair to show. Newspapers were warned not to print news about social movements or economic problems. Anyone with ties to the West came under suspicion.

Iran's anti-Western positions have hardened since Mahmoud Ahmadinejad became president in 2005. He supports terrorism and calls for the destruction of Israel.

Three Iranian-Americans were imprisoned while visiting Iran, accused of spying. They were released after several months.

In October a new report from the IAEA confirmed that Iran was ready for large-scale production of nuclear fuel. The country would soon be able to make a nuclear bomb. And it still hadn't answered questions about suspicious nuclear activities. The report led to a new push for stricter sanctions.

Then, in a surprising twist, U.S. intelligence services concluded in December that Iran had most likely stopped its secret efforts to design and build nuclear weapons back in 2003. That finding weakened the case for stricter sanctions—or for military action. But Iran continued to openly enrich uranium. It was also building a reactor that could produce plutonium, another fuel for nuclear weapons. Nuclear experts said that there was still cause for concern.

A boy seeks shelter behind a U.S. soldier after a suicide car bombing in a busy area of Baghdad. Despite some improvements in security, the violence in Iraq continued.

THE WAR IN IRAQ

The U.S. war in Iraq entered its fifth year in 2007, and Americans were increasingly divided over it. In March 2003, when the United States and a small number of allies had invaded Iraq to drive the brutal dictator Saddam Hussein from power, officials had predicted a short fight. That prediction and others had turned out to be false.

Saddam Hussein was quickly overthrown, but the fighting didn't stop. Iraqi factions turned on each other, and Islamic extremists launched terrorist campaigns against civilians and U.S. soldiers. Violence kept the country from rebuilding. Iraqis elected a new government in 2006, but it was unable to bring the country together. And the human and dollar costs of the war mounted.

U.S. TROOP SURGE

In early 2007, U.S. President George W. Bush ordered a "surge" in U.S. troop levels in Iraq. About 30,000 additional soldiers were sent, bringing the total to more than 160,000.

The goal of the surge was to establish security in some of the areas where violence was worst. That, it was thought, would give the new Iraqi government time to build unity among the country's rival ethnic and religious groups. The main groups are the Shi'ite Muslims, who form the country's largest group but were persecuted by Saddam; the Sunni Muslims, who make up about 20 percent of the population and controlled Iraq under Saddam; and the Kurds, who live in northern Iraq. The government that was elected in 2006 was led by the Shi'ites but included representatives of the other groups.

Extra U.S. troops were sent into Baghdad, the capital, and other areas where Shi'ite and Sunni militias were attacking each other and civilians. One early result was an increase in U.S. casualties—as more Americans moved into high-risk situations, more were wounded and killed. The total of American deaths in April and May was the highest of any two-month period since the war began.

As U.S. troops fanned out in Baghdad and other areas, some Sunni militants fled north. Violence increased in Mosul, a northern city with a mixed population. Sunni Arabs drove at least 70,000 Kurds out of the city. Terrorist bombs killed more than 300 people in the northern towns of Amerli and Tal Afar. In August, a series of truck bombs killed more than 500 in two villages near the Syrian border. It was the deadliest such attack yet. Most of the victims were members of a Kurdish-speaking sect.

REPORTS TO CONGRESS

By fall there were signs that the surge was having some effect. In September, General David Petraeus, the senior U.S. commander in Iraq, reported to Congress that killings between Sunnis and Shi'ites were down by 50 percent. These groups were still fighting each other, and terrorists were still attacking civilians and U.S. soldiers. But in Anbar Province and some other Sunni areas, tribal leaders had stopped supporting terrorists. They were helping U.S. troops instead.

The general said that it might be possible to end the surge by the summer of 2008, leaving about 130,000 U.S. soldiers in Iraq. It was too soon to bring U.S. troops home, he said, as Iraqi forces weren't yet ready to provide security.

Ryan Crocker, the U.S. ambassador to Iraq, also reported to Congress in September. Gains in security hadn't been matched by political progress, he said. The Iraqi government had failed to take some important steps to unify the country. It hadn't disbanded militias or decided how Shi'ites, Sunnis, and Kurds would share the income from the country's vast oil fields. But he urged patience. If the United States withdrew quickly, Iraq could collapse and become a haven for international terrorists.

As a Kurdish shepherd herds sheep, a Turkish soldier patrols near Turkey's border with Iraq. Kurdish guerrillas have attacked Turkish forces in the area.

The Kurdish Question

Kurds have lived in a region that includes parts of northern Iraq, southeastern Turkey, and northwestern Iran for thousands of years. Kurdistan, as the region is called, has never been independent. But many Kurds want their own country. At various times, they have rebelled against the governments that rule them. In 2007, Kurdish conflicts with Turkey and Iran threatened to draw those countries into the Iraq war.

The Kurds of Iraq had been persecuted under Saddam Hussein. After Iraq was defeated in the Persian Gulf War of 1991, the terms of the peace gave the Kurds some protection. And in 2006 they won a large number of seats in the Iraqi legislature.

Within their part of Iraq, the Kurds now enjoy a degree of self-government. Kurdish guerrilla groups from other countries have taken advantage of that. Pezak, a group that opposes the Iranian government, staged attacks in Iran from bases in Iraqi Kurdistan. In 2007, Iran responded by shelling Iraqi Kurdish villages.

Some Turkish Kurds have also used bases in Iraq to strike at the Turkish military. In October, Kurdish guerrillas killed a dozen Turkish soldiers. The Turkish government responded in December with airstrikes against the Kurdish bases. Several hundred Turkish soldiers then crossed the border into Iraq to pursue the guerrillas and wipe out their bases.

Millions of Iraqis have fled their homes since the war began. Many—mostly women and children—are in refugee camps, in urgent need of basic care.

In contrast, U.S. allies continued to pull troops out of Iraq in 2007. Britain, which had sent as many as 40,000 troops early in the war, still had about 5,000 soldiers in southern Iraq. In October, the new British Prime Minister, Gordon Brown, said that the number would be down to 2,500 by the spring of 2008. U.S. officials worried that the reductions might weaken security along vital supply routes from Kuwait.

U.S. officials were also concerned about Iran's role in the conflict. During the year they presented evidence that Iran's Shi'ite government was helping to arm extremist Shi'ite militias in Iraq. Iran denied the charge.

REFUGEE CRISIS

Daily life was a struggle for many Iraqis. Despite the more than $100 billion that has been spent to rebuild the country, many areas were short of basics like electricity and clean water. The aid group Oxfam International reported in July that poverty, hunger, and public health were getting steadily worse in the country. About 4 million Iraqis, many of them children, needed food and other aid.

And most of the country's hospitals needed basic medical and surgical supplies.

Problems were worst for the more than one million Iraqis who were forced from their homes by the violence. Families fled mixed neighborhoods, with Shi'ites heading toward Shi'ite areas in the south, and Sunnis toward Sunni regions west and north of Baghdad. This deepened the divisions between the groups.

An estimated 2.5 million Iraqis had fled the country since the war began. Most Iraqi refugees went to neighboring countries, especially to Syria and Jordan. Social services were stretched in those countries. In fall 2007, Syria closed its borders to all but small numbers of Iraqis. Fewer than 500 of the refugees were resettled in the United States. U.S. officials promised to take in more refugees, especially Iraqis who had worked with Americans as translators and in other roles. In Iraq, their lives were in danger from extremists.

By November, as security improved in Baghdad, some refugees began to trickle back to neighborhoods there. It was a hopeful sign. But returning families needed shelter, food, and other aid. They often found others living in their homes. There were concerns that property disputes might set off yet another wave of violence.

DEBATE IN THE UNITED STATES

In the United States, polls showed that public opinion had turned against the war. A majority of Americans thought that U.S. troops should leave Iraq as soon as possible.

Some people questioned why U.S. troops should keep fighting when the Iraqi government wouldn't take the steps needed to bring the country together. And they pointed out that the reasons U.S. leaders had given for the war—that Saddam was hiding weapons of mass destruction and had links to Al Qaeda, the terrorist group behind the September 11, 2001, attacks on the United States—had been false. Other people said that, having invaded Iraq, the United States had an obligation to make the country stable. Withdrawing U.S. troops too soon would risk losing whatever gains in security had been made.

Meanwhile, the costs of the war kept rising. As of mid-December, nearly 3,900 U.S. soldiers had died in Iraq since the start of the war, and more than 28,600 had been wounded in action. More than 890 troops were killed in 2007, making it the deadliest year yet for Americans. And since 2001, the United States had spent $800 billion on the wars in Iraq and Afghanistan. Late in 2007, President George Bush asked Congress for $196 billion more. Democrats agreed to $50 billion, tied to a schedule to bring troops home by the end of 2008. But Republicans blocked the measure, leading to a year-end stalemate.

Bush did agree to bring home about 18,000 soldiers by July 2008. Still more troops would come home as more gains were made, he said. But exactly how and when the war would end wasn't clear.

Helicopters of the Blackwater private-security firm patrol over Baghdad.

Blackwater in Trouble

The 160,000 U.S. troops in Iraq in 2007 were only part of the effort to bring stability to the country. About 180,000 private contractors were also there, working for U.S. government agencies. Among them were some 30,000 heavily armed guards—soldiers in all but name. Their role came under investigation after an incident in September.

The incident involved guards working for Blackwater USA, one of several private firms that provide security for U.S. diplomats and other civilian officials. On September 16, Blackwater guards opened fire on a car that failed to slow down as it approached their convoy in Baghdad. Seventeen civilians in and around the car were killed. Blackwater said that the convoy had come under fire, but the Iraqi government said the shooting was unprovoked. Blackwater guards had been involved in other incidents over the years. After this incident, the Iraqi government said it would ban the company from the country.

U.S. investigators later found that the shootings were unjustified. But it wasn't clear if the guards could be charged with a crime under U.S. law for actions in a war zone. That led Congress to take up a bill that would place all contractors operating in war zones under the military code of justice.

In existence less than 20 years, the World Wide Web has become a way for everyone to share everything, everywhere.

THE WEB EXPLOSION

Learn on it, work on it, shop on it, play on it. Use it to keep up with friends, meet new people, share information, and express yourself. In 2007 the World Wide Web was more things to more people than ever.

The Web has been around for less than 20 years. It began as a way for computer users to quickly share information of all kinds through the worldwide super-network called the Internet. Today millions of computers, in thousands of networks, are linked to the Internet. And new gadgets and technology have made the Web part of everyday life in ways that people couldn't have imagined just a few years ago.

THE WEB EXPLOSION

Scientists at the European Organization for Nuclear Research (CERN) started the Web in 1990 as a way to share research. The idea was that a researcher would post a document on a Web site. Then other scientists around the world could go online, connect to the site, and read it. But it didn't take long for people to figure out other ways to use the Web.

Since 1990 the number of Web sites has grown to about 110 million—and it continues to grow. Anyone, from the U.S. government to your Aunt Tillie, can decide to create a site. Schools, museums, and libraries post information and present programs on the Web. Businesses promote products, offer services, and sell merchandise on the Web. Individuals maintain sites that reflect their personal interests.

Programs called Web browsers let computer users access the sites, or "surf" the Web. Other programs—search engines—help them find what they want among the millions of possibilities. And some new developments have helped turn the Web into a way for everyone to share everything, everywhere.

Broadband systems, including fiber-optic cable and wireless networks, are one major advance. These systems allow huge quantities of data to flash through the Internet at incredible speeds. Just a few years ago, it took minutes to download (receive) a single picture over the Internet. Now it takes seconds. You can download music, videos, even entire movies. You can also capture streaming media—live video and audio.

Wireless networks, in which computers communicate with radio signals, are bringing high-speed Internet access even to remote places. With a laptop or hand-held computer equipped for wireless networking, people can surf the Web from any point where such a network is set up. Some devices will even let users access Web sites through cellular-phone networks. The hottest new gadgets let you make phone calls, take pictures, hear music, watch video, send and receive e-mail, get driving directions, and surf the Web—all with one hand-held device.

The technology behind these new developments is amazing. But many people are less interested in how they work than in how they can be used. And people are finding all kinds of ways to put the Web to work. Here are just a few of them.

With a laptop equipped for wireless networking, you can surf the Web from any place where such a network is set up.

STARRING YOU!

Thanks to the Web, anyone with a video camera can become a celebrity. The Web site YouTube is a "virtual video village" where anyone can post a video. Anyone can log on and watch.

YouTube was started in 2005 by three young Californians—Chad Hurley, Steve Chen, and Jawed Karim. They figured out an easy way to post and share home videos on the Web. At first there were just a few videos, mostly of rock bands hoping for a break. Now there are about 100 million videos!

YouTubers have posted home videos of their friends, families, and pets. They have posted short films that they've produced themselves. They have posted clips from their favorite films, TV shows, and music performances (sometimes in violation of copyright laws). Above all, they have posted videos of themselves—singing, performing sports or stunts, creating art, and more. Just posting a video doesn't guarantee fame and fortune, of course. Perhaps millions of people will watch it. Then again, with so many videos on the site, no one may notice it.

YouTubers also use the site to sound off on topics of the day. Often other people answer—with videos of their own. And now YouTubers are becoming a force in national politics. In July 2007 the Web site teamed up with the cable news network CNN to present a debate among eight candidates for the 2008 Democratic presidential nomination. (Later in the year, Republican candidates held a similar debate.) The questions were all presented in videos made by ordinary people. Instead of just listening as candidates spoke in front of a television camera, people had a chance to talk directly to them.

Millions of people have posted videos of all kinds on YouTube (left). In 2007, YouTube partnered with CNN and presented debates among candidates for the 2008 presidential nominations (above).

Many blogs provide news on specific subjects; others function as personal online diaries. This blog presents "small bites" of news on nutrition.

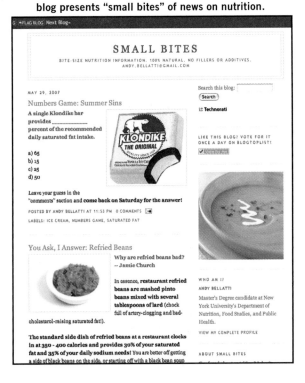

BLOG, MEET POD

Are you taking a vacation? Working on a project? Have some ideas about world peace? You can share it all with the world in a blog— a Web log.

Some bloggers (blog posters) dish out news, gossip, and opinions about the worlds of politics or entertainment. Often readers post replies, agreeing or arguing with the blogger. A blog can also be more personal. Bloggers may write about anything they want others to know about. That might be a daily report of events at school, updates on a favorite sport, or a blow-by-blow account of a family trip to the beach. Personal blogs are like diaries—but, unlike a diary, they can be read online by anyone in the world.

Many blogs consist of only text postings. Other bloggers add pictures. And now that video and sound can be easily put online, people are posting video blogs and podcasts.

A podcast is like a radio show posted on a Web site. People can download the show to a computer or a portable music player, like the

This Maryland teenager produces a weekly podcast called "Alan's Yak" from his home studio. To be a podcaster, all you need is a microphone and a sound-recording feature on your computer.

Wiki-Web

You can learn about almost anything online, from abbreviations to zucchini squash. But today Web users aren't just downloading content from the Web. They are also *adding* content to the Web. Anyone who puts up a blog or a Web page is a "content creator." So is anyone who posts photographs, videos, or stories online—or contributes to a wiki.

A wiki is a Web site that allows visitors to add, remove, and edit content. At least, that's how the term is defined by Wikipedia. This huge (and growing) online encyclopedia is probably the best-known example of user-created content. Volunteers from all around the world create the articles. Anyone can add information to any article, within certain guidelines. There are many other wikis, including wiki dictionaries, textbooks, and other reference tools. Some wikis have a very narrow focus. Wookieepedia (right), for example, focuses on *Star Wars* films.

The term "wiki" comes from a Hawaiian word for "quick." Information on a wiki is

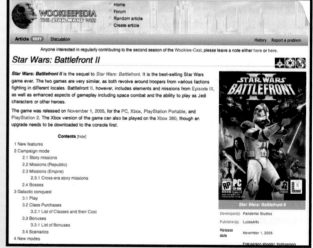

quickly updated because users are always working on the site. But how accurate are wikis? That varies. Sometimes people add incorrect information out of ignorance, bias, or malice. It's generally up to other users to spot and correct these errors. Wiki users say these sites reflect "collective intelligence" and that errors are corrected quickly. Still, if you get information from a wiki, it's smart to check it against another source.

Game On!

Broadband and streaming media have taken games to a new level. On the Web, games can now include complex graphics and animation. Many people can play at the same time, interacting with each other. Some games draw millions of players from countries around the world. The players take on characters, called avatars, and meet with others in virtual worlds.

Many online multiplayer games are designed for adults. But some are designed for younger players. In Neopets, for example, players create, name, and care for virtual pets. They travel with their pets around the Neopets site, meeting other pets and players and taking part in a range of activities. They can earn NeoPoints, the virtual money of the game, in contests and games. They can exchange their NeoPoints for food and other items for their pets. They can also invest the points in the site's virtual stock market, among other things.

Neopets has become hugely popular with kids. In 2007 its Web site had more than 30 million members. The game even jumped to television—the Nickelodeon cable network introduced a series of short cartoons based on Neopets characters.

popular iPod, and listen to it whenever they want. (The name "podcast" is a combination of "iPod" and "broadcast.") Some professional programming is podcast. National Public Radio and other broadcasters offer podcasts on their Web sites. There are also services that "host" podcasts created by people who don't have Web sites of their own. Using these services, anyone can be a podcaster. All you need is a microphone, a computer with a sound-recording feature—and something to say.

A number of schools have brought podcasting into the classroom. At these schools, kids work together to create weekly shows focusing on student news, school sports, and the like. For each episode, they must do research, conduct interviews, write stories, and then record the show. The kids love the project, and that makes teachers love it too.

DIGITAL BUDDIES

On social-networking sites, users can create personal profiles and build networks that connect them to other users. They are hugely popular with teens and young adults, who see them as one of the best features of the Web. More than half of all American teens ages 12 to 17 with Internet access use online social-networking sites, according to a survey released early in 2007.

Young people use the sites mainly to keep up with friends, but they may also meet new people online. Friends contact each other in several ways. A network member can post messages to another member's page or "wall," send a group message to his or her network, post comments to a friend's blog, or send a private message through the network.

MySpace and Facebook are the two most popular social-networking sites, although they aren't the only ones. Facebook networks are mostly organized around specific communities—college campuses, high schools, certain employers, geographic regions. MySpace users can create whatever type of network they like. People post a variety of things on their profiles, including videos. It was the largest social-networking site, with more than 130 million members, in 2007.

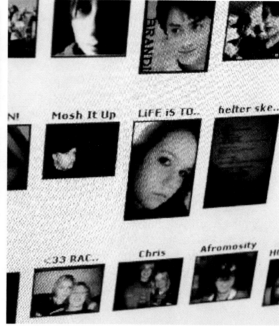

Social-networking sites like MySpace (above) and Facebook (left) are hugely popular with teens and young adults. But they should be cautious about giving out personal information online.

The latest twist on social networking is MoSoSo—Mobile Social Software. MoSoSo lets users access their network anywhere, through a cell phone. If the phone is also equipped with global positioning software (GPS), they can even locate other network members—and be located by them.

That might be a good feature if, for example, you got lost while trying to meet up with a friend. But it might not be so good if strangers could also find you. Many network users already restrict access to all or part of their profiles, so they can't be viewed by everyone. Many profiles also have false or incomplete information. People do this mainly to protect their privacy and to keep strangers from locating them.

Strangers have used these sites to locate and victimize young people. And if you meet someone on a social-networking site, you can't be sure who the person really is. That's why smart people are cautious about using these sites. It's just common sense never to give out personal information online.

DOWNSIDES AND DISTRACTIONS

Many people believe that the Web is changing society—in some good ways, and in some ways that may not be so good. Strangers who may have harmful intentions are certainly one downside to the Web.

There are other downsides, too. You can find all kinds of information online, but the information you find may not be accurate. Web-based games are great, but they won't keep you fit the way playing sports can. It's great to express yourself in a blog—but not if you're blogging when you're supposed to be paying attention in class. And posting messages to friends online can't take the place of seeing them. Spending more time in cyberspace may mean spending less time face to face with family and friends. That can make you feel isolated.

Every year, it seems, the World Wide Web has more to offer—more exciting possibilities, and more distractions. The Web is a wonderful tool. It's sure to grow even better as people find more ways to use it. But as with any tool, it's important to use it wisely.

An ailing Fidel Castro, the Communist leader of Cuba for nearly 50 years, turned over the running of the country to his brother, Raúl. People wondered what changes this might bring to the country, which has long been at odds with the United States.

CUBA: LOOKING AHEAD

Cuba was poised on the brink of change in 2007. For almost half a century, this small island nation in the Caribbean Sea had been ruled by Fidel Castro. But Castro, who turned 81 during the year, was too ill to govern. He had turned over the day-to-day work of running the country to his younger brother, Raúl. People were looking ahead to a new era for Cuba and wondering what it would bring.

Cuba is one of the United States's closest neighbors. It's only about 90 miles (145 kilometers) from the southern tip of Florida. Its history has been closely linked to that of the United States—and under Castro, relations with the United States haven't been good. Castro's Cuba was the first Communist state in the Americas, and it remains one of the few Communist countries in the world today. This has led to friction between Cuba and its large and powerful neighbor to the north.

REVOLUTION

Spain colonized Cuba in the early 1500's and ruled it for nearly 400 years. A struggle for independence began in the late 1800's, and the United States became involved. In 1898, the United States defeated Spain in the brief Spanish-American War. U.S. troops then occupied Cuba for four years.

Cuba became a republic in 1902. But an amendment to the U.S. constitution gave the United States the right to intervene in Cuba's internal affairs and to establish a naval base at Guantánamo Bay. This amendment, the Platt Amendment, was later repealed. But the United States kept permanent rights to the naval base.

The new country faced many problems. A few Cubans—those who owned profitable sugar and tobacco plantations and other industries—grew rich. But most people were desperately poor. U.S. companies also profited from Cuban sugar plantations and other businesses. The country alternated between periods of dictatorship and democracy. Many leaders were corrupt and more interested in gaining wealth and power than in helping the poor.

Unrest grew during the 1950's, under the dictator Fulgencio Batista. And that was when Fidel Castro came on the scene. Castro was practicing law in Havana, the capital, in 1952, when Batista staged a coup to take power for the second time. Castro was outraged, and the next year he and a small band of followers staged an armed attack on an army barracks in southeastern Cuba. He was taken prisoner and sentenced to 15 years in prison, but he was released after two years.

Castro then went to Mexico and began to organize a small rebel force. In 1956 he and his band launched an attack on Cuba's north coast. Most were killed or captured, but Castro and a handful of other survivors fled into the mountains. They continued the fight, and word of his campaign spread. More fighters came to join him.

In 1958 the United States ended its support of Batista and refused to sell arms to him. Batista's regime collapsed, and he fled the country on January 1, 1959. Castro entered Havana to form a new government.

CASTRO'S CUBA

It was soon clear that the new government would be Communist. It seized private land, property, and businesses, eventually including property owned by foreigners. The economy came under government control. Castro also developed close ties with the Communist government of the Soviet Union, which began to provide aid to Cuba.

Poor people benefited in many ways. The government provided education and health care for all. Housing projects were built. Land was allotted to farm workers. But middle-class Cubans lost out, and many fled the country. Most settled in the United States, especially in southern Florida, where there are now about one million Cubans. Castro's

Cuba and the United States: Two Crises

Soon after Fidel Castro came to power, two incidents deepened the rift between Cuba and the United States. These incidents were the Bay of Pigs invasion and the Cuban missile crisis.

In 1960, the United States trained and armed a band of about 1,500 Cuban exiles who hoped to overthrow Castro. The force landed at the Bay of Pigs, on Cuba's south coast, on April 17, 1961. The exiles expected the invasion to touch off an anti-Castro revolution, but that didn't happen. Castro's forces easily defeated the invaders.

A U.S. Navy ship intercepts a missile-carrying Soviet ship during the Cuban missile crisis in 1962.

The next year the Soviet Union began to place long-range nuclear missiles—which were capable of striking the United States—in Cuba. When a U.S. spy plane discovered the missile sites, President John F. Kennedy imposed a naval blockade on Cuba. He also told the armed forces to prepare for a possible nuclear war. In the end, the Soviets backed down and removed the missiles. Many historians believe that the Cuban missile crisis was the most dangerous moment of the Cold War.

The island of Cuba has good resources and great natural beauty. But most of the people are poor, and many of the cities and towns are in need of modernization. Raúl Castro (below) made some reforms in 2007, but it wasn't clear what Cuba would be like after Fidel Castro's death.

government also didn't allow dissent. Those who opposed the government were jailed or exiled.

The changes in Cuba caused tensions with the United States, which opposed Communism. This was the height of the Cold War, the period of intense rivalry between the democratic countries of the West, led by the United States, and the Communist countries, led by the Soviet Union. In 1961 the United States

ended diplomatic relations and stopped all travel and trade with Cuba. The restrictions were kept in place through the long years of Castro's rule that followed.

In 1991, Communism collapsed in the Soviet Union, and the country broke apart. Cuba no longer received the aid it depended on. Even before this, food and consumer goods were often rationed or unavailable. Now the island was thrown into an economic crisis.

Many people expected that Castro's regime would fall, but it didn't. Castro showed no signs of stepping down. Although some Cubans had always defied government restrictions against emigration, their numbers increased as conditions worsened. Thousands of Cubans tried to reach the United States in small boats.

Then, in 2006, Castro fell ill. On July 31 he temporarily transferred control of the country to his brother Raúl, who had been defense minister, and underwent intestinal surgery. Over the next year he had several other operations and remained too weak to govern.

A NEW ERA?

It seemed clear that the Castro era couldn't last much longer. But what would Cuba—a country where most people are employed by the government—be like without him?

When reports of Castro's illness first reached Florida, Cuban exiles danced in the streets. Many expected to soon return to the island and reclaim the property they had lost so many years before. But experts cautioned that Cuba after Castro wasn't likely to be very different from Cuba under Castro. Change, if it came, would probably come slowly.

Cuba desperately needs reform. Cubans earn about $12 a month on average, and most of that is spent on food. Goods are rationed, and there are chronic shortages. As acting president, Raúl Castro, 76, has taken steps suggesting that some change is coming. He has paid debts that the government owed to private farmers, and he has raised the prices the government pays farmers for milk and meat. He has announced plans to fix up hotels, marinas, and golf courses in the hope of attracting more tourists.

Raúl has also offered to begin talks with the United States in the hope of improving relations. And fewer government critics have been arrested since he took charge. Will there be bigger changes after Fidel Castro's death? Perhaps. But no one can say what Cuba's post-Castro era will be like.

Maybe the country will return to the corruption and dictatorship of the Batista era. Or Cuba may become like China, allowing free enterprise but with the Communist Party in firm political control. Many people hope for democracy. The U.S. government has formed a commission and set aside $80 million to promote that goal.

Cubans have several important advantages as they enter the next chapter in their history. Their island home has good land, natural resources, and great beauty. They are well educated, and they take pride in their culture. All those things will stand them in good stead, whatever the future brings.

A suspected terrorist captured in Afghanistan is held at the Guantánamo detention center.

Guantánamo Bay

Guantánamo Bay, on the southeastern coast of Cuba, is the site of the only U.S. military installation in Communist territory. The bay is among the world's largest and best-sheltered natural harbors, and the United States has controlled it since the Spanish-American War in 1898. After that war, the United States occupied all of Cuba. The right to lease land at Guantánamo Bay and build a naval base there was part of the agreement that ended U.S. occupation and allowed Cuba to gain its independence.

The arrangement has continued ever since, through all the changes that have come to Cuba. After Fidel Castro took power and relations with the United States soured, Cuba sought to get the base back. But the treaty can't be ended unless both countries agree. The Cuban government has cut off water to the base and isolated it from the rest of the country. Supplies arrive by ship, and water is shipped in or provided by desalination plants. Wind turbines supply some of the electricity used on the base.

As a naval base, Guantánamo Bay is no longer very important to the United States. But closing it would be seen as giving in to the Castro regime, so the United States has maintained it. Since 2001 the base has become the site of a controversial detention center. About 350 suspected terrorists captured in Afghanistan and other places have been detained there as "unlawful enemy combatants."

Russian President Vladimir Putin continued to increase his power to such an extent in 2007 that people questioned whether democracy in Russia would survive.

AROUND THE WORLD

Strong rulers tried to tighten control in Russia and several other nations in 2007. Conflict continued in two of the world's "hot spots"—the Middle East and Darfur, in Sudan. But negotiations brought a breakthrough in efforts to keep North Korea from building a stockpile of nuclear weapons.

RUSSIA: PUTIN CONSOLIDATES HIS POWER

When the Soviet Union disbanded in 1991, Russia set out on a new path. The Soviet Communist regime had controlled every aspect of society. The new Russia was to be a democracy, with a free-market economy and freedom of expression. But in 2007, many people wondered if democracy could last in Russia—or if it was already dead.

Since taking office in 2000, Russian President Vladimir Putin had steadily consolidated his control over the government. His United Russia Party controlled parliament. He appointed the governors of Russia's 89 federal regions. He extended government control over businesses. And he cracked down on the media, silencing his critics. In 2007, police used force to break up peaceful protests in Moscow and St. Petersburg.

Several of Putin's critics, including journalists and the deputy head of the Russian Central Bank, have been assassinated. The government has blamed exiled Russians for these deaths. Perhaps the most bizarre killing was that of Alexander Litvinenko, a former Soviet intelligence agent living in Britain. He died in late 2006 in London, poisoned by radioactive plutonium. British police charged a Russian businessman, Andrei Lugovoi, with the crime. But Russia refused to send Lugovoi to Britain to stand trial.

Other incidents strained Russia's relations with the West in 2007. During the Cold War, from the end of World War II to 1991, there had been fierce rivalry between the Soviet Union and the West. After the Soviet collapse, relations had warmed. But now a definite chill was creeping in.

Russia firmly opposed a U.S. plan to build a missile defense system in Eastern Europe, seeing it as a threat. Putin said he would point Russian missiles at Europe if the United States installed the system there. He also threatened to withdraw from a European treaty that limited conventional weapons and troops in Europe. That move would leave Russia free to build up forces near its borders. Russia also rejected a plan for independence of the Serbian province of Kosovo, which the United States supported.

These actions led Westerners to wonder if Putin was taking Russia back to the days of the Cold War. But Putin remained hugely popular in Russia. His second term as president was ending, and under Russia's constitution he couldn't serve a third. Yet it seemed he would find a way to stay in power.

In parliamentary elections on December 2, 2007, Putin led the list of candidates for the United Russia Party. The party won overwhelmingly. The outcome wasn't a surprise—not only was Putin popular, but new election rules were stacked against opposition parties. Liberal, pro-Western parties didn't win any seats, and European observers said the vote wasn't free or fair.

The victory led many people to wonder if Putin would be the next premier or stay on in some other role. Either way, whoever he backed for the presidency would certainly win that election, in March 2008.

VENEZUELA: ON A RADICAL SOCIALIST COURSE

In Venezuela, President Hugo Chávez also tightened his grip on power in 2007. Venezuela is an important oil producer, supplying about 12 percent of U.S. oil imports. Under Chávez, the country has become a center of anti-American feeling in Latin America.

A former Army officer, Chávez tried but failed to take power in a coup in 1992. Six years later he was elected president. The government had long represented wealthy and middle-class Venezuelans, but Chávez won the vote by promising to help the poor.

In his first term, Chávez made some controversial decisions, including firing the managers of the state-run oil company. He set up price controls to keep inflation in check. Income from oil exports allowed him to spend lavishly on social programs, and his support grew.

In 2002 his opponents tried to overthrow him in a coup. They failed, and Chávez blamed the United States for the attempt. He became increasingly outspoken in his opposition to the United States. And he developed strong ties with Cuba and Iran, countries that also oppose the United States.

Chávez easily won re-election in December 2006. He then steered the country on a more radical socialist course. The government took over the country's electrical and telephone companies. It also took control of oil projects being developed by foreign companies. Chávez cracked down on the media. And he proposed sweeping changes to Venezuela's constitution.

The changes would give far more power to the president, allowing him to control government down to the local level. He would be able to suspend civil liberties indefinitely, if he chose. And he would be able to serve an unlimited number of terms. There were some popular changes, too. The workday would be shortened to six hours. And homemakers and street vendors would get state pensions.

Chávez campaigned hard for his plan. He rallied his supporters with speeches criticizing the United States and other foreign countries. Government workers flooded into

Venezuelan President Hugo Chávez cast a vote for constitutional changes that would have made him president for life. But a majority of Venezuelans voted "No!"

The Monks of Myanmar

Myanmar, a Southeast Asian nation formerly called Burma, has been under various forms of military rule since 1962. It is one of the poorest countries in the world. The generals who run the country use force and fear to stay in power. They have arrested thousands of their opponents. The leader of the opposition, Aung San Suu Kyi (a Nobel Peace Prize winner), has been in jail or under house arrest on and off since 1989.

The military rulers faced a serious challenge in 2007. The challenge came from thousands of Buddhist monks, who led massive street protests against the government for a week in September.

The monks are honored and respected in Myanmar, where nearly all the people are Buddhists. There are about 400,000 monks—about as many monks as soldiers. Most are young. Many remain monks for life, but others spend only a few years in the monastery. The monks are supported by alms.

The protests started with small student demonstrations against increases in the price of fuel. But on September 5, security officers beat a group of Buddhist monks during a demonstration in the northern city of Pakokku. That sparked wider protests, in which thousands of red-robed monks marched through the streets of Yangon (Rangoon) and other major cities (above).

The protesting monks marched with their begging bowls upside down, to show that they rejected the military government. That was a powerful signal in this deeply religious country. Pro-democracy protesters joined the monks. As many as 100,000 people marched in Yangon on September 26. But security forces cracked down. They fired shots and tear gas into the crowds, killing several people. They also raided homes and monasteries, rounding up political activists. Thousands of monks and their supporters were jailed.

Western countries condemned the arrests. But the military rulers seemed unlikely to listen. Myanmar has few ties to any country except China.

poor districts to get out the vote. But even some of Chávez's supporters thought he had gone too far. Some of the president's policies were starting to backfire, too. There were shortages of basic goods like milk and eggs because, with strict price controls, farmers couldn't produce these items at a profit. And violent crime was on the rise.

In a referendum held on December 2, voters narrowly rejected Chávez's plan, with 51 percent voting against it. It was the first electoral defeat for Chávez in his 10 years in power.

NORTH KOREA: NO NUCLEAR WEAPONS?

After years of on-again, off-again talks, North Korea agreed to disable its nuclear facilities and give a full accounting of its nuclear programs in 2007. The agreement raised hope that this secretive Asian country might end its quest to build an arsenal of nuclear weapons.

North Korea, which has been ruled by a Communist dictatorship since the end of World War II, spent years developing nuclear weapons in secret. In 2003 the North Koreans admitted to the program, and in 2006 they

A team of international inspectors traveled to North Korea in July to confirm that the country's nuclear-weapons program had been halted.

tested a nuclear bomb for the first time. They said that they needed nuclear weapons to defend their country against the United States.

U.S. officials have labeled North Korea a terrorist nation, but they say they have no plans to attack it. Bad feelings between the two nations go back to the 1950's, when North Korea fought a bitter war with South Korea. The United States fought on South Korea's side and remains a strong ally.

Many people worry that North Korea may use its nuclear weapons against South Korea or another neighbor, such as Japan, or sell them to terrorists. Thus the North Koreans have been under growing pressure to give up the program. Beginning in 2003, China, Japan, Russia, South Korea, and the United States met with the North Koreans in six-way talks. But North Korea had repeatedly walked out of the talks.

In 2006, the United Nations imposed economic sanctions against North Korea. The North Koreans then returned to the negotiations. And in February 2007 there was a breakthrough. North Korea agreed to disable the reactor it used to provide plutonium fuel for weapons. It also agreed to provide a complete list of its nuclear programs. In exchange, the country would get food, fuel, and other aid. North Korea is desperately poor and relies heavily on basics from abroad.

International inspectors confirmed that the reactor was shut down in July. In further talks, the North Koreans agreed to disable all their nuclear facilities by the end of the year. In return, North Korea would get almost one million tons of fuel oil, or equivalent aid. And the United States would take steps to remove North Korea from the list of terrorist nations.

However, the North Koreans had gone back on agreements in the past. And many questions remained. North Korea hadn't agreed to give up the nuclear weapons it already had. In addition, the United States has long believed that North Korea has a secret program to produce enriched uranium as weapons fuel. The country is thought to have many deep mountain tunnels where such activities could be hidden.

THE MIDEAST: SMALL STEPS TOWARD PEACE

A split between rival Palestinian factions snarled efforts to settle the conflict between Israel and the Palestinian Arabs in 2007. This conflict has been going on since 1947, when the United Nations split the territory of Palestine into separate Jewish and Arab states. Israel was created the next year as the Jewish homeland. Arab countries rejected the plan and immediately attacked Israel. Years of bloodshed followed. In 1967, during one of several Arab-Israeli wars, Israel took control of the Gaza Strip (a narrow band of land along the Mediterranean coast), the West Bank (on the west side of the Jordan River), and parts of Jerusalem.

The Palestinians have long demanded their own state. In 1993, after a series of peace talks brokered by the United States, they won limited self-rule in parts of the West Bank and Gaza Strip. They set up a government, the Palestinian National Authority (PNA). Although violence erupted again, moderates on both sides continued to work for peace.

In 2005, Mahmoud Abbas, a moderate, was elected president of the PNA. He signed

Hamas, a militant Islamic party in the Palestinian territories, consolidated their control over one of the territories—the Gaza Strip—in 2007.

a truce with Israel, and Israeli troops and settlers left the Gaza Strip. But the next year a militant Islamic party, Hamas, defeated Abbas's Fatah Party, and won a majority in the PNA parliament. That dashed hopes for peace—Hamas, which gets support from Iran, refuses to recognize Israel's right to exist. Soon Gaza militants were firing rockets into Israel and carrying out other terrorist attacks. Israel closed Gaza's borders. That and an international boycott caused great hardship for the Palestinian people.

Abbas was still president of the PNA, but the rise of Hamas left his Fatah Party with less power. By early 2007, armed clashes were breaking out between the two factions. Hamas and Fatah formed a new "unity" government in March, hoping to head off a civil war. But fighting flared up again. In June, Hamas gunmen seized key sites in the Gaza Strip and blew up Fatah's headquarters there. The Palestinian territories were left divided, with Hamas controlling Gaza, and Fatah controlling the West Bank.

Abbas formed a new, Fatah-led government in the West Bank. He called for peace talks with Israel to resume. Israel, the United States, and European nations eased the boycott, allowing aid and goods to

enter the West Bank. Moderate Arab nations also backed Fatah. Egypt hosted a regional peace conference in late June, inviting Abbas, Israeli President Ehud Olmert, and Jordan's King Abdullah II.

Israeli and Palestinian leaders met again on November 27 in Annapolis, Maryland, at a conference sponsored by the United States. Syria, Saudi Arabia, and other Arab nations were also at the conference, showing support for a peaceful solution to the Palestinian problem. Abbas and Olmert pledged to negotiate a peace treaty by the end of 2008. But neither leader had strong support at home. And after 60 years of conflict, many issues would have to be settled before Palestinians and Israelis could live in peace.

DARFUR: A TROUBLED REGION IN SUDAN

In August 2007 the nations of the world took an important step toward ending violence in Darfur, in the African nation of Sudan. The U.N. Security Council voted to send a 26,000-member peacekeeping force to this troubled region, where fighting has killed at least 200,000 people since 2003. It would be the largest peacekeeping effort ever. But by year's end the force still hadn't arrived. Meanwhile, the violence continued.

Israeli Prime Minister Ehud Olmert and Palestinian President Mahmoud Abbas attended a multi-nation Middle East peace conference in Annapolis, Maryland, in November. It was hosted by U.S. President George W. Bush.

Darfur is in western Sudan, at the southern edge of the Sahara desert. Its problems began with conflicts between two main ethnic groups—Arab tribes, who traditionally are nomadic traders and camel herders; and non-Arab Africans, who are mostly farmers. Some years ago, Arab nomads began to raid farming villages. Sudan's government was said to be arming the raiders, who were known as the janjaweed. In 2003, when non-Arabs rebelled and fought back, the government took military action against them. And the janjaweed stepped up attacks against civilians. Some 2.5 million people were driven from their homes. Many fled to refugee camps in Darfur and in Chad, just over Sudan's western border.

In 2006 the government reached a partial peace agreement with the largest of several rebel groups. But by that time dozens of armed groups were roaming Darfur, attacking civilians, aid workers, and each other. Talks between the groups made little progress. Meanwhile, aid groups struggled to help the refugees who remained crowded into camps.

Sudanese children at a refugee camp in Darfur wait their turn to get containers of water.

Women Peacekeepers

The first all-woman U.N. peacekeeping force (above) went on duty in Liberia in January 2007. The 103 members, all female soldiers from India, joined a force of about 15,000 peacekeepers there. U.N. troops have been in Liberia since 2003, when they stepped in to halt a civil war.

In their sharp blue uniforms, the female peacekeepers patrolled the streets of Monrovia, the capital. They helped control crowds at rallies. And they provided backup for Liberia's police, who don't carry weapons.

Liberians elected Africa's first female president, Ellen Johnson-Sirleaf, in 2005. But women aren't always treated well there. Many are victims of violent crime. It was hoped that the sight of female soldiers on patrol would help reduce crimes against women—and inspire young women to become police officers.

The new peacekeeping force was a joint effort by the United Nations and the African Union (AU). Its main goal was to protect civilians. It was to replace an AU force of about 7,000 soldiers—far too few to cover Darfur, which is the size of France. But the U.N. force was delayed by lack of equipment and lack of cooperation from the Sudanese government. U.N. officials warned that if these problems weren't solved, violence was likely to increase.

ELAINE PASCOE
Author, *Freedom of Expression: The Right to Speak Out in America*

NEWSMAKERS

Most North American kids go to school every day. But millions of kids throughout the world—especially girls—don't have those educational opportunities. The talk-show host **Oprah Winfrey,** 53, hopes to help. In 2007, Oprah, who is one of the best-known TV personalities, opened two schools in South Africa. Causes that Oprah takes up receive lots of attention, and her new schools were no exception.

Poverty is the main reason that many girls don't get an education. In many countries schools charge fees that poor families can't afford. If a family scrapes together the money for school, often it's a son who goes. Daughters stay home to help with chores like cooking, cleaning, fetching water, and caring for younger kids.

"When you change a girl's life, it's not just that life," Oprah says. "You start to affect a family, a community, a nation." In January she opened her Leadership Academy for Girls (below) in a small town south of Johannesburg, South Africa's largest city. It's a boarding school for 152 girls, ages 11 and 12. And in March she opened the Seven Fountains Primary School (right) in a remote town in eastern KwaZulu-Natal province. Both schools were funded by her Angel Network, a charity that supports projects focused on education and literacy.

On January 4, 2007, Representative **Nancy Pelosi** took the gavel as the new Speaker of the U.S. House of Representatives. Children and grandchildren of members of Congress were at her side at the event. Pelosi, 67, was the first woman ever to hold this powerful position. A Democrat, Pelosi had represented San Francisco, California, in the House for 20 years.

Former U.S. Vice President **Al Gore** shared the 2007 Nobel Peace Prize for his efforts to spread knowledge about the threat of global warming. The co-winner was the Intergovernmental Panel on Climate Change (IPCC), a U.N. network of scientists formed to assess the impact of climate change. Gore, 59, served as vice president under President Bill Clinton (1993–2001). In 2000, as the Democratic candidate for president, Gore lost one of the most controversial presidential elections in U.S. history to George W. Bush. But he rallied from that disappointment to become a world leader on the issue of climate change. His award-winning 2006 documentary film *An Inconvenient Truth* showed how the use of coal, oil, and other fossil fuels is spurring global warming, and how the change is likely to cause havoc worldwide. (Left: Gore at the opening of the film in Japan.)

Gordon Brown, 56, became Great Britain's prime minister and head of the Labour Party after Tony Blair resigned from those positions in June 2007.

Brown, 56, is a native of Glasgow, Scotland. He was first elected to the British parliament in 1983 and has served continuously since then. In 1997, when the Labour Party won a majority in parliamentary elections, he was named Chancellor of the Exchequer in a new government headed by Blair. That made him the second most powerful person in the government, responsible for financial and economic affairs.

Some Labour Party members came to see Brown as a likely replacement for Blair, and he stepped into the prime minister's position when he was named the new party leader. As prime minister, Brown has promised to improve education and health care and to provide more affordable housing.

Tony Blair left office after serving ten years as British prime minister and 13 years as leader of the Labour Party. He was the first Labour leader ever to win three terms as prime minister.

Blair, 54, was born in Edinburgh, Scotland. Like Gordon Brown, he was first elected to parliament in 1983. He became Labour leader in 1994 and prime minister three years later, when his party won a majority in parliament. Labour won again in 2001 and 2005.

As prime minister, Blair's greatest accomplishment was bringing peace and self-rule to Northern Ireland. He also breathed new life into Britain's schools and health service. Abroad, he was a steadfast ally of the United States. But his decision to send British troops to join the 2003 U.S.-led invasion of Iraq proved to be deeply unpopular in Britain. After leaving office in 2007, Blair became a special ambassador working for peace in the Middle East.

In May 2007, French voters chose **Nicolas Sarkozy,** a conservative, as their new president. Sarkozy, 52, was the first person born after World War II to be elected president of France.

The son of Greek and Hungarian parents, Sarko, as he is known, was born in Paris. He was mayor of Neuilly-sur-Seine from 1983 to 2002. He came to national attention when he successfully negotiated the release of a group of kindergarten students who had been taken hostage. Later, he held a number of government positions under President Jacques Chirac.

Sarkozy pledged to reduce crime and unemployment, to fight intolerance and racism, and to revive the work ethic. He took a tough stand against illegal immigration but supported helping legal immigrants adjust to French society. He also promised to improve relations with other European countries and with the United States.

Jacques Chirac, 74, stepped down after two terms as president of France. He had been a leading conservative politician since the 1970's.

Chirac was born in Paris. In the late 1950's he served with the French military in Algeria, then a French colony. He entered politics in the early 1960's and rose quickly. He was premier twice (1974–76 and 1986–88) and mayor of Paris (1977–95). In 1995, he was elected president.

As president, Chirac steered France on a conservative course. But in 1997, Socialist leader Lionel Jospin became premier. In France, the president and premier share power. There were conflicts between Chirac and Jospin. However in 2002, Chirac was reelected with more than 80 percent of the votes, the widest margin in French history. Chirac opposed the 2003 U.S.-led invasion of Iraq. His position was hailed by many Europeans but strained relations with the United States.

In September 2007 **Yasuo Fukuda,** 71, became Japan's second new premier in a year. The Liberal Democratic Party, which holds a majority in Japan's parliament, named him to succeed Premier Shinzo Abe. Abe's government had been plagued by scandals, and that had led to losses for the Liberal Democrats in June elections. While the party kept its majority in parliament, its leaders put pressure on Abe to resign. He did so abruptly on September 12, after just under one year in office.

An experienced politician, Fukuda had served in Japan's parliament since 1990. From 2000 to 2004 he was chief cabinet secretary, a government position considered to be a steppingstone to the post of premier. Fukuda is known for his ability as a behind-the-scenes negotiator, and he was expected to help steady the scandal-plagued government. In the past, he had emphasized the importance of strong ties with China and the rest of Asia.

Drew Gilpin Faust, a historian who has specialized in the Civil War and the American South, became the first woman president of Harvard University on July 1, 2007. She was the 28th president of the prestigious Cambridge, Massachusetts, university, which was founded in 1636.

The appointment capped an outstanding academic career for Faust, 59, who was born in New York City and raised in Virginia's Shenandoah Valley. She is a graduate of Bryn Mawr College and has advanced degrees in American civilization from the University of Pennsylvania. Previously, she was the founding dean of the Radcliffe Institute for Advanced Study. In that role she helped shape the former Radcliffe College, which merged with Harvard, into one of the country's foremost scholarly institutes. She is also the author of five books, including *Mothers of Invention: Women of the Slaveholding South in the American Civil War.*

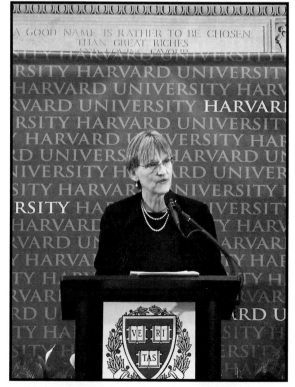

The tenth anniversary of the death of **Diana, Princess of Wales,** was marked in several ways during 2007. The former Diana Spencer, she had become an international celebrity when she married Prince Charles, the heir to the British throne, in 1981. Her youth and beauty had inspired millions of fans worldwide. They were thrilled when Charles and Diana became the parents of two sons, William and Harry. But the marriage was troubled, and the royal couple was the focus of constant media attention. They separated and then divorced in 1996. A year later Diana, 36, died in a car crash in Paris. Her death touched off a huge public outpouring of grief.

In 2007, princes William and Harry celebrated Diana's memory with a huge rock concert on her birthday, July 1. Some 70,000 fans poured into Wembley Stadium in London for the event. "This evening

is about all that my mother loved in life," William (below, left, with Harry) told the crowd. The princes also helped organize a solemn memorial service on August 31, the anniversary of her death. On hand were family members, friends, and representatives of charities that Diana had supported.

ANIMALS

A mother panda munches a snack of tasty bamboo while her young cubs play in the snow at a reserve in China. The roly-poly cubs are clearly having a great time. However, their games are much more than fun. As the cubs wrestle and tumble around, their muscles become stronger. Their reflexes become quicker. And their coordination becomes better and better. In these ways, the cubs' cute panda-play helps them develop strengths and skills. And those strengths and skills will help them survive in the wild as they grow up. Throughout the world, for young animals of many different kinds, play serves the same important purpose.

Young animals, like these wrestling lion cubs, have a great time playing with each other. But their rough-and-tumble games are also teaching them important skills that will help them survive as adults.

ANIMAL ANTICS

Wolf cubs wrestle outside their den, play-biting and not really hurting each other. A cheetah cub pounces on a stick and begins to bat it around. A young antelope bounds into the air, runs, and leaps up in the air again. A mother gorilla covers her face, playing peek-a-boo with her baby.

What are these animals doing? They are all playing, and having a wonderful time at it. But animal play is more than fun. Play serves a serious purpose: It helps animals develop the skills that they will need to survive in the wild.

Rough-and-tumble antics help animals grow strong and develop quick reflexes. Scientists think play may even help animals' brains develop, especially the parts of the brain involved in coordination. Play also helps animals learn patterns of behavior that they will use throughout their lives—hunting,

fleeing from predators, courting a mate, besting a rival. For some animals, play helps form bonds among members of a group.

Not all animals play. No one has yet seen snails frolicking, or ants playing tag. With very few exceptions, all playful animals are mammals and birds. Some adult animals play, especially among species that are generally considered intelligent, such as dolphins and primates. But most of the fooling around is done by youngsters. That makes sense, in light of play's role as a sort of natural survival school. And different kinds of animals play in different ways—ways that, in each case, will help them survive.

RUN-AWAY PLAY

Have you ever seen young horses playing in a field? They race back and forth, chasing each other, leaping, bucking, and kick-

Through its playful leaps, a mountain goat develops the balance it needs to stay alive in its mountain home.

ing up their heels. Even though they're safe in the field, they are practicing moves that would help them escape from predators in the wild.

Horses, sheep, goats, antelopes, and other herbivores (plant-eaters) instinctively run away at the first hint of danger. But that instinct to run isn't enough. In the wild, animals must also be quick on their feet, or they'll wind up as dinner for wolves, lions, or other predators. That's where play comes in. High-speed chase games help the youngsters develop strong running muscles and stamina. As they dodge this way and that, they fine-tune their reflexes and learn to run evasive patterns, like a football player running downfield. Bucking and kicking are defensive actions that would help drive away a predator that was getting too close.

Some animals are famous for this kind of "run-away" play. Pronghorns race in circles

Young squirrels are very playful, often chasing each other up and down a tree. The game will help them evade enemies when they are older.

and make fantastic leaps. Mountain goats and their relatives, ibexes and chamois, scamper across steep, rocky slopes. They jump from ledge to ledge and vault straight up into

Toys and Games

Animals not only play with each other—they also play with toys. A young wolf will use a stick to start a chase game, "daring" another wolf to take it and then running away with it. Naturalists have seen whales playing with balls of kelp, and elephants hurling clods of earth with their trunks. A raven will carry a stick into the air, drop it, and dive to catch it before the stick hits the ground. In New Zealand, people sometimes wake up to the sound of stones landing on their roofs. The culprits are parrots called keas, which toss rocks for fun and sometimes drop them on rooftops below.

Dolphins are famous for playing with toys in the water. But visitors to the Amsterdam zoo were amazed one day to see a hippopotamus playing with a leaf that had landed on the surface of its pond. The hippo went underwater and blew the leaf into the air with a blast from its nostrils. As soon as the leaf floated back down to the water surface, the hippo went down and blew it up again. Lethargic on land, hippos can really cavort in the water. They have even been seen doing underwater backflips.

Naturalists who have studied gorillas in Africa have seen these animals playing a version of football by tossing and kicking fruit. Sometimes primates even make toys. A chimp will poke a hole in a leaf and peer through it,

for a new view of the world. And young Japanese macaques—the snow monkeys of Japan—make snowballs. The monkeys carry the snowballs around as toys (above). But, so far as anyone knows, they don't throw them!

the air, just for the fun of it. All the while, they are developing the keen balance and coordination that they must have to stay alive in their rugged mountain homes.

Small animals play chase games, too. Maybe you've seen squirrels or chipmunks racing around, playing their own version of tag. Mice and rats play in the same way. They are practicing moves that will help them evade their enemies—predators such as cats, owls, and hawks. A little extra speed, a

slightly bigger leap, or a turn that's just a bit quicker can make all the difference between life and death for prey animals.

GOTCHA!

Predators have their own kinds of play. If you have watched a kitten or a puppy, you've seen some of these games. Toss a stick, and a puppy will be off and running, racing after it. The puppy pounces on the stick, grasps it in its teeth, and shakes its head. Wiggle a string or a feather in front of a kitten, and the little animal can't resist the game—it pounces on the moving object or reaches out to bat at it with its paws. Wolf cubs, lion cubs, and other wild members of the cat and dog families play similar games. They stalk, chase, pounce, bat, and "catch" sticks, stones, feathers, leaves, grasshoppers, and whatever else catches their eye—including their own tails. Often, litter mates stalk and chase each other. It's great fun, but it's also a way for these young animals to sharpen essential hunting skills. When they grow up, they will have to stalk and capture prey to survive.

Adult predators are generally too busy finding food to spend much time in play. But they'll tolerate a lot of playful nipping, swatting, and freshness from their youngsters, and sometimes they get in the act. Lionesses twitch their tails to give their cubs something to chase. Cheetahs and other hunting cats sometimes bring their young small prey before it's killed. The kittens play with the still-living prey, getting paws-on practice for the hunt.

You might be surprised at some of the other animals that play hunting games. When young dolphins frolic in the waves and play underwater tag with each other, they are honing skills that will help them

Wolf cubs chase and pounce and "catch" their prey. This helps them sharpen their hunting skills. Dolphins sharpen their fishing skills as they frolic in the waves and play underwater tag.

Mock fighting teaches animals social skills such as how and when to give in. Elephants play-wrestle with their trunks (above). Dall sheep play head-butting games (right).

catch fish. Bears go play fishing, too, splashing in mountain streams where, later, they'll catch dinner. When young bats start to fly, they chase each other through the air, learning to make the loops and dives they'll need to catch flying insects.

SOCIAL PLAY

When lion cubs wrestle and tumble around with each other, they're doing more than practicing hunting skills. Many kinds of play serve important social purposes, especially for animals that live in groups. Through play, young animals bond with other members of their group and learn to get along. They also learn to understand body language and other cues that group members use to communicate.

Mock fighting can help establish rank in the group. It can help youngsters learn how and when to give in, and how to control

A baby rhino plays with its mom by running rings around her and butting her—until she grunts, "Stop that!"

aggression. Wrestling matches, butting contests, and other games teach these skills. In Africa, lion cubs play "king of the hill" on termite mounds. Elephants bump heads and wrestle with their trunks. Sheep and goats play butting games, too. When they grow up, they will use the same moves to fight off rivals during breeding season. And young rhinos, who don't have many playmates, still find a way to play. A young rhino will run rings around its mother and then suddenly butt her—until she lets out a grunt that says, "Stop that!"

Bears are also known for their playful ways. There's nothing a bear likes better than giving a big bear hug—to another bear. Litter mates and even mothers and cubs hug tight and roll around, having a great time. Animals that most people don't think of as playful also kick up their heels at times. The collared

Let's play! Bears like to wrestle, chase each other, and give each other big bear hugs.

The Language of Play

Are these hippos fighting or playing? Animal play mimics serious behavior—fleeing, hunting, fighting. But animals can tell each other that they are just having fun! Animal play has its own language, made up of special signals called play markers. Here are some examples of the many ways animals have to say, "let's play!"

■ Mountain goats rear up on their hind legs or lean to one side.

■ Horses leap, buck, or shake their heads.

■ A dog or wolf does a play bow, crouching down in front with its tail waving in the air.

■ A kitten taps another kitten with its paw.

■ A weasel arches its back and hops.

■ A playful panda turns a somersault to let others know that it wants to romp.

■ A frolicsome rat flips over on its back.

■ Animals of many species, including dogs and primates, have a special play face, which is usually a relaxed, open-mouthed grin. When they're play-fighting, the grin says, "I'm not really angry—I'm just kidding around!" However, chimpanzees, baby gorillas, and baby orangutans are the only animals (besides people) that actually laugh.

peccary, a wild pig that lives in the southwestern United States, is best known for its quick temper. But bands of peccaries have been known to engage in frantic play sessions. All the members of the group tumble and leap around until they are exhausted; then they pile up together and nap. Naturalists think that these group games help forge tight bonds within the band.

Monkeys and other primates are among the most playful animals. Some monkey youngsters spend half their waking hours in play. They race through the treetops, playing hide-and-seek or follow-the-leader. They spin and twirl and wrestle with each other. Adults often get into the act, too: Chimpanzee moms make funny faces at their babies and tickle them under the chin. Young chimps tickle back.

SERIOUS BUSINESS

Play is risky in the wild. Monkeys that scamper through the trees, and young mountain goats that leap for joy, can fall and be injured. An animal may be so distracted while playing that it falls victim to a predator. But the skills that animals learn through play are important. Animal games look like fun—but they are really serious business.

And it seems that some animals just have to play, even in the most unlikely ways. No one knows, for example, why dolphins often

An orangutan tumbles in the treetops. Apes and monkeys are among the most playful of all animals.

In Canada's far north, this polar bear and sled dog spent a week romping with each other. Bears and dogs are known enemies—but sometimes odd playmates come together.

seek out boats and even swimmers, and frolic alongside them in the water. Some playmates are even odder. In Alaska, a naturalist watched a bear and a raven play tag with each other.

From Canada's far north comes the story of a polar bear that played with sled dogs. Polar bears and dogs are sworn enemies, and this big bear was definitely hungry. But for more than a week, the bear lumbered over to a place where about 40 dogs were tethered and romped with them. The two species seemed to understand each other—through the universal language of play.

Billions of honeybees have simply vanished from colonies across the United States and parts of Canada—and no one knows why!

WHERE HAVE ALL THE HONEYBEES GONE?

Beekeepers and farmers across North America faced a mystery in 2007. Honeybees were vanishing, and no one could figure out why. If the mysterious disappearance continued, scientists warned, it might affect food supplies—and not just supplies of honey!

Honeybees are important pollinators. The bees visit flowers to gather nectar and pollen. As they move from flower to flower, they spread grains of pollen from male to female flower parts. This pollinates the flowers, allowing the plants to form fruit. By pollinating crops, honeybees help produce every third bite of food that we eat.

COLONY COLLAPSE

Farmers rely on honeybees to pollinate some 90 crops, from apples to watermelons. Each spring, commercial beekeepers truck colonies of domestic honeybees, housed in hives, to farms and orchards around the country. They start in California, where the bees pollinate groves of almond trees. Then they move on to other crops in other places.

In domestic honeybee colonies, just as in wild honeybee colonies, each member has a job. Worker bees forage in fields, gardens, and orchards, carrying nectar and pollen back to the hive. Other workers remain in the hive, making honey, caring for larvae (young), and performing other tasks. The queen bee is the most important member. Her job is to lay eggs.

Many honeybees die at the end of summer, but thousands winter over. A colony that has 60,000 bees in summer might have 20,000 in winter. The bees stay in the hive, living on their stores of nectar and pollen until warm weather returns in the spring.

But since 2004, beekeepers have been reporting something strange. They have opened hives in the spring to find that the bees have disappeared. The hives are packed with food stores; but few adult bees, living or dead, remain. Often only the queen and a few young bees are left. The rest have simply vanished. The remaining bees are often sick, but they have a variety of different diseases—none of which would kill off a colony.

Scientists call this "colony collapse disorder" (CCD). In late 2006 and early 2007, beekeepers reported a sharp increase in CCD. The mysterious problem had spread to at least 27 states and parts of Canada. Many beekeepers lost more than 50 percent of their hives over the winter. Some reported losses of 90 percent.

SEARCHING FOR A CAUSE

What caused the wave of CCD? Scientists were determined to find out. The surviving bees in affected colonies had no signs of pesticide poisoning. Nor did they show signs of parasitic mites, which have caused problems for beekeepers in the past.

After months of tests, scientists zeroed in on a virus found in many of the affected colonies. This virus became a leading suspect. But scientists noted that that the virus occurs in many parts of the world. In other countries, it produces symptoms different from those seen in CCD. Thus it may not be the only cause.

Many researchers think that stress plays a role. Stress can interfere with the immune system, the body's natural defense against disease. Stressed bees easily fall victim to infections. Being trucked around the country could stress commercial colonies. Poor nutrition could also be a factor. Many affected colonies were in areas that had suffered drought. The drought hurt plants, so there was less flower nectar for bees.

Perhaps a combination of factors weakens the bees. Scientists continue to hunt for answers.

From Nectar to Honey

Golden honey begins with nectar, a watery liquid found in flowers. Foraging honeybees gather nectar and take it back to their hive. There, they pass the nectar to other workers, called house bees. The house bees mix the nectar with enzymes, which they produce in their bodies. Then they deposit it into a honeycomb—a mass of six-sided cells made of beeswax, which the bees also produce.

At first, the cells stay open, to let some of the water in the nectar evaporate. The bees fan the open cells with their wings to speed this up. The enzymes and evaporation change the nectar to honey. Then the bees cap the honey cells with beeswax.

Stores of honey and pollen (called beebread) feed the colony, but the bees make more honey than they need. Beekeepers collect the extra honey—about 80 pounds (36 kilograms), on average—for sale. The honey's flavor and other characteristics reflect the flowers where the bees gathered the nectar.

Honeybee colonies dying out

Bee colonies have been dying rapidly and in large numbers across the nation. The cause is unknown.

Colony Collapse Disorder, Feb. 2007

☐ Non-reported states
■ Affected states

D.C.

☐ Alaska
☐ Hawaii

SOURCE: United States Department of Agriculture

Not just honey

Many valuable agricultural products are dependent on honeybee pollination.

Crop and value in billions, 2006		Percentage pollinated by honeybees
Soybeans	$19.7	50%
Alfalfa	7.5	60
Cotton	5.2	80
Almonds	2.2	100
Apples	2.1	90
Oranges	1.8	90
Peaches	0.5	80
Cherries, sweet	0.5	90
Grapefruit	0.4	90
Tangerines	0.1	90

SOURCE: U.S. Dept. of Agriculture; Roger A. Morse and Nicholas W. Calderone, Cornell University

For centuries, mythical creatures—such as fierce, fire-breathing dragons—were imagined by people all over the world. They created these beasts as a way of making sense of actual but strange creatures they had never seen before.

MYTHICAL CREATURES: ANIMALS THAT NEVER WERE

The dragon stretched 17 feet (5 meters) from the tip of its huge fanged jaws to its scaly rump, and its snakelike tail was just as long. Enormous batlike wings rose from its scaly green back, which was studded with sharp, bony spines. Its powerful claws were poised to strike. Its orange eyes were filled with menace. It seemed ready to breathe fire at any minute as it crouched, guarding the entry.

The entry to an enchanted castle? No. This was the entrance to "Mythic Creatures: Dragons, Unicorns, and Mermaids," an unusual exhibit that opened at the American Museum of Natural History in New York City in May 2007 and ran to January 2008. It was scheduled to travel to Chicago, Illinois; Canada; Australia; and Atlanta, Georgia.

Visitors who were brave enough to pass the dragon at the entrance door discovered many other creatures of land, water, and air—all of which lived only in myths and legends. In years gone by, when great parts of the world were still unexplored, people believed that all kinds of outlandish beasts lived just over the horizon. Some were monstrous. Some were kind. And most had magical powers that they might use to help—or snare—the people who encountered them.

How did these imaginary animals take shape in people's minds? Some mythical beasts were likely based on reports from confused travelers who thought (or wished) they had seen such animals in distant places. Some may have been inspired by fossils of dinosaurs or other prehistoric animals. In many cases the legends are so old that it's hard to know what might have started them. But stories about strange and magical beasts are shared by many cultures, and often the creatures in stories from different parts of the world are strikingly alike.

CREATURES OF THE LAND

The unicorn is one of the most famous mythical creatures. It has appeared in stories from many lands. In China and Japan, tales of the unicorn (called the ki-lin or kirin) go back thousands of years. The ancient Greeks believed unicorns lived in India.

In Europe, unicorns were thought to be white. Asian unicorns came in all the colors of the rainbow. But the general appearance was similar—a graceful animal that looked like a horse, a deer, or sometimes a goat, with a single horn growing from its forehead. In most sto-

Myths about the unicorn (above) and its magical horn came from many parts of the world. The long spiraled tusk of an actual sea creature—the narwhal (left)—may have contributed to the legend.

ries the unicorn was a gentle, shy creature. It lived in deep forests and was hardly ever seen.

Stories about unicorns may have begun with travelers who saw real but unfamiliar animals. The travelers returned home with reports that were inaccurate or misunderstood. For example, travelers may have sighted an oryx, an Arabian antelope that has two long straight horns. If they saw the animal in profile, the two horns might have looked like one. Or perhaps travelers tried to describe a rhinoceros, and listeners imagined something that looked like a unicorn.

The horn of a unicorn was believed to have magical properties, able to protect a person from poison or the plague. In medieval Europe kings, queens, and nobles were willing to pay small fortunes to obtain these marvelous magical horns—and traders were happy to supply them. The horns were real enough, but they didn't come from unicorns. Many were the tusks of the male narwhal, a small whale that is sometimes called the unicorn of the sea. The tusk (actually an incredibly enlarged tooth) spirals straight out in front of the narwhal, growing up to 10 feet (3 meters) long. Vikings hunted the narwhals and sold these "unicorn horns" without revealing where they came from.

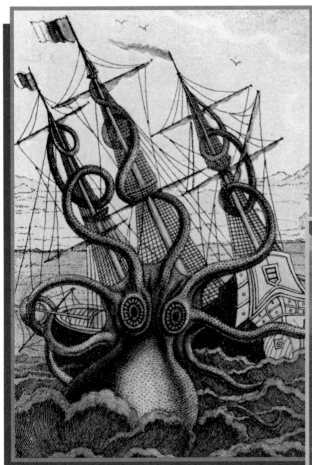

mate this ape weighed about 800 pounds (350 kilograms)! The last *Gigantopithecus blacki* are thought to have died out about 300,000 years ago. But if a few survived a little longer, perhaps early people in the region caught sight of them. That might have given rise to the legend. Or people may have come across giant ape fossils long ago, without knowing how old the bones really were. They may have believed that such huge creatures still roamed the land, and they began to spin tales about them.

Long ago, sailors told of a monstrous sea creature called the kraken (above). That imaginary water beast was probably inspired by a real giant squid (right), which can grow longer than a school bus.

No one has ever seen an actual unicorn, but for thousands of years people were convinced that they were real. The same can be said for other legendary creatures. Many people around the world still tell stories about huge primates, half human and half ape, said to roam remote forests and mountains. The yeti of the Himalayas, the almas of Mongolia, the yowie of Australia, and the sasquatch, or Bigfoot, of the American Pacific Northwest are just some of many examples. Many people claim to have caught glimpses of these hairy giants or heard their eerie howls. But no one has produced solid evidence that the creatures exist—no bones or other remains have been found.

However, people have found fossil teeth and jawbones of a giant ape, *Gigantopithecus blacki*, that once lived in Asia. Scientists esti-

CREATURES OF THE WATER

Long ago, people believed that all kinds of dangers lurked in oceans, rivers, and lakes. The borders of old maps were filled with pictures of sea serpents and other water monsters. And sailors often returned from voyages claiming to have seen such creatures.

The most fearsome sea creature was the kraken. More than 800 years ago, this monster was said to dwell in the waters between Norway and Iceland. The kraken was unbelievably huge—it supposedly measured more than 1.5 miles (2.4 kilometers) around. Each of its multiple arms was as big as a ship's mast. The kraken could easily toss a ship into the air, but it rarely attacked people. Still, it was dangerous. If it surfaced near a ship, the ship might capsize. And when the kraken sank, it would create a huge whirlpool that could suck a ship into the depths.

Many reports of sea monsters had simple explanations. Sea serpents might be oarfish, strange ribbonlike fish that can be 36 feet (11 meters) long. One immense "sea serpent" was nothing but seaweed. Several reports of dead sea monsters turned out to be carcasses of basking sharks, huge fish that grow to be nearly as long as the oarfish.

The legendary kraken may have been inspired by real animals—the giant squid and the colossal squid. The giant squid can grow longer than a school bus. Its even bigger cousin, the colossal squid, is the largest living invertebrate. Both are deep-sea dwellers, seldom seen alive. It's easy to see how sailors, finding bits of these animals' huge tentacles, might weave stories to explain them.

Sailors also told of mermaids (right), creatures with the upper body of a woman and the tail of a fish. What they actually saw were probably manatees, marine mammals that have paddlelike flippers and tails that allow them to gracefully move through the water.

Sailors also sighted mermaids, half human and half fish. A mermaid might appear to be a beautiful woman, swimming alongside the ship. But when she turned and dived beneath the waves, the sailors caught a glimpse of her fish's tail. Christopher Columbus reported sighting a mermaid in the ocean near the island of Haiti in 1493. He wrote that these creatures were "not as pretty as they are depicted, for somehow in the face they look like men."

Perhaps Columbus needed glasses. Modern scholars suspect that he actually saw a manatee. These large aquatic mammals live in shallow waters and swim near the surface, often popping up to breathe. Their bodies taper to a paddlelike tail, and their two forelimbs look something like arms. Manatees are found in the waters around the West Indies, West Africa, and a few other places, and Europeans weren't familiar with them in Columbus's time.

phant off the ground and stir up storms with its wings. It was said to live near Madagascar, an island off the southern coast of Africa. Some stories of the roc are based on the Garuda, a mythical creature found in Hindu stories dating back thousands of years. But a giant bird called Aepyornis did once live on Madagascar. The bird weighed half a ton and was the largest ever seen, although far smaller than the legendary roc. Long extinct, it has been identified from fossil bones and eggs.

Magical birds appear in myths from many lands. One of the best known is the legendary phoenix, a beautiful bird with feathers of

Tales were told of the roc (above), a bird so huge it could lift an elephant off the ground. Perhaps some imaginary flying creatures were based on fossils of dinosaurs with birdlike features (right).

Whether manatees or something else gave rise to European tales of mermaids, European sailors carried these tales with them all over the world. People in other places adapted the stories to fit their own cultures. Sailors also brought home proof—preserved specimens of little mermaids. The great showman P. T. Barnum put one such specimen on display at his museum in New York City in 1842. Crowds of people lined up and paid admission to see his "FeGee Mermaid." Like other such mermaid specimens, it was just a dried monkey's body stitched to a dried fish's tail.

CREATURES OF THE AIR

Arab traders told tales of a fabulous bird called the roc, so huge that it could lift an ele-

every color imaginable. The phoenix was said to live anywhere from three hundred to a thousand years, depending on the story. At the end of that time, at night, the bird would build a nest of fragrant spices. When the first light of day struck the nest, it would burst into flames and the phoenix would be consumed. But then the ashes would miraculously come to life, and the phoenix would be reborn. Even today the phoenix is a symbol of hope and renewal.

The skies of legends are filled with many other magical beasts. For example, there is Pegasus, the winged horse of Greek mythology. No mortal could hope to catch this wonderful horse. But the hero Bellerophon tamed Pegasus using a golden bridle given to him by a goddess. Then he rode his magical steed to battle the chimera, a three-headed mythical monster, by firing arrows from the air.

The griffin was a cross between a lion and an eagle, with the lion's powerful body and the head, claws, and wings of the eagle. (A similar creature, called the hippogriff, had the body of a horse.) Griffins were said to roost in high mountains, where they built nests lined with gold and precious gems. Sometimes a fortune-hunter would try to steal a griffin's gold, but none succeeded. A griffin was fierce—and powerful enough to carry off horses and cattle.

The ancient Greeks said that griffins guarded huge supplies of gold in Central Asia. A Greek author wrote, "The place where the griffins live and the gold is found is a grim and terrible desert. Waiting for a moonless night, the treasure-seekers come with shovels and sacks and dig. If they manage to elude the griffins, the men reap a double reward, for they escape with their lives and bring home a cargo of gold—rich profit for the dangers they face."

In fact, gold was mined in the Gobi Desert. And ancient gold miners might have seen something else—dinosaur fossils, which are common there. Some dinosaurs had birdlike beaks and bodies with four legs. If people dug up fossils of such a dinosaur, they may have thought they had found a monstrous animal that was half bird.

In the same way, dinosaur fossils may have helped give rise to the idea of dragons.

DRAGON TALES

Like unicorns and magical birds, dragons have appeared in stories from around the world. Often dragons were said to fly. But some had no wings and lived on land or in water.

In medieval Europe, dragons were thought to be evil creatures that soured wells, spread plague, and burned down homes with their fiery breath. In many medieval tales, dragons preyed on people and terrorized the countryside. Medieval heroes, it seemed, were constantly rescuing fair damsels from dragons that hoped to devour them.

While European dragons were fierce, Chinese dragons (above) were kinder and more gentle. But all dragon myths may have been inspired by fossils of dinosaurs.

But in Chinese legends, dragons could be kind, even helpful. They were honored as wise and powerful beings that supported the palaces of the gods in the skies, guarded buried treasure, and controlled forces of nature—wind and weather, streams and rivers. Helpful dragons would bring gentle rains, to help crops grow. But if dragons were angry, devastating floods and storms would occur.

With their sharp teeth and claws, huge size, and lizardlike bodies, dragons look like relatives of some dinosaurs. Of course, all the dinosaurs disappeared millions of years before there were people on Earth. But long ago, it's likely that people came across fossils of dinosaurs or other huge animals that had died out in prehistoric times, such as giant cave bears. These people may have thought they had found the bones of real dragons.

Today people know better. But it's still fun to imagine that these and other mythical creatures might be real.

WHAT'S IN A NAME?

Imagine! You've discovered an animal never before seen by people. How do you choose a name for it?

An animal's name usually shows its relationship to other animals. For example, an animal with feathers and wings is called a bird. Another part of the name may describe the animal's color—blackbird or bluebird. Where the animal lives may be part of the name, too—as with the European blackbird.

I belong to a certain group of beetles. My neck is so long that I've been named after a tall mammal of the African plains. My head is rather long, too, because of my very large snout.

I live on Madagascar, an island off the southeastern coast of Africa. And I'm a male. My female relatives don't have long necks.

But the females have an interesting method of laying eggs. They use their jaws to cut the ends of leaves, forming pieces that hang from the main part of the leaves by only a fiber or two. Then they roll the hanging pieces into little packages and lay an egg in each package. This protects the eggs from enemies and bad weather.

ANSWER: giraffe beetle or giraffe weevil

I'm a small, furry creature with a long tail. Indeed, my tail is longer than my body! My large eyes are a clue to my name.

All my relatives are active during the day. But my eyes are blinded by the sun, so I sleep during the day. As dusk falls, I wake up. Then I wake up my parents, brothers, and sisters.

We live high in the trees of South and Central American forests. We're very hungry when we wake up, and Mom or Dad scampers off to find fruit, tender leaves, insects, or other food. If none of our enemies are around, we soon follow them. After we've finished eating, we like to play. We chase each other from tree to tree and swing on vines—just like Tarzan!

ANSWER: night monkey or owl monkey

Many names describe unusual features. There's a fish with a long snout shaped like a tube, which it uses to suck up food. It's called the tube-mouthed fish. Other names are based on behavior. Retrievers are dogs that are skilled at retrieving, or bringing back, dead and wounded birds from wherever they may fall.

Look at and read about the four animals on these pages. Can you guess their names?

I'm a large bird that lives in Australia, New Guinea, and nearby islands. I was named by people on New Guinea, who speak the language called Papuan. My name, in Papuan, refers to the impressive bony crest on top of my head—think of the bony structures on the heads of cattle and goats.

I'm about 5 feet (1.5 meters) tall. But my wings are very small, and I can't fly. I can run fast though—much faster than any human. The crest protects my head as I run through dense rain forests at speeds of up to 30 miles (48 kilometers) per hour.

I'm quite shy, and if I see you I'll try to run away. But if you corner me, I'll fight—and my powerful legs and long, sharp claws can really hurt!

ANSWER: cassowary (which in Papuan means "horned head")

My name tells you three things: the continent near where I live, the habitat in which I live, and the type of animal I am.

The continent lies in the Southern Hemisphere between the Pacific and Indian oceans. The habitat is made up of salty water. My relatives and I are sometimes called snails without shells. Many of my relatives live on land; these dull-colored, slow-moving critters are pests in people's gardens. But the only people who see *me* are snorklers and divers. They like to photograph me because I'm very beautiful, with bright, colorful markings.

ANSWER: Australian sea slug

93

Australia's cuddly koalas are in danger because their natural habitat is being destroyed.

KOALAS: LIVING TEDDY BEARS

With its plump pear-shaped body, sleepy eyes, big ears, and cuddly fur, the koala is one of the cutest animals in the world. These tree dwellers almost look more like stuffed toys than real animals. And they are so beloved by people everywhere that they have been promoted as a national symbol by their homeland, Australia.

Yet despite their enormous popularity, koalas are in danger. In the past they were hunted nearly to extinction. Today they are threatened by disease and by the destruction of their natural habitat—the eucalyptus forests of eastern Australia.

TREE-DWELLING MARSUPIALS

Koalas look like little bears. In fact, the classic toy "teddy bear" looks a lot more like a koala than a bear. But koalas aren't bears at all. They are marsupials—mammals that raise their young in pouches outside the body. And they are distantly related to some of the other marsupials of Australia, such as the wombat. Like the wombat but unlike most other marsupials, the koala has a pouch that opens downward, toward the feet, rather than toward the head.

Koalas spend most of their lives in the eucalyptus trees that provide their food, and they are expert climbers. They have long, sharp claws, and their hands and feet are great for grasping. The first and second fingers of each hand oppose the other three fingers—which means that they essentially act as thumbs. This allows the koala to grip tightly to branches. And the feet have rough pads and opposable first toes, for gripping tree bark. Two toes are joined together, forming a handy comb for grooming the koala's thick, warm, grayish or rusty brown fur. Koalas can weigh up to 30 pounds (14 kilograms), although sizes vary and females generally weigh less. This makes them one of the largest tree-dwelling mammals in the world.

A koala can bite and scratch to defend itself, but these animals are mostly docile and good-tempered. A koala's life is a quiet one. For as much as 20 hours a day, the animal sleeps tucked securely in the fork of a tree. You may think this would be an uncomfortable bed, but a koala rests easily on a thick pad of gristle and fur on its rump.

Koalas are active mostly at night and at dusk, although they sometimes wake up for a midday snack. Most of their waking hours are spent eating. And koalas are among the pickiest eaters in nature. Their diet is made up almost entirely of eucalyptus leaves—and not just any eucalyptus leaves at that. Of the 600 different kinds of eucalyptus in Australia, koalas will eat leaves from only about 120 of them. A koala that eats a pound or two of leaves a day may sort through ten times that much to find ones it likes, sniffing each carefully with its big black nose. The animal stuffs those it chooses into its ample cheek pouches. Because of the large amounts of eucalyptus they eat, these little animals have an odd, medicinal smell—a bit like cough drops.

Koalas rarely go down to the ground. On the ground, they waddle along and are open to attack from dogs and other predators. And as long as enough eucalyptus leaves are on hand, there is little need for a koala to go to the ground. Koalas seldom if ever drink water; they get all the moisture they need from their leafy diet. But they do occasionally round out their diet by eating small amounts of dirt, which may provide minerals or help them digest the leaves.

Koalas make a variety of sounds. Males grunt like pigs, while females make a higher-pitched noise. Frightened koalas howl and wail, and the cries of lost baby koalas sound like

This "bed" may look uncomfortable, but it's just perfect for a koala! Koalas sleep about 20 hours a day, tucked in the fork of a tree.

the cries of human babies. And groups of koalas have been heard murmuring to each other in the trees.

KOALA FAMILIES

Koalas mate during the Australian summer—September to January. At that time males can be heard calling loudly to attract a harem of females, and they may fight with each other over territory. Females generally mate and give birth once a year.

Young koalas are born singly (twins are very rare) about 35 days after mating. A koala is only about the size of a jellybean at birth, and it is blind and hairless. It immediately crawls into its mother's pouch and attaches itself to a nipple.

A koala munches on a juicy eucalyptus leaf. The leaves provide these finicky eaters with all the food and water they need to survive.

KOALAS IN DANGER

Koalas were once widespread throughout eastern Australia. Today they are confined to a few pockets of their former range, and the areas where they live are shrinking. Although not everyone agrees, some people believe they are in danger of dying out.

The Australian aborigines hunted koalas for food for many, many years, but koalas didn't become endangered until the late 19th and early 20th centuries. At that time, hunters found that there was great demand for the koalas' soft fur. Each year more and more koalas were killed, and their skins were shipped overseas for sale. At the height of the slaughter, in 1924, as many as two million skins were exported. By then, it was clear that the koala would be wiped out if the killing continued. The United States banned the import of koala skins, and after 1927 koala hunting was banned in Australia.

But koalas soon faced new threats. As the number of people in Australia grew, more land was taken over for farms and houses and malls. Eucalyptus forests were cut down. By some estimates, as much as 80 percent of the eucalyptus habitat of eastern Australia has been destroyed over the years. And because the koala's diet is so specialized, it hasn't been able to adapt—a koala *must* have eucalyptus trees to live. When the animals don't have a large enough territory in which to find their food, they will strip all the leaves from the few trees they find, killing them. And when those few trees are dead, the koalas starve.

The destruction of the koalas' habitat continues. And as more people move into what was once koala territory, koalas face other dangers. They may be hit by cars or attacked by dogs, or they may drown in backyard swimming pools. In recent years, koalas have also been plagued by disease. Forest fires pose another deadly threat for the little marsupials—in 2002, forest fires around Sydney, Australia, killed many koalas and destroyed much of their habitat.

There it stays, sucking milk and growing into a furry young koala. As it grows larger, it begins to poke its head out of the pouch and then to climb out for short periods of time.

After about six months, the koala leaves the pouch for good. Until it is about a year old, it rides around on its mother's back, learning to eat leaves and clamber around in the trees. Then it becomes more independent. When a young koala is about eighteen months old, it usually leaves its mother's home range and heads off to find its own territory.

Except during the mating season, koalas tend to be solitary animals—they live alone. In the wild, they usually live about 12 years, but they can live to be 20 or more.

Until they are about a year old, baby koalas ride on their mothers' backs, learning to eat leaves and scramble in the trees.

For these reasons, people are taking special steps to protect koalas. Laboratory researchers are working to find treatments for the diseases that affect the animals. In the field, wildlife specialists are studying koalas to find out how much land they need and what kind of habitat and diet suit them best. Other researchers are trying to develop an artificial diet that can replace eucalyptus leaves. And still others are studying plans both to move koalas to unpopulated areas and to preserve koala habitats alongside suburban developments.

No one is sure how much danger koalas are in. This is because no one knows how many koalas lived in Australia originally, or even how many koalas are alive today (estimates range from 100,000 to 400,000). But most experts agree that the number of koalas is declining.

Crazy for Koalas

The koala's adorable looks have made it famous around the world. In fact, the craze for koalas has given rise to a multi-billion-dollar industry, especially in Australia. The furry marsupial is the best-known national symbol of its country. Its image appears on T-shirts, mugs, and dozens of other souvenirs. Thousands of stuffed toy koalas are sold every year. And Australia's national airline has made the koala its official emblem.

Koalas have long been the favorites of zoo-goers around the world. Most recently, they have become a big hit in China. In May 2006, the Xiangjiang Safari Park in the city of Guangzhou imported three male and three female koalas from Australia. Before long, four cubs, including a pair of twins, were born. These were China's first koalas.

Koalas are a major attraction for the thousands of tourists who visit Australia each year. At privately run preserves, visitors have a chance to view these fascinating animals up close—and can sometimes even cuddle them.

Other Australian animals may be rarer and in greater danger of dying out. But Australians want to be sure that the cuddly koala, their country's greatest goodwill ambassador, will always be around for the world to love.

ANIMALS IN THE NEWS

Bald eagles had reason to soar in 2007. For more than 30 years, this bird—a national symbol of the United States—was on the nation's list of endangered and threatened species. But the eagle has made a dramatic comeback, and in June officials removed it from the list.

In 1782, when the bald eagle became the national bird, there may have been 75,000 breeding pairs of these birds in what is today the continental United States. But people took over eagle habitats as they moved into wild areas. Hunters killed many eagles. And the use of DDT and other insecticides took a heavy toll. These chemicals contaminated fish that the eagles ate, causing the birds to produce fragile eggs that broke before hatching. By 1963, only 417 breeding pairs of bald eagles remained in the lower 48 states.

The government banned DDT in 1972. A year later, under the Endangered Species Act, bald eagles in states south of Alaska were listed as endangered and protected by law. Before long, their numbers began to grow. In 1995, the government upgraded the bird from "endangered" to "threatened," a less severe status.

In 2007 there were almost 10,000 breeding pairs of bald eagles in the lower 48 states. The government decided that it was time to "delist" the bird. The eagles still face threats, so wildlife officials will monitor their health carefully. And large areas of eagle habitat will still be protected.

When a tiger at a Chinese zoo rejected her newborn cubs in spring 2007, **a dog named Huani** stepped in. Huani, a mixed-breed farm dog, nursed the tiger triplets alongside her own pup for about a month—until they grew too large. Zoo officials said it wasn't the first time that Huani had cared for tiger cubs.

Knut, a cuddly polar bear cub, was the talk of Germany in 2007. Born in December 2006 at the Berlin Zoo, Knut was abandoned by his mother. Zookeepers took over his care, feeding him with a bottle. News media reported his daily progress. And before long, Knut was a star. He was featured on the cover of a major magazine. There were stuffed Knut toys for kids. He even starred in a music video! Attendance at the zoo doubled—twice a day, visitors lined up to watch the little bear play with his keepers. The play sessions would end as Knut grew up, the zoo said. Polar bears are among the largest predators in the world.

What makes people love baby bears and certain other animals? These animals are cute. And just what is it that makes them so cute? Scientists have asked that question, and they have come up with a list of **"cute cues"**—traits that make people respond with coos and squeals.

Bright, forward-facing eyes are high on the list, especially if they are set low on a big round face. The panda (top right) is a perfect example. Its black-and-white markings make its eyes seem extra big and extra low, and its big round ears add to the cute factor. People also fall for floppy limbs and a waddling walk—like the young penguins (top left). And animals with folds of loose skin are often deemed cute. The manatee (bottom right) is an example. The manatee also shows that cuteness has little to do with beauty.

The animal that best illustrates all the cute cues, of course, is a human baby. In fact, scientists say, people respond to cute cues precisely because they mimic the traits of babies. Like a panda, a baby has a round face and low, forward-facing eyes. Like a manatee, a baby has folds of loose skin. And a waddling penguin looks like a toddler dressed up in a tuxedo. People naturally want to cuddle and care for babies. And that carries over to anything that shares these cute traits.

The **Yorkshire terrier** weighs only about 7 pounds (3 kilograms). But it bested much bigger dogs in 2007. The American Kennel Club (AKC), which registers purebred dogs in the United States, said that the Yorkie was the nation's second most popular breed. It was the first time in almost 70 years that a small breed had ranked so high.

The Labrador retriever has topped the list since 1991. About 124,000 Labs were registered with the AKC in 2006. There were about 48,000 Yorkies. German shepherds ranked third. The Yorkie's rise is part of a trend toward smaller dogs. Big dogs are great pets, but they need lots of exercise. Pint-sized pets like Yorkies are perfect for people in apartments.

The English springer spaniel may not rank highest in popularity, but that didn't bother a handsome spaniel named James in 2007. In February, James—whose full name is **Champion Felicity's Diamond Jim**—won the top award at the Westminster Kennel Club Dog Show in New York City. Westminster is America's most prestigious dog show. James's win, then, made him the nation's new top dog. Springer spaniels like James are medium-sized sporting dogs, originally developed for bird hunting. They are friendly, eager to please, and excellent hunters.

Flora, a female Komodo dragon at the Chester Zoo in Great Britain, surprised scientists when she became a mom. Flora was raised at the zoo and
had never mated with—or even met—a male Komodo dragon. Yet she laid
a clutch of eggs. And baby dragons hatched from seven of them in late
December 2006.

Komodo dragons are the world's largest lizards. Like most animals, they
reproduce sexually. A male sperm cell fertilizes a female egg, and the egg
develops into an embryo. But Flora fertilized her own eggs. No one knew
that Komodo dragons could do this. However, in reviewing records,
researchers found one earlier case in which a Komodo dragon at a London zoo reproduced this way.

Self-fertilization occurs in some other lizards, but it's more common in
insects and other invertebrates (animals without backbones). Females that
develop this ability do so when they can't find males. Self-fertilization may
have helped Komodo dragons in their homeland, Indonesia, which is
made up of islands. A female that swam to an island alone could start a
new dragon colony.

Thumbelina, a miniature horse from Missouri, trotted into the record books in 2007. Weighing just 57 pounds (26 kilograms), she was the world's smallest living horse. Thumbelina stood just a bit over 17 inches (43 centimeters) tall at the shoulder, about a foot shorter than most miniature horses. The largest living horse, a draft horse named Radar in Texas, was about five times taller and 40 times heavier! Despite her small size, Thumbelina had a big job. She toured the United States in the summer of 2007 to raise money for children's charities.

A month-old tiger cub and a baby orangutan make an odd couple. You would never see this pairing in the wild. But two orangutan babies became best buddies with twin tiger cubs at an Indonesian zoo in early 2007. Both sets of babies were abandoned by their mothers. They were placed in the same nursery to be hand-raised at the zoo. Soon they were fast friends, romping and playing together. But the friendship couldn't last. Zookeepers were careful to separate the buddies as they grew bigger—before the tigers' natural hunting instincts appeared.

SCIENCE

In 1807, onlookers were amazed by the sight of a steamboat as it chugged up the Hudson River from New York City to Albany. The boat was the creation of Robert Fulton. Fulton didn't invent the first steamboat, but he was the first person to build one that was commercially successful. The 200th anniversary of the maiden voyage of his boat (later named the Claremont) was celebrated in 2007.

CLIMATE CHAOS!

Global warming—it's an issue that people have been debating for years. Is the world's climate really getting warmer? If so, what's causing the change? How will it affect people and all the other living things on Earth?

For most people, debate over these questions ended. A series of reports from a United Nations panel of some 2,000 of the world's leading scientists confirmed what many experts have been saying for a long time: Not only is Earth's climate changing, but people are responsible. Rising temperatures are having effects worldwide, and the effects are likely to get worse.

Now attention is shifting to questions that may be even more important. What can be done to stop or slow global warming? What can be done to help people and other living things adapt to climate change? There are growing calls for action. Scientists have many ideas, but they warn that fighting climate change will take a lot of effort. And the world's nations don't agree about what to do.

THE FORECAST: WARMER

The United Nations group, the Intergovernmental Panel on Climate Change (IPCC), was formed in 1988 to alert nations about risks from climate change. Two years later, in its first report, the panel confirmed that Earth's climate was warming due to a process called the greenhouse effect. In this process, carbon dioxide and certain other gases in the air act like the glass in a greenhouse. They trap heat from the sun and prevent it from escaping back into space. Throughout Earth's history, a natural greenhouse effect has helped regulate the climate, allowing life to flourish. But the greenhouse effect was growing, and the IPCC scientists worried that human activities were the cause.

In 2007, IPCC scientists released four new reports. They concluded that people were almost certainly the cause of climate change—mainly through the use of gasoline, oil, coal, and other fossil fuels. These fuels release carbon dioxide and other greenhouse gases

In 2007, a group of the world's leading scientists confirmed that Earth's climate is getting warmer—and people are largely responsible. Rising temperatures could cause melting ice sheets; increased droughts, floods, and wildfires; and damage to coral reefs.

into the air as they burn. The gases build up in the atmosphere, and the atmosphere traps more heat. That makes temperatures rise around the world. The experts drew a grim picture of the results.

Global warming is already changing weather patterns, the panel said. The changes are affecting everything from supplies of drinking water to glaciers and ice sheets, which are melting. If greenhouse emissions keep growing at current rates, global temperatures could rise 11°F (6°C) by 2100. Even an increase of 3.6°F (2°C) by 2050 could bring huge problems, the panel said. Some 20 to 30 percent of the world's species could be driven to extinction.

Among the changes that warming might bring, the panel said, are these:

■ Warming will cause the melting of ice sheets, and this will cause sea levels to rise. Low-lying islands and coastal areas worldwide—from the Louisiana coast to the river deltas of Africa and Asia—could see floods affecting millions of people.

■ Freshwater supplies will shrink in dry regions. Areas prone to drought will expand. But wet areas could see heavier snow and rainfall, bringing increased flooding.

■ A modest rise in temperatures would mean longer growing seasons in some areas, and farmers could benefit. But in other areas, drought and flooding will damage crops.

International Polar Year

Climate change is having dramatic effects in Antarctica and the Arctic. Glaciers and ice sheets are shrinking. Sea ice and snow cover are melting more and earlier each year. Even the permafrost—the layer of permanently frozen soil that underlies Arctic lands—is starting to melt.

The changes have prompted a huge international scientific research effort, called International Polar Year (IPY). IPY is actually two years—from March 2007 to March 2009. Scientists from some 60 countries are taking part, carrying out over 200 research projects.

Many of these scientists are focusing on the impact of climate change on polar lands and peoples and on the ways in which melting ice sheets will affect the rest of the world. Others want to learn more about the polar regions even as they are in the process of changing. For example, IPY scientists who are studying the collapse of huge ice shelves along the Antarctic coast have found exotic ocean animals, including new species, living in places that were once covered by ice. They saw a psychedelic octopus (below left), bright orange sea stars (below right), blue ice fish with fanned fins, and roving bands of sea cucumbers.

How does life survive in the harsh polar conditions? What clues to Earth's past are locked in the ice? IPY scientists hope to find answers to these and many other questions before the polar regions change.

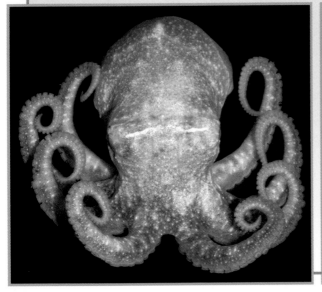

■ Rising ocean temperatures will harm coral reefs. Warming will also damage other delicate ecosystems. Increases in wildfires and insect pests will put forests at risk.

■ Poor areas are likely to feel the effects of global warming most severely. In these areas, clean water, health care, and other services are already scarce.

Too little is being done to prevent or prepare for the effects of warming, the IPCC warned, and the panel outlined what needs to be done.

CAN WARMING BE STOPPED?

Just to keep the temperature rise to a moderate 3.6°F, the panel said, the world will need to cut greenhouse emissions dramatically—to 50 percent of 1990 levels by 2050. That will require efforts on many fronts.

People need to switch from fossil fuels to alternative energy sources. Power plants and factories could convert from coal to natural gas, nuclear power, or renewable energy sources such as wind and solar power and biofuels (fuels made from plants). People can design new facilities to use these energy sources. In years to come, technologies such as hydrogen fuel cells and advanced hybrid and electric vehicles could end reliance on gasoline.

People also need to use energy more efficiently. Better insulation, lighting, and other changes in design and materials could cut greenhouse emissions from buildings by about 30 percent by 2020, the panel said. People can do more to make motor vehicles more fuel-efficient, too. These steps would have an immediate payoff—people would spend less on energy.

Other actions can help, the panel said. For example, trees act as carbon "sinks"—they absorb carbon dioxide from the air. But the world's forests are shrinking as people cut trees for timber and clear land for development. Reducing deforestation, as this trend is called, and planting more trees would help limit carbon dioxide in the air. In the future, a technology called carbon sequestration, in which carbon emissions are stored underground, might also help. So would capturing methane, another greenhouse gas, which is released by livestock and manure.

Most of these ideas have been on the table for a while, but they haven't been widely adopted. Cost is one reason. It costs money to convert power plants to new fuels or add insulation to buildings. In the end, the effects of climate change will cost more than the steps taken to fight it. But governments can make such steps more appealing in several ways, the IPCC said. They can impose "carbon taxes" on fossil fuels. They can adopt "cap-and-trade" systems, like a system being used in Europe. There, industries are given emissions quotas. Efficient companies that don't use all their quotas can sell the excess to less efficient companies.

INTERNATIONAL ACTION

Emissions of greenhouse gases have risen 70 percent since 1970 and could rise an additional 90 percent by 2030 if nothing is done. It will take a huge effort just to keep the concentration of carbon dioxide in the atmosphere at about the current

Bear Trouble

Polar bears are among the largest predators in the world. They are the rulers of the Arctic ice—but their survival is in doubt. In May 2006, the World Conservation Union designated the polar bear as a threatened species. And in 2007, the United States proposed adding the polar bear to its list of threatened species.

Shrinking sea ice is the main reason. Polar bears spend most of their time on the Arctic pack ice, hunting for seals and other prey. They also den and raise their cubs on the ice. But the pack ice is melting more and earlier each summer, and most scientists agree that climate change is the main cause. In the summer of 2007, the extent of the Arctic pack ice shrank more than ever recorded.

Less ice means less habitat for polar bears. It's harder for them to find food and den sites. More bears are starving, and fewer cubs are surviving. As a result, their numbers are declining. In September 2007, U.S. government scientists said that two-thirds of the world's polar bears will likely disappear by 2050.

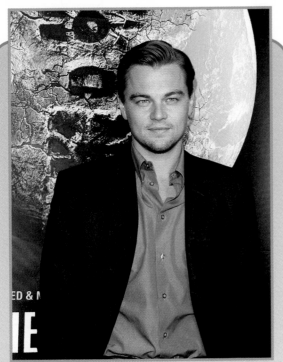

Leonardo DiCaprio's documentary film about global warming—*The 11th Hour*—opened in August.

Celebrity Climate Crusaders

Some big names from the worlds of politics and entertainment helped draw attention to the climate crisis in 2007.

● Former Vice President Al Gore continued to speak out about climate change. Gore shared (with the IPCC) the 2007 Nobel Peace Prize for this work. And his 2006 documentary on climate change, *An Inconvenient Truth,* won two Academy Awards in 2007.

● The Clinton Climate Initiative (CCI), launched by former U.S. President Bill Clinton, focused on cutting greenhouse emissions in the world's largest cities. In May 2007, the CCI announced a plan under which banks agreed to provide loans for new energy-efficient heating, cooling, and lighting systems in older city buildings.

● Actor Leonardo DiCaprio produced and narrated a documentary, *The 11th Hour*, that opened in theaters in August. Much of the movie focused on ways to combat global warming.

● Singer Sheryl Crow and Hollywood producer Laurie David toured colleges in a biodiesel bus to raise awareness about global warming. They urged the U.S. government to impose mandatory curbs on carbon dioxide and other greenhouse gases within two years.

level, the panel said, and much more must be done. All nations will have to take action, and quickly. Yet some of the world's biggest producers of greenhouse emissions have yet to sign on to the effort.

Under a treaty called the Kyoto Protocol, 35 industrialized countries agreed to cut greenhouse emissions to 5 percent below 1990 levels. But U.S. President George W. Bush rejected the treaty, saying it would slow the U.S. economy. And the treaty didn't cover developing countries such as China.

The United States has been the world's largest emitter of greenhouse gases, but China was expected to take the lead in 2007. China, which is undergoing huge growth, burns lots of coal.

The Kyoto limits are set to expire in 2012. In August 2007 representatives of 158 countries agreed to press for much steeper cuts to replace them. They called for reducing emissions by 25 to 40 percent of 1990 levels by 2020. Those targets were taken up at the U.N. Climate Change Conference, a major international climate summit in December 2007 in Bali, Indonesia. Just before the meeting, the IPCC released its fourth report, summarizing its findings. This report stated the risks of climate change in the starkest terms yet. The report was a call to action. But China and the United States still didn't accept the idea of mandatory cuts.

Even if countries cut emissions by the amounts required, the climate will grow warmer for many years. It will take time to put the cuts into effect, and carbon dioxide stays in the atmosphere for decades. Thus countries must also prepare for the effects of climate change, the IPCC warned.

GETTING INVOLVED

The IPCC reports sparked a chorus of calls for the U.S. government to adopt a stronger climate policy. Meanwhile, people took action on many levels.

■ Activist groups staged demonstrations and other events. In April, a group called Step It Up! organized 1,400 rallies in locations chosen to show how climate change would affect daily life.

Shrink Your Carbon Footprint

How big is your carbon footprint? The footprint is a measure of the greenhouse gases you put in the air. You can estimate your footprint on line, at Web sites such as *www.carbonfootprint.com.* Chances are you'll be shocked at your footprint's size—and want to make it smaller. Here are 10 ways to do that.

1. Ride your bike. For every mile you ride your bike instead of driving a car, you avoid the production of about 1 pound (0.5 kilograms) of carbon dioxide.

2. Turn off electronics. Video-game boxes and many other electronic gadgets keep using power even when they're off. Plug them into a power strip, and switch the power strip off when you aren't using them.

3. Use recycled paper products. If every household in the United States replaced one roll of toilet paper with recycled paper, that would save 424,000 trees—which could soak up lots of carbon dioxide from the air.

4. Take shorter showers. You'll use less hot water and less energy, and produce less carbon dioxide.

5. Change your lightbulbs. Replace three frequently used lightbulbs with compact fluorescent bulbs, which use about 70 percent less energy.

6. Muscle-mow your lawn. A gasoline-powered lawn mower can produce more carbon dioxide than a car. A push-mower just burns calories.

7. Change your thermostat. In winter, turn down the heat at night and when you're not home. In summer, set the thermostat for air conditioning at 75 degrees. You'll save money and reduce pollution.

8. Reduce, reuse, recycle. Buy products with less packaging and recycle paper, plastic, and glass. Take reusable cloth bags to the store, instead of using disposable paper or plastic. You'll help save trees and produce fewer greenhouse gases.

9. Line-dry laundry. Hang your laundry to dry, instead of using a dryer, to save energy and cut carbon-dioxide emissions.

10. Drink tap water. Bottled water is popular today, but producing and shipping those bottles uses lots of oil—and produces lots of carbon dioxide.

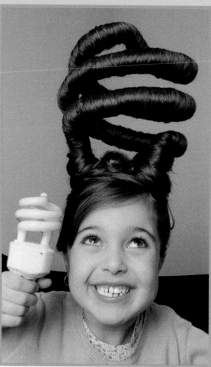

This youngster's hairdo resembles the new compact fluorescent lightbulb she is holding. She appeared in a commercial promoting the benefits of these energy-efficient lightbulbs.

■ States stepped up to the plate. Groups of states in the Northeast, Southwest, Midwest, and West Coast signed regional agreements to cut greenhouse emissions. California pledged to cut greenhouse emissions by one-third by 2020, through steps ranging from cleaner-burning cars to smarter development. The governors of California, Montana, and Utah appeared in nationwide ads urging Congress to act.

■ Local leaders took action. By 2007, the leaders of 435 U.S. cities had agreed to meet the greenhouse-gas reductions of the Kyoto Protocol. They were installing low-energy streetlights and solar-powered trash compactors, adopting "green" building standards, and taking many other steps.

A 2007 poll showed that most Americans think climate change is a serious issue that calls for immediate action. Will enough be done, quickly enough, to prevent the worst effects of climate change? That question will be answered, yes or no, in the years ahead.

Robert Fulton's steamboat made its first trip up the Hudson River in 1807, becoming the world's first commercially successful steamboat. The 200th anniversary of that voyage was marked in 2007.

FULL STEAM AHEAD!

When Robert Fulton launched a steamboat at New York City in 1807, people gathered on shore—to laugh! A boat powered by a steam engine? "Fulton's Folly" would never run, they said. "There were not perhaps thirty persons in the city who believed that the boat would ever move one mile an hour, or be of the least utility," Fulton later wrote in a letter to a friend.

But Fulton had the last laugh. On its maiden voyage, his steamboat traveled up the Hudson River to Albany and then returned to New York City. The trip was a complete triumph. And before long, Fulton's steamboat was making regular runs up and down the river, carrying paying passengers.

In 2007, people celebrated the 200th anniversary of that famous trip. Fulton wasn't the first person to build a steamboat, but his boat was the first to be a commercial success. It marked the start of a new age in travel.

FROM SAIL TO STEAM

In Fulton's day, ships depended on the wind for long trips. Sailing ships carried people and goods along rivers and across oceans around the world. The best of these ships were sleek and fast, with tall masts and huge canvas sails. But they all shared one drawback: If the wind didn't blow, the ships couldn't go. Travel, then, was often left to chance.

With steam power, ships wouldn't need to wait for the wind—they could travel anytime. Robert Fulton wasn't the first person to recognize how important this might be. The American inventor John Fitch hit on the idea in the 1780's, and he demonstrated a steamboat on the Delaware River in 1787. Members of the Constitutional Convention at Philadelphia, Pennsylvania, were among the onlookers.

Later, Fitch built several other steamboats and started a passenger service between Philadelphia and Trenton, New Jersey. But

Fitch's boats cost more to build and run than they could earn, and the venture failed. Many people decided that the steamboat was a joke—a ship powered by a "teakettle"—and would never be practical.

Among the few who thought otherwise were Fulton and Robert R. Livingston, a wealthy and powerful merchant. Fulton believed steamboat travel could be practical. And Livingston had secured exclusive rights to develop steamboat routes in New York State. He agreed to back Fulton in an attempt to build a steamboat that could travel at least 4 miles (6.4 kilometers) an hour. In 1806, Fulton began work on the project at a boatyard on the East River in New York City.

FULTON'S STEAMBOAT

Fulton's boat was 133 feet (41 meters) long, with a wedge-shaped bow and stern. It had two masts and could put out sails if need be, but steam was the main power source. On the deck was a large boiler, mounted on fireproof brickwork and topped by a tall smokestack. The boiler burned pine wood to heat water and produce steam for the boat's 24-horsepower engine, which was mounted just in front of it. The engine would turn two large side paddle wheels, which would push the boat through the water.

On August 17, 1807, the steamboat was finally ready for its first trip up the Hudson River. Fulton and a group of invited passen-

Robert Fulton: Artist and Inventor

As a boy, Robert Fulton had two great interests—drawing and mechanical inventions. Those interests would shape his life.

Born in Lancaster, Pennsylvania, in 1765, Fulton was fascinated by machines of all kinds. While still in school, he designed a rocket and a hand-powered paddle-wheel boat. He was also a talented artist, and at one time he thought of making a living as a painter. As a young man he traveled to England to study under the well-known American painter Benjamin West. But his real talent lay in figuring out how things worked—and how to make them work better. In England, Fulton invented a machine to dig canals, and he worked on several canal projects. A few years later, in France, he built a "diving boat"—a submarine—and a torpedo.

In Paris, Fulton met Robert R. Livingston, a wealthy merchant who was then serving as the U.S. minister to France. With Livingston's encouragement, he began to work on designs for a steamboat. The two men formed a business partnership in 1802, and the next year they launched a small steamboat on the Seine River. The work continued back in New York with the building of the *Claremont.*

After the success of the *Claremont* in 1807, Fulton married Harriet Livingston, a young relative of Robert Livingston. Fulton and Robert Livingston expanded their business, beginning steamboat service on the Raritan, Potomac, and Mississippi rivers as well as the Hudson. Fulton didn't enjoy his success for long, however. He fell ill and died in February 1815, at age 49.

Steam Power!

The steam engine is based on a simple idea: When water turns into steam, it expands. The energy of the expanding steam can be harnessed to do work. In the engine that powered Robert Fulton's boat, the force of expanding steam drove a piston back and forth inside a closed cylinder, and the piston turned the paddle wheels.

This engine was an improved version of one developed by Scottish inventor James Watt. He didn't invent the first steam engine, but he improved earlier designs so much that his engines helped usher in the Industrial Revolution.

In Watt's first steam engine, introduced in 1769, steam (made by heating water in a boiler) was let into a cylinder to push a piston down. Then the piston was raised, using a weighted lever. This "single-acting" engine produced short spurts of power with each downstroke. It was used mainly to pump water.

Later, Watt developed a "double-acting" engine. It had a sliding valve that delivered steam alternately to each end of a cylinder, pushing the piston back and forth (see diagram). This powered both the upstroke and the downstroke. Now the moving piston could be hooked up to gears and used to run machines in factories and turn the wheels of locomotives—or the paddle wheels of steamboats.

Steam engines were improved in many ways in later years and were the major source of power for machines of all kinds until the 1900's. Then they began to be replaced by electric motors, internal-combustion engines, and other more efficient sources of power.

How a Simple Steam Engine Works

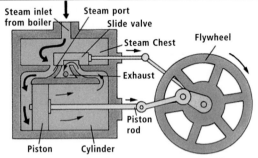

Steam entering the left-hand side of the chamber will move the piston to the right.

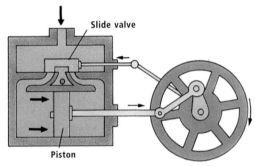

As expanding steam continues to push the piston to the right, the slide valve closes and no more steam enters the chamber.

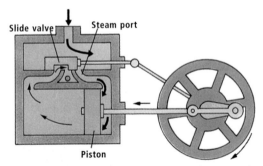

When the piston is all the way to the right again, the steam rushes into the right-hand side of the chamber and pushes the piston back to the left.

gers were on deck, and the wharf was crowded with spectators. "I heard a number of sarcastic remarks," Fulton later recalled. The steamboat put off from the wharf, lurched forward—and stopped. Fulton quickly fixed the engine. Then, to the surprise of the doubting crowd, the boat chugged upriver, riding low in the water due to the weight of the machinery and brickwork on board.

Traveling against the current, the steamboat took 32 hours to make the 150-mile (240-kilo-meter) trip from New York City north to Albany. It completed the return trip in 30 hours. Its sails were never hoisted, and it made an average speed of 5 miles (8 kilometers) an hour. That wasn't very fast even for 1807, when transportation of all kinds was much slower than it is today. With a fair wind, a Hudson River sloop (one of the fast sailing ships on the river) could easily beat the time. But Fulton's boat didn't need wind. He wrote, "The power of propelling boats by steam is now fully proved."

After its successful maiden voyage, the steamboat was quickly fitted out with cabins for passengers. It began regular runs in September. At first, the sound of its noisy engine and splashing paddles frightened animals and startled people all along the river. So did the sight of black smoke—and, at night, glowing sparks—pouring from its smokestack. But by late November the steamboat had already turned a profit. That winter it was given more alterations and a name—*North River Steam-*

single paddle wheel mounted on beams between the hulls. While the *Claremont*'s engine had been made in England, Fulton also began to design and build his own steam engines.

By the time of Fulton's death, in 1815, his boats were providing regular service on several rivers, including the Mississippi. His steamboats cut the cost of shipping goods between New Orleans, Louisiana, and Natchez, Mississippi, by 25 percent.

A steam engine powered the *Claremont*. It turned two big paddle wheels, one on each side, pushing the boat through the water.

boat of Claremont. Fulton always called it the *North River,* which was an alternate name for the Hudson River. Most people called it the *Claremont* (or *Clermont*), which was the name of Robert Livingston's estate on the banks of the Hudson.

A NEW ERA

Fulton went on to design more than a dozen steamboats, including a warship. One of his boats had two separate hulls, with a

Others were quick to see the advantages of these vessels—their major advantage being speed. As new and better steamboats began to ply the rivers, they helped the country grow. Steamboats linked towns far from the sea with ports on the coast, allowing people to send and receive goods from around the world. By 1838 steamboats were even crossing oceans.

The age of sailing ships was beginning to draw to a close.

"I scream, you scream, we all scream for ice cream!" And one of the most popular ice-cream concoctions is the super-duper banana split.

THE INSIDE SCOOP ON ICE CREAM

Smooth and sweet, cool and creamy—nothing tops ice cream as a treat. In fact, ice cream and other frozen dairy desserts—such as frozen yogurt, sherbet, ice milk, and gelato—are so popular, they are eaten in practically every country of the world.

Ice cream may seem like a simple food, but this tasty dessert is actually quite complicated. It took centuries to develop ice cream as we know it, and a lot of modern technology and scientific knowledge go into the making of the ice cream we enjoy today.

A SWEET HISTORY

Ice cream has a long history. The idea of frozen desserts is said to have begun with the Roman emperor Nero, who lived in the 1st century A.D. Nero was known for his lavish banquets. One special treat was snow, brought by runners from nearby mountains and flavored with honey, fruit juices, and wine. But Nero's ices didn't catch on, and they were forgotten after the fall of the Roman Empire.

Meanwhile, the Chinese developed a dessert much closer to ice cream as we know it. They added milk to honey-and-fruit-flavored ices, producing something similar to sherbet. When the Italian explorer Marco Polo returned from China in the late 1200's, he brought a recipe for this Chinese sherbet back to his native Venice. Soon delicious ices were being served throughout Italy, and by the 1500's their popularity had spread to the rest of Europe.

This was the time when Europeans first began to cross the Atlantic Ocean to the Western Hemisphere. Their conquests and colonies in the New World led to many changes on both sides of the ocean. Even ice cream changed.

The Ice Cream Factory

The ice-cream mixture—milk, cream, and sugar—is made (1). The mix is pasteurized (2) and homogenized (3). It is then cooled (4) and flavorings are added (5). The mix is frozen and whipped (6). Other flavorings are added (7). The ice cream is dispensed into containers (8) and hardens in a very cold room (9). Then it's trucked and delivered (10).

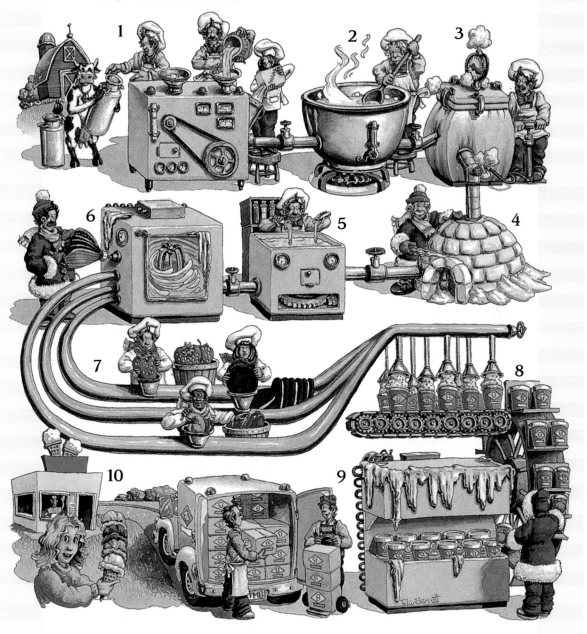

Before electric refrigeration, people used a hand-cranked ice-cream freezer to stir ice cream as it froze.

Huge plantations in the New World now supplied Europe with sugar, which replaced honey as a sweetener. And chocolate, from the New World cacao bean, became a popular flavoring.

Chefs also developed a new way of making frozen desserts: Instead of mixing crushed ice with milk, sweeteners, and flavorings, they packed ice around a container of sweetened and flavored milk and froze the milk directly, producing a much richer and smoother confection. This was the beginning of true ice cream.

At first, ice-cream recipes were the closely guarded secrets of chefs who served kings and nobles. But nothing so good could remain a secret for long. In 1670, a Parisian cafe became the first restaurant to serve ice cream to the general public. By the mid-1700's, recipes for ice cream were included in popular cookbooks. And by 1786, ice cream was being produced commercially.

THE ICE-CREAM FACTORY

Early recipes for ice cream reveal the basic principles that allow this wonderful dessert to be made. If you were to take a container of milk and just put it in the freezer, the result wouldn't resemble ice cream at all. It would be a block of frozen milk, and as it melted it would be watery and full of chunky ice crystals.

Why does this happen? Milk and cream are made up of water and milk fat. As it comes from the cow, each drop of milk contains millions of microscopic fat globules, spread evenly through the liquid. But when milk freezes, the water and milk fat separate, and the water forms big ice crystals. To keep this from happening, the ingredients in ice cream must be handled in a very special way. They must be frozen very quickly, and they must be mixed during freezing. Mixing breaks up the ice crystals and adds air to the ice cream, making it smooth.

Before the days of electric refrigeration, people would shake or stir ice cream while it froze. Hand-cranked ice-cream freezers were an easier way to do this. The ingredients— cream, sugar, flavorings, and sometimes eggs— were put in a metal pail that fit inside a larger wooden bucket. A mixture of crushed ice and rock salt was packed in the space between the pail and the bucket. (Salt lowers the freezing temperature of water, so it helped the ice cream freeze faster.) A paddle, or dasher, fit inside the pail. It was turned by a crank to stir the ice cream while it froze.

Today, commercial ice-cream factories still rely on the principles of freezing ice cream quickly and mixing it while it freezes. But they have refrigeration and machines to do the work, and they have made other changes to the basic procedure.

First, the ice-cream mix is made, usually in a huge stainless-steel tank. The mix consists of milk, cream, and liquid sugar. Sometimes a chemical called a stabilizer is added, to help prevent big ice crystals from forming. The mix is then pasteurized (heated to destroy harmful bacteria) and homogenized (a procedure that uses pressure to break up globules of milk fat and spread them throughout the liquid). After the mix is cooled in refrigerated storage tanks, flavorings may be added.

Now the freezing process begins. In big vats (or in some cases long tubes) surrounded by liquid ammonia, the mixture is frozen and, at the same time, whipped. Liquid ammonia is much colder than ice and freezes the mixture faster. Stainless-steel dashers whip the mixture while it freezes, and a compressor forces air into it. Some ice-cream makers also add chemicals called emulsifiers, which help break up the milk fat.

The Old-fashioned Soda fountain

From the 1860's to the 1960's, the favorite place to enjoy ice cream was the soda fountain. Most drug stores had soda fountains, which were often elegant creations of marble, mirrors, glass, and shining metal. Their original purpose was to dispense healthful mineral waters—but seltzer and sweet treats soon replaced the mineral waters.

Behind the counter, white-jacketed "soda jerks" mixed seltzer with any of dozens of sweetened, flavored syrups—everything from chocolate to wintergreen. Cream was often added to the drinks. And ice cream supposedly made its way into the mix in 1874, when a Philadelphia soda-fountain operator ran out of cream and substituted the frozen dessert.

Soon soda fountains were creating ice-cream sodas in numerous varieties, as well as milkshakes and other fabulous ice-cream treats. Soda fountains became a center of social life, especially for young people. But not everyone approved—some Midwestern towns banned the sale of sodas on Sundays. According to one story, ice-cream sundaes were developed as a way to get around this ban—the sundaes were made of ice cream and syrup, but no soda.

Today most of the old soda fountains are gone. But a few remain, and so do the wonderful treats they created. Here is how to make one popular old-fashioned ice-cream soda, the Brown Cow:

1. Fill a glass three-fourths full with root beer.
2. Add a scoop of vanilla ice cream.
3. Top with whipped cream, and enjoy!

Visitors to this old-fashioned ice-cream parlor at the Smithsonian Institution in Washington, D.C., could treat themselves to a Brown Cow.

The Whole Scoop!

How many licks do you need to polish off an ice-cream cone? What's the favorite ice-cream topping? Where do the top ice-cream eaters live? Read on, and you'll find the answers to these questions—and more!

■ The United States produces 1.6 billion gallons (6.1 billion liters) of ice cream and related frozen desserts each year.

■ On average, every American eats about 48 pints (23 liters) of ice cream a year.

■ The top ice-cream producing states are California, Indiana, Texas, Minnesota, Illinois, and New York.

■ Le Mars, Iowa, is known as the Ice Cream Capital of the World. It is home to the Wells Dairy, the largest family-owned dairy processor in the United States.

■ The people of Portland, Oregon, eat more ice cream per capita than the people of any other U.S. city.

■ More ice cream is sold on Sunday than any other day of the week.

■ July is National Ice Cream Month; the 3rd Sunday of July is National Ice Cream Day.

■ After the United States, the top per-capita ice-cream-consuming countries are New Zealand, Denmark, and Australia.

■ The favorite ice-cream topping is chocolate syrup.

■ It takes about 50 licks—or 26 licks and 10 bites—to polish off a single-scoop ice-cream cone.

■ The longest banana split in the world was 4.55 miles (7.32 kilometers) long. It was created by the residents of Selinsgrove, Pennsylvania, in 1988. It contained 2,500 gallons (9,464 liters) of ice cream, 24,000 bananas, 600 pounds (272 kilograms) of chopped nuts, and 24,000 cherries. Yum!

The ice cream is only about half frozen when it comes out of the freezer. Nuts, chunks of chocolate, and some flavorings may be added at this stage. Then the ice cream is dispensed right into the containers it will be sold in.

Finally, the ice cream is sent to harden in a room where the temperature is as low as –30°F (–34°C).

The biggest enemy of ice cream is heat. When ice cream melts, the air that was beaten into it escapes. When it refreezes, big ice crystals form. Ice-cream makers and stores go to great lengths to prevent so-called "heat shock," storing ice cream at temperatures ten degrees colder than other frozen foods. Even so, ice cream is best when it's eaten as soon as possible after it has been made.

Gelato—an Italian version of ice cream—comes in a great variety of flavors and is very popular today.

COOL VARIETY

The basic steps in making ice cream don't vary a great deal. But ice-cream makers certainly have come up with variety in their products. Ice cream and other frozen desserts come in a range of forms, from soft-serve cones to ice-cream bars to ice-cream sandwiches.

Ice-cream cones originated at the 1904 Louisiana Purchase Exposition in St. Louis, Missouri. From a booth at the fair, Ernest Hamwi, a Syrian immigrant, was selling *zalabia*, a crisp pastry baked with a waffle iron. Next to him was an ice-cream vendor. When the ice-cream vendor ran out of dishes, Hamwi rolled a *zalabia* into a cone, let it cool and harden, and offered it to his neighbor, who put ice cream in it and served it to a customer. The treat turned out to be the hit of the fair, and the ice-cream cone was born.

Chocolate-covered ice-cream bars were invented in 1919 by Christian Nelson, an Iowa candy-store owner. His creation became famous as the Eskimo Pie. At an ice-cream parlor in Ohio, Harry Burt took the idea a step further and put an ice-cream bar on a stick. He founded the Good Humor company and sold his creations from a white truck.

The number of ways people have found to serve ice cream is nothing compared to the hundreds of flavors that have been created. The old standbys—vanilla, chocolate, and strawberry—are still the most popular. In fact, vanilla accounts for about one-third of all ice-cream sales each year. Chocolate accounts for almost 10 percent; and strawberry, butter pecan, and neapolitan each account for about 5 percent.

But the trend is toward ever more exotic flavors: Some of 2007's innovative flavors were blueberry cobbler, chocolate cream pie, mango pomegranate surprise, and sticky toffee pudding. There are regional favorites, too. In the Midwest, ice-cream eaters love blue moon, which tastes like Fruit Loops. Philadelphians enjoy a treat called Gadzooks!—caramel-laced chocolate ice cream laden with chunks of chocolate, pieces of brownies, and peanut butter. In the Southwest, the sweet and spicy taste of peach sorbet with habanero peppers thrills and chills Arizonans. If some of these flavors sound odd to you, consider a few of the top-selling ice creams in Japan: sweet potato, oolong tea, tomato, cactus, chicken-wing, and octopus.

Even if octopus ice cream isn't for you, chances are there's a flavor of ice cream you adore. Just about everyone loves this cool and creamy treat!

Shallow lakes and streams are home to one of nature's most beautiful plants—the water lily.

WATER LILIES—FLOATING GARDENS

Imagine discovering a floating garden filled with colorful flowers atop clusters of round, green leaves. A frog basks happily in the sun on a leaf it uses as a small raft. Fish weave patterns beneath the leaves. Dragonflies dart from blossom to blossom. You might not think of a shallow lake or a slow-moving stream as a garden, but these are the habitats of water lilies—some of nature's most beautiful creations.

Water lilies come in many sizes and colors and are found in many parts of the world. There is a great variety of wild species, and many others are hybrids that have been specially cultivated by botanists. Despite their name, water lilies aren't members of the lily family. Long ago, before scientists had classified all the plants, "lily" was used to describe any especially beautiful flower. And that is how water lilies were given their popular name.

HOW THEY GROW

Although they live in water, water lilies have the same basic parts as flowering land plants. Most species of water lilies grow from a thick underground stem buried in the mud bottom of a pond, lake, or stream. The stem produces roots that grow down into the mud. And it sends long, flexible stalks up through the water. Some stalks support leaves; other stalks support flowers.

The leaves are large, flat, and nearly circular. They are often called lily pads. Usually the leaves float on the surface of the water, but in some species they are slightly beneath the surface.

Water lilies have many petals. They come in a multitude of colors—white, yellow, pink, blue, apricot, purple, even green. They may be as large as dinner plates or as small as your

Water lilies come in a great many varieties, and they are found in many parts of the world. The large, flat leaves are sometimes variegated in color. The flowers come in most every shade of the rainbow. They either float on the leaves or rise above the surface of the water.

thumbnail. Supported by their stalks, the flowers float or rise somewhat above the surface of the water.

Each plant produces only one flower at a time, and the flower lives about three days. But one plant may continue to blossom throughout the course of the growing season. Some water-lily plants bear more than 100 blooms a year. In tropical lands, water-lily flowers can be seen all year round. In cooler climates, they blossom from early spring until the first frosts of autumn.

123

The leaves of the royal water lily look like enormous pie plates. They are strong enough to support a child. And the flowers are pollinated in a very unusual way.

Some water lilies bloom during the day, then close up as darkness falls. Others are night bloomers, opening their petals only after the sun has passed beyond the horizon. At one time, night-blooming varieties were called husband lilies—because they opened as the man of the house returned home from work.

The purpose of the flowers is to attract insects, which pollinate the flowers. Pollination of water lilies takes place when pollen from the male part of one flower is transferred to the female part of another flower. Pollination is necessary for the formation of seeds.

Many water lilies use their colorful petals to attract insects. Some species smell sweet, and they depend on their scent to lure insects. Beetles, flies, and other insects crowd around for a free lunch. They feed on nectar, a juice produced by the flower. As the insects crawl over the flowers, pollen sticks to their bodies. Later, when they crawl over other flowers, they leave behind the pollen picked up from the water lilies they visited earlier.

After the flowers have been pollinated, and when they finish blooming, they close up like buds and sink to the bottom of the water. There, they produce seeds, which will eventually grow into new water-lily plants.

ROYAL WATER LILIES

A spectacular water lily is a giant species called the royal water lily. The plant's scientific name is *Victoria amazonica,* and it is a native of the Amazon River basin of South America. It was named in honor of Queen Victoria, the 19th-century ruler of Britain.

The leaves of the royal water lily look like enormous pie plates. They may be 7 feet (2 meters) in diameter. The leaves have upturned edges that prevent water from getting on top. A network of narrow ribs crisscrosses the underside of each leaf. The ribs make the huge leaves so strong that they can support the weight of a child. In Peru, Indian mothers sometimes left their babies on the leaves while they gathered water-lily seeds. One bird—the jacana, or lily trotter—often builds its nest and raises its young on these leaves.

The flowers of the royal water lily may be 1 foot (30 centimeters) or more in diameter. They open on two successive nights. On the first night, the flowers are creamy white. By the second night they have changed to a reddish purple. But the flowers have done more than change color. They have also been pollinated. And this they have achieved in a most unusual way.

When the flowers first open, they have a strong fruity odor. The smell is said to resemble a mixture of pineapple and butterscotch. This strong scent attracts large scarab beetles. In the dark of night, the beetles crawl deep into the flower in search of nectar. Toward morning, the scent slowly disappears. The flower closes, trapping the beetles inside. The flower stays closed all day long. By the time it

Claude Monet's Water Lilies

Claude Monet was a famous Impressionist artist, and some of his greatest paintings were of water lilies. He painted them from the late 1800's until his death in 1926, during his years at the little village of Giverny, France. It was there, in the garden of his home, that he built a lily pond with a Japanese arched bridge and began to paint one of his most magnificent series— *Les Nymphéas* ("The Water Lilies"). These masterpieces have long been admired for their beauty and serenity.

In an early work in the series, *Bridge Over a Pool of Water Lilies* (right), you can see how Monet applied thick paint in broad, skillful strokes. The graceful arch of the bridge frames the delicate water lilies in the soft blue-green water of the pond. Color shows how light falls on the pond, and the water lilies shimmer with white and a rainbow of tints.

Monet painted more than 15 views of the footbridge, all with differing light conditions. This painting's soft green foliage suggests it was painted in early summer.

Many of Monet's paintings of water lilies can be seen in the Musée de l'Orangerie in Paris, France, and in the Museum of Modern Art in New York City. And many people travel to Giverny to see Monet's pond with its beau-

Bridge Over a Pool of Water Lilies

tiful water lilies surrounded by banks of irises, rhododendrons, and azaleas. The garden and his paintings are memorials to a great artist.

The ancient Egyptians believed that the Egyptian white lotus, a night-blooming water lily, was sacred.

become dusted with pollen. They fly off, in search of white, sweet-smelling flowers. And as they crawl into the newly opened blossoms, they deposit the pollen from the flowers that had trapped them the night before.

During times of drought, a lakebed may dry up. The water lilies seem to completely disappear. But the roots and stems buried in the mud survive. When the rains return, new leaves begin to grow, and soon the water is filled with lily pads and colorful flowers.

Ancient peoples witnessed the return of the water lilies, and they believed that the plants were sacred. They saw water lilies as symbols of immortality—the ability to live forever. And they considered water lilies to be symbols of resurrection—the ability to return to life after death.

The favorite sacred plant of the ancient Egyptians was a night-blooming water lily called the Egyptian white lotus *(Nymphaea lotus)*. It was the flower of Isis, the goddess of motherhood. The Egyptians often decorated their buildings with drawings and sculptures of lotus flowers. They also made coins decorated with these flowers. And when an important Egyptian nobleman entertained, his guests were often given lotus flowers. The guests held the blossoms or wore them in their hair.

reopens the next evening, the captured beetles are eager to escape. They are all covered with a sticky substance produced by the flower. And as they leave the flower, they cannot help but

The seed pod of the sacred lotus is pierced with holes containing the seeds. In ancient China and India, the people believed their gods sat in the center of the blossoms.

The lotus also played an important role in funerals. Petals of lotus flowers have been found in ancient graves. They were found in the funeral wreath of Ramses II, an Egyptian ruler who died more than 3,000 years ago.

In China and India, people worshipped the sacred lotus *(Nelumbo nucifera).* The large but delicate pink flowers of this plant are on stalks that rise several feet out of the water. The people believed that their gods sat in the center of these lotus blossoms.

The seed container of the sacred lotus is very attractive. It is bowl-shaped, with a flat top. The top is pierced with holes, and in the holes are the seeds. Birds pick the seeds out of the holes. Many seeds are dropped by the birds as they fly. If they fall into water, they sink to the bottom, and some of them will grow into new plants.

USES PAST AND PRESENT

Throughout history, water lilies have served several purposes. In Ireland and Scotland, people made a blue-black dye from the roots of the plants. They used the dye to color wood.

Various parts of water-lily plants have been used to treat illnesses, although there is no scientific proof that such medicines really work. The powdered roots of one kind of water lily have been used to treat digestive problems. The leaves of another are said to be good for curing fevers. And, said one writer, "The syrup of the flowers produces rest and settles the brain of frantic persons."

Every part of the water-lily plant can be eaten. In China, people eat the stem, either raw or cooked. They wrap fresh water-lily leaves around meat, and then steam the combination. In South America, the seeds are ground to make flour, which is used to make a delicious pastry. The ancient Egyptians also made flour from water-lily seeds, then used the flour to make bread.

Today water lilies are appreciated chiefly for their beauty. Many people plant them in ponds or in small tubs. Special aquatic nurseries can advise you on getting the correct balance of plants and water creatures, and you can create your own lovely floating garden.

The Poetry of Water Lilies

Broad water-lilies lay tremulously,
And starry river-buds glimmered by,
And around them the soft stream did glide
  and dance
With a motion of sweet sound and radiance.
            Percy Bysshe Shelley

The water-lily starts and slides
Upon the level in little puffs of wind,
Tho' anchor'd to the bottom.
            Alfred, Lord Tennyson

Those virgin lilies, all the night
Bathing their beauties in the lake,
That they may rise more fresh and bright,
When their beloved sun's awake.
            Thomas Moore

Rapaciously we gathered flowery spoils
From land and water; lilies of each hue,
Golden and white, that float upon the waves,
And court the wind.
            William Wordsworth

But out upon the central pool there blow
The lily-legions these dull waters hold,
With hollowed petals dropping curves of snow
Back from the large fragrant stars of mossy gold,
All gleaming stainless on the unbroken sheen
Of heart-shaped leaves, in blended bronze and
  green.
And as I watch them, in serene array,
And muse, while scenting their delicious balm,
Of how they burst from soilure and decay,
  In taintlessness of alabaster calm,
And blossoming from this grim half-stagnant
  lake,
What sweet pure incongruity they make.
            Edgar Fawcett

LIGHT FOR HEALTH

Good morning! The sun is shining, and you bounce out of bed eager to be up and doing things. Most everybody loves a sunny day—sunshine just naturally seems to go along with good times and happy feelings.

Light from the sun makes life on our planet possible. It warms the Earth. Green plants use it to produce food. And people have always sought the sun. In ancient times, they often worshipped it as a god. Today, on sunny summer days, they flock to beaches, parks, and any other place where they can catch its rays.

However, scientists have discovered that sunshine—and light in general—may affect us in ways we never dreamed of. The amount and kind of light we are exposed to may help govern our moods, our behavior, and even our efficiency at school and on the job. And light may play a bigger role in our physical health than was previously thought.

LIGHT-HEARTED FEELINGS

The most interesting discoveries about light are in the area of mood and behavior. Some people, for example, become deeply depressed in winter. They are very sad and irritable and have difficulty concentrating. And they suffer from fatigue, anxiety, and headaches. But at the same time, they eat a lot, sleep a lot, and crave carbohydrates—activities that aren't usual symptoms of depression. Then, in the spring, the symptoms disappear. Mental health professionals have a name for this pattern of behavior: Seasonal Affective Disorder, or SAD. (The word "affective" means "emotional.") Many researchers believe that SAD is related to the amount of light people are exposed to in winter.

In the Northern Hemisphere—especially the northern parts of the hemisphere—winter is the time when people have the least exposure to natural light. Winter days are shorter. People spend more time indoors—and artificial lighting isn't the same as natural light. In fact, most artificial light has less than 10 percent the intensity of sunlight. And it doesn't contain the full spectrum, or range of wavelengths, that natural light contains. Even the light that comes through a window isn't the same as light outdoors, because the window glass filters out some of the wavelengths.

In experiments, researchers asked patients with SAD to increase their exposure to light for a few hours each morning, by turning on special bright lamps that produced full-spectrum light. In most cases, the depression ended within a few days. But when the light treatments stopped, the patients became depressed again.

Research indicates that SAD has a physical basis. Bright light appears to suppress the body's production of a hormone called melatonin. When a person isn't exposed to bright light—in winter, for example—the body produces more melatonin. Having too much of this hormone seems to set off depression in SAD patients.

Not all depressed people respond to light; SAD is only one kind of depression. But for those who suffer from it, the discovery of light's role has been an important breakthrough. Today the main treatment for people with SAD is sitting under ultra-bright light—light that's at least ten times brighter than ordinary house lamps—for at least 30 to 60 minutes each day. This treatment is called bright-light therapy.

The studies of SAD have also produced new ideas about how light can help people with less severe problems. Some people, for instance, have sleep problems. "Larks" wake up too early in the morning and become sleepy too early in the evening. "Owls" have insomnia at night, and they can't get up in the morning. Research has shown that both groups could reset their schedules by increasing their exposure to bright light. Larks can stay alert longer if they take a long walk outdoors late in the day. And owls find it easier to go to sleep at night if they force themselves to get up and go outside early in the morning.

Besides affecting sleep patterns, light—especially its brightness—seems to play a

A person suffering from Seasonal Affective Disorder (SAD) is usually treated with bright-light therapy.

role in the way people act toward one another. In dimly lit rooms, people tend to sit close together and speak softly. Their conversations are friendlier and more intimate than they are in brightly lit rooms.

Light can also have a big effect on the way you work. Bright lights increase productivity. And some research indicates that people are more productive when they work under lights that reproduce the full spectrum of natural light.

This fisherman lives in a light-deprived northern climate and works mostly at night. He suffers from SAD. To help him, he has been outfitted with a special headset that supplies him with daylight frequencies.

Bright light can help "larks"—people who wake up too early in the morning and become sleepy too early in the evening. They can stay alert longer if they take a long walk outdoors late in the day.

The invisible ultraviolet wavelengths in sunlight are responsible for many of these physical effects. They can also harm vision, damaging the retina of the eye or causing cataracts. That's why, when you're heading for the beach or the ski slopes, sunscreens and sunglasses that filter out ultraviolet light are strongly recommended.

But light can also promote good physical health. People have long known about some of its beneficial effects. For example, ultraviolet light reacts with chemicals in your skin to produce vitamin D, which allows your body to absorb calcium and build strong bones. However, don't get too much exposure to ultraviolet light. Ten to 15 minutes of sunshine a day is usually enough to produce the vitamin D you need.

Many doctors have done research on the helpful effects of sunlight. Niels R. Finsen, a Danish researcher, won a Nobel Prize in 1903 for his discovery that light reduced scarring in smallpox and helped cure a tuberculosis skin infection. Since then, scientists have found that strong ultraviolet light acts as a disinfectant, killing germs.

LIGHT'S PHYSICAL BENEFITS

You are probably familiar with one of the harmful effects of overexposure to the sun: a painful sunburn. Too much sunlight can also age the skin so that wrinkles develop, and it can promote skin cancer. Sunlight can even react with soaps and cosmetics on the skin, changing them and producing an allergic reaction.

People tend to speak more softly and be more intimate in a room that's dimly lit (below). Bright light seems to increase people's productivity (right).

Doctors have also discovered that a special light therapy can cure a type of jaundice that's common in premature infants. Jaundice is a yellowing of the skin caused by the buildup of a waste product, bilirubin, in the blood. The bilirubin can have other, more harmful effects, including brain damage. But when fluorescent light is shined on the jaundiced infant, the light changes the molecules of bilirubin so that the body can easily excrete them.

Light also affects the actions of certain medicines. For example, it has been used with ointments and internal medicines to treat a serious skin condition called psoriasis. The ultraviolet rays in the light seem to trigger the action of such medicines. Doctors have also discovered that the combination of light and medicines may help other diseases, especially those that are treated with powerful (and sometimes harmful) chemicals.

Scientists say that they are only beginning to discover all the ways, mental and physical, that light affects us. But one thing is already clear: There are good reasons to be happy when the sun is shining.

Prism Breakout

We seldom think of light as having color. Yet natural light contains all the colors of the rainbow. The English scientist Sir Isaac Newton discovered this in 1665, when he directed a beam of light through a triangular piece of glass called a prism. The prism split the light into an array of different colors, which Newton called a spectrum.

Scientists during and after Newton's time developed a theory to explain the prism's effect. According to this theory, light travels in waves, and its wavelength (the distance between the crest of one wave and the next) determines its color. Natural light is made up of many different wavelengths. When the light passes through a prism, each wavelength is bent at a slightly different angle. Thus the light is split up into various colors, from violet (the shortest waves) through blue, green, yellow, orange, and red (the longest ones).

This theory explains all the colors we see. A piece of blue cloth, for example, appears blue because it absorbs all the wavelengths except the blue ones, which are reflected. A piece of blue glass allows only blue wavelengths to pass through. Some colors are mixtures of different wavelengths; green, for example, is a mixture of blue and yellow.

You may have noticed that colors look different under natural light and artificial light. This is because most artificial lights don't reproduce the full spectrum of nature's light. Regular incandescent lightbulbs send out a lot of red wavelengths. Most fluorescent lights emit mostly green, yellow, and orange wavelengths.

Today we know that the full spectrum also includes wavelengths we cannot see. Ultraviolet wavelengths are shorter than those of visible violet light. Ultraviolet light can have powerful affects, from producing a suntan to killing germs. Infrared wavelengths are longer than those of visible red light. Although they can't be seen, they can be felt—as heat.

Fossils are ancient traces of living things, and they help us learn about the history of Earth. The fossil above is of an ammonite, a mollusk with a pearly shell that became extinct about the same time the dinosaurs did.

FOSSILS: RECORDS OF EARTH'S PAST

Fossils are the remains of life that existed in ancient times. A fossil may be just a sign left behind by some ancient animal—the impression of a dinosaur's foot or the remains of a primitive mammal's burrow. A fossil may be a shadowy mark left in rock by an ancient leaf that disappeared millions of years ago. Or a fossil may be the actual remains of a living thing, such as the bones of ancient animals—including prehistoric humans.

Fossils are found all over the world. They are usually found in sedimentary rocks. They are sometimes found frozen in the ice of glaciers or perfectly preserved in amber.

To be considered a fossil, the remains must be more than 10,000 years old. Scientists use fossils to chart the history of Earth.

HOW FOSSILS FORM

Many fossils were formed by plants and animals that died and were quickly covered by silt, mud, clay, or perhaps the ash from a volcanic eruption. Over millions of years, the sediments hardened into rock. And, since they were sealed up before they had a chance to decay, the once-living things were preserved in various ways.

In some cases, plant and animal tissues became mineralized, or petrified. That is, the tissue changed to rock as water washed away its components and minerals seeped in to replace them. In other cases, minerals filled tiny air spaces in bones and shells, strengthening these tissues and preserving them through the ages. And sometimes minerals formed a mold around the outside of a shell or another hard structure. The shell eventually dissolved, leaving a perfect image embedded in the rock.

The delicate skeletal structure of this ancient fish has been forever preserved in stone.

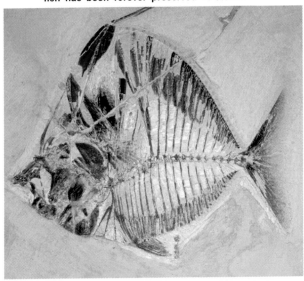

Some fossils are simply ghostly traces of things that once were. When a plant or animal decays, it may leave behind a deposit of carbon—a thin film that reveals its outline and structure. But some living things have been preserved nearly intact. Leaves and insects (and even some tiny vertebrates) have been found encased in amber, the fossilized resin of ancient coniferous trees. Larger animals have been preserved for millions of years in deposits of tar and in the year-round ice of Arctic regions.

Usually, however, only bits and pieces are found—a few bones or teeth, or fragments of plant leaves and stems. Hard tissues such as bones and shells, or the stems and veins of plants, are more likely to become fossils than soft tissues. This is because soft tissues decay quickly.

Amber: A Golden Window to the Past

Since ancient times, amber has been valued as a precious stone. Artisans from all over the world have created beautiful objects with this gold-colored substance. But amber is especially valued by scientists.

Amber is actually fossilized plant resin, a kind of sap. It came from pine trees and other conifers—now extinct—in prehistoric forests. If conditions were right, the gummy resin would slowly change into a hard, translucent, golden material—amber. Often trapped within the amber were the remains of ancient living things—feathers, leaves, insects—all millions of years old. Thus amber is a treasure chest of information about the prehistoric world.

As many as one in 100 amber specimens contains a bit of ancient animal or plant life. These have included tiny flowers, ants, bees, caterpillars, moths, termites, mushrooms, pollen grains, and the bones of small mammals.

Amber fossils are unlike most other fossils. Most fossils are stone molds or casts of ancient bones and other hard tissues. But amber preserves everything, even soft tissue and the structures inside cells. Scientists have even extracted bits of DNA, the genetic code in the cells of every living thing, from amber specimens.

In the famous book and movie *Jurassic Park,* scientists extracted dinosaur DNA from a bloodsucking fly trapped in amber and used it to clone living dinosaurs. That was pure fiction. But prehistoric DNA preserved in amber can help scientists unravel the secrets of how life on Earth evolved.

Wonderful scientific treasures are locked inside this beautiful prehistoric material.

This tree frog has been perfectly preserved in a chunk of amber for 25 million years. It was discovered in Mexico, and its actual size is less than half an inch.

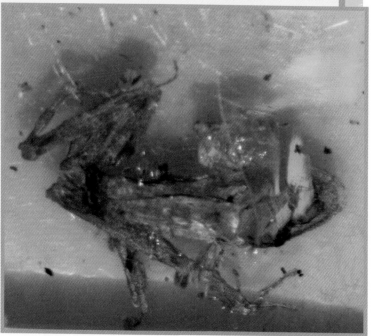

Above: This fossilized sea urchin, still armed with its spines, is a rare find. Below: Encased in rock, a 20-million-year-old poplar leaf still retains the lovely pattern of its veins.

Whatever form a fossil takes, the process that leads to its creation can take thousands of years. And conditions must be exactly right. Thus, of all the billions of creatures that have lived on Earth, relatively few have left fossil remains. And many of those remains are buried in rock that's deep below Earth's surface, where they may never be found.

Still, Earth has changed greatly during its long history. Areas that once lay on the floor of ancient oceans have been pushed up to form mountains—and to reveal fossils. Fossils have been found on every continent, including Antarctica. Where they have been exposed to wind and rain, erosion has taken its toll and sometimes made the fossil record difficult to read. But people have been fascinated by fossils since early times.

FOSSIL THEORIES

When the ancient Greeks discovered the delicate forms of fossilized shells embedded in rocks, they correctly concluded that these fossils revealed the sites of ancient oceans. But other early theories about fossils weren't anywhere near as accurate. In the Middle Ages, some people believed that fossils were stones that fell to Earth during storms or lunar eclipses. Others thought that these lifelike forms actually developed inside rock, perhaps growing from tiny seeds.

The fossilized tusks of woolly mammoths were once thought to be unicorn horns. Certain fossils were also thought to have magical or medicinal powers—the ability to cure snakebite or the plague, for example. And American Indian legends held that the petrified trunks of ancient trees found in what is now Arizona were bones left from a battle between gods and giants.

Gradually, however, people began to reject such theories. Leonardo da Vinci, the Italian Renaissance scholar and artist, was among the first to realize that fossils

Artists based this drawing of Giganto on its fossil remains—segments of jaw, ribs, legs, and tail. The birdlike dinosaur lived in China some 70 million years ago.

Dinosaur Fossils: On All the Continents

Dinosaurs roamed Earth for 165 million years. Dinosaur fossils were first discovered in the 1820's, in Europe. Since then, thousands of fossils have been found on all the continents.

One of the most recent finds was the fossil skeleton of a birdlike dinosaur called *Gigantoraptor erlianensis* that lived 70 million years ago. The "Giganto" part of the name indicates that the beast was large—25 feet (8 meters) long, 16 feet (5 meters) tall, and weighed 3,000 pounds (1,361 kilograms); it would have gotten much larger had it not died when it was young. The "raptor" part means it's related to the oviraptor, a dinosaur that was beaked and birdlike and probably had some feathers. And "erlianensis" tells that Giganto was found in the Erlian basin of Inner Mongolia, the northernmost part of China.

Many scientists believe that Giganto and other members of the oviraptor family may have been an early step in the evolution of birds.

Here are some other recent dinosaur fossil finds:

■ Scientists recovered protein from the thighbone of a *Tyrannosaurus rex* that died about 68 million years ago in what is now Montana. The dinosaur protein most closely matches the protein of a chicken—further evidence that dinosaurs and birds were evolutionary cousins.

■ In Argentina, scientists found thousands of fossil eggs the size of grapefruits, and the fossil remains of unhatched dinosaurs. Some were so well preserved that even the scales on their skin could be seen. The eggs were laid 70 to 90 million years ago by dinosaurs called titanosaurs.

■ The fossil of a baby dinosaur that died more than 100 million years ago was found in Italy, with its internal organs intact. For the first time, scientists had a clear picture of a dinosaur's insides, including its intestines, liver, windpipe, and muscles. The dinosaur was related to the fierce *Tyrannosaurus rex*.

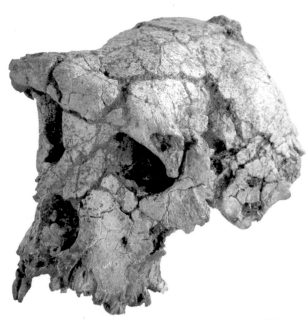

This 7-million-year-old skull was found in the African country of Chad. It is believed to be the oldest fossil from a member of the human family. It belonged to a hominid (a humanlike primate). Scientists have nicknamed it Toumai, which means "hope of life" in the local language.

were the remains of ancient animals that had been buried in sediment—sediment that had turned to stone.

It was many years before others adopted this view. But by the mid-1800's, many scientists accepted fossils as the remains of ancient life. And at about that time, Charles Darwin's work on the theory of evolution paved the way for the modern understanding of fossils.

READING THE RECORD

"Fossil" comes from a Latin word meaning "dug up." And scientists who study life through fossils are called paleontologists, from Greek words meaning "existing long ago." These scientists date fossils by studying rocks and other materials that encase them and by noting their place in the layers, or strata, of rock that have been laid down over the ages.

In the time scale that paleontologists use, even primitive mammals are newcomers—they appear in the fossil record less than 200 million years ago. The oldest fossils known are those of certain bacteria, one-celled organisms so simple they lacked even a cell nucleus. These creatures lived almost 3.5 billion years ago.

It took millions of years for structures such as the cell nucleus to develop, and millions more for multi-celled plants and animals to appear. Some 600 million years ago, animals with shells and skeletons and plants with stems developed. At this point, the fossil record becomes truly rich, revealing how life proliferated first in the oceans and then on land.

Fossils have helped scientists piece together the story of evolution and discover how the forms of life we know developed from earlier forms. But there are still many gaps in the story—and many mysteries.

Among the mysteries are the many great extinctions that took place in the past. Over millions of years, countless strange and fantastic creatures have appeared, walked the Earth, and vanished. The most spectacular of these were the dinosaurs. These reptiles dominated all other life forms for 165 million years. But then, some 65 million years ago, they died out.

Dinosaurs weren't the only creatures to vanish. Ammonites were mollusks with pearly shells that developed long before the dinosaurs and died out at about the same time they did. Trilobites, distant relatives of today's spiders and crustaceans, were even more ancient. More than 10,000 species of these armor-plated ocean creatures developed before they disappeared some 230 million years ago. The fossil record doesn't explain why these and other creatures died out. It shows only that they once lived.

Still, fossils have revealed much of what life was like in ancient times. Scientists have found the fossilized nests, eggs, and young of dinosaurs. The fact that the young of some kinds of dinosaurs were more or less defenseless at birth indicates that their parents had to care for them. Thus we know that these dinosaurs, unlike most reptiles, were caring parents.

Fossils have also shown that some dinosaurs migrated in large herds and that, later in Earth's history, herds of camels and rhinoceroses roamed North America. And fossils have helped produce a picture of the ways in which Earth's climate and land surfaces have changed.

Thanks to fossils, scientists know that frigid Antarctica once had a warm climate and that

Hunting for Fossils

If you want to search for fossils, look first for an area where sedimentary rocks have been pushed up to Earth's surface. Sediments are particles of material that come from the weathering of rock and are carried and deposited by wind, water, or ice. Sedimentary rocks are slowly built up in layers, and include sandstone, shale, and limestone. Most fossils are found in these rocks.

Sedimentary rocks can be found almost anywhere. But scientists who study fossils often make their richest finds near ancient bodies of water—in cliffs along dry streambeds, or in areas that were once covered by the ocean, for example. This is because water speeds the process of mineralization by which many fossils form.

Fossil hunters may split open rocks in a search for traces of ancient plants or tiny animals. Or they may find fragments of fossilized teeth or bones. When such bits and pieces are found, the searchers comb the area for more fossils. The bones of a skeleton may be found together, relatively undisturbed. But more often, they are scattered. The workers may use heavy equipment to move large amounts of soil and rock at first. But around the delicate fossils (and especially around fragile fossilized bones) they use fine instruments to chip away rock.

Hunting for fossils at the Caesar Creek Lake spillway near Waynesville, Ohio.

When scientists find a fossil, they make careful records of where it was found. Then they usually move it—to a university, a museum, or some other site—for further study. If enough pieces are found, scientists are sometimes able to reconstruct the skeleton of an ancient animal. This allows them to picture what the animal actually looked like—even though it may not have walked the Earth for millions of years.

an inland sea once covered areas of the United States. Fossils have also helped scientists develop the theory of continental drift, which explains how the continents have moved to their present positions over millions of years. For example, fossils found in some of the older rock layers of South America are very similar to fossils found in India and southern Africa. This has led scientists to suppose that these landmasses were once joined.

As scientists continue to search out fossils and study them, they will no doubt learn more secrets of Earth's past.

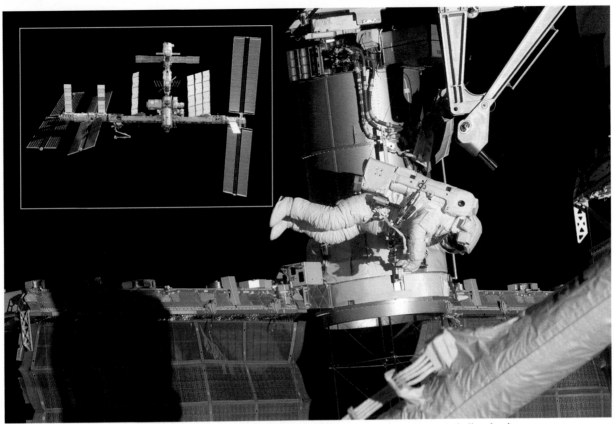

The October-November *Discovery* build-and-repair mission was among the most challenging in space-shuttle history. Above, in a long and difficult space walk, astronauts repair a damaged solar array. Inset: the *International Space Station* photographed by the *Discovery* crew at the end of the mission.

SPACE BRIEFS

Work at the *International Space Station* highlighted the 2007 year in space. Other exciting developments involved spacecraft exploring Earth's moon and distant planets.

PEOPLE IN SPACE

The *International Space Station (ISS)* is a giant structure that orbits 240 miles (386 kilometers) above Earth. Construction, which began in 1998, is expected to be completed by 2010.

The *ISS* is continually staffed by the United States and Russia, who send crews back and forth aboard U.S. space shuttles and Russian *Soyuz* craft. Each crew includes at least one U.S. astronaut and one Russian cosmonaut, and most crewmembers stay on the space station for about six months. The Expedition 14 crew arrived at the *ISS* in September 2006 and stayed until April 2007. It was replaced by Expedition 15, which remained until October, when it was replaced by Expedition 16.

The Expedition 16 crew was the first in which a woman—astronaut Peggy Whitson—was in command of the *ISS*. Barely had Whitson taken charge of the space station when women made history again. On October 25, the space shuttle *Discovery* docked with the *ISS*. *Discovery*'s commander was astronaut Pamela Melroy. It was the first time in the 50-year history of spaceflight that two women were in charge of two spacecraft at the same time.

The *Discovery* mission was one of three space-shuttle missions conducted by the United States during 2007. The primary objective of all the missions was to continue building the *ISS*. The year's first shuttle mission, aboard *Atlantis*, occurred in June. Its purpose was to add more electrical power capability to the *ISS*.

In August, *Endeavour*'s crew added another truss segment to the station. (A truss serves as a rigid framework to which other structures—such as modules and solar arrays—can be attached. It provides power, cooling, data, and communications to the structures.) The crew also attached a platform for spare parts. And they activated a new system that allows docked shuttles to draw electrical power from the *ISS*. This will enable shuttles to extend their visits to the space station. Barbara Morgan, the first educator-astronaut in space, operated the robotic arm that was used to transfer cargo to the space station. Morgan, a former school-teacher from Idaho, talked with students on Earth via ham radio during her spare time.

The main objective of the fall *Discovery* mission was to install the Italian-built Harmony module. This closet-sized module increased the *ISS*'s living and working space. It also provided attachment points for laboratory modules from Japan and Europe. Harmony is similar to the Unity module, attached several years earlier, linking the U.S. and Russian sections of the *ISS*.

Installing Harmony was among the most challenging assignments ever handled by astro-

The Space Age Turns 50

On October 4, 1957, Russia (then part of the Soviet Union) launched *Sputnik,* the first artificial satellite to orbit Earth. The little aluminum sphere had four spiky antennas; it weighed just 184 pounds (83 kilograms) and was less than 2 feet (0.6 meter) wide—about as big as a basketball. One month later, the Russians launched a second satellite—*Sputnik 2*—which carried Laika, a live dog.

The little satellites stunned the world—and the Space Age was born! In the next 50 years, thousands more space vehicles were launched, most by the United States and Russia. Some were sent into Earth orbit. Others traveled to the moon and distant planets. Most were unmanned, but others—including some that visited the moon—carried men and women.

These voyages have vastly increased our knowledge and understanding of the universe. We saw how beautiful Earth looks from outer space. And the voyages provided benefits on Earth. When *Sputnik* was launched, news spread around the world rather slowly,

A Soviet newspaper announces the launch of *Sputnik,* the world's first artificial satellite, on October 4, 1957.

through undersea phone lines and dial telephones. Today, such news spreads almost instantaneously, thanks to cell phones and a network of communications satellites. Other satellites monitor weather, analyze crop growth, and help ships navigate.

Who knows what the next 50 years of the Space Age will bring. Perhaps factories on the moon. . .people on other planets. . .discoveries of intelligent beings elsewhere. Only time will tell.

Educator-astronaut Barbara Morgan is on the aft flight deck of the space shuttle *Endeavour* while docked with the *ISS*. During the mission, she spoke with schoolchildren on Earth about her experiences in space.

nauts, requiring moving it from one location to another. The astronauts also had to move an enormous solar array and the truss it stands on from its temporary location on top of the space station to its permanent location on the station's far left side. (Solar panels collect sunlight and turn it into heat and electricity.) And there were some unexpected problems—a torn solar panel had to be mended, and metallic shavings found in a joint had to be dealt with. The difficult 15-day mission involved four spacewalks and extensive use of the robotic arms.

A fourth shuttle flight, *Atlantis,* had been scheduled for December. However, problems with sensors inside a fuel tank delayed the flight until early 2008. The mission of that flight is to deliver the European-built Columbus module to the *ISS* and attach it to the Harmony module. Columbus will allow scientists all over Europe to participate in their own experiments in space.

THE MYSTERIES OF AURORAS

Early in 2007 the United States launched the *THEMIS* mission. It consisted of five identical space probes—all sent aloft aboard a single rocket. The mission, which is scheduled to last two years, will help scientists solve mysteries of the Northern Lights, or aurora borealis.

Auroras are spectacular light displays that are usually seen in the night sky in polar regions. They look like dancing sheets, shimmering with colors.

Auroras are created during magnetic storms in the upper atmosphere, much as thunder and lightning are created by weather storms closer to the ground. In both cases there is a sudden release of energy, called a substorm.

The *THEMIS* satellites are lined up in a row over the North American continent. Scientists expect the satellites to observe about 30 substorms during the two-year mission. Data collected by instruments aboard the satellites should allow scientists to pinpoint when and where each substorm begins. The data will also help scientists determine the exact sequence of events that triggers auroras.

TO THE MOON AND BEYOND

Moon. Until 2007 only the United States and Russia had sent space ships into orbit around the moon. In 2007 the number of countries putting vehicles into lunar orbit doubled. In September, Japan launched the *Kaguya* probe, named after a fairytale princess. A month later, China launched *Chang'e 1,* named after a mythical Chinese goddess who flew to the moon. Both probes are expected to spend about a year collecting information about the moon's land features and gravity fields.

Asteroids. In September, the United States launched *Dawn* on a 3-billion-mile (4.8-billion-kilometer) trip to study the asteroids Vesta and Ceres. The probe will reach Vesta in 2011 and Ceres in 2015. Instruments aboard *Dawn* will measure the asteroids' mineral composition, shape, surface features, and gravity fields, and will look for water-bearing minerals. This will enable scientists to more accurately compare the two asteroids.

Far-Out Fashion

Space suits have changed very little since people first started traveling into space some 40 years ago. But this may soon change. Designers are creating sleek outfits to replace today's bulky space suits.

In the next 10 or 15 years, the United States hopes to again send astronauts to the moon. From the moon, the astronauts will begin to stage a mission to Mars—farther than explorers have ever gone before. Current space suits are too heavy and stiff for such exploration. On the moon, astronauts may be building stations. On Mars, they may be scaling red-rock walls. For that kind of work, they will need a suit they can easily move around in.

A team at the Massachusetts Institute of Technology (MIT) is designing a space suit called the BioSuit, which will be lightweight and flexible. But it will still protect astronauts from the hazards of outer space.

A critical function of a space suit is to maintain pressure around the astronaut's body when he or she steps out of a spacecraft. Without this pressure, oxygen and other essential gases can escape through the skin. Today's space suits create pressure by surrounding an astronaut's body with a large air-filled bag. The BioSuit is different—it uses tightly fitting fabric to squeeze the skin. Current designs use

Above: The new BioSuit will be lighter and more flexible than the standard oxygen-pressurized space suits used today. Left: A researcher makes adjustments to the knee of the BioSuit.

many layers of fabric, one on top of another, but this makes it difficult to put the suit on.

Eventually, the researchers plan to make BioSuits from materials that change shape when electricity is applied to them. That way, an astronaut could easily zip into a suit. Just before going outside, the suit could be activated to shrink around the astronaut's body. When the astronaut returns to the safety of a space station, the shrinking mechanism would be deactivated to remove the suit.

Mars. The Red Planet is the only planet in the solar system besides Earth where scientists believe life may have existed. Life as we know it depends on water, and spacecraft continue looking for evidence that water was once plentiful on Mars.

In August, the United States launched *Mars Phoenix Lander,* which is scheduled to reach the planet in mid-2008. *Phoenix* will be the first spacecraft to land in the planet's north-pole region. In winter this area is covered with ice, but in summer the ground is mostly exposed. Scientists think this ground is a mixture of soil and ice—similar to the permafrost in Earth's Arctic regions. The craft's robotic arm is designed to dig into the ground

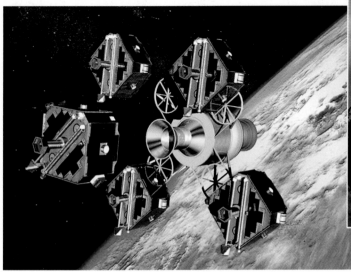

The *THEMIS* mission consists of five identical space probes that will help scientists learn more about the beautiful and mysterious Northern Lights, or auroras.

and pick up samples. These can then be examined in an on-board laboratory for evidence of water.

Spirit and *Opportunity,* the two U.S. robot rovers that began exploring the Martian surface in early 2004, continued their amazing adventures in 2007. *Spirit* found a patch of soil that's about 90 percent silica—the chemical that makes up sand on Earth. On Earth, water is required to produce such a concentrated deposit of silica. *Spirit*'s discovery suggests that Mars had abundant water within the last 10 million years.

The *Mars Reconnaissance Orbiter,* another U.S. spacecraft, began orbiting the planet in 2006. Recent photographs showed evidence of ancient underground streams of water or gas, as well as surface streams. The pictures also indicated that the surface streams flowed long enough to have supported at least simple forms of life, such as bacteria.

Jupiter. *New Horizons,* launched by the United States in 2006 on a mission to Pluto, swung past Jupiter in 2007. That giant planet's gravity acted like a slingshot, speeding up the spacecraft and hurling it on its way to Pluto, which it will reach in 2015. While in the vicinity of Jupiter, *New Horizons'* cameras zoomed in on the planet's Little Red Spot (a small version of the famous Great Red Spot) and on its thin rings. The cameras also photographed volcanic eruptions on Io, one of Jupiter's moons.

Saturn. The U.S. *Cassini* mission, designed to study Saturn's rings and moons, celebrated

Left: The *Dawn* probe will study two asteroids, Vesta and Ceres. Below: The *Mars Phoenix Lander* will be the first spacecraft to land in the planet's north-pole region.

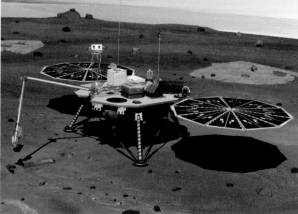

Space Junk

We see "Don't Litter!" signs on streets, in parks, and in many other places on Earth. But there are no such signs in space. There should be! The area from 100 to 22,000 miles (160 to 35,400 kilometers) above our planet is littered with space junk.

Some of the junk has been there for 50 years. Some is brand new. It comes from the satellites, shuttles, and space stations that orbit Earth. It includes non-working satellites, burned-out rocket stages, damaged solar panels, camera lens caps, space gloves, and nuts and bolts. More than 9,000 pieces are larger than a softball. In addition, there are millions of tiny bits of debris, like paint flakes. All together, the space junk weighs more than 5,500 tons.

The worst litterers are the United States and Russia. But in 2007, China created the messiest space event. In January, a Chinese missile test purposely smashed an aging weather satellite, adding more than 1,500 large scraps of debris to the junkyard.

Space debris travels through space at about 17,400 miles (28,000 kilometers) an hour—ten times faster than a bullet from a high-powered rifle. It can be very dangerous. Hundreds of bits of debris have dented and chipped some of the space shuttles. Dozens of shuttle windows have been replaced because debris has become embedded in them. If a large piece of debris were to pierce a space shuttle, it could destroy it. And if one of the bits hit an astronaut during a spacewalk, it could kill him or her.

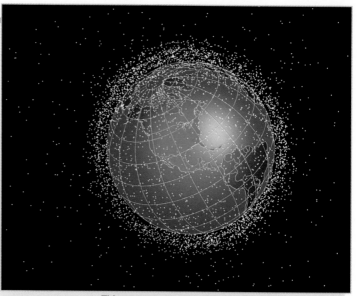
This computer artwork shows space debris traveling around Earth. All together, the space junk weighs more than 5,500 tons!

Scientists have "mapped" the large pieces of debris. That is, they know where all the big pieces are. So if a space shuttle seems to be on a collision course with a large object, the shuttle is maneuvered out of the way. Scientists are also changing the orbits of some old satellites so that they will enter Earth's atmosphere and burn up.

In addition, special protective shields have been installed on spacecraft, including the *ISS*. However, these shields protect the spacecraft from only tiny bits of debris. For holes created by somewhat larger debris, there's a puncture repair kit. For still-larger holes, Japanese scientists are working on a special shield that would slow the leak of air from a spacecraft, giving astronauts time to escape. And perhaps someday there will be a giant laser or other device to get rid of space junk. Until then, the best way to prevent a disaster is to stop littering in space!

ten years in space. The craft went into orbit around Saturn in 2004 and has sent back spectacular photographs and huge amounts of data. In 2007, scientists reported that Hyperion—Saturn's eighth-largest moon—resembles a giant sponge. The moon is very porous, with about 40 percent empty space. Perhaps because of this spongelike nature, Hyperion is the only moon in the solar system with a chaotic rotation: It doesn't spin as much as it tumbles on its journeys around Saturn.

Radar images from *Cassini* show that the surface of Titan, Saturn's largest moon, is much like that of Earth, with mountains, dunes, and lakes. It was discovered that the lakes are made up of liquid methane. This chemical is present in large quantities in Titan's atmosphere, giving the atmosphere a smoggy appearance.

144

Use lots of imagination—and have lots of fun—as you make a colorful collage like this one out of many scraps of fabric. Begin by drawing a picture on a piece of heavy paper, such as posterboard. Then glue on the background fabrics—the sky and grass. Glue on the remaining fabrics, working with the larger pieces first, and then the smaller ones. Decorate your picture with bits of lace, tiny buttons, and bright sequins. You can also paint details onto your picture. Now frame it, and wait for the ooohs and aaahs!

Some birds will go anywhere for a handful of tasty seeds! Attracting wild birds to your yard is easy and fun, and it helps the birds survive.

INVITING BIRDS TO YOUR BACKYARD

A robin hops across the lawn, searching for a tasty worm to feed her growing babies. By the garden, a sparrow takes a dust bath. A kingbird sits motionless on a fence, while a pair of tiny warblers rustles in the bushes. A woodpecker works its way up a tree trunk, tapping and probing with its beak in search of insects.

Would you like to see all this and more right outside your window? All you need to do is let birds know they are welcome in your backyard. Shrubs that offer shelter, good nesting sites, a feeder or two, and a source of water are what birds look for. As soon as they spot these, they'll be quick to make themselves at home.

Backyard bird watching is an easy, inexpensive hobby that you can enjoy all year. Birds are a pleasure to see and hear. And if you take time to observe them, you can learn many things. Where do different birds like to feed and nest? When do they lay their eggs? What are their favorite foods? Which ones are brave and daring? Which are shy? Which ones act as sentinels, using alarm calls to warn other birds that an enemy is approaching?

You can attract birds to your yard no matter how large or small it is. If you have lots of space, you may want to plant trees and shrubs that birds like. If you have very little space, you may decide to just place a feeder near a window. You can buy feeders and birdhouses. Or you can build them from kits or from scratch, following plans or making your own designs. They can be plain or fancy, made from new or recycled materials. Check your library for books that give information about feeders and birdhouses for various types of birds, as well as plans for building them.

GARDENING FOR BIRDS

One of the best ways to bring birds to your backyard is to plant trees, shrubs, and flowers that they like. Large areas of lawn provide little food for birds and no place to raise their young. But a yard filled with berry bushes, evergreens, and flowers will appeal to many species.

Shrubs provide protective cover, where birds can hide from predators and rear their young. Trees and shrubs that bear fruits, nuts, and berries are natural feeding stations. So are garden plants like sunflowers, which form huge seed heads. You can attract hummingbirds with plants that have red, tubular flowers, such as trumpet honeysuckle, flame vine, trumpet creeper, and fuchsia. And many flowers attract flying insects, which in turn attract insect-eating birds.

If you want birds and other wildlife in your yard, don't use pesticides. They kill useful as well as harmful insects, and they harm the birds that feed on insects. Instead, invite animals that feed on pests, such as toads and ladybugs. And let the birds help control the insect population.

PLACES TO NEST

Birds use birdhouses mainly to lay eggs and raise their young. Even in gardens with lots of trees, nesting sites may be limited. Birdhouses are excellent substitutes. Some birds will also use birdhouses as shelters at night and during cold winters.

You can buy fancy birdhouses, but a plain box is fine with most birds. The roof should slant, to shed water. A few small holes under the eaves will provide ventilation. And the entrance should be a round hole. When you put the box up, tilt it forward slightly, so that rain won't enter the hole.

Attach your birdhouses to trees or walls. Choose locations where the houses can be easily reached for cleaning, where they are sheltered from wind and hot sun, and where cats and other predators can't reach them. Put the houses out in late winter or early spring, so that they'll be in place when birds start to hunt for nesting sites. Each summer, after a bird family has left a house, clean it out. Then it will be ready for the next tenants!

Single-Family Homes. Birds that may use these houses include sparrows, finches, wrens, nuthatches, titmice, chickadees, swallows, woodpeckers, flickers, and sparrow hawks. Birds have strong preferences when it comes to the size of a birdhouse, the diameter of its entrance, its location, and the height at which it should be placed above the ground. For example, song sparrows nest close to the ground, but downy woodpeckers prefer to be at heights of 12 feet (3.6 meters) or more. Wrens nest just about anywhere, but they like small houses with entrance holes just 1 inch

Build a House for Bluebirds

Bluebirds like to nest in hollow trees. But in many places, people have cut down trees with nesting holes. That was bad news for bluebirds—until young people all across North America began to put up simple nest boxes for them. Now these pretty birds are making a comeback.

Would you like to help, too? Libraries and nature centers have plans for bluebird nest boxes. You can also search the Internet for plans. Here's one Web site with helpful instructions: *birding.about.com/library/weekly/aa010703a.htm*

After you put up your box, watch it from a distance. Once a week, you may quietly—and briefly—open it to look for a nest, eggs, and chicks. Keep a diary of what happens in the box.

Birdhouses come in almost every shape and color. The size of a birdhouse and its entrance hole determine which birds will nest in it. Most birds want "single-family" homes. Other birds, such as purple martins, prefer "condos." And sometimes a birdhouse will double as a shelter when the nesting season is over.

(2.5 centimeters) across. Flickers want bigger houses than house finches, which want bigger houses than chickadees.

Condominiums. Purple martins are attracted to multi-unit dwellings in which each nesting pair has its own separate "apartment." These houses have a central airshaft and an elevated roof for ventilation. Some are only one or two stories high but are designed so that additional floors can be added if needed. Others are elaborate structures that reflect the creativity of their builders. Purple martins are picky—they want their condos to be in an open area near water.

Nesting Shelves. These are just planks of wood on which birds can build their nests. Barn swallows, robins, and phoebes are birds that will use nesting shelves. The shelves should be placed beneath the eaves of a building or protected from rain in some other way.

DINING OUT

Most people think of feeding birds only in winter, but birds will come to feed all year long if food is available. Some birds will come almost every day. Others will visit only occasionally or only at certain times of the year when their preferred foods are scarce.

148

Robins, for example, feed mainly on earth-worms, insects, and spiders. In fall, however, they may visit if you provide fruits and seeds.

One very easy way to feed birds is to place seeds and other foods on a windowsill or a deck, or simply toss them on the ground. In fact, sparrows, doves, quails, and certain other birds actually prefer to eat on the ground. But you will attract more kinds of birds if you put out feeders.

Feeders should be placed where you can easily reach them for cleaning and filling, in spots where they are protected from wind and rain. And try to place them near bushes that provide perches and cover for the birds.

To attract a variety of birds, provide a variety of food, including fruits, suet (animal fat), and a mix of seeds. Some birds will enjoy foods from your kitchen. Try cheese, cooked peas, bacon grease, cereal, and bread broken into small pieces. If you are consistent in putting out food, birds will make your backyard a regular dining spot.

In fact, you may find that your feeder attracts more than birds. Squirrels are often unwanted visitors—one squirrel can quickly gobble up enough food for dozens of birds. Many commercial feeders are designed to prevent squirrels from reaching the food. If your feeder is mounted on a pole, attach a metal cone that will keep squirrels from climbing up.

Clean feeders regularly to remove spoiled food and prevent the growth of mold. This is especially important during warm weather. Use warm soapy water and rinse thoroughly. Never use insecticides around bird feeders.

Bird Tables. The simplest type of feeder is a flat wooden board or tray, set on a post. You

What to Feed Your Fine-Feathered Friends

Bobwhites (quail)	cracked corn, millet, peanut hearts, canary seed
Buntings	grass seed, sunflower seed, thistle (niger) seed, canary seed
Cardinals	sunflower seed, cracked corn, millet
Chickadees	sunflower seed, suet, peanut butter
Dickcissels	millet, sunflower seed, cracked corn
Doves	corn, millet, hulled sunflower seed
Finches	sunflower seed, thistle (niger) seed, millet, peanut hearts, canary seed
Flickers	suet, peanut butter, sunflower seed
Grosbeaks	sunflower seed, peanut hearts, cracked corn
Jays	cracked corn, sunflower seed, suet, peanut hearts
Juncos	millet, thistle (niger) seed, canary seed, cracked corn
Nuthatches	sunflower seed, suet, peanut butter
Orioles	sugar water, oranges and other fruits
Robins	apples, sunflower seed, suet
Sparrows	millet, sunflower seed, canary seed, peanut hearts, cracked corn
Towhees	millet, sunflower seed, cracked corn, oats, peanut hearts
Woodpeckers	suet, sunflower seed, oranges, peanut hearts
Wrens	peanut hearts, millet, dried fruits

can stock a bird table with every type of food—a bird buffet of everything from fruits to seeds to suet. A roof over the tray will help keep rain off the food.

Seed Feeders. These feeders are long tubes that are easy to fill with a supply of seeds, and they keep the seeds dry in all sorts of weather. Birds eat from the tube at one or several openings. Different types of seed feeders may be mounted on posts or hung

To bring different birds to your yard, offer a variety of foods, and place feeders in several locations. Here, an indigo bunting snacks at a hanging feeder, chickadees check out a table feeder, and an oriole nibbles at a fruit feeder.

from branches. Hanging types are especially popular with chickadees, titmice, cardinals, and finches, and other nimble little birds—they can hang on when the feeder sways in the wind! You can buy seed feeders, but you

can make your own, too. For example, a metal adapter and a wire hanger (both available from stores and nature catalogs) can turn a large plastic soda bottle into a bird feeder.

Suet and Peanut Butter. Suet and peanut butter provide fat, an important part of a bird's diet, particularly during cold weather. Make suet feeders from plastic mesh bags, such as those used by supermarkets to package onions and oranges. Buy suet at a supermarket, place it in the bag, and hang the bag from a tree. Change suet often, especially in warm weather—it can spoil in just a few days.

Make a peanut-butter feeder by spreading peanut butter onto the scales of a pine cone. Add some seeds, too. Tie one end of a piece of heavy string around the cone and the other end around a tree branch.

Fruit Feeders. Orioles, thrushes, warblers, wrens, and certain other birds enjoy fruits.

Even a clay saucer filled with water will provide a welcome drink or bath for a visiting bird, such as this brown thrasher.

Put apples, oranges, bananas, and raisins on table feeders or in a mesh bag hung from a branch. Large fruits should be cut open. You can also make special holders for fruits. To make an orange feeder, take a stiff wire and turn up the bottom end to form a U. Cut an orange in half. Push the wire through one half, sliding the orange down to the U. Then push the wire through the other orange half, and slide it down next to the first. Twist the top of the wire into a loop that can be hung from a nail.

WATERING HOLES

Birds need water to survive. Some birds, such as colorful warblers, that never nest in your yard or visit your feeders may be attracted by birdbaths, ponds, and running water. Even a shallow plastic container filled with water and a few perching stones will draw a flurry of feathery activity. Other animals—squirrels, chipmunks, lizards, butterflies, frogs—may also stop by for a drink or a bath. Where winter temperatures fall below freezing, put out warm water twice a day.

Now that you have provided your fine-feathered friends with plants, a birdhouse, food, and water, sit back and enjoy the action!

Welcoming Hummingbirds

Tiny, colorful hummingbirds are fascinating to watch. Their fast-beating wings are a blur as the birds fly forward and backward and hover in place.

Hummingbirds feed mainly on nectar, using their long, thin bill and extendable tongue to draw this sweet, sugary liquid from flowers. In summer, you can attract them to your backyard with a feeder filled with sugar water, like the one shown here.

You can also make a hummingbird feeder by using a hamster's water bottle. Hummingbirds are attracted to red, so place red tape or ribbon around the drinking tube. To fill your feeder, mix one part sugar with two parts hot water, and stir until the sugar dissolves. Then add two more parts cold water.

Hang the feeder near red flowers, where hummingbirds will be most likely to discover it.

IT'S GAME TIME...

SAILING ON A HISTORIC MISSION

In April 1607, after a journey of almost five months, a fleet of three merchant ships arrived on the banks of a North American river. They were the *Susan Constant*, the *Godspeed*, and the *Discovery*. The 104 passengers, all men and boys, began building what was to be America's first permanent English colony.

In 2007, historical pageants, musical performances, fireworks, and a visit by Great Britain's Queen Elizabeth II marked the 400th anniversary of this settlement's founding. To learn its name and location, you need a pencil and a sheet of paper. Carefully follow the directions given below.

1. Print the words SUSAN CONSTANT. Keep the words separated as you continue to work.

2. Erase the C.

3. Find the first vowel in the first word. Change it to an E.

4. Add an I before each vowel in the second word.

5. Delete both Ts from the second word.

6. Put a T after the third letter of the first word.

7. Change the first S to the letter that comes after L in the alphabet.

8. Move the O between the T and A.

9. Substitute R-G-I for the N-S combination.

10. Locate the third vowel in the first word. Transfer it to the beginning of the same word.

11. Insert a W inside the O-N combination.

12. Move the last letter to the inside of the I-I combination.

13. Put a J in front of the first vowel of the first word.

14. Attach a V to the beginning of the second word.

> *Re-creations of the three ships that brought the colonists to America are moored near the colony's original site. Visitors can try steering with a whipstaff, climb into a sailor's bunk, and explore the contents of a "see" chest.*

ANSWER: Jamestown Virginia

A SCOOP OF COOPS

Here's a detective puzzle for you: What happens when an "S" jumps from the beginning of a word to the end? In many cases, a new word forms. For example, SCOOP is changed to COOPS, and SLAP becomes LAPS.

Below are the definitions for 12 pairs of words. Can you detect what the words are? Both words in each pair contain exactly the same letters. The only difference is the position of the letter "S."

1. Your backbone
   Trees with needles

   S _ _ _ _ _
   _ _ _ _ _ S

2. Fire a gun
   Sounds made by an owl

   S _ _ _ _ _
   _ _ _ _ _ S

3. It twinkles in the sky
   Black, sticky substances used on roads

   S _ _ _ _
   _ _ _ _ S

4. The final result of a baseball game
   Centers of apples

   S _ _ _ _ _
   _ _ _ _ _ S

5. A small animal with a coiled shell
   Things on the tips of your fingers

   S _ _ _ _ _
   _ _ _ _ _ S

6. What a sword or knife is
   Stringed musical instruments

   S _ _ _ _ _
   _ _ _ _ _ S

7. Ouch! To hurt your toe
   People take baths in these

   S _ _ _ _
   _ _ _ _ S

8. A seat found at a playground
   Birds have two

   S _ _ _ _ _
   _ _ _ _ _ S

9. Clean with a broom
   Sheds tears

   S _ _ _ _ _
   _ _ _ _ _ S

10. Partly close your eyes in bright light
    Five children born in a single birth

    S _ _ _ _ _ _
    _ _ _ _ _ _ S

11. A home for horses
    Kitchen furniture

    S _ _ _ _ _ _
    _ _ _ _ _ _ S

12. The opposite of big
    Places with lots of shops

    S _ _ _ _ _
    _ _ _ _ _ S

ANSWERS: 1. spine, pines; 2. shoot, hoots; 3. star, tars; 4. score, cores; 5. snail, nails; 6. sharp, harps; 7. stub, tubs; 8. swing, wings; 9. sweep, weeps; 10. squint, quints; 11. stable, tables; 12. small, malls

PAPER
STAINED GLASS

Stained-glass windows consist of pieces of colored glass held together by strips of black lead, to form a picture or design. They are among the most beautiful and dramatic of all arts and crafts. Paper versions of these windows are fun to create, and they can be used in a variety of ways: as pictures, greeting cards, bookmarks, even tree ornaments.

A paper stained-glass window is made by cutting out a design from a sheet of black paper, and then placing colored paper behind each cutout area. You'll need the following materials: black paper, colored papers, graph paper, a glue stick, and scissors.

Begin by creating your design on graph paper that's the same size as the black paper. Working on graph paper makes it easier to draw symmetrical and uniformly thick black strips. As you draw the design, make certain that every black strip connects to at least one other black strip.

When your design is completed, place the graph paper on the black paper. Use the glue stick to lightly attach them around the edges. Then carefully cut out the design. When you are finished, gently remove the bits of graph paper still attached to the black paper. What you are looking at will be the back of your picture. Continue working on the back.

Next, cut pieces of colored paper to fit each cutout area of the design; each piece should be a bit larger than the cutout, so that it slightly overlaps the black strips. Glue the edges of each colored piece onto the black strips. Keep working until all the cutout areas have been filled. Then cover the back of the picture with a sheet of paper to protect it. Finally, turn your creation over—and enjoy your eye-catching version of a stained-glass window!

If you'd like to hang your pictures in a window, use colored cellophane instead of colored paper in the cutouts. Experiment with layering one color of cellophane atop another to create a new color.

STAMP COLLECTING

Popular books and movies, historic events, cartoons, nature, art, and pure fun inspired new stamps from many nations in 2007. Here are some highlights.

U.S. STAMPS

A postage-rate increase in May 2007 prompted a first-class "first" from the U.S. Postal Service. As the cost of mailing a letter first class rose from 39 cents to 41 cents, the Postal Service issued a "Forever" stamp. This stamp carried a picture of the Liberty Bell but bore no denomination. It cost 41 cents, like other new first-class stamps. But those who bought it could be sure that even if rates go up again, they could use this stamp without paying extra postage.

The Postal Service released plenty of other new stamps during the year. Among the most popular were stamps based on the *Star Wars* films. A pane of 15 *Star Wars* stamps issued in May showed various char-

acters, including Darth Vader, Luke Sky-walker, Boba Fett, C-3PO, and Obi-Wan Kenobi. The Postal Service went all out for the release, even disguising mailboxes to look like the *Star Wars* android R2-D2. Customers were asked to vote for their favorite *Star Wars* stamp, and the design showing Yoda was the winner. A slightly smaller version of that stamp was reissued later in the year, in panes of 20.

Another popular release marked the 400th anniversary of the founding of Jamestown, the first permanent English settlement in North America. This unusual 41-cent stamp showed the three English ships that brought the first Jamestown settlers to the wild coast of Virginia in May 1607. It was three-sided— only the third such stamp in U.S. postal history—to represent the three-sided fort that the settlers had raised there.

A new stamp in the American Treasures series showed a beautiful stained-glass win-

2008 STAMPS
FROM AROUND
THE WORLD

dow designed by Louis Comfort Tiffany around 1908. Tiffany was a master of the art of glass. The window shown on the stamp depicted irises and magnolia trees framing a distant landscape, with a river winding toward a glowing sunset.

Disney characters worked their magic on four new stamps. The Art of Disney: Magic stamps featured Mickey Mouse as the Sorcerer's Apprentice, Dumbo and Timothy Mouse, Peter Pan and Tinker Bell, and Aladdin and Genie. This was the fourth group of stamps in the Art of Disney series, which started in 2004.

Ten Marvel Comics superheroes turned their talents to delivering mail. The stamps, sold in sheets of 20, featured portraits and comic-book covers showing Captain America, Elektra, Iron Man, Silver Surfer, Spider-Man, Spider-Woman, Sub-Mariner, The Incredible Hulk, The Thing, and Wolverine.

Flowers were showcased on several releases. Reproductions of vivid color photographs showed nine different garden flowers on the 41-cent Beautiful Blooms stamps, sold in booklets and coils. And four stamps highlighted the importance of pollinators, animals that transfer pollen among flowers, allowing seeds to form. The stamps showed four pollinators—a bumblebee, a bat, a butterfly, and a hummingbird—visiting four wildflowers. The sheets emphasized their interdependence by arranging the four designs in two alternate blocks that fit together like a puzzle. In one block the pollinators formed a central starburst; in the other block the flowers were in the center.

STAMPS AROUND THE WORLD

The year 2007 marked the 100th anniversary of the Scouting movement, started by Robert Baden-Powell in Britain in 1907. A number of countries, including Britain, celebrated the anniversary on stamps. Canada Post's Scouting stamp showed five Scouts, boys and girls of various ethnic groups, forming a human fleur-de-lis similar to the Scouting symbol. In the background were modern and historical scenes showing Scouts camping,

cycling, and canoeing. Scouting was also the theme for the 2007 Europa issue. The more than 40 members of PostEurop, the association of European public postal administrations, release this omnibus issue each year.

It was the Year of the Pig in the Chinese lunar calendar, and so pigs paraded on many stamps. Jersey, one of the Channel Islands, released a series of souvenir sheets each containing a single stamp. The designs showed happy pigs wearing colorful winter scarves. Vietnam and Canada were among the other countries that depicted playful pigs on stamps to mark the new year. South Korea featured a cute pig printed in special glow-in-the-dark ink.

To mark the publication of the seventh and final volume in the *Harry Potter* series, several countries issued stamps showing characters from those hugely popular books. Stamps from France showed Harry and his friends Hermione and Ron as they appeared in the film version of the fifth book, *Harry Potter and the Order of the Phoenix*, which came out in 2007. Britain released seven

stamps showing the jackets of the British editions of the books. Five other British designs showed the crests of Harry's school, Hogwarts, and its four houses. Self-adhesive versions of these stamps were sold in panes bearing labels printed in heat-sensitive ink. Rubbing the label revealed the meaning of magic spells from the stories.

Peter Rabbit, Benjamin Bunny, Squirrel Nutkin, and other characters from the tales of Beatrix Potter appeared on a set of six stamps from the Pacific nation of Solomon Islands. The books of this British author-illustrator have been popular with young children around the world ever since they first came out in the late 1800's. Mauritius featured popular children's games, including hopscotch and marbles.

Friendship was the theme of a clever stamp from Finland. It showed the tops of two faces—a blond boy and a brown-haired girl—in a design that looked correct no matter which was on top. Streamers and confetti set the mood for a cheerful new "Celebration"

A TOPICAL COLLECTION OF LOVE STAMPS

stamp from Canada. And Canada celebrated spring on a pair of stamps showing white and purple lilacs against complementary backgrounds.

Belgium released a pane of ten stamps celebrating its famous foods, including delicious chocolates. Britain highlighted summer fun with Beside the Seaside, a group of stamps in various denominations. One of the stamps in the group featured a treat called a 99—a soft-serve ice-cream cone with a chocolate candy bar sticking out of it.

Among the releases from the United Nations Postal Administration was a set of six stamps called Peaceful Visions. The colorful watercolor designs showed symbols of peace such as doves and olive branches alongside fanciful human figures representing nurturing, unity, freedom, and other themes. Graceful dancers appeared on four stamps from Israel, depicting ballet, modern dance, and folk and ethnic dances.

Many countries depicted the wonders of the natural world on stamps. Britain high-lighted animals found in its coastal waters on ten stamps. The designs, based on eye-popping underwater photographs, showed a sun star, a moon jellyfish, a gray seal, and other creatures. The African nation of Namibia celebrated its biodiversity—the huge variety of living things found within its borders. Animals shown on these stamps ranged from bullfrogs to zebras.

A TOPICAL COLLECTION

Do you love collecting stamps built around a single theme? Then collect stamps that send messages of love! The U.S. Postal Service began issuing its popular Love stamps in 1973. Its 2007 design, With Love and Kisses, was the 23rd in the series. Several other countries, including Australia and Ireland, issue Love stamps around Valentine's Day each year. Whether you concentrate on Love stamps from one country or many, you'll have warm feelings and happy thoughts whenever you look through your collection.

A ROOT IN YOUR SOUP

The next time you eat vegetable soup, look closely. You'll find roots and stems and maybe even fruit in it. This is because we eat different parts of different plants.

Most plant foods are grouped as fruits or vegetables. But this doesn't necessarily tell us what part of the plant is being eaten. We eat the underground stem of a yam plant; the seeds of a pea plant; the fruit of an orange tree; the bark (stem covering) of a cinnamon tree; and the leaves of an onion plant. (Onions are leaves wrapped around one another, forming a bulb.)

The names of 33 plants are listed below. Match each to the part that you normally eat.

a. LEAF   **b.** STEM   **c.** ROOT   **d.** FLOWER   **e.** FRUIT   **f.** SEED

1. apple	**12.** coconut	**23.** potato
2. artichoke	**13.** collards	**24.** pumpkin
3. asparagus	**14.** corn	**25.** quince
4. banana	**15.** cucumber	**26.** radish
5. beet	**16.** eggplant	**27.** spinach
6. broccoli	**17.** fig	**28.** squash
7. cabbage	**18.** green pepper	**29.** strawberry
8. carrot	**19.** lettuce	**30.** tomato
9. cauliflower	**20.** parsley	**31.** turnip
10. celery	**21.** pear	**32.** walnut
11. cherry	**22.** pineapple	**33.** watermelon

ANSWERS: 1.e; 2.d; 3.b; 4.e; 5.c; 6.d; 7.a; 8.c; 9.d; 10.a; 11.e; 12.f; 13.a; 14.f; 15.e,f; 16.e,f; 17.e,f; 18.e; 19.a; 20.a; 21.e; 22.e; 23.b; 24.e; 25.e; 26.c; 27.a; 28.e,f; 29.e,f; 30.e,f; 31.c; 32.f; 33.e.

Next, go on a hunt. All 33 plants are hidden in this word-search puzzle. Try to find them. Cover the puzzle with a sheet of tracing paper. Read forward, backward, up, down, and diagonally. Then draw a neat line through each plant as you find it.

E	C	N	I	U	Q	R	W	A	T	E	R	M	E	L	O	N
B	O	S	E	A	E	G	A	B	B	A	C	T	I	N	G	I
R	T	P	R	Y	R	E	L	E	C	L	O	M	I	B	N	K
O	A	A	G	A	A	T	N	H	E	E	T	E	N	O	E	P
C	T	R	R	S	E	R	U	T	Z	B	A	G	A	E	G	M
C	O	A	E	F	C	B	T	J	L	E	M	T	O	P	G	U
O	P	G	E	C	A	U	L	I	F	L	O	W	E	R	P	P
L	T	U	N	O	C	O	C	O	C	R	T	A	P	P	L	E
I	T	S	P	E	G	I	R	U	R	H	R	B	F	D	A	H
N	U	S	E	H	T	O	D	A	M	H	O	I	E	N	N	S
O	R	S	P	I	N	A	C	H	I	B	G	K	A	E	T	I
V	N	X	P	I	N	E	A	P	P	L	E	N	E	S	T	D
L	I	U	E	V	Y	R	R	E	B	W	A	R	T	S	N	A
Q	P	A	R	S	L	E	Y	E	R	B	C	O	R	N	A	R
A	S	P	A	R	A	G	U	S	D	R	A	L	L	O	C	R
Y	C	H	E	R	R	Y	N	H	S	A	U	Q	S	L	V	O

Dressed in her finest, Miss Penelope Pig is so charming that she can sit with you at the breakfast table! And she's just one of the cool crafty characters that you can make.

CRAFTY CHARACTERS

Need something to do on a lazy afternoon? Here's a crew of amusing characters that you can create, using various techniques and materials. You'll have lots of fun while you're crafting—and lots of opportunities to use your imagination.

PENELOPE PIG

Did anyone ever warn you that if you ate too much you'd swell up like a balloon? Well, that's exactly what's happened to Penelope Pig. This chubby pink pig is made by blowing up balloons, and then covering them with lots and lots of thread.

You'll need a large balloon for Penelope's body, a medium one for the head, and four small ones for the feet. You'll also need pink crochet thread, thread stiffener, glue, a plas-

tic cup, a large bowl, beads, pieces of pink and black felt, and a pink pipe cleaner.

Blow up the balloons and knot the ends. For the body, tie one end of the thread to the knot of the large balloon. Wrap the thread around the balloon, crisscrossing it in all directions so that the balloon is completely covered. Tie the thread to the balloon knot, leaving a "tail" for hanging. Follow the same procedure for all the other balloons.

Make a snout from the bottom of the plastic cup. Wrap thread around the cup, just as you did around the balloons.

Now comes the messy part, so be sure your work surface is covered with a plastic bag or newspaper. One by one, hold each balloon and the snout over the large bowl and pour thread stiffener over it, repeating the process

Funky Fish Magnets

until all the threads are saturated. Hang the balloons and snout by their "tails" over a protected surface for one to two days, until the threads are completely dry. Then cut off the "tails" and puncture the balloons. Remove the plastic cup from the snout.

Gently press an indentation into one side of the body and glue on the head. Follow the same procedure for the feet. Glue the open end of the snout to the head. Glue felt nostrils onto the snout, beady eyes and felt ears onto the head, and the pipe-cleaner tail onto the body.

To turn Penelope into a perfect little pig, dress her in a lace collar and a little straw hat. Now she's ready to charm family and friends.

FUNKY FISH

Find a piece of fabric that's "swimming" with tropical fish and use it to create colorful fish magnets. In addition to the fabric you'll need felt, iron-on adhesive, glue, fiberfill stuffing, clear fabric paint, clear fabric glitter, and round magnets.

Cut a fish shape from the fabric, leaving a bit of background fabric around the edges. Use this cutout as a pattern to cut a matching fish from a piece of felt.

Place the fabric fish, right side up, on the iron-on adhesive. Using an iron preheated at medium setting, press the fish onto the adhesive for about five seconds. Don't move the iron during pressing! When cool, trim the excess fabric around the fish.

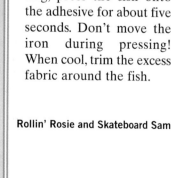

Rollin' Rosie and Skateboard Sam

Glue a magnet to the center of one side of the felt fish. Place the felt fish, magnet side down, on the ironing board. Put a small amount of fiberfill stuffing in the center. Place the fabric fish on top. Press with the warm iron for a few seconds. Use the tip of the iron to press around the outside edges, to make certain the pieces are sealed together. Trim the excess felt, leaving a thin felt border around the outside of the fish.

Outline the fish, its fins, and other details with the fabric paint. While the paint is still wet, sprinkle on glitter. After the fish dries, it's ready to swim across your refrigerator!

ROLLIN' RACERS

With hair standing on end, Rollin' Rosie and Skateboard Sam (page 163) show off their nimble-footed skills. Each of these teenage speedsters is made from a miniature seagrass broom (hair), a wooden craft spoon (face and body), a pipe cleaner (arms), two wooden craft sticks (legs), and two wooden ovals (feet).

Paint the front and side edges of the wooden spoon. Add details to the face. Let dry. Place the broom on your work surface. Center the pipe cleaner on the back of the handle, just below the bristles; glue it on the handle to form the arms. Glue the spoon to the front of the broom handle, placing it so the face is centered in a halo of hair. Glue the craft sticks atop the lower part of the handle, so that they are even with the bottom of the spoon, to form the legs. Glue the oval feet to the bottoms of the craft sticks.

Make Rosie's skates from painted wooden circles, and Sam's skateboard from a jumbo craft stick, with four wooden circles for wheels. Dress the pair in clothes made from brightly colored felt or construction paper, and these kids will be ready to race!

SLIM 'N' JIM

These smilin' cowpokes look mighty cute in their ten-gallon hats and nifty bandannas. The hats can be purchased at a craft store, but the bandannas and other clothing can be made from old jeans and scraps of fabrics.

To make Slim—he's the tubby one—you'll need a wooden bead for the head, two craft spoons for the arms, a large foam ball for the body, and a large wooden heart for the feet. Skinny Jim is made from a head bead, two short dowels for the arms, a clothespin for the body, and a small wooden heart for the feet. You'll also need doll hair and glue.

Slim 'n' Jim Cowpokes

164

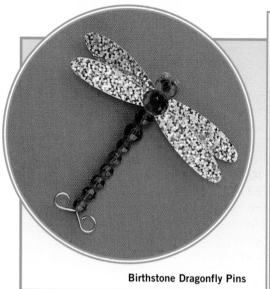

Birthstone Dragonfly Pins

January	February	March	April
May	June	July	August
September	October	November	December

Paint faces on the head beads, and paint the hearts brown. While these dry, make the cowboys' clothes. Begin with the shirt sleeves: Wrap pieces of fabric around the arms; glue the fabric edges together; and glue the fabric to the arms. In a similar fashion, attach fabric around each cowboy's body, first the shirt and then the pants.

Glue the arms, head, and heart onto each body. Glue doll hair and then a hat onto each head. Wrap a bandanna around each neck, and add button belt buckles. Your cowboys are gettin' ready to rustle up some fun!

DAZZLING DRAGONFLIES

Dragonflies are among nature's most beautiful insects. They look like sparkling jewels as sunlight reflects from their bodies. You can re-create this splendor by making a birthstone dragonfly pin—it's a great birthday present for friends or family.

Here are the birthstone colors for each month: January, dark red; February, purple; March, light blue; April, crystal; May, green; June, light purple; July, red; August, light green; September, blue; October, rosy pink; November, amber; and December, turquoise.

To make a pin you'll need eight faceted beads, two slightly larger than the others; and four faceted stones—a large round one, two small round ones, and a large heart-shaped one. You'll also need adhesive-backed glitter

paper, posterboard, beading wire that's 8 inches (20 centimeters) long, jewelry glue, and a pin back.

Bend the wire in half and twist it two or three times to form a small loop, as shown in the diagram at right. This will be the body.

To make the dragonfly's tail, insert both wire ends through the eight beads, beginning with the two larger ones. Push the beads up to the loop, and then bend the bottom ends of the wire into small curls.

Remove the backing from the glitter paper and press the paper to the poster board. Cut out two pairs of wings. Glue the front wings onto the front of the wire loop. Glue the back wings so that they overlap the front wings and touch the first bead of the tail.

The heart-shaped stone is the dragonfly's head. Glue the two small round stones onto the curves of the heart, to create eyes. Glue the heart to the body so that it slightly overlaps the wings. Glue the large round stone atop the wings. Glue the pin back on, and your dragonfly is ready to fly onto a T-shirt or sweater!

MANY FRIENDS COOKING

BANANA NIBBLES
from the Philippines

Time for a snack. Have a fried banana, Philippine style. These banana chips are often dipped in batter and then fried. Or you can simply slice and fry them quickly in oil. Bananas thrive in tropical climates, so it's no wonder they crop up in Philippine foods as often as they do—in soups, stews, desserts, and snacks. (Have an adult help you with this recipe.)

INGREDIENTS

6 bananas
oil for deep frying
salt

EQUIPMENT

knife
high-sided frying pan
slotted spoon
oven mitts
paper towels

HOW TO MAKE

1. Peel the bananas and cut them into ½-inch slices.
2. Heat the oil until it bubbles.
3. Carefully drop several banana slices at a time into the hot oil and fry until golden brown. Use oven mitts to protect your hands.
4. Remove the bananas with the slotted spoon and drain on paper towels.
5. Sprinkle with salt and serve hot.

This recipe serves 6 people.

Note: *This recipe works best with plantains, which are green and less sweet than yellow bananas.*

GAZPACHO
from Spain

Cool off in hot summer weather. The Spanish know how, with a cold soup-salad—gazpacho. Chop and mix fresh tomatoes, cucumbers, and green peppers. Season and chill. You're set for a drinkable feast. In Spain, different towns make different versions of this soup. After you make this one, invent your own gazpacho by adding any of your favorite vegetables.

INGREDIENTS

- 2 cucumbers
- 5 medium tomatoes
- 1 onion
- 1 green pepper
- 2 cloves garlic
- 2 cups cold water
- 2 cups tomato juice
- ¼ cup olive oil
- 1 tablespoon salt

EQUIPMENT

- paring knife
- 2 large mixing bowls
- mixing spoon
- measuring cups
- blender or food mill
- fork

HOW TO MAKE

1. Peel the cucumbers and cut into pieces. Peel the tomatoes and onion and chop coarsely. Cut the green pepper into small pieces. Mince the garlic.
2. In a large mixing bowl combine the chopped cucumbers, tomatoes, onion, green pepper, and garlic. Mix well.
3. Stir in the water and tomato juice.
4. Pour the mixture into a blender 2 cups at a time. Blend at a high speed for 1 minute. If using a food mill, pour the mixture in small amounts and purée.
5. Pour the blended mixture into another mixing bowl. Beat in the olive oil with a fork. Add salt.
6. Cover the bowl and refrigerate. Serve cold.

This recipe serves 6 people.

COIN COLLECTING

Coin collectors had many options in 2007. There were new coin series from the United States and Canada. And there were collector coins from countries around the world.

U.S. COINS

Five new coins joined the U.S. Mint's state quarters series in 2007. All honored western states. Montana's quarter showed a bison skull above a rugged mountain landscape. Millions ored the first four presidents—George Washington, John Adams, Thomas Jefferson, and James Madison. The obverse designs showed their portraits and the dates they served; the Statue of Liberty was on the reverse. The mottoes "In God We Trust" and "E Pluribus Unum," along with the date and mintmark, were on the coins' edges. This was the first time since 1933 that circulating U.S. coins displayed edge lettering.

U.S. state quarters representing Montana, Washington, Idaho, Wyoming, and Utah.

of bison once roamed Montana's eastern plains, and the bison skull was a powerful symbol for the American Indians there. Washington, the Evergreen State, showed two state symbols—a leaping salmon and towering Mount Rainier.

A peregrine falcon graced the Idaho quarter. The state's official raptor, the peregrine reflected respect for nature. A bucking horse and rider appeared on Wyoming's coin, which carried the legend "The Equality State." Wyoming was the first state to grant women the right to vote. The completion of the transcontinental railroad at Promontory Summit, Utah, in 1869 was marked on that state's quarter.

The Mint kicked off another new series of coins: presidential dollars. The 2007 coins hon-

Four half-ounce gold $10 collector coins began another new series, this one honoring First Spouses. Three showed First Ladies—Martha Washington, Abigail Adams, and Dolley Madison. Thomas Jefferson's wife died before he took office, so the coin for his presidency showed an image of Liberty. The reverse designs were different on each coin. Martha Washington was shown sewing a button onto her husband's Revolutionary War uniform. Abigail Adams was shown writing to her husband, asking him to "remember the ladies" when creating the new Republic. And Dolley Madison was shown saving items from the White House before the British burned it in 1814. The Jefferson coin showed his epitaph, which he wrote.

A dollar coin of George Washington (from the U.S. presidential series); a gold $10 coin showing Dolley Madison (from the First Spouses series); a silver dollar marking the founding of Jamestown; a silver dollar commemorating the desegregation of a high school in Little Rock, Arkansas.

Canada's 25-cent coin celebrating the 2010 Vancouver Olympics; and its silver dollar honoring native hero Joseph Brant.

U.S. commemoratives included a silver dollar and a gold $5 coin marking the 400th anniversary of the founding of Jamestown, the first permanent English settlement in North America. Another silver dollar honored the 50th anniversary of the desegregation of Little Rock Central High School, in Little Rock, Arkansas. In 1957, facing threats and taunts, nine brave students became the first African Americans at this school. The coin showed their legs as they walked to school, accompanied by a soldier. The reverse showed an image of the school.

CANADIAN COINS

The Royal Canadian Mint launched a three-year coin program celebrating the 2010 Vancouver Olympic and Paralympic Winter Games. Five 25-cent circulation coins honored the sports of alpine skiing, biathlon, curling, ice hockey, and wheelchair curling. Seventeen circulation coins and 36 collector coins are planned in all.

Among the many other Canadian releases was a silver dollar marking the 200th anniversary of the death of the Native American hero Thayendanegea (Joseph Brant). A $20 silver coin marked the International Polar Year, a multi-nation research effort. It featured Sir Martin Frobisher, who sailed into Arctic waters in 1576. A special "plasma" coating gave an icy blue sheen to 7,000 of the coins.

Canada also issued two 25-cent colored coins depicting birds—a red-breasted nuthatch and a ruby-throated hummingbird. Dinosaur fossils appeared in a new series of silver $4 coins. The first coin showed the bones of a Parasaurolophus, a plant eater that lived in Alberta around 75 million years ago.

WORLD COINS

The world's first artificial satellite, *Sputnik,* was launched in 1957 by the former Soviet Union. Several nations, including Russia and the Cook Islands, issued coins to mark the 50th anniversary of the event.

Bermuda issued two triangular $3 silver coins honoring ships lost in the Bermuda Triangle, an area known for shipwrecks. The coins showed the *San Pedro,* which went down in 1505, and the *Colonel William G. Ball,* which sank in 1943.

Russia's coin honoring *Sputnik*; the Bermuda Triangle coin; the Year of the Pig coin from China; Tuvalu's coin featuring a great white shark.

The 100th anniversary of scouting was celebrated on coins of several nations, including Britain and New Zealand, and the Isle of Man. To mark the 400th anniversary of Jamestown, the British Virgin Islands issued silver and gold coins showing an English lion and an American eagle.

It was the Year of the Pig in the Chinese lunar calendar, and several countries celebrated with coins. Among them were China, Singapore, and Canada. Other animals appeared on coins from many lands, including a great white shark that seemed to jump off a colored dollar coin from Tuvalu.

ROBERT VAN RYZIN
Editor, *Coins* magazine

SPORTS

Switzerland's Roger Federer falls to the ground in joy—and relief—after defeating Rafael Nadal of Spain at Wimbledon in July. This was his fifth consecutive Wimbledon championship. Earlier in the year, Federer won the Australian Open for the third time. And after Wimbledon he went on to win the U.S. Open for the fourth time. In all, Federer has won 12 Grand Slam titles. He is considered the best player of his generation, and one of the all-time great tennis players.

Boston third baseman Mike Lowell scores a run in Game 4 of the World Series. The Red Sox swept the Colorado Rockies to win the Fall Classic. Lowell was named Series MVP.

BASEBALL

Pitching. Hitting. Fielding. The Boston Red Sox had them all in 2007, amply provided by proven veterans and some superb youngsters. After wrapping up the American League pennant, the Sox ripped through the Colorado Rockies in the World Series, sweeping the National League champs in four games. Boston had last won the Fall Classic in 2004.

Supplying much of Boston's power throughout the season were David Ortiz, who led the Sox in batting (.332) and home runs (35); Mike Lowell, team leader in runs batted in (RBI's; 120); and Manny Ramirez, who cracked 20 four-baggers. Joining them were rookie second baseman Dustin Pedroia; catcher Jason Varitek; first baseman Kevin Youkilis; Julio Lugo at shortstop; centerfielder Coco Crisp; and J. D. Drew in right field. The pitching staff included Josh Beckett, the only major-league hurler to win 20 games in 2007; 17-game-winner Tim Wakefield; rookie Daisuke ("Dice-K") Matsuzaka, who notched 15 victories; veteran Curt Schilling; and bullpen ace Jonathan Papelbon. Terry Francona was the Boston manager.

In the regular season, Boston finished first in the American League (AL) Eastern Divi-sion. The New York Yankees finished second and qualified for the playoffs as the AL's wild-card team. The other division titlists were the Cleveland Indians (Central Division) and the Los Angeles Angels of Anaheim (Western Division).

The Red Sox swept the Angels in the best-of-five Division Series in three games, while the Indians whipped the Yankees, three games to one. In the best-of-seven American League Championship Series (ALCS), Cleveland took a lead of three games to one, but the Sox captured the next three to win the AL pennant. Josh Beckett won two games and was named Most Valuable Player (MVP) of the ALCS.

In the National League (NL), Colorado finished second behind the Arizona Diamondbacks in the NL West. The Rockies had to win a one-game "mini-playoff" over the San Diego Padres in order to secure the wild card. The NL Central winners were the long-suffering Chicago Cubs, who hadn't won a World Series since 1908. The Philadelphia Phillies topped the NL East.

In the NL Division Series, the Rockies rocked the Phillies in three straight, while the Diamondbacks clobbered the Cubs, also in three. In the NLCS, Colorado swept again, ousting Arizona, four games to none. Matt Holliday was named MVP of the NLCS.

2007 WORLD SERIES RESULTS

		R	H	E	Winning/Losing Pitcher
1	Colorado	1	6	0	Jeff Francis (L)
	Boston	13	17	0	Josh Beckett (W)
2	Colorado	1	5	0	Ubaldo Jimenez (L)
	Boston	2	6	1	Curt Schilling (W)
3	Boston	10	15	1	Daisuke Matsuzaka (W)
	Colorado	5	11	0	Josh Fogg (L)
4	Boston	4	9	0	Jon Lester (W)
	Colorado	3	7	0	Aaron Cook (L)

Visiting team listed first, home team second.

Regular-season MVP's: New York Yankee Alex Rodriguez (above); Philadelphia Phillie Jimmy Rollins (below).

The Rockies entered the 2007 World Series having won seven consecutive playoff games. But then they met the Red Sox.

The Fall Classic began on October 24 at Fenway Park in Boston, Massachusetts. Game 1 was a rout; the Sox won, 13–1, bashing 17 hits, including three apiece by Ortiz and Ramirez, and a homer by Pedroia. Beckett was the winning pitcher. Game 2, also in Boston, was closer, a 2–1 victory for the Sox; Lowell and Varitek drove in Boston's runs. Schilling got the win.

Matsuzaka pitched into the sixth inning for Boston in Game 3, played at Coors Field in Denver, Colorado, and was credited with the victory; "Dice-K" also contributed a two-run single in Boston's six-run third inning. The final score was 10–5. Mike Lowell and pinch-hitter Bobby Kielty hit home runs for Boston in Game 4, also played in Denver. The Sox finished their sweep with a 4–3 win. Lowell was named MVP of the Series; he batted .400, collected 4 RBI's, and scored 6 times.

New York Yankee third baseman Alex Rodriguez was MVP of the AL regular season; "A-Rod" blasted 54 homers and drove in 156 runs—almost one per game! Jimmy Rollins of the Phillies was the NL MVP; he won the Gold Glove Award at shortstop and was an excellent leadoff hitter, rapping out 212 hits, including 30 homers, stealing 41 bases, and batting .296 with 94 RBI's.

Cleveland's C.C. Sabathia took the Cy Young Award as the AL's top pitcher; the lefthander posted a 19–7 won-lost record and a 3.21 ERA. The NL Cy Young went to San Diego righty Jake Peavy, who won 19 games, lost only 6, recorded a 2.54 ERA, and struck out 240 in 223.1 innings.

Rookie of the Year Awards went, in the AL, to Boston's Pedroia, who batted .317. In the NL, it went to Ryan Braun, third baseman for the Milwaukee Brewers, who compiled 34 home runs, 97 RBI's, and a .324 batting average.

San Francisco Giant Barry Bonds became baseball's all-time home-run leader in 2007, surpassing Henry Aaron's total of 755; Bonds finished the year with 762. But allegations that he had used steroids overshadowed his achievement. And in November, a federal grand jury indicted Bonds on charges of perjury and obstruction of justice for allegedly lying under oath about his use of steroids.

2007 MAJOR LEAGUE BASEBALL FINAL STANDINGS

AMERICAN LEAGUE

Eastern Division

	W	L	Pct.	GB
* Boston	96	66	.593	—
New York	94	68	.580	2
Toronto	83	79	.512	13
Baltimore	69	93	.426	27
Tampa Bay	66	96	.407	30

Central Division

	W	L	Pct.	GB
Cleveland	96	66	.593	—
Detroit	88	74	.543	8
Minnesota	79	83	.488	17
Chicago	72	90	.444	24
Kansas City	69	93	.426	27

Western Division

	W	L	Pct.	GB
Los Angeles	94	68	.580	—
Seattle	88	74	.543	6
Oakland	76	86	.469	18
Texas	75	87	.463	19

*World Series winner

NATIONAL LEAGUE

Eastern Division

	W	L	Pct.	GB
Philadelphia	89	73	.549	—
New York	88	74	.543	1
Atlanta	84	78	.519	5
Washington	73	89	.451	16
Florida	71	91	.438	18

Central Division

	W	L	Pct.	GB
Chicago	85	77	.525	—
Milwaukee	83	79	.512	2
St. Louis	78	84	.481	7
Houston	73	89	.451	12
Cincinnati	72	90	.444	13
Pittsburgh	68	94	.420	17

Western Division

	W	L	Pct.	GB
Arizona	90	72	.556	—
Colorado	90	73	.552	0.5
San Diego	89	74	.546	1.5
Los Angeles	82	80	.506	8
San Francisco	71	91	.438	19

MAJOR LEAGUE LEADERS

AMERICAN LEAGUE

Batting
(top 10 qualifiers)

	AB	H	Avg.
M. Ordóñez, Detroit	595	216	.363
I. Suzuki, Seattle	678	238	.351
P. Polanco, Detroit	587	200	.341
J. Posada, New York	506	171	.338
D. Ortiz, Boston	549	182	.332
C. Figgins, Los Angeles	442	146	.330
M. Lowell, Boston	589	191	.324
V. Guerrero, Los Angeles	574	186	.324
D. Jeter, New York	639	206	.322
D. Pedroia, Boston	520	165	.317

Home Runs

	HR
A. Rodriguez, New York	54
C. Peña, Tampa Bay	46
D. Ortiz, Boston	35
J. Thome, Chicago	35
P. Konerko, Chicago	31
J. Morneau, Minnesota	31

Pitching
(top qualifiers, based on number of wins)

	W	L	ERA
J. Beckett, Boston	20	7	3.27
C.C. Sabathia, Cleveland	19	7	3.21
C.-M. Wang, New York	19	7	3.70
F. Carmona, Cleveland	19	8	3.06
J. Lackey, Los Angeles	19	9	3.01

NATIONAL LEAGUE

Batting
(top 10 qualifiers)

	AB	H	Avg.
M. Holliday, Colorado	636	216	.340
C. Jones, Atlanta	513	173	.337
C. Utley, Philadelphia	530	176	.332
E. Rentería, Atlanta	494	164	.332
H. Ramírez, Florida	639	212	.332
A. Pujols, St. Louis	565	185	.327
D. Wright, New York	604	196	.325
M. Cabrera, Florida	588	188	.320
T. Helton, Colorado	557	178	.320
D. Young, Washington	460	147	.320

Home Runs

	HR
P. Fielder, Milwaukee	50
R. Howard, Philadelphia	47
A. Dunn, Cincinnati	40
M. Holliday, Colorado	36
L. Berkman, Houston	34
R. Braun, Milwaukee	34
M. Cabrera, Florida	34

Pitching
(top qualifiers, based on number of wins)

	W	L	ERA
J. Peavy, San Diego	19	6	2.54
B. Webb, Arizona	18	10	3.01
C. Zambrano, Chicago	18	13	3.95
J. Francis, Colorado	17	9	4.22
B. Penny, Los Angeles	16	4	3.03
A. Harang, Cincinnati	16	6	3.73
T. Hudson, Atlanta	16	10	3.33

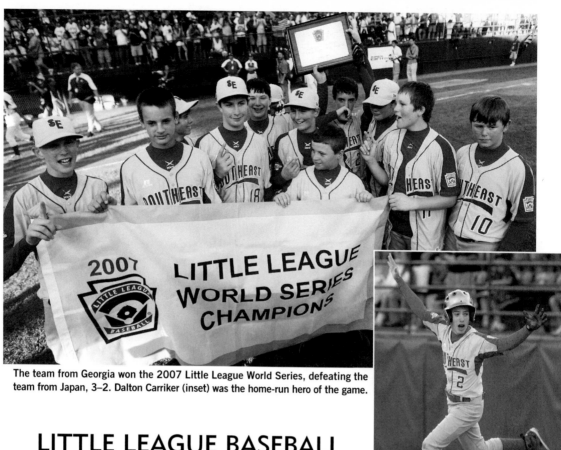

The team from Georgia won the 2007 Little League World Series, defeating the team from Japan, 3–2. Dalton Carriker (inset) was the home-run hero of the game.

LITTLE LEAGUE BASEBALL

Few plays in baseball are as dramatic as a "walk-off" home run—the four-bagger that ends a game with a victory. It's even more dramatic when a homer wins a championship in extra innings. On August 26, 2007, shortstop Dalton Carriker from Warner Robins, Georgia, lifted his team to the Little League World Series title, cracking a solo homer in the bottom of the eighth inning of the final game. (Little League contests are normally six innings long). The Georgia youngsters, the U.S. champions, defeated a Japanese team, Tokyo Kitasuna, the International champions, by the score of 3–2.

Japan had captured an early 2–0 lead, but the United States tied the score in the bottom of the second inning. Kendall Scott entered the game as a relief pitcher for the United States; he struck out 10 batters while permitting only one hit over the next 5⅓ innings. Leading off for the United States in the eighth, Dalton Carriker launched his winning blast—his fourth homer of the tournament—over the right-field wall off Japanese pitcher Junsho Kiuchi.

Georgia's Little League World Series title was the second in a row for a team from the Peach State, and the third straight for a U.S. squad. The 2006 champs represented Columbus, Georgia; and the 2005 winners were from Ewa Beach, Hawaii.

Each August, 16 teams travel to Williamsport, Pennsylvania, to compete in the Little League World Series. Eight teams are from the United States, and eight are International. The U.S. teams battle one another for the chance to play the final game against the winner of the International bracket of the tournament.

Besides Japan, the International teams were from Willemstad, Curaçao; White Rock, British Columbia, Canada; Dhahran, Saudi Arabia; Mexicali, Mexico; Taichung, Chinese Taipei (Taiwan); Maracaibo, Venezuela; and Apeldoorn, the Netherlands.

The other U.S. teams were from Walpole, Massachusetts; Lake Oswego, Oregon; Hamilton, Ohio; Salisbury, Maryland; Chandler, Arizona; Lubbock, Texas; and Coon Rapids, Minnesota.

Led by guard Tony Parker (#9), the San Antonio Spurs beat the Cleveland Cavaliers to notch their fourth NBA championship. Parker was named MVP of the finals.

BASKETBALL

For the third time in five seasons and the fourth in nine years, the San Antonio Spurs captured the National Basketball Association (NBA) championship in 2007. In the playoff finals, the Spurs swept the Cleveland Cavaliers in four straight games. The Spurs have now joined the list of great teams in NBA history. Only the Boston Celtics, the Los Angeles (formerly Minneapolis) Lakers, and the Chicago Bulls have won as many crowns.

San Antonio coach Gregg Popovich balanced his squad around a talented trio: center-forward Tim Duncan, a 10-year pro who averaged 20.0 points and 10.6 rebounds per game during the regular season; 25-year-old guard Tony Parker, who averaged 18.6 points and 5.5 assists per game; and guard Manu Ginobili, who contributed 16.5 points and 3.5 assists per game.

In the 2006–07 NBA regular season, the Spurs finished second in the Southwest Division, behind the Dallas Mavericks. The other playoff qualifiers from the Western Conference were the Houston Rockets; the Utah Jazz, who led the Northwest Division; the Denver Nuggets; the Phoenix Suns, who

Dallas Maverick forward Dirk Nowitzki won the MVP award for the NBA's regular season. A German, he was the first European-born player to win that award.

2007 NBA FINAL STANDINGS

EASTERN CONFERENCE
Atlantic Division

	W	L	Pct.
Toronto	47	35	.573
New Jersey	41	41	.500
Philadelphia	35	47	.427
New York	33	49	.402
Boston	24	58	.293

Central Division

	W	L	Pct.
Detroit	53	29	.646
Cleveland	50	32	.610
Chicago	49	33	.598
Indiana	33	47	.427
Milwaukee	28	54	.341

Southeast Division

	W	L	Pct.
Miami	44	38	.537
Washington	41	41	.500
Orlando	40	42	.488
Charlotte	33	49	.402
Atlanta	30	52	.366

WESTERN CONFERENCE
Northwest Division

	W	L	Pct.
Utah	51	31	.622
Denver	45	37	.549
Portland	32	50	.390
Minnesota	32	50	.390
Seattle	31	51	.378

Pacific Division

	W	L	Pct.
Phoenix	61	21	.744
L.A. Lakers	42	40	.512
Golden State	42	40	.512
L.A. Clippers	40	42	.488
Sacramento	33	49	.402

Southwest Division

	W	L	Pct.
Dallas	67	15	.817
San Antonio	58	24	.707
Houston	52	30	.634
New Orleans	39	43	.476
Memphis	22	60	.268

NBA Championship: San Antonio Spurs

COLLEGE BASKETBALL

Conference	Winner
Atlantic Coast	North Carolina and Virginia (tied, regular season) North Carolina (tournament)
Atlantic 10	Massachusetts and Xavier (tied, regular season) George Washington (tournament)
Big East	Georgetown (regular season and tournament)
Big Ten	Ohio State (regular season and tournament)
Big 12	Kansas (regular season and tournament)
Big West	Long Beach State (regular season and tournament)
Ivy League	Pennsylvania
Missouri Valley	Southern Illinois (regular season) Creighton (tournament)
Pacific-10	UCLA (regular season) Oregon (tournament)
Southeastern	Eastern: Florida Western: Mississippi State (regular season) Florida (tournament)
Southwestern Athletic	Mississippi Valley State (regular season) Jackson State (tournament)
Western Athletic	Nevada (regular season) New Mexico State (tournament)

NCAA, men: Florida
   women: Tennessee

NIT: West Virginia

Cleveland, coached by Mike Brown, featured a superstar: forward LeBron James. The 22-year-old averaged 27.3 points, 6.7 rebounds, and 6.0 assists in the regular season. The "Cavs" were runners-up to the Detroit Pistons in the Central Division. The other Eastern Conference teams in postseason competition were the Chicago Bulls; the Toronto Raptors, first in the Atlantic Division; the New Jersey Nets; the Southeast Division-leading Miami Heat, the defending NBA champs; the Washington Wizards; and the Orlando Magic.

In round one of the playoffs, Cleveland swept Washington in four games. The Cavaliers felled the Nets in six games in round two.

topped the Pacific Division; the Los Angeles Lakers; and the Golden State Warriors.

The Spurs buried the Nuggets, four games to one, in the first round of the playoffs, and then downed the Suns, four games to two, in round two. In the Western Conference finals, San Antonio ousted Utah in five games.

behind Parker's 17 points. Game 4 was closest of all, an 83–82 San Antonio triumph. Ginobili tallied 27 points, Parker had 24, and Duncan snared 15 rebounds. The Spurs were champs, just as in 1999, 2003, and 2005. Parker was named Most Valuable Player (MVP) of the finals.

Dallas forward Dirk Nowitzki became the first European to be named MVP of the NBA regular season. The 7-footer averaged 24.6 points and 8.9 rebounds per game.

Laker Kobe Bryant was the league's top scorer—31.6 points per game—for the second straight year. Portland Trail Blazer guard Brandon Roy won rookie-of-the-year honors; and Toronto's Sam Mitchell was coach of the year.

WNBA. The Phoenix Mercury won their first-ever championship of the Women's National Basketball Association in September, defeating the Detroit Shock, three games to two, in the playoff finals. Phoenix guard Cappie Pondexter scored 26 points in Game 5 and was named MVP of the finals. The MVP of the WNBA regular season was Lauren Jackson, a forward for the Seattle Storm.

College Play. The University of Florida repeated as men's champs of the National Collegiate Athletic Association (NCAA). Coach Billy Donovan's Gators defeated Ohio State, 84–75, in the NCAA tournament final, on April 2. Corey Brewer was named the Final Four's Most Outstanding Player (MOP).

The Lady Vols of Tennessee were the women's champs, besting Rutgers, 59–46, in the NCAA final on April 3. Tennessee's Candace Parker was named the Final Four's MOP. It was the seventh NCAA title for Hall-of-Fame coach Pat Summitt.

In the Eastern Conference finals, Cleveland dropped the first two games to Detroit but then powered back to take the next four. The Cavs were on their way to their first NBA finals.

The finals began in San Antonio on June 7. In Game 1, Parker poured in 27 points, and Duncan added 24. LeBron James managed only 14, and the Spurs won, 85–76. Game 2, also in San Antonio, ended at 103–92, Spurs. Parker notched 30 points, and Ginobili 25.

Home in Cleveland for Game 3, the Cavs came closer, but San Antonio won, 75–72,

Green Bay Packer quarterback Brett Favre broke Dan Marino's records for most passing yards and career touchdown passes as he led the Packers to a division title and the 2007–08 playoffs.

FOOTBALL

The Indianapolis Colts stood atop the National Football League (NFL) in 2007, defeating the Chicago Bears in the Super Bowl in February. In the Canadian Football League (CFL), the Saskatchewan Roughriders claimed the Grey Cup in November. And in U.S. college football, Ohio State and Louisiana State were to vie for the national championship.

THE NFL PLAYOFFS AND SUPER BOWL XLI

Coach Tony Dungy guided the Colts to an American Conference (AFC) division championship in the 2006–07 season. The other AFC division champs were the New England Patriots, the Baltimore Ravens, and the San Diego Chargers; wild-card playoff berths went to the New York Jets and the Kansas City Chiefs.

In the first round of the playoffs in January 2007, the Colts clipped the Chiefs, 23–8, and the Patriots took down the Jets, 37–16. The following week, Indianapolis bested Baltimore,

15–6, and New England edged San Diego, 24–21. The Patriots mounted a late rally for the victory.

The AFC title game matched Indianapolis and New England. Down 21–3, the Colts fought back to win, 38–34. Indianapolis quarterback Peyton Manning completed 27 passes for 349 yards. The Colts were headed to their first Super Bowl since Super Bowl V in 1971, when they played in Baltimore, Maryland.

In the National Conference (NFC), the division titlists were the Chicago Bears, the Philadelphia Eagles, the New Orleans Saints, and the Seattle Seahawks. Qualifying for the postseason as wild cards were the Dallas Cowboys and the New York Giants.

Chicago drew a "bye" in the first week of the NFC playoffs; Seattle stopped Dallas, 21–20, while Philadelphia foiled New York, 23–20. In week two, the Bears ousted the Seahawks in overtime, 27–24, and the Saints eliminated the Eagles, also by 27–24.

In the NFC title game, Chicago clobbered New Orleans, 39–14. The Bears, coached by Lovie Smith, returned to the Super Bowl for the first time since Super Bowl XX in 1986.

Miami, Florida, Sunday, February 4, 2007: For the first time in the game's four-decade history, rain fell on the Super Bowl. Also for the first time in Super Bowl history, the opening kickoff was returned for a touchdown—Chicago's Devin Hester hastened 92 yards for the score. The Colts countered some 8 minutes later on a 53-yard touchdown pass from Manning to Reggie Wayne; the extra point attempt failed. At the end of the first quarter, the Bears led, 14–6.

But after that, Indianapolis dominated. The Colts collected 10 unanswered points in the second period, on a field goal by Adam Vinatieri, a 1-yard touchdown run by Dominic Rhodes, and a Vinatieri extra point. Vinatieri added two more 3-pointers in the third quarter; entering the final period, Indianapolis led, 22–17. Early in the fourth quarter, Colt defensive back

Kelvin Hayden intercepted a Chicago pass and returned it 56 yards for the game's last touchdown. The Colts had won their first Super Bowl in 36 years—and their first for Indianapolis. The final score was 29–17.

Manning was named the game's most valuable player (MVP). He completed 25 passes, including the one touchdown toss, for 247 yards. Coach Dungy exulted—it was his first Super Bowl title as a coach; he was a player in the Pittsburgh Steelers' win in Super Bowl XIII in 1979.

THE 2007–08 REGULAR SEASON

Indianapolis continued its success, taking the title of its division in 2007–08. The other AFC playoff teams were division champions New England, Pittsburgh, and San Diego; and the wild cards, the Jacksonville Jaguars and the Tennessee Titans. The NFC qualifiers were division winners Dallas, Seattle, the Green Bay Packers, and the Tampa Bay Buccaneers; and the wild cards, the New York Giants and the Washington Redskins.

THE CANADIAN FOOTBALL LEAGUE (CFL)

Prior to 2007, Saskatchewan had won only two Grey Cups. But in Toronto on November 25, in the 95th Grey Cup game, the Roughriders captured the CFL title by downing the Winnipeg Blue Bombers, 23–19. Saskatchewan cornerback James Johnson intercepted three passes, a Grey Cup record, returning one for a touchdown; he was named the game's outstanding player. Saskatchewan was piloted by rookie coach Kent Austin, who had quarterbacked the Roughriders to their last Grey Cup victory in 1989.

COLLEGE PLAY

Ranked numbers one and two at the end of the regular season, Ohio State and Louisiana State University were set to meet in the national championship game in January 2008. Kansas defeated Virginia Tech in the Orange Bowl; USC overwhelmed Illinois in the Rose Bowl; Missouri crushed Arkansas in the Cotton Bowl; Georgia routed Hawaii in the Sugar Bowl; and West Virginia outscored Oklahoma in the Fiesta Bowl.

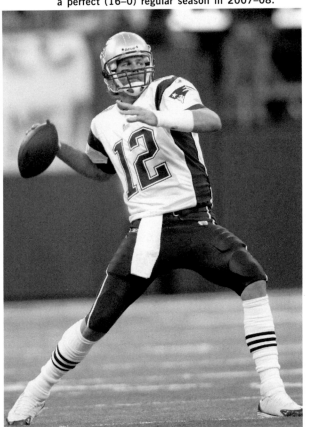

With quarterback Tom Brady calling the offensive signals, the New England Patriots fashioned a perfect (16–0) regular season in 2007–08.

Florida quarterback Tim Tebow won the 2007
Heisman Trophy as the best college player.

The Heisman Trophy went to Florida quarterback Tim Tebow, the first sophomore ever to win the coveted award. He was also the first player in the history of the National Collegiate Athletic Association to exceed 20 touchdowns passing and 20 touchdowns rushing in the same season.

COLLEGE FOOTBALL

Conference	Winner
Atlantic Coast	Virginia Tech
Big Ten	Ohio State
Big 12	Oklahoma
Pacific-10	USC
Southeastern	LSU
Western Athletic	Hawaii

Cotton Bowl: Missouri 38, Arkansas 7
Fiesta Bowl: West Virginia 48, Oklahoma 28
Gator Bowl: Texas Tech 31, Virginia 28
Orange Bowl: Kansas 24, Virginia Tech 21
Rose Bowl: USC 49, Illinois 17
Sugar Bowl: Georgia 41, Hawaii 10

Heisman Trophy: Tim Tebow, Florida

2007–08 NFL FINAL STANDINGS

AMERICAN CONFERENCE

East

	W	L	T	Pct.	PF	PA
New England	16	0	0	1.000	589	274
Buffalo	7	9	0	.438	252	354
N.Y. Jets	4	12	0	.250	268	355
Miami	1	15	0	.063	267	437

North

	W	L	T	Pct.	PF	PA
Pittsburgh	10	6	0	.625	393	269
Cleveland	10	6	0	.625	402	382
Cincinnati	7	9	0	.438	380	385
Baltimore	5	11	0	.313	275	384

South

	W	L	T	Pct.	PF	PA
Indianapolis	13	3	0	.813	450	262
Jacksonville	11	5	0	.688	411	304
Tennessee	10	6	0	.625	301	297
Houston	8	8	0	.500	379	384

West

	W	L	T	Pct.	PF	PA
San Diego	11	5	0	.688	412	284
Denver	7	9	0	.438	320	409
Kansas City	4	12	0	.250	226	335
Oakland	4	12	0	.250	283	398

NATIONAL CONFERENCE

East

	W	L	T	Pct.	PF	PA
Dallas	13	3	0	.813	455	325
N.Y. Giants	10	6	0	.625	373	351
Washington	9	7	0	.563	334	310
Philadelphia	8	8	0	.500	336	300

North

	W	L	T	Pct.	PF	PA
Green Bay	13	3	0	.813	435	291
Minnesota	8	8	0	.500	365	311
Detroit	7	9	0	.438	346	444
Chicago	7	9	0	.438	334	348

South

	W	L	T	Pct.	PF	PA
Tampa Bay	9	7	0	.563	334	270
Carolina	7	9	0	.438	267	347
New Orleans	7	9	0	.438	379	388
Atlanta	4	12	0	.250	259	414

West

	W	L	T	Pct.	PF	PA
Seattle	10	6	0	.625	393	291
Arizona	8	8	0	.500	404	399
San Francisco	5	11	0	.313	219	364
St. Louis	3	13	0	.188	263	438

Morgan Pressel: Teen Golf Star

Morgan Pressel became the youngest golfer ever to win a Ladies Professional Golf Association (LPGA) major tournament. She was 18 years, 313 days old when she won the LPGA Kraft Nabisco Championship on April 1, 2007. (It certainly wasn't an April Fools' Day for her!)

Pressel was born in Tampa, Florida, and began playing golf when she was 8 years old. As an amateur, she won 11 American Junior Golf Association (AJGA) titles. In 2001, when she was 12, she became the youngest golfer ever to qualify for the U.S. Women's Open Championship.

The young golfer had a remarkable year in 2005. She won the U.S. Women's Amateur Golf Championship, and she was named AJGA Player of the Year. And after again qualifying for the U.S. Women's Open, she tied for second place.

Pressel became a pro in November 2005, turning down a college golf scholarship at Tufts University. She graduated from high school in May 2006. After her 2007 record-setting performance, she moved into the top five in world rankings.

Has stardom changed Morgan Pressel? "With all her success, she hasn't changed a bit," said her best friend. "Honestly, that's what I admire the most about her."

GOLF

PROFESSIONAL		AMATEUR	
	Individual		**Individual**
Masters	Zach Johnson	**U.S. Amateur**	Colt Knost
U.S. Open	Angel Cabrera	**U.S. Women's Amateur**	Maria Jose Uribe
Canadian Open	Jim Furyk	**British Amateur**	Drew Weaver
British Open	Padraig Harrington	**British Ladies Amateur**	Carlota Ciganda
PGA	Tiger Woods	**Canadian Amateur**	Nick Taylor
U.S. Women's Open	Cristie Kerr	**Canadian Ladies Amateur**	Stephanie Sherlock
Ladies PGA	Suzann Pettersen		
			Team
		Walker Cup	United States

The Anaheim Ducks defeated the Ottawa Senators, four games to one, for their first Stanley Cup. Anaheim defenseman Scott Niedermayer (left) was named Most Valuable Player of the playoffs.

HOCKEY

The Anaheim Mighty Ducks joined the National Hockey League (NHL) in 1993. They dropped the "Mighty" from their name in 2006, and in 2007 they won their first league title. In the Stanley Cup finals, Anaheim outmatched the Ottawa Senators by four games to one.

Anaheim's leading scorer during the regular season was right-wing Teemu Selanne. The 36-year-old native of Finland tallied 94 points (48 goals, 46 assists). His teammates included goalie Jean-Sebastien Giguere; captain Scott Niedermayer, a defenseman; and his brother Rob, a center. Others on the roster were defensemen Chris Pronger, François Beauchemin, and Sean O'Donnell; wings Travis Moen, Dustin Penner, and Corey Perry; and centers Andy McDonald, Samuel Pahlsson, Ryan Getzlaf, and Todd Marchant. Randy Carlyle was the Ducks' coach.

Anaheim led the Pacific Division during the regular season, finishing with 48 victories, 20 losses, and 14 overtime losses for 110 points. Also making the playoffs from the NHL's Western Conference were the Detroit Red Wings, champs of the Central Division, whose 113 points topped the Conference; the Vancouver Canucks, leaders of the Northwest Division; the San Jose Sharks; the Dallas Stars; the Nashville Predators; the Minnesota Wild; and the Calgary Flames.

In the first round of postseason play, the Ducks tamed the Wild, four games to one. Anaheim next vanquished Vancouver, also in five games, in round two. Then, facing the Red Wings in the Western Conference finals, the Ducks emerged victorious in six games.

In the Eastern Conference regular season, Ottawa finished second in the Northeast Division. The Buffalo Sabres, who compiled a conference-leading 113 points, were first. The Eastern Conference's other playoff qualifiers were the New Jersey Devils, the titlists of the Atlantic Division; the Pittsburgh Penguins; the New York Rangers; the New York Islanders; the Atlanta Thrashers, who snared the Southeast Division crown; and the Tampa Bay Lightning.

Ottawa outplayed Pittsburgh, four games to one, in the first round of the playoffs. They dropped the Devils, four games to one, in round two. In the Eastern Conference finals, again needing only five games, the Senators stopped the Sabres.

The Stanley Cup finals began in Anaheim, California, on May 28. The Ducks took Game 1 by the score of 3–2, on goals by McDonald, Getzlaf, and Moen.

Game 2, also at Anaheim, was scoreless for more than 45 minutes. Finally, Duck center Pahlsson popped the puck into the Ottawa net. The final score was 1–0; goalie Giguere turned away 16 Senator shots. Anaheim was up, two games to none.

Ottawa won its only contest of the finals, Game 3, at home, by the score of 5–3. Game 4, also at Ottawa, went to the Ducks, 3–2. Anaheim's McDonald notched two goals, 60 seconds apart, in the second period. Penner collected the winning tally in the third period.

Back home for Game 5, Anaheim exploded for two goals in each period. The scores were provided by McDonald, Rob Niedermayer, Moen, Beauchemin, Moen again, and Perry. The final score was 6–2, and the Anaheim

In only his second year as a pro, 19-year-old Pittsburgh center Sidney Crosby (left) won the Hart Trophy (MVP, regular season), the Ross Trophy (top scorer), and the Lester B. Pearson Award (outstanding player, regular season). Detroit defenseman Nicklas Lidstrom (below) won his fifth Norris Trophy (outstanding defenseman).

2007 NHL FINAL STANDINGS

EASTERN CONFERENCE

Atlantic Division

	W	L	OL	Pts.
New Jersey	49	24	9	107
Pittsburgh	47	24	11	105
N.Y. Rangers	42	30	10	94
N.Y. Islanders	40	30	12	92
Philadelphia	22	48	12	56

Northeast Division

	W	L	OL	Pts.
Buffalo	53	22	7	113
Ottawa	48	25	9	105
Toronto	40	31	11	91
Montreal	42	34	6	90
Boston	35	41	6	76

Southeast Division

	W	L	OL	Pts.
Atlanta	43	28	11	97
Tampa Bay	44	33	5	93
Carolina	40	34	8	88
Florida	35	31	16	86
Washington	28	40	14	70

WESTERN CONFERENCE

Central Division

	W	L	OL	Pts.
Detroit	50	19	13	113
Nashville	51	23	8	110
St. Louis	34	35	13	81
Columbus	33	42	7	73
Chicago	31	42	9	71

Northwest Division

	W	L	OL	Pts.
Vancouver	49	26	7	105
Minnesota	48	26	8	104
Calgary	43	29	10	96
Colorado	44	31	7	95
Edmonton	32	43	7	71

Pacific Division

	W	L	OL	Pts.
Anaheim	48	20	14	110
San Jose	51	26	5	107
Dallas	50	25	7	107
Los Angeles	27	41	14	68
Phoenix	31	46	5	67

Stanley Cup: Anaheim Ducks

OUTSTANDING PLAYERS

Hart Trophy (most valuable player)	Sidney Crosby, Pittsburgh
Ross Trophy (scorer)	Sidney Crosby, Pittsburgh
Vezina Trophy (goalie)	Martin Brodeur, New Jersey
Norris Trophy (defenseman)	Nicklas Lidstrom, Detroit
Selke Trophy (defensive forward)	Rod Brind'Amour, Carolina
Calder Trophy (rookie)	Evgeni Malkin, Pittsburgh
Lady Byng Trophy (sportsmanship)	Pavel Datsyuk, Detroit
Conn Smythe Trophy (Stanley Cup play)	Scott Niedermayer, Anaheim

For the regular season, 19-year-old Sidney Crosby of Pittsburgh captured the Hart Trophy as MVP. He was the second youngest (after Wayne Gretzky) to be so honored. Crosby also took the Art Ross Trophy as the NHL's leading scorer (120 points on 36 goals and 84 assists). He was also the youngest team captain in league history.

Nicklas Lidstrom of Detroit collected the fifth Norris Trophy (best defenseman) of his career. Named top goalie (Vezina Trophy) was New Jersey's Martin Brodeur. And Crosby's Pittsburgh teammate Evgeni Malkin, a 20-year-old left wing, won the Calder Trophy as the NHL's best rookie. Vancouver's Alain Vigneault took the Adams Award as top coach.

College Play. On March 18, the University of Wisconsin captured the women's hockey championship of the National Collegiate Athletic Association (NCAA). They had also won in 2006. In the final game of the "Frozen Four," the Badgers defeated Minnesota-Duluth, 4–1. Senior Sara Bauer was named the tournament's Most Outstanding Player.

Michigan State was the men's NCAA champ, topping Boston College in the April 7 final by the score of 3–1. Spartan sophomore Justin Abdelkader took Most Outstanding Player honors.

Ryan Duncan, a sophomore forward at the University of North Dakota, was honored with the Hobey Baker Award as the top men's player in NCAA Division I.

Ducks became the first California team ever to win the Stanley Cup. Captain Scott Niedermayer was awarded the Conn Smythe Trophy as the playoffs' Most Valuable Player (MVP).

Kimmie Meissner. American figure-skater Kimmie Meissner, 17, won the gold medal at the 2007 U.S. Figure Skating Championships. It was her first victory in this event. She also won the prestigious Four Continents Championships in 2007, and was the gold medalist at the 2006 World Figure Skating Championships.

Brian Joubert. Brian Joubert of France won the 2007 World Figure Skating Championships. With his strong jumping skills, he has been a consistent winner at major figure-skating events. Joubert, 22, has won the French Championships five years in a row, including in 2007.

ICE SKATING

FIGURE SKATING

World Championships

Men	Brian Joubert, France
Women	Miki Ando, Japan
Pairs	Xue Shen/Hongbo Zhao, China
Dance	Albena Denkova/Maxim Staviski, Bulgaria

United States Championships

Men	Evan Lysacek
Women	Kimmie Meissner
Pairs	Brooke Castile/Benjamin Okolski
Dance	Tanith Belbin/Benjamin Agosto

SPEED SKATING

World Championships

Men	Sven Kramer, Netherlands
Women	Ireen Wüst, Netherlands

SKIING

WORLD CUP CHAMPIONSHIPS

Men	Aksel Lund Svindal, Norway
Women	Nicole Hosp, Austria

WORLD ALPINE CHAMPIONSHIPS

Men

Downhill	Aksel Lund Svindal, Norway
Slalom	Mario Matt, Austria
Giant Slalom	Aksel Lund Svindal, Norway
Super Giant Slalom	Patrick Staudacher, Italy
Combined	Daniel Albrecht, Switzerland

Women

Downhill	Anja Pärson, Sweden
Slalom	Sarka Zahrobska, Czech Republic
Giant Slalom	Nicole Hosp, Austria
Super Giant Slalom	Anja Pärson, Sweden
Combined	Anja Pärson, Sweden

SWIMMING

Michael Phelps: Swimming Sensation

At the 2007 World Swimming Championships in Melbourne, Australia, Michael Phelps won seven events, shattering world records in five. His seven gold medals tied the record seven golds won by legendary swimmer Mark Spitz at the 1972 Summer Olympics.

Phelps, 21, won individual golds in the 100- and 200-meter butterfly, the 200-meter freestyle, and the 200- and 400-meter individual medley. His team golds were for the 400- and 800-meter freestyle relays.

Born in Baltimore, Maryland, Phelps began swimming competitively when he was 7. He was just 15 when he qualified for the 2000 U.S. Olympic team that went to the Summer Olympics in Australia—the youngest member of a U.S. Olympic team since 1932. Phelps finished fifth in the 200-meter butterfly at that Olympics. But the following year he set a new world record in the event at the World Championships in Japan, becoming the youngest world-record-holder in history.

At the 2003 World Championships in Spain, Phelps won six medals, including four golds, and broke three world records. The following year, at the Summer Olympics in Greece, he won six gold medals. And at the 2005 World Championships in Canada, he won five more.

Michael Phelps is considered one of the world's greatest athletes. What's next for him? The 2008 Summer Olympics in China!

TENNIS

In 2007, for the second straight year, Roger Federer of Switzerland won three of tennis's four Grand Slam titles. Justine Henin of Belgium took a pair on the women's side, while sisters Serena and Venus Williams of the United States split the other two.

Federer, 26, captured the **Australian Open** in January with a victory in the final over Fernando Gonzalez of Chile: 7–6 (2), 6–4, 6–4. The champion won all seven of his matches at Melbourne in straight sets. The last man to win the Australian Open without losing a set was Tennis Hall-of-Famer Ken Rosewall, in 1971. And not since all-time-great Bjorn Borg of Sweden, in the 1980 French Open, had any man taken a Grand Slam event without dropping a single set.

Serena Williams, 25, overpowered 19-year-old Maria Sharapova in the 2007 Australian women's final, winning 6–1, 6–2. The triumph was Williams's first "major" since the 2005 Australian, but the eighth of her career. Bedeviled by injuries, she had played little in 2006 and entered 2007 ranked 81st in the world. Williams jumped to 14th after this victory.

In June, Justine Henin collected her fourth **French Open** title, and her third in a row. She defeated the 19-year-old Serbian Ana Ivanovic in the final by 6–1, 6–2. The 25-year-old Henin had first won in Paris in 2003.

Roger Federer collected three Grand Slam titles in 2007: the Australian Open, Wimbledon, and the U.S. Open.

TOURNAMENT TENNIS

	Australian Open	French Open	Wimbledon	U.S. Open
Men's Singles	Roger Federer, Switzerland	Rafael Nadal, Spain	Roger Federer, Switzerland	Roger Federer, Switzerland
Women's Singles	Serena Williams, United States	Justine Henin, Belgium	Venus Williams, United States	Justine Henin, Belgium
Men's Doubles	Bob Bryan, United States/ Mike Bryan, United States	Mark Knowles, Bahamas/ Daniel Nestor, Canada	Arnaud Clement, France/ Michael Llodra, France	Simon Aspelin, Sweden/ Julian Knowle, Austria
Women's Doubles	Cara Black, Zimbabwe/ Liezel Huber, South Africa	Alicia Molik, Australia/ Mara Santangelo, Italy	Cara Black, Zimbabwe/ Liezel Huber, South Africa	Nathalie Dechy, France/ Dinara Safina, Russia

Davis Cup Winner: United States

The men's French champ was Spain's Rafael Nadal, 21. In a repeat of 2006, he gave Federer his only Grand Slam loss of the year. The score of the final was 6–3, 4–6, 6–3, 6–4. A left-hander, Nadal became the first man since Borg—who won four straight from 1978 to 1981—to win at least three consecutive French titles.

Federer rebounded at **Wimbledon,** contested in London in June-July. He fought off Nadal in the five-set final, 7–6 (7), 4–6, 7–6 (3), 2–6, 6–2. The Swiss star thus won his fifth Wimbledon in a row, tying Borg's record (1976–80) for consecutive All-England championships.

The last time 27-year-old Venus Williams won a major was at Wimbledon in 2005. In 2007, she topped Marion Bartoli of France in the final, 6–4, 6–1. She thus collected her fourth Wimbledon crown, and the sixth Grand Slam singles title of her career. Listed only 31st in the world tennis rankings when the tournament began, Williams became the lowest-ranked woman ever to win at Wimbledon. The victory improved her standing to 17th.

At the **U.S. Open** in New York City in September, Henin secured the seventh major singles title of her career. And she put a lock on her number-one rank in the women's tennis world. In the final, she overmatched Svetlana Kuznetsova, a 22-year-old Russian, by 6–1, 6–3. Henin won every set she played in the tournament; she defeated both Williams sisters on her way to her second U.S. crown. (Her first was in 2003.)

Federer set a record in New York by appearing in his tenth consecutive Grand Slam final. He downed talented Novak Djokovic, a 20-year-old Serbian, in straight sets: 7–6 (4), 7–6 (2), 6–4. It was Federer's fourth straight U.S. singles title, and the 12th major of his career. This tied him with Roy Emerson for second place behind American Pete Sampras, who holds the all-time men's record of 14.

As of September 2007, Federer, Nadal, and Djokovic stood atop the men's rankings. Henin, Kuznetsova, and Jelena Jankovic of Serbia led the women.

Justine Henin: Tennis's Number-One Woman

At the end of 2007, Justine Henin was ranked as the world's number-one women's tennis player. During the year, the 25-year-old Belgian had won the French and U.S. Opens, two of tennis's four Grand Slam events.

Henin has now won seven Grand Slam events—four French Opens, two U.S Opens, and one Australian Open. Overall, she has won 36 singles titles and two doubles titles, as well as the 2004 Olympic singles gold medal.

Her mental toughness on the court—as well as her power and great footwork—have made her a formidable player. While she is relatively small by the standards of women's tennis, her strong and accurate single-handed backhand (most players use two hands) has left opponents standing in their tracks. And her serve has reached 124 miles (200 kilometers) an hour!

Off the court, Henin funds Justine's Winners' Circle, which helps children with cancer. "If I can let them forget a little bit of their problems," she says, "that's wonderful. That's probably my finest victory."

U.S. gymnast Shawn Johnson, 15, won the all-around title at the Pan American Games in July.

SPORTS BRIEFS

A number of sports stories received special attention during 2007. The 15th Pan American Games were held in Brazil. The women's World Cup soccer tournament was held in China. English soccer superstar David Beckham moved to the United States, joining the Los Angeles Galaxy of Major League Soccer. A record was set by a veteran runner in the marathon, and two teenagers set records in sailing and mountain climbing. Cheerleading was also in the news after a report detailed how dangerous that sport was becoming.

THE PAN AMERICAN GAMES

The 15th Pan American Games were held in Brazil from July 13 to July 29. About 5,500 athletes from 42 countries in the Americas competed in 41 sports. Most of the sports were the same as Olympic sports, but some were not: badminton, bowling, squash, water skiing, and futsal (indoor soccer). The competitions were held in and around Rio de Janeiro. The opening and closing ceremonies and many events were held in Maracanã Stadium, one of the largest soccer stadiums in the world.

The Pan American Games have been held every four years since 1951. The United States has dominated in most of the Games, and U.S. teams were the big winners in 2007. They won 237 medals, 97 of them gold. They did especially well in swimming (18 golds) and wrestling (6 golds).

The other big winners at the Pan Am Games were Cuba (135 medals/59 gold), Brazil (161/54), and Canada (137/39).

SOCCER: THE MAIN EVENTS

Two important soccer events made headlines in 2007.

▪ Soccer star **David Beckham** moved from England across the Atlantic to the United States to play for the Los Angeles Galaxy. The Galaxy is one of the 13 teams in Major League Soccer, the U.S.–Canadian professional soccer league.

"I'm coming [to Los Angeles] not to be a superstar," Beckham, 31, said. "I'm coming there to be part of the team, to work hard and to hopefully win things."

But Beckham *is* a superstar—he's the world's most famous soccer player. He played for Real Madrid, Europe's most glamorous team; and for Manchester United of England's Premier League, winning six league titles. Adding to his celebrity status is his wife Victoria, the former Posh Spice of the pop-music group the Spice Girls.

Beckham joined the Galaxy in July 2007 and made his league debut in August. However, he injured his knee late in the month and played in just one more game at the end of the season. Beckham said he was hoping to raise the profile of soccer in the United States and to inspire more kids to take up the sport.

▪ The **women's World Cup soccer** championship, like the men's World Cup, is held every four years, but not during the same year. First played in 1991, it's the most important women's soccer tournament. In 2007, the tournament was held in China, from September 10 to September 30.

Germany defeated Brazil 2–0 in the final game. The two scores were made by Birgit Prinz and Simone Laudehr, whose stunning header came in the 86th minute of play. Germany's defense was also superb. In six games, it didn't yield a single goal, enabling the team to outscore the opposition 21–0. This was Germany's second women's World Cup championship. Its first win was in 2003.

The U.S. women's team was defeated by Brazil in the semifinals, but it outplayed Norway to capture third place in the tournament. The United States is the only other country to have won two women's World Cups, in 1991 and 1999.

Soccer star David Beckham, shown here playing for Real Madrid of Spain, joined the Los Angeles Galaxy in 2007.

Germany's Birgit Prinz (left), in the final game of the women's World Cup soccer championship in September.

Jackie Robinson, in 1947, with his Brooklyn Dodgers teammates Spider Jorgensen, Pee Wee Reese, and Ed Stanky.

Honoring Jackie Robinson

When Jackie Robinson stepped onto the Brooklyn Dodgers' Ebbets Field in Brooklyn, New York, on April 15, 1947, he made history. Robinson was the first African American to play in modern Major League Baseball, thus ending the color barrier in America's national sport. The 60th anniversary of that event was celebrated on April 15, 2007.

Robinson's courage made him an American hero. At first, he endured taunting, boycotts, beanballs, and even death threats. It would have been easy for him to give up, but he persevered. During his 10-year career, he helped lead the Dodgers to six National League pennants and the 1955 World Series. In 1962 he became the first African American to be elected to the Baseball Hall of Fame. Robinson died in 1972.

To honor Robinson, his number—42—was officially retired in 1997; no other Major League Baseball player will ever be given that number again. But on April 15, 2007, also to honor this great athlete, more than 200 players wore Robinson's number 42 just for that special day.

RECORD-BUSTERS

Three people set records in 2007: high in the mountains, at sea, and on land.

■ Mountain climber **Samantha Larson** reached new heights in 2007. The 18-year-old from Long Beach, California, became the youngest American woman to reach the top of Mount Everest, the world's tallest mountain. With that success, she also became the world's youngest person—male or female—to climb the Seven Summits, the highest mountains on all seven continents!

Samantha's first big climb was Mount Kilimanjaro in Africa. She scaled its peak in 2001, when she was just 12 years old. She then set her sights on the other six summits: Denali, Elbrus, Aconcagua, Kosciusko, Vinson Massif, and Everest. In 2002, Samantha and her father climbed Mount Aconcagua in South America. Next, the father-and-daughter team tackled Mount Elbrus in Europe; Denali in North America; Mount Kosciusko in Australia; and Vinson Massif in Antarctica. Finally, in May 2007, they reached Mount Everest in Asia, at 29,035 feet (8,850 meters) the world's hightest peak.

Samantha was exhilarated when she reached the top of that mountain in the breathtaking Himalyas. "I had a wild mix of emotions at the summit," she said. "I actually cried in a mix of exhaustion, taking in the beauty of my surroundings, and recognition that I had just achieved my goals of not only climbing Everest, but all of the Seven Summits."

■ Sailor **Michael Perham,** a 14-year-old from Hertfordshire, England, became the youngest person to sail solo across the Atlantic Ocean. Over a six-week period, from November 18, 2006, to January 3, 2007, he sailed from the southern coast of Spain to St. John's, Antigua, in the Caribbean Sea—a distance of 3,500 miles (5,630 kilometers). "It feels absolutely fantastic to be back on dry land," Michael said after docking at Antigua.

Michael didn't get any help crossing the ocean in the *Cheeky Monkey,* his 28-foot (8-meter) sailboat. But Michael's father was never far behind. Peter Perham followed Michael in his own sailboat and stayed in radio contact with him throughout the trip. They stopped briefly off the coast of Africa at the Canary Islands and at Cape Verde for repairs. Other than that, Michael was without direct human contact during his voyage.

To pass the time when he wasn't working on his boat, Michael studied, read books, and practiced playing the guitar. And, like most teens, he spent several hours on the phone; he had a satellite phone.

Michael broke the record of 15-year-old Britisher Sebastian Clover, who crossed the Atlantic by himself in 2003.

■ Marathoner **Haile Gebrselassie** proved once again that he is one of the greatest distance runners in history. In September, in Berlin, Germany, the 34-year-old Ethiopian broke the world record for the marathon. His time— 2 hours, 4 minutes, 26 seconds—was 29 seconds faster than the record set by Kenyan Paul Tergat on the same course in 2003.

Gebrselassie has set more than 20 running records— in everything from 2 miles to 20 kilometers. And he won gold medals in the 10,000 meters at both the 1996 Atlanta Summer Olympics and the 2000 Sydney Summer Olympics. But Gebrselassie considers his marathon victory to be the most satisfying because, he says, "it is the king of distance."

Watch for him in China, at the 2008 Summer Olympic Games!

Eighteen-year-old Samantha Larson became the youngest person to climb the Seven Summits.

Fourteen-year-old Michael Perham became the youngest person to sail alone across the Atlantic.

Haile Gebrselassie of Ethiopia broke the world record for the marathon.

CHEERLEADING: A DANGEROUS SPORT?

Many people would say that football is the most dangerous high-school sport. But another sport is climbing the high-risk list: cheerleading. A recent study showed that cheerleading injuries doubled between 1990 and 2002. And the report showed only injuries that sent cheerleaders to emergency rooms. Those treated in doctors' offices weren't included.

Why is cheerleading so risky? In the past, cheerleaders didn't do much more than jump and shake pom-poms. But cheerleading has changed. It's more athletic—and dangerous. Squads practice all year for cheerleading competitions, and some events are televised.

To win, squads have to perform daring routines. They form human pyramids and they do flips and tosses. In the basket toss, a very difficult stunt, a cheerleader is hurled some 20 feet (6 meters) into the air and then caught by teammates.

Cheerleading has become extreme tumbling. If the routines don't go exactly right, a cheerleader can be seriously hurt or even killed. But cheerleaders often don't get the same supervision as gymnasts and other athletes. That's because many states still don't recognize cheerleading as an official school sport, so there are no state safety standards. And many coaches aren't well trained. They let kids try routines that are too advanced.

In addition, many schools don't have the right equipment and practice spaces. Cheerleaders end up practicing in hallways and on hard surfaces, instead of on mats. That increases the chance that they'll be badly injured if they fall.

As cheerleading is soaring in popularity, more people are calling for higher safety standards.

Daredevil routines have made cheerleading a risky sport.

Sochi, a resort city in Russia, was selected to host the 2014 Winter Olympic Games.

WAGNER, PITTSBURG

ON TO THE OLYMPICS

On July 4, 2007, the International Olympic Committee selected the host city for the 2014 Winter Games—Sochi, Russia. This resort city is on the northwestern shore of the Black Sea. Sochi has a subtropical climate, so the luge, bobsled, skeleton, skiing, and snowboarding events will take place in nearby Krasnaya Polyana, a ski resort high in the Western Caucasus Mountains.

But you won't have to wait until 2014 to watch exciting Olympic competitions. The next Summer Olympics will be held in 2008 in Beijing, the capital of China, the world's most populous nation.

The 2010 Winter Games will be held in Vancouver, British Columbia, a city in southwestern Canada with majestic snow-covered mountains on its northern fringes.

The 2012 Summer Games will be staged in London, the capital of Great Britain.

The Mona Lisa of Baseball Cards

A 1909 Honus Wagner baseball card was sold twice in 2007—first for $2.35 million and then for $2.8 million. Both sales shattered all records for a baseball card. This highly collectible piece of baseball memorabilia was in near-mint condition and is often referred to as the Mona Lisa of baseball cards.

In the early 1900's, baseball cards were distributed in packs of cigarettes, not packs of bubble gum. It is said that Wagner, a nonsmoker, objected to his card being used in this way because he didn't want to encourage kids to smoke. As a result, his cards were withdrawn. Today, there are no more than 70 of them, and none in as good condition as the one sold in 2007.

Honus Wagner, nicknamed "the Flying Dutchman," played during the 1890's until the 1910's, mostly for the Pittsburgh Pirates. He is considered Major League Baseball's greatest shortstop ever. To some, he was the greatest all-around baseball player ever. He was one of the Baseball Hall of Fame's first five members.

English colonists step ashore in Virginia on May 14, 1607. The colony they founded, Jamestown, would become the first successful English settlement in North America. The year 2007 marked the 400th anniversary of Jamestown's founding, and the event was celebrated in many ways.

English settlers arrive at Jamestown, Virginia, in May 1607, and begin to cut trees to build a fort. The founding of the first successful English colony in the New World was commemorated in 2007.

THE 400TH ANNIVERSARY OF JAMESTOWN, AMERICA'S FIRST COLONY

In April 1607, three ships arrived off the coast of what is now Virginia. They were the *Susan Constant, Godspeed,* and *Discovery.* Of 105 passengers and 39 crew, only one passenger died during the stormy five-month voyage from England. The men found a safe place to set anchor at a site they named Jamestown. On May 14, 100 men and four boys went ashore to settle the new colony. Jamestown became the first successful English settlement in the New World.

In May 2007, Jamestown celebrated the 400th anniversary of its founding.

ESTABLISHING THE COLONY

The Jamestown colonists had been sent by the Virginia Company of London (or London Company), a trading company that had been granted a charter by King James I.

Almost half of the ships' passengers were "gentlemen" who had never worked with their hands. Their mission in Virginia was to establish a colony, search for gold and raw materials needed in England, and try to find a westward passage to the Orient. At that time, "Virginia" was the name for all the land claimed by England that extended from present-day Maine to North Carolina.

The Englishmen chose to settle on a point of land up a wide river. They named the river James in honor of their king. Then they built a fort, called James Fort, facing the river. The fort was shaped like a triangle. Guns were mounted at each corner. Several public buildings, including a church, a storehouse, and a guardhouse, were built inside the fort. Houses were built along the inside fort walls.

John Smith: Jamestown Leader

John Smith was an English soldier and explorer who helped found Jamestown, Virginia. He was born in Willoughby, England, in 1580. While still in his teens he became a soldier and had many adventures. By his own account, he defeated three Turks in duels and killed yet another who had made him a slave.

In 1606, Smith joined a group of colonists bound for Virginia. On the voyage, he was accused of mutiny and arrested. When the ships reached America, the sealed orders of the Virginia Company of London were opened. They revealed that Smith had been appointed to the colony's governing council. At first, he wasn't allowed to serve, so he went on an exploring expedition.

In his *General Historie of Virginia* (1624), Smith said that during this time away from the colony, he and some companions were captured by Indians. As he was about to be killed, he was saved by Pocahontas, the daughter of Chief Powhatan. Though no one knows if the tale is true, it is known that Pocahontas later befriended the colonists and accompanied the Indians who brought them food.

On Smith's return to Jamestown, he was again arrested but was soon freed. Eventually he became the colony's most successful leader. He set the colonists to work building houses, making glass and pitch and tar, and planting crops. During the severe winter of 1608–09 he saved them from starvation by persuading the Indians to give them corn.

In 1609, Smith was injured in an explosion and returned to England. Five years later he came back to America, explored New England, and made the first accurate map of the coast. His book *A Description of New England* (1616) gave the region its name. The Pilgrims later used his books and maps. Smith returned to England, where he died on June 21, 1631.

In 2006, the Captain John Smith Chesapeake National Historic Trail was established. It commemorates his exploratory voyages on Chesapeake Bay and its tributaries.

In June 1607 the ships sailed back to England, leaving the settlers behind. The colonists set about digging for gold in the sandy soil. But there was no gold. In August, famine and disease struck. By January 1608, all but 38 of the group had died.

In 1608 one of the original settlers, Captain John Smith, took charge of the situation. He persuaded Powhatan, the powerful Indian chief who controlled most of the tribes in the region, to give corn and meat to the desperate colonists.

Under Smith's leadership, about 20 houses and a glassworks were built. He made the gentlemen make wooden clapboards (used for siding) and produce pitch and tar to send back to England. Most important, however, Smith made them stop looking for gold and strengthen their defenses. He also made them hunt, fish, and plant corn.

However, without experience as farmers, their harvests were poor. The settlers were starving when they should have had plenty. Ships brought supplies, but never enough. Instead they brought more mouths to feed. Then disaster struck. Smith was wounded in a gunpowder explosion and returned to England. Without a strong leader to protect them,

The settlers trade with the Powhatan Indians at Jamestown. Without the help of the Indians, the colony probably wouldn't have survived.

the colonists were attacked by Indians. They also faced disease and starvation. Jamestown was almost wiped out. Only about 90 settlers survived the dreadful winter of 1609–10. That period became known as "the starving time." In May 1610, Sir Thomas Gates, the appointed lieutenant governor, arrived. It was decided that the colonists would return to England and the colony would be given up as a failure. They had sailed about 14 miles (23 kilometers) down the James River when Lord de la Warr, Virginia's first official governor, arrived with supplies and fresh colonists. The settlers turned back, determined to try again.

Under the leadership of Sir Thomas Dale, who became deputy governor in 1611, the colonists carried on. They repaired the church, built a bridge and a munitions house, dug a new well, and planted gardens. Dale was said to be a tyrant. But strong discipline was needed to keep the colony going.

Around 1612 a Jamestown settler, John Rolfe, began growing tobacco, a West Indian plant. His experiments were successful. At last the colony had a cash crop that might begin to return profits to the London Company investors. Tobacco, not gold, became the real wealth of Virginia. But this didn't happen in time to pay the investors, so the London Company gave them their profits in the form of land grants. And a peace was made between the settlers and the Powhatan Indians after a period of four years of occasional warfare.

Eventually, new settlements sprang up along the James River. Jamestown remained the capital of the colony, but settlers began moving to less swampy locations with more-fertile land.

In 1619 the first representative assembly in the New World met at Jamestown. It was called the General Assembly. It included the governor, his council, and two elected representatives from each of the major settlements. Records from that year also indicate that the first Africans were brought to Virginia. They were probably treated initially as indentured servants—slavery wouldn't begin in the colony for several more decades.

Powhatan: Indian Leader

Powhatan (POW-ah-tan) was the supreme chief of the Powhatan Indians of eastern Virginia. He ruled at the time of the English settlement in 1607. Powhatan's given name was Wahunsonacock. He took the name Powhatan from his birthplace, near present-day Richmond.

Near the end of the 1500's, six tribes came under Powhatan's leadership through his mother's ancestors. He then began bringing other tribes under his control, either through warfare or intimidation. Eventually he controlled about 14,000 people belonging to 30 different tribes.

When the English first arrived, Powhatan was headquartered at Werowocomoco, on the York River. But he moved twice during his lifetime to avoid the growing numbers of settlers. His response was to wait and see what the English would do and how long they planned to stay. He also wanted to see what goods they would trade.

In December 1607, one of the settlers' leaders, John Smith, was captured and brought before Powhatan. Powhatan wanted to demonstrate his authority over the English. Stories have it that Powhatan's daughter, Pocahontas, begged her father to spare Smith's life. However, historians believe that either Powhatan was testing Smith to show his authority before allying with the English, or the rescue never happened. Smith wrote of Powhatan's dignity, wisdom, and defiance.

Powhatan is entreated by his daughter, Pocahontas, to spare the life of John Smith.

Powhatan rarely met directly with the English. Nevertheless, he formed an initial alliance with them. The uneasy relationship between the two groups broke down in early 1609 after the English forced the Indians to give them food. Powhatan decided to try to starve the English and attacked their fort. In 1613 the English kidnapped Powhatan's daughter, Pocahontas. They hoped to exchange her for English prisoners. But Powhatan wouldn't give in to their demands. He never went to Jamestown. The English always had to come to him.

When Powhatan died in 1618, his younger brother Opechancanough (o-pee-CAN-can-oh) took control of his empire.

JAMESTOWN TODAY

Today the original Jamestown site, Historic Jamestowne, is jointly administered by the Association for the Preservation of Virginia Antiquities (APVA) and the National Park Service. The archaeological remains of the original 1607 Jamestown fort were discovered here in 1994. More than a million other artifacts dating to the 1600's have been found, including a church tower, the remains of the colony's glass factory, and the foundations of a number of buildings.

A short distance from the original site is Jamestown Settlement, a living-history museum operated by the Commonwealth of Virginia's Jamestown-Yorktown Foundation. The Settlement features replicas of James Fort and a Powhatan Indian village, as well as life-size replicas of the three ships that brought the first settlers from England. Jamestown Settlement, established in 1957 for the 350th anniversary of Jamestown, was originally called Jamestown Festival Park.

Pocahontas: Jamestown's Indian Friend

Pocahontas was the favorite daughter of the powerful Indian chief Powhatan. She befriended the English settlers in Virginia in the early 1600's.

She was born about 1596 to one of her father's numerous wives. Pocahontas probably spent her early childhood in her mother's village, playing and learning women's chores. When she was about 10, she moved back to her father's household. The English called her a princess because her father was the supreme chief. But in her society, status was inherited through the mother's, not the father's, line.

Pocahontas had several names, in keeping with Powhatan Indian tradition. Her nickname was Pocahontas, meaning "playful one." But she also had a formal name, Amonute, and a personal name, Matoaka.

Pocahontas first met Captain John Smith, one of Virginia's early English leaders, in December 1607, when he was captured and brought before her father. Smith wrote that Pocahontas rescued him from death. But no one knows if that story is really true. Later, Powhatan sent Pocahontas with Indian messengers to bring food to the Jamestown settlers. Once she warned Smith of a possible ambush.

After Smith left Virginia in late 1609, Pocahontas no longer visited Jamestown. One source says she married a warrior named Kocoum. In 1613 the English settlers kidnapped Pocahontas to ransom English prisoners held by Powhatan. But she remained with them, studying English customs and religion. She met John Rolfe, a planter who introduced tobacco to Virginia and made it the colony's most important cash crop. In 1614, Pocahontas was baptized with the Christian name Rebecca and married Rolfe. A year later they had a son, Thomas.

In 1616 the Rolfe family was sent to England to raise funds in support of the Virginia colony. In London, Pocahontas met many prominent people, including King James I and Queen Anne. But she became ill, and Rolfe moved her to the countryside, where she met her old friend John Smith. As the Rolfes prepared to return to Virginia in early 1617, Pocahontas died. She was buried at St. George's Church, Gravesend, England.

ANNIVERSARY CELEBRATIONS

The 2007 celebration of the establishment of Jamestown colony was appropriately called "America's 400th Anniversary." Jamestown was, after all, the start of the America we know today. Celebratory events began in 2006 and continued throughout most of 2007.

The commemorative events were coordinated by a special Virginia state agency called Jamestown 2007. Sandra Day O'Connor, a former Associate Justice of the U.S. Supreme Court, was the honorary chairwoman of the celebration.

The first event was the *Godspeed* Sail. From May to July 2006, this replica of one of the ships that had landed at Jamestown 400 years earlier toured six East Coast ports. Half a million people visited the ship at Alexandria, Virginia; Baltimore, Maryland; Philadelphia, Pennsylvania; New York City; Boston, Massachusetts; and Newport, Rhode Island. The *Godspeed* then sailed across the Atlantic to London, England. It docked outside the Museum in Docklands, which had mounted an exhibition about the connections between London and Jamestown.

Jamestown Settlement features a replica of James Fort as well as life-size models of the three ships that brought the settlers from England. Actors in Colonial costumes play the parts of settlers, Indians, and sailors from 17th-century Jamestown.

Also in 2006, Virginia's Native Americans, whose ancestors had been instrumental in Jamestown's survival, held a meeting at Williamsburg, Virginia, to discuss "Virginia Indians: 400 Years of Survival." They met again in Hampton, Virginia, at an American Indian Intertribal Festival in July 2007.

African Americans, too, played a role in Jamestown. The first Africans arrived in 1619 as indentured servants. By 1649, a few years after slavery began there, there were about 300 African Americans in Jamestown. Their skills, labor, and culture, essential to the colony's development, were discussed in 2006 and 2007 at conferences that stressed the "African-American Imprint on America."

The highlight of the celebrations took place on May 11–13—America's Anniversary Weekend. This three-day event was held at all of the Jamestown sites. It included pageantry, musical performances, cultural presentations, and celebrity appearances. President George W. Bush and First Lady Laura Bush attended. Queen Elizabeth II and her husband, Prince Philip, Duke of Edin-

burgh, had visited Jamestown earlier in May. "This 400th anniversary," the Queen said, "marks the deep friendship that has grown between our two countries."

In the years following the establishment of Jamestown, the number of England's New World colonies grew—to thirteen in 1733. They became states of the United States following the Declaration of Independence in 1776. And from Jamestown's 100 colonists, the population of the United States has grown to 300 million. In the colonial period, most of the people were from the British Isles—England, Scotland, Ireland, and Wales. Today, the United States is a nation of immigrants, with people from every country of the world settling there. From its shaky start at Jamestown, the United States has become a major world power.

ARE YOU SUPERSTITIOUS?

Did you see the new moon over your left shoulder last night? Well, keep your fingers crossed—it looks like you might be in for some good luck. Things don't look so bright, though, if you spilled the salt at dinner or if you broke a mirror recently. Then, some people say, your luck will be bad.

These are superstitions—beliefs based on faith in magic or chance. People who are superstitious believe that certain actions will influence events in their lives, even when those actions have no logical connection to the events.

Many superstitions date back to ancient times, when people didn't understand why or how things happened. But even though we may know better today, many people are still superstitious.

Knock on Wood

Touching or knocking on wood is another custom that's thought to help good things happen. This belief has its roots in ancient folklore. In early times, trees were often thought to be the homes of friendly spirits. People touched or knocked on a tree to ask a favor of the spirit that lived there. Some people also thought that knocking loudly on wood would keep evil spirits from hearing them talk about good news—so that the spirits wouldn't step in to spoil things for them.

Don't Break a Mirror

The belief that mirrors have special magical powers is an ancient one. Early peoples thought that they were seeing their souls when they saw their reflections in lakes and ponds—how else, they wondered, could there be "other beings" exactly like themselves? When people began to make mirrors, they thought that the mirror actually held the other self, or soul, of whoever looked into it. If the mirror broke, then, something bad would surely happen to that person.

The ancient Romans added the notion that breaking a mirror would bring seven years of poor health. They believed that life renewed itself every seven years, so after that time a person's health would be renewed. Thus if a person's other self were shattered in a mirror, his or her health would also be "broken," and it would take seven years to get well. Gradually the superstition changed from poor health to poor luck. But superstitions aside, a person in ancient times had good reason not to break mirrors—they were expensive and rare.

Keep Your Fingers Crossed

When you hope something good will happen, do you ever cross your fingers? Ancient peoples believed that the cross was a powerful symbol, with the ability to prevent evil and bring good. By crossing their fingers when they made a wish, they thought they could trap the wish at the place where the two fingers met, so it couldn't slip away before it came true. At first, two people made the sign—the wisher would hold out one finger, and a friend would place a finger on top to form the cross. Later the custom changed, and people made the sign themselves with their index and middle fingers.

Don't Spill Salt

Salt was hard to get and very expensive in ancient times. If people spilled it, they thought that evil spirits must have been around to cause the unhappy accident. And these evil spirits would surely cause more trouble before they were done. Some people thought that their bad luck would last until they had cried a tear for every grain of salt that had spilled. But there was a way to ward off the bad luck. Evil spirits were thought to always stand behind a person to the left. So if you took a pinch of salt and threw it over your left shoulder, you could bribe the spirits into leaving you alone.

Reaching for Bread at the Same Time

In early times, bread was considered sacred. It stood for the essentials of life—water and grain (used in making the bread) and the earth and sun (needed to grow the grain). As a result, many superstitious beliefs grew up about bread. One was that it was bad luck to cut a loaf

at both ends. Another was that it was good luck to accidentally drop bread—and if you made a wish as you picked it up, your wish would come true. This superstition didn't apply if you dropped your bread butter-side down, though—that was bad luck. People also thought that if two people reached for the bread at the same time, someone would visit the house soon. And dreaming about bread was considered a sign of a happy event to come in the future.

Make a Wish. . .

. . .on a star, on the new moon, on the breastbone (wishbone) of a chicken, on the candles of your birthday cake. Each of these superstitions has a long history.

first saw it over your left shoulder, you were sure to be lucky. And any wish made at first sight of the new moon was certain to come true.

The custom of making a wish on a chicken's "wishbone" dates to early Roman times. The Romans sacrificed chickens to their gods and hung the breastbones up to dry for luck. This grew into another custom—two people would grasp the ends of the bone and snap it as they each made a wish. Whoever got the longer piece would also get his or her wish.

And when you blow out the candles on your birthday cake, you are following still another ancient superstition. Long ago, people lit fires as protection from cold and from wild animals. Gradually any fire—even a candle—came to be a symbol of magical protec-

The belief that the stars govern luck goes back to the ancient Middle East, where people thought that each person's destiny was ruled by the stars. If a person was born under an evil star, bad things would happen. But if a good star ruled, it would bring good luck.

The new moon was thought to be a symbol of good luck by people in many places. If you

tion. For example, the ancient Greeks and Romans lit candles when they prayed, so that the flames would carry their prayers to the gods. Later, candles were placed on birthday cakes to ward off evil spirits. And today many people try to blow out all their birthday candles with one puff—to make their wishes come true.

World-famous aviator Amelia Earhart was the first woman to fly solo across the Atlantic Ocean. The 75th anniversary of that achievement was celebrated in 2007.

AMELIA EARHART—PIONEER PILOT

In the early days of aviation, it took a strong heart and a true sense of adventure to take off into the skies. Flying wasn't considered a woman's sport—women were supposed to stay safely at home. Yet one of the most daring flyers of the 1920's and 1930's was a woman: Amelia Earhart.

Earhart's career was tragically short, however. While attempting a round-the-world flight in 1937, she disappeared over the Pacific Ocean. Her disappearance remains a mystery to this day.

But her accomplishments are no mystery. Amelia Earhart set many aviation records, and in May 1932 she became the first woman to fly solo across the Atlantic Ocean. The 75th anniversary of that historic event was marked in 2007—as well as the 70th anniversary of her disappearance.

A SENSE OF ADVENTURE

The daughter of a railroad attorney, Amelia Earhart was born in Atchison, Kansas, on July 24, 1897. As she grew into a tall, freckled, smiling girl, her sense of adventure was already evident. She wore bloomers, could shoot a .22-caliber rifle, and played football. She also developed an interest in science. She left college in her senior year to work as a nurse in Toronto, Canada, during World War I, and she later briefly studied medicine.

But medicine wasn't to be her life's work. In 1920, while living with her parents in California, she visited an air show and was fascinated by what she saw. She immediately decided she would learn to fly, and she began to work to earn money for lessons. By 1922, she had her first airplane, and she soon set a new women's altitude record by flying to 14,000 feet (4,200 meters).

Earhart's flying career went on hold for a few years when her family suffered financial problems. She moved to Boston and found a job as a social worker, but she continued to fly in her spare time. Then, in 1928, came an offer: A group that was sponsoring a transatlantic flight asked her to go along as the first woman to make the trip. The idea was as dangerous as it was exciting. Charles Lindbergh had made the first solo crossing the year before, but 19 other people had died attempting the trip that year.

THE MYSTERY LINGERS ON

The disappearance of Amelia Earhart on July 2, 1937, became one of the most intriguing mysteries of aviation history. Ever since that event, people have sought answers, even traveling to the remote part of the Pacific Ocean where she crashed. There are two main theories today: One is set forth by The International Group for Historic Aircraft Recovery (TIGHAR); the other by Nauticos, a company that specializes in deep-ocean search.

In 1992, investigators from TIGHAR announced that they had found evidence that Earhart had been forced to land on the uninhabited island of Nikumaroro (then called Gardner Island). Nikumaroro is about 350 miles (563 kilometers) south of Howland Island, Earhart's intended destination.

On the island, the investigators found a ragged sheet of aluminum with rows of rivet holes. The aluminum was identical to the type used to build Earhart's two-engine plane. The investigators also found the heel and sole of a woman's shoe, size 9, from the 1930's—the same size and style worn by Earhart.

TIGHAR researchers made three other expeditions to Nikumaroro Island, including one in the summer of 2007. They conducted archaeological digs to discover artifacts from Earhart's ill-fated flight.

TIGHAR's claims have been challenged by other experts, especially by Nauticos. Nauticos has been involved in hi-tech underwater search projects since the 1990's. Their researchers believe that Earhart and Noonan ran out of fuel and ditched their plane at sea

Earhart and her navigator, Fred Noonan, discuss the flight plan for their trip around the world.

in the vicinity of Howland Island. They are supported by Elgen Long, a renowned pilot who has written a book on Earhart's disappearance. In 1971, during his record round-the-world flight, Long duplicated Earhart's approach to Howland Island. He based her approach on the radio messages she sent to a U.S. Coast Guard ship that was anchored at Howland. It was this experience that led Long to investigate what had happened to Earhart.

Nauticos, with Long on board their research ship, mounted two expeditions to the waters around Howland Island, in 2002 and 2006. They didn't find Earhart's plane, but they planned a third expedition. Using immersible radar to search the ocean floor 18,000 feet (5,486 meters) below the surface, they hope to find Earhart's plane and solve the mystery surrounding the world's most famous woman aviator.

Earhart took up aviation as a hobby while living in California. She earned her pilot's license in 1922.

With her sense of adventure, however, Earhart needed only moments to decide—the answer, of course, was yes.

In June, Amelia Earhart, Wilmer Stultz, and Lou Gordon made the 2,500-mile (4,025-kilometer) flight, from Newfoundland to Wales. Although she was named commander of the *Friendship,* the men actually flew the plane.

Still, the crossing was hailed as a great achievement, and Earhart became a celebrity. She wrote a book about the trip, and married her publisher, George Putnam, in 1931.

Despite her fame, Earhart wasn't satisfied. "I was just baggage, like a sack of potatoes," she said of her historic voyage. She continued to fly, and she set a new women's autogiro altitude record of 18,415 feet (5,615 meters) in

1931. (An autogiro was an early helicopter.) But she knew she would have to repeat the Atlantic crossing at the controls of her plane. And she did so in May 1932, piloting her single-engine craft from Newfoundland to Ireland to become the first woman to fly across the Atlantic alone.

Awards and honors showered down on her. She was wined and dined by heads of state, and the press followed her everywhere. But she didn't rest on her laurels. Later in 1932, she flew from California to New Jersey to set a new women's transcontinental speed record—and then broke her own record the next year. In 1935, she made the first solo flight from Hawaii to the U.S. mainland, crossing 2,400 miles (3,860 kilometers) of the Pacific Ocean. She told her friends that she did it for fun.

AROUND THE WORLD

By 1937, Earhart was ready to attempt her greatest challenge: a flight around the world. Her first try, on an east-west route along the Equator, ended in Hawaii when the plane was damaged on takeoff. She set off on her second attempt on June 1, just a couple of months before her 40th birthday. She and her navigator, Fred Noonan, took off from Miami and headed east. "Amelia is a grand person for such a trip," Noonan had said. "She is the only woman flyer I would care to make such an expedition with. Because in addition to being a fine companion and pilot, she can take hardship as well as a man—and work like one."

Flying in stages, Earhart and Noonan crossed Africa, India, and Southeast Asia. On July 2, they left New Guinea for the most difficult part of the trip, a long stretch over the Pacific to Howland Island. Somewhere near Howland, radio contact with their plane was lost.

The U.S. Navy mounted an exhaustive, 17-day search of the area. Nine ships and 66 aircraft scoured the area. But nothing was found—Earhart had simply vanished. It was

Just before Earhart disappeared, the U.S. Coast Guard ship *Itasca,* off Howland Island, received this radio message from her: "We must be on you but cannot see you but gas is running low."

assumed that the plane had gone down in the ocean. But in the years that followed, rumors and theories about the disappearance kept cropping up. Some people claimed that Earhart and Noonan had been captured by Japanese soldiers and had died in captivity. There was even a story that they had been on a secret spying mission for the United States. Other people contended that the famous woman aviator was still alive, living on some Pacific isle. One recent theory is that Earhart and Noonan landed on the island of Nikumaroro, south of Howland Island. Another is that they crashed into the ocean in the vicinity of Howland Island, her destination.

To date, none of these theories has been proved—or disproved. But Earhart's true legacy isn't the mystery she left behind but the example she set. She showed that women, through courage and commitment, could accomplish anything. Today, her daring feats are still inspiring.

DID YOU KNOW?

Amelia Earhart was one of the most famous women of her day, and her name and exploits were constantly in the news. There are many interesting facts that relate to her life—and her disappearance.

■ Amelia Earhart was nicknamed Lady Lindy, not only because she was as daring a pilot as Charles Lindbergh, but also because many people thought she resembled him.

■ Earhart was the aviation editor of *Cosmopolitan* magazine.

■ Earhart was a friend of First Lady Eleanor Roosevelt, wife of President Franklin D. Roosevelt, and was going to teach her to fly. Mrs. Roosevelt had gotten her student permit.

■ Although Amelia Earhart's body was never found, she was legally declared dead by a California court on January 5, 1939, just 1½ years after she disappeared.

■ Actress Rosalind Russell played Earhart in *Flight for Freedom* (1943), a fictionalized account of the famed aviator's life.

■ Earhart has been the subject of more than fifty nonfiction books.

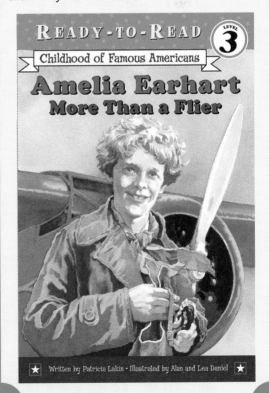

READY-TO-READ — LEVEL 3

Childhood of Famous Americans

Amelia Earhart
More Than a Flier

★ Written by Patricia Lakin • Illustrated by Alan and Lea Daniel ★

India's Taj Mahal is one of the New Seven Wonders of the World selected by 100 million global voters in 2007. The famous tomb has attracted visitors from many nations over the centuries.

THE NEW SEVEN WONDERS OF THE WORLD

About 2,200 years ago, ancient Greek writers and historians compiled a list of marvels they saw as they traveled around the Mediterranean region and the Middle East. The statues and monuments they described came to be known as the Seven Wonders of the World: the Pyramids of Giza, the Hanging Gardens of Babylon, the Statue of Zeus at Olympia, the Temple of Artemis at Ephesus, the Mausoleum at Halicarnassus, the Colossus of Rhodes, and the Pharos lighthouse of Alexandria. Of these ancient wonders, only the Pyramids of Giza, in Egypt, exist today.

But what other wonders are there in the world today? Bernard Weber, a Swiss businessman, asked that question. And he formed the New7Wonders Foundation, an organization that conducted a global vote to come up with seven wonders that still exist.

On July 7, 2007 (07/07/07), more than 100 million people around the world voted on the Internet and with cellphone text messages for their favorite new wonders, selected from a list of 21 sites. Among those not included in the "lucky seven" were the Statue of Liberty, the Eiffel Tower, and the Kremlin. The Pyramids of Giza were given honorary status.

Here are the marvels chosen by the voters as the New Seven Wonders of the World:

The Taj Mahal, in Agra, India, is a stunning white marble tomb. It was built by Shah Jahan, a Mogul ruler of India, for his favorite wife, Arjumand Banu, when she died. He wanted it to be the most beautiful tomb in the world. The monument was completed about 1648 by 20,000 laborers under the direction of skilled artisans. It stands on a large white marble terrace overlooking the Jumna River. Four slender minarets, each in a corner of the terrace, rise into the sky. The front of the Taj Mahal is reflected in the waters of a long pool. Lush gardens surround the marble building.

Petra, in Jordan, is a unique 2,500-year-old city. Its 800 ancient monuments—temples, royal tombs, monasteries, and elaborate buildings—were entirely carved into the red sandstone cliffs. Because of this, Petra is also known as the "rose red city." Petra was the capital of the Nabataean kingdom until it was occupied by Rome in A.D. 106. Over the centuries, the city seemed to disappear. But in 1812, Johann Ludwig Burckhardt, a Swiss explorer, rediscovered it. Petra's natural beauty and enormous stone carvings have made it one of the most remarkable ancient cities remaining in the modern world. (At right is the Urn Tomb.)

The Great Wall of China, an architectural and engineering marvel, was built to protect ancient China from attacks by its northern neighbors. More than 2,000 years ago, it stretched across northern China for about 4,000 miles (6,400 kilometers). But over the centuries, half the wall disappeared. War, weather, and a spreading desert did most of the damage. In addition, people took stones to build houses, and parts of the wall were demolished to make room for new roads. Recently, however, the Chinese government has taken steps to preserve this great monument to the Chinese people.

❧Petra · Jordan❧

❧The Great Wall of China❧

Chichén Itzá · Mexico

Chichén Itzá, in Mexico, was a Maya city on the Yucatán Peninsula. From A.D. 900 to 1100, it was the political and economic center of Maya civilization. In the middle of the city was a huge plaza, dominated by the Temple Pyramid of Kukulcan. Kukulcan was a feathered serpent god called Quetzalcoatl by the Aztecs. The pyramid has square terraces, and staircases rise up each of the four sides to the temple at the top. Other structures at Chichén include the Great Ball Court, the Temple of the Warriors, and the Court of the Thousand Columns. The ruins are now a major archaeological site.

The Colosseum, in Rome, Italy, is among the most important monuments remaining from the days of ancient Rome. It was built between 70 and 80 A.D. by emperors of the Flavian Dynasty who gave it its original name—the Flavian Amphitheater. The four-story stadium, oval in shape, stood 160 feet (49 meters) high with an arena measuring 280 by 175 feet (85 by 53 meters). Built as an entertainment complex, it held more than 50,000 spectators, who gathered there to watch gladiator battles, mock sea battles, and other spectacles. It is an example of ancient Rome's outstanding architecture.

The Colosseum · Italy

❧Machu Picchu · Peru❧

Machu Picchu, in the Andes mountains of Peru, is an Inca town built around 1450. The ruins are one of the world's most famous archaeological sites. Machu Picchu was abandoned when the Spanish conquered the Incas in the 1530's. The site became covered with dense vegetation and remained basically unknown until its discovery in 1911. The "lost city" of the Incas, as it is called, contains fine stone buildings, such as the Temple of the Sun and the Room of the Three Windows, as well as extensive agricultural terraces. The Intihuatana, or Hitching Post of the Sun, is a carved rock whose shape is similar to that of a sacred peak near the ruins.

Christ the Redeemer, in Rio de Janeiro, Brazil, is a giant statue of Jesus. It is 130 feet (40 meters) tall, and its arms are open and welcoming as it overlooks the city. The statue sits atop Corcovado ("hunchback") mountain. One of the world's best-known monuments, it was built between 1926 and 1931 and was designed by Brazilian engineer Heitor da Silva Costa and created by French sculptor Paul Landowski. In 2006, Christ the Redeemer's 75th anniversary, a chapel was built under the statue.

❧Christ the Redeemer · Brazil❧

THE INS AND OUTS OF FADS

Some fads may come, and some may go—and some stay around so long they become permanent fixtures in the popular culture. The Frisbee is one of these fads: The flying disc celebrated its 50th anniversary in 2007.

College students at Yale and other universities had long been sailing pie tins through the air. The tins were made by the Frisbie Baking Company of Bridgeport, Connecticut, and the students would yell out "Frisbie" whenever they launched one.

Years later, in 1957, the Wham-O toy company bought a Frisbie-like plastic disc called the Pluto Platter from Walter Morrison, its inventor, and renamed it the Frisbee. Sales soared. Today, the Frisbee is not only a top-selling toy, it's also used in competitive sports play. The World Flying Disc Federation regulates the sport and sponsors competitions.

Every era seems to have its fads—toys, activities, foods, clothes—that come in, suddenly are all the rage, and just as quickly go out again. It's almost impossible to predict what will catch on next. It's just as hard to predict which fad will continue for such a long time that it becomes an icon. The Frisbee did it!

On the following pages, you will read about ten of the hundreds of fads that have been popular in the last 100 years. Some, like the pet rock, are out. But many, like the Teddy Bear and Pokémon, are still in—and are still delighting us.

The **Teddy Bear** is one of the best-loved toys of all time. It was named for Theodore "Teddy" Roosevelt, the 26th president of the United States. On a hunting trip in 1902, President Roosevelt refused to kill a captive bear. The *Washington Post* reported the story, along with a cartoon that showed Roosevelt refusing to shoot a cute bear cub. A candy-store owner in New York City saw the cartoon, and he and his wife began making toy bears, modeled on the cartoon bear cub, for sale in their store. He wrote to Roosevelt, asking for permission to call the toys "Teddy's bears." Roosevelt agreed—and the teddy bear was born. Before long, teddy-bear fever swept the country. Teddy bears have won hearts in every generation since then. The teddy bear has real staying power!

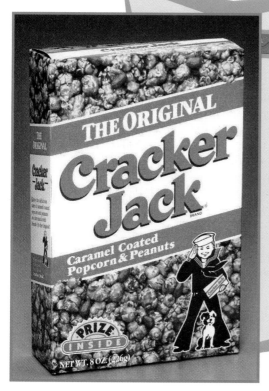

"Take me out to the ball game, Take me out to the park, Buy me some peanuts and Cracker Jack, I don't care if I never get back."

This 1908 baseball song ensured **Cracker Jack**'s place in American pop culture. But F. W. Rueckheim's popcorn, peanut, and molasses confection was a popular treat long before. He made it in the 1870's and sold it to retailers. When a salesman tasted it, he shouted, "That's crackerjack!"—a phrase of the time meaning "fantastic." Rueckheim soon put his confection into boxes to sell to the public, calling it Cracker Jack. The box featured a boy, Sailor Jack (modeled after Rueckheim's grandson); and a dog, Bingo (which stood for the prize in every box).

They had names like "Singing Tower" and "Luxury Light-Up." They featured brilliantly colored molded plastics and bubble tubes. They glowed and bubbled and flashed. And if you put a nickel in the slot, they played jazz, blues, and big-band music. These were the magnificent **jukeboxes** of the 1930's and '40's. When jukeboxes were installed in soda fountains, diners, and bars, people got up to dance to their favorite tunes. African Americans called dance halls "juke joints," so the new machines were called jukeboxes. The high-tech CD jukeboxes of later years could play many more songs—but for sheer beauty, they couldn't compare to the originals.

In 1958 the Wham-O toy company handed out colorful plastic hoops, 3 feet (1 meter) in diameter, to some young Californians. Soon the kids were rotating their hips to make the hoops whirl around their waists. When their antics were shown on television, the **Hula-Hoop** fad was born. Wham-O called the hoops "Hula-Hoops" because the movements that were used to make them twirl around the waist were similar to the movements used in the Hawaiian hula dance. By the time the fad ended, more than 100 million hoops had been sold in the United States alone. And the hoops have retained some popularity to this day.

The **pet rock** craze was started in 1975 by advertising executive Gary Dahl. Rocks, he said with a straight face, were cleaner, better behaved, and less expensive to care for than dogs, cats, birds, fish, and other pets. He sold the rocks for $3.95 each, packaged in a cardboard box that looked like a small pet carrier. Also included was a *Pet Rock Training Manual*, which taught commands such as "sit" and "stay." Pet rocks were soon rolling into people's homes, and before the short-lived fad ended, more than five million of them had been sold.

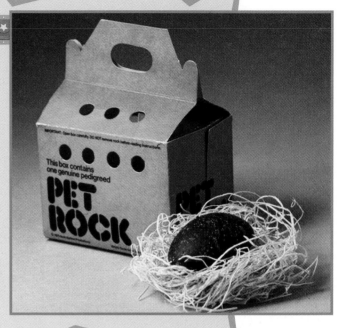

What can be moved into billions of different positions—and can drive people crazy? It's **Rubik's Cube**, the enormously popular puzzle of the early 1980's. Invented by Hungarian professor Erno Rubik, it's a six-sided plastic cube with three rows of nine colored squares on each side. Initially, each of the six sides is a different solid color. The colors are scrambled by twisting the cube in different directions. To solve the puzzle, one has to rotate the squares until all nine squares of the same color are again on one side of the cube—something that's frustratingly difficult to do!

The first **Cabbage Patch Kids** were handmade by Xavier Roberts, a Georgia sculptor, in the late 1970's. His chubby soft-sculpture dolls had large, round cloth faces, detailed fingers and toes, and even a belly button. Each doll was unique, and each came with a name, birth certificate, and "adoption papers." In 1983, the Coleco toy company began mass-producing the dolls with vinyl faces, but the appeal was the same. Cabbage Patch Kids were hugely popular for more than five years—and they even appeared on U.S. postage stamps.

Humphrey the Camel. . .Fleece the Lamb. . .Squealer the Pig. Is this a group of animals at a zoo? Nope! These are **Beanie Babies**, the tiny, squishy beanbag animals that sold in the hundreds of millions. Introduced in 1994 by Ty Inc., Beanie Babies were huggable and cuddly, and their bodies—which are filled with plastic pellets, not real beans—could be posed. Kids loved them, and people of all ages collected them. The fad peaked in 1999, but Ty Inc. still offers special Beanie Babies at summer toy shows.

Monsters from Japan invaded America in 1999. They were **Pokémon**—short for "pocket monsters." And Pokémon video games and trading cards—along with movies, a TV show, and toys—turned out to be one of the biggest crazes ever. Most of the nearly 500 monsters are more cute than scary. But each one has certain powers, and they use weapons such as water, fire, and electricity. In the video games, the goal is to capture and "train" as many Pokémon as possible. The Pokémon fad is still popular today.

The **sudoku** craze hit the United States in 2005. Now you can find these puzzles everywhere. People of all ages love them because they're challenging—and addictive. You don't have to know math to solve sudoku. But you do have to think. These puzzles caught on in Japan in the 1980's, which is where they picked up the name sudoku—which comes from words meaning "single number." The name refers to the fact that the numbers 1 through 9 are used just once. There are versions for beginners and experts. There are also versions especially for kids. Solving sudoku takes time and patience. But chances are that you, too, will be hooked!

Franklin Delano Roosevelt may have had a greater influence on life in the United States than any other 20th-century president. The 125th anniversary of his birth was marked in 2007. (He is shown here with the cigarette holder that became one of his trademarks.)

FRANKLIN DELANO ROOSEVELT: A REMARKABLE LEADER

The Great Depression of the 1930's and World War II were two of the greatest crises of the 20th century. One president—Franklin Delano Roosevelt—led the United States during both. Roosevelt was the only U.S. president ever to serve more than two terms. He was first elected in 1932 and then re-elected three times, serving until his death in 1945.

FDR, as he is often called, had great personal courage. He achieved success even after an illness left him without the use of his legs. He also had great warmth and charm, which he used to rally the country through some of its darkest hours. Millions of Americans loved him. But those who disagreed with the course he charted for the country detested him. Almost no one was neutral about FDR.

The year 2007 marked both the 125th anniversary of Roosevelt's birth, and the 75th anniversary of his victory in the 1932 presi-dential election. It was a time to look back at the life and times of this remarkable leader.

A CAREER IN POLITICS

Roosevelt grew up surrounded by wealth and comfort. He was born on the family estate in Hyde Park, New York, on January 30, 1882, and educated at home by a governess and private tutors. Later he attended Groton, a prestigious prep school in Massachusetts, and Harvard University. In 1904 he enrolled at Columbia University Law School. The next year he married Eleanor Roosevelt, a distant cousin. At their wedding, President Theodore Roosevelt (Eleanor's uncle and Franklin's fifth cousin) gave her in marriage.

FDR passed the New York bar exam in 1907 and left school for a job with a leading New York City law firm. After practicing law for three years, he entered politics. In 1910 he was

Left: FDR married Eleanor Roosevelt in 1905. She was a niece of President Theodore Roosevelt. Above: Roosevelt with a young friend and his beloved dog, Fala. (This is one of the few photos showing him in a wheelchair.)

elected to the New York State Senate, running as a Democrat from his traditionally Republican home district. In 1912 he supported Woodrow Wilson for the presidency; when Wilson won, the new president named him Assistant Secretary of the Navy. FDR was successful and popular in that job—so much so that, in 1920, he won the Democratic nomination for vice-president. But the Democrats lost the election to a Republican ticket headed by Warren G. Harding.

The 1920 election was a setback. But real tragedy struck the next summer, while the Roosevelts were vacationing at Campobello Island, in New Brunswick, Canada. FDR was stricken with what was believed to be polio. The disease left him without the use of his legs. For the rest of his life he would be unable to walk without heavy leg braces and crutches. But he didn't give up. He exercised every day. And he visited Warm Springs, Georgia, to swim in the mineral springs there. He found it so helpful that he bought the resort and set up a foundation to provide therapy for other polio victims.

No one would have been surprised if Roosevelt had dropped out of politics after his ill-

ness. But in this, too, he didn't give up. His wife, Eleanor, and his aide, Louis Howe, encouraged him. By this time Franklin and Eleanor had five children. Eleanor was shy by nature. However, she overcame this and began to attend political events in her husband's stead.

In 1924, Roosevelt gave his first public speech since his illness. At the Democratic National Convention, he nominated New York governor Alfred E. Smith for president. Smith didn't win the nomination that year, but he did get it four years later. The Democrats then nominated Roosevelt to succeed him as governor of New York. In the 1928 election, Smith lost to Herbert Hoover, a Republican. But Roosevelt was elected governor.

During FDR's first year as governor, the infamous stock market crash of 1929 occurred. Overnight, people who had invested in stocks saw their life savings disappear. The crash was followed by a nationwide economic depression. People lost confidence and stopped investing. Factories cut production and laid off workers.

Under Roosevelt, New York became the first state in the country to provide jobs and relief for the unemployed. His bold steps were popular, and in 1932 he won the Democratic nom-

Many of Roosevelt's New Deal programs were known by their initials—referred to as his "alphabet" agencies.

work in forest conservation and road building. The NRA (National Recovery Administration) set up business codes that regulated production, prices, and working conditions and gave workers the right to join unions. Other agencies insured bank deposits, regulated the stock market, and helped jobless workers. The TVA (Tennessee Valley Authority) was set up to provide flood control and cheap electricity to a large area of the South.

To explain his programs, Roosevelt gave regular press conferences. He invited reporters into his office and let them fire questions at will. He also broadcast radio talks, or "fireside chats." Commercial radio stations had begun to appear in the 1920's, and by the 1930's millions of Americans had home radios. FDR's broadcasts let him speak to them directly.

More New Deal programs followed in 1935. The Works Progress Administration (WPA) gave jobs to laborers, as well as artists, writers, and musicians. The Social Security Act provided unemployment insurance, pensions for the aged, and aid to widows and orphans. To help pay for these programs, income-tax rates were raised for the wealthy.

Critics said Roosevelt would bankrupt the government and turn the country into a welfare state. In 1935 the Supreme Court ruled that parts of the NRA and AAA programs were unconstitutional. But the New Deal helped millions of people, and it was popular. Roosevelt was easily re-elected in 1936.

ination for the presidency. In his acceptance speech, he pledged "a new deal for the American people." He campaigned on that theme and defeated Herbert Hoover in November.

THE NEW DEAL

Meanwhile, the Depression worsened. Farms and businesses went bankrupt. Thousands of banks failed as panicky depositors withdrew their money. By the time Roosevelt took office as president in March 1933, one out of every four American workers was unemployed.

Roosevelt set out an ambitious recovery program in his first 100 days as president. One of his first actions was to declare a temporary bank "holiday." This halted withdrawals and kept more banks from failing. Then he called a special session of Congress to pass emergency banking legislation. The new laws restored confidence. When the banks reopened, people once again deposited money.

Congress also passed laws establishing a cluster of "alphabet" agencies. The AAA (Agricultural Adjustment Administration) supported farm prices. The CCC (Civilian Conservation Corps) put jobless young men to

WORLD WAR II

The U.S. economy didn't recover quickly. Roosevelt continued to press for reforms, including a minimum-wage law. But by the end of the decade, his attention was turning overseas. Japan invaded northern China in 1937. Two years later, World War II broke out in Europe, when Nazi Germany attacked Poland.

The United States was officially neutral, and many Americans hoped to stay out of the war. But when German troops overran France in June 1940, it was clear that U.S. help was needed. Roosevelt won election to a third term that fall. Early in 1941 the United States began to send military aid to Britain and other countries at war with Germany. It became the "arsenal of democracy." Factories were finally as busy as they had been before the Depression.

In February 1945, Allied leaders met in Yalta, then a Soviet city, to discuss the war and the postwar period. Left to right: British Prime Minister Winston Churchill, an ailing FDR, and Soviet dictator Joseph Stalin.

On December 7, 1941, Japan staged a surprise attack on the U.S. Navy base at Pearl Harbor, Hawaii. Within days, the United States was at war with the Axis powers—Japan, Germany, and Italy. Roosevelt was an active commander-in-chief, making decisions about strategy. He also forged an alliance among the nations fighting the Axis powers. They pledged to found a peacekeeping organization after victory.

The strain of the war took a toll on Roosevelt. By 1944 he was suffering from health problems. Nevertheless, he ran for a fourth term and won. By April 1945, Allied forces were advancing against Japan in the Pacific. Victory in Europe seemed certain. But Roosevelt didn't live to see it. He suffered a stroke and died on April 12.

Roosevelt made a huge impact on his times. That impact didn't end with his death. His policies helped lead to the founding of the United Nations, and they shaped the society that Americans live in today.

FDR IN QUOTES

FDR was known for his ability to inspire others with his words. Here are some quotations from his speeches and writings.

■ It is common sense to take a method and try it. If it fails, admit it frankly and try another. But above all, try something. (1933)

■ Let me assert my firm belief that the only thing we have to fear is fear itself—nameless, unreasoning, unjustified terror which paralyzes needed efforts to convert retreat into advance. (First inaugural address, March 1933)

■ Those words freedom and opportunity do not mean a license to climb upwards by pushing other people down. (1935)

■ To some generations much is given. Of other generations much is expected. This generation of Americans has a rendezvous with destiny. (1936)

■ The test of our progress is not whether we add more to the abundance of those who have much; it is whether we provide enough for those who have too little. (Second inaugural address, March 1937)

■ We look forward to a world founded upon four essential human freedoms. The first is freedom of speech and expression—everywhere in the world. The second is freedom of every person to worship God in his own way—everywhere in the world. The third is freedom from want. . .everywhere in the world. The fourth is freedom from fear. . .anywhere in the world. (1941)

From the mid-1600's through the 1700's, pirates menaced the Caribbean Sea and the Atlantic Ocean, seizing any ship that came within their grasp. The most notorious pirate of all was Blackbeard.

PORTRAIT OF A PIRATE

His name alone—Blackbeard—made sailors' blood run cold, for he was the most ruthless pirate ever to sail the high seas. For a few years in the early 1700's, Blackbeard terrorized the Caribbean Sea and the Carolina coast. Then his luck turned. In June 1718, his flagship, the *Queen Anne's Revenge,* ran aground on a sandbar and sank off North Carolina. Blackbeard survived, but just a few months later the pirate was cornered and killed by British soldiers.

For almost 280 years, the rotting hulk of the *Queen Anne's Revenge* lay under the murky coastal waters, its location known only to passing fish. Then, in March 1997, a team of marine archaeologists announced that they had found, off Beaufort, North Carolina, a wreck they were sure was that of Blackbeard's ship.

It was an exciting discovery. The archaeologists didn't expect to find chests of pirate gold aboard—Blackbeard and his crew would have had time to get valuables off the ship before it went down. But the searchers did hope to find treasure of another sort: information.

By the fall of 2007, the searchers had recovered and restored more than 2,000 artifacts, from cannons to everyday items such as bottles and pewter plates. Archaeologists hoped that these artifacts would yield the information they were looking for. There are scores of tales and legends about Blackbeard and other pirates, but little is known about their real lives.

THE GOLDEN AGE OF PIRACY

A Spanish galleon, carrying a cargo of silver, is bound for home when a strange ship approaches. Is it friend or foe? The galleon's lookout can't tell. The ship sails closer, and then suddenly a flag rises to the top of her mast—a black flag, bearing a skull and crossbones. Pirates!

There have been pirates as long as people have been traveling in ships, and there are still pirates in some parts of the world. But the pirates most people in North America think of preyed on ships in the Caribbean Sea and Atlantic Ocean from the mid-1600's through the 1700's. At the start of that golden age of piracy, Spain controlled an empire in the Americas. Ships crossed the Caribbean and the Atlantic, carrying the riches of the New World back to Spain. Soon, English, French, and other European sailors settled in the Caribbean area and began to loot the Spanish ships. These sailors were called buccaneers.

In those days, nations that were at war often licensed private ships to attack enemy vessels. The people who served on these ships were known as privateers. And while buccaneers had no formal licenses, their actions were often supported by their governments. However, both privateers and buccaneers often crossed the line into piracy, seizing *any* ship that came within their grasp.

Some pirates were former navy sailors or deserters who "jumped ship" to escape harsh conditions. Some had lost their jobs on land and turned to crime. Piracy seemed to offer easy money and wild living, and it was easier to escape capture at sea than on land. Pirates faced harsh punishment, usually hanging. But only a few of them were ever caught.

In books and movies, pirates are bloodthirsty villains or swashbuckling romantic heroes. Neither picture is correct, historians say. New evidence from the ocean floor is helping to change some of the ideas people have long held about pirates. Much of the evidence comes from the wreck of the *Whydah,* a pirate ship that sank in 1717 off Cape Cod and was discovered in 1984.

Pirates seldom, if ever, buried treasure or made their victims "walk the plank." Piracy was certainly violent, but it wasn't as murderous as people have come to believe. Some pirates were fierce criminals who tortured and killed their victims. But most wanted to capture valuable ships, not sink them. Prisoners might be set ashore or invited to join the pirate crew. When a pirate was known for mercy, ships were more likely to surrender without a fight. Still, those who didn't give up when they saw the "Jolly Roger"—the black pirate flag usually showing a skull and crossbones—had to be prepared to fight.

Pirates had a strict society, with its own rules and quite a bit of democracy. On many ships, the crew elected the captain. Crews signed on for a share of the loot, and shares were measured out meticulously. But piracy didn't always pay well. Instead of piles of gold doubloons, the booty might be a cargo of cotton, or some supplies for the ship.

Blackbeard (right) was said to be one of the cruelest pirates ever to brandish a cutlass. And like other pirates, he devised his own flag (inset). While it didn't show the usual skull and crossbones, his flag was a dreaded sight to sailors.

This replica of Blackbeard's flagship, the *Queen Anne's Revenge,* is on display at the Maritime Research Institute in Beaufort, North Carolina.

Pirates were considered criminals, but some became legends. Henry Morgan's adventures were so celebrated that he was knighted and made lieutenant governor of Jamaica. Fame didn't help William Kidd, though, who was captured and hanged in 1701. Bartholomew Roberts (Black Bart) was known for his plumed hats and strict rules—he frowned on drinking, gambling, and swearing. John Avery, called Long Ben, stole a fortune on the seas but died without a doubloon. And, of course, there was Blackbeard.

THE NOTORIOUS BLACKBEARD

By all accounts, Blackbeard was one of the cruelest pirates ever to wave a pistol. Actually, Blackbeard carried six pistols, draped across his chest. In battle, he stuck lighted cannon wicks under the brim of his hat, so that his head was wreathed in smoke. He boasted of torturing his prisoners, kept his crew on their toes by firing randomly at them, and was said to drink a mixture of rum and gunpowder.

Blackbeard's real name was Edward Teach. He was nicknamed for his long black beard, which he

sometimes wore in braids. Teach was born in England, perhaps in Bristol, but his early life is a mystery. He was a privateer in the Caribbean in the early 1700's, when Britain was at war with France and Spain. After the war ended in 1713, he turned to piracy. Although his first known raid was made in 1716, historians think he was probably seizing ships long before that.

Among his prizes was a French merchant ship that he turned into his flagship, outfitting it with 40 cannons and renaming it the *Queen Anne's Revenge.* A fleet of smaller vessels was also under his command. With these ships, Blackbeard terrorized the Caribbean and the coasts of Virginia and the Carolinas, attacking towns as well as ships. He based his ships in North Carolina and kept them safe by sharing his spoils with that colony's governor.

After the *Queen Anne's Revenge* sank in 1718, Blackbeard turned his attention to the North Carolina coast. He demanded supplies from planters and tolls from passing ships. Since their governor wouldn't help them, North Car-

An 8-foot-long cannon was pulled from the underwater excavation site of the *Queen Anne's Reveng*e in October 2007. A pewter syringe (inset) was recovered earlier.

Modern-Day Pirates

Blackbeard. Black Bart. Captain Kidd. Sir Henry Morgan. These pirates who terrified travelers on the high seas during the 1600's and 1700's are long gone. But pirates are still operating in the 21st century. Not many people know their names, but they are just as terrifying as the pirates of long ago.

Experts estimate that modern-day pirates—who use speedboats, not sailing ships—hijack more than $10 billion worth of goods a year! The booty? Oil, gas, foodstuff, and everything else carried by commercial ships. In addition, the ships themselves and their crews are sometimes ransomed.

Today's pirates operate around the world. Major trouble spots include the waters around Indonesia in Asia; Nigeria and Somalia in Africa; the port of Chittagong, Bangladesh, in Asia; and the port of Santos, Brazil, in South America.

Tracking and keeping records of the pirates is the job of the International Maritime Bureau (IMB). Chasing and catching them is mostly the job of the countries where the pirates operate. But the United States is also actively involved, using U.S. Navy high-tech guided missile destroyers. That's a far cry from the

A U.S. Navy destroyer follows a pirate vessel in the Indian Ocean, off the eastern coast of Somalia. The American sailors boarded the ship and seized a cache of small arms.

1790's, when U.S. Navy frigates, small sailing ships, battled Barbary Coast pirates in the Mediterranean Sea. In late 2007, U.S. ships went to the aid of Japanese and Korean vessels being attacked by pirates off the coast of Somalia. In the first nine months of the year there were 198 reported attacks, 24 more than during the same period in 2006. It seemed that modern-day pirates were getting bolder.

olinians turned to Virginia's governor. He sent British troops, who caught up with the pirate on Ocracoke Island on November 22, 1718. There, Blackbeard was killed in hand-to-hand fighting.

SUNKEN TREASURE

The discovery of the *Queen Anne's Revenge* came after a ten-year-long search. Archaeologists consulted old documents, including reports by witnesses of the ship's sinking, to narrow down the location. Then they combed the water off Beaufort with an underwater metal detector.

In November 1996, they found what they were looking for—the ship's 40 metal cannons gave its location away. Divers quickly confirmed the find: The ship was sitting under just 20 feet (6 meters) of water. "If you could have

seen through that dirty water, it was right there," one of the searchers said.

The search team brought up still more artifacts that pointed to the identity of the ship—a ship's bell with the date 1709, the brass barrel of a blunderbuss, a cannonball. By 2007, many of the ship's cannons had been brought up and restored. Other retrieved items included navigational instruments and four anchors. There were many smaller pieces, too, including dishes, bottles, jewelry, small arms, straight pins, a tobacco pipe, a button, and even gold dust.

The archaeologists expect to bring up tens of thousands of individual artifacts by the time the excavation is completed, which may be by 2010. They hope that as the sea gives the items up, they will be able to learn the truth behind the legend of Blackbeard.

Gym class is going high-tech! In 2007 about 2,000 schools in some 35 states had "exergaming" fitness centers like this one at Kirksey Middle School in Rogers, Arkansas. The centers let kids exercise by doing something they love—playing video games. These games are a good workout because players control the action with their whole bodies, using motion sensors, touch-sensitive floor mats, and other devices.

CAREERS WITH PLANTS

Do you love growing things—flowers, trees, and plants of all kinds? Do you have a "green thumb"—that is, do plants grow well when you care for them? Maybe you would like to make plants your career.

Perhaps you would enjoy developing new strains of plants, caring for trees, or arranging and selling flowers. There are many other careers that involve plants, too. These careers are especially appealing because most of the people who work with plants have jobs they truly enjoy, often outdoors or in pleasant surroundings such as in greenhouses and nurseries.

PLANT SCIENCE

If you are fascinated by plants and curious about the way plants grow, perhaps you should be a **botanist,** a scientist who studies plants. Botanists usually specialize in a particular aspect of plant life, and there's quite a range of specialties.

Some botanists focus on certain types of plants, such as ferns or flowers. Some study plant nutrition and photosynthesis—the process by which plants make their own food. Some study plant genetics—the way traits are passed from one generation to another. Through genetic engineering, they may try to improve a plant by altering these traits.

Some botanists focus on roots, stems, and leaves. Botanists called systemists study the relationships between plants. Paleobotanists study the fossil remains of plants that died out many millions of years ago.

A four-year degree in botany is a starting point for these careers. Most botanists have at least a master's degree. Those who teach or direct research hold doctorates. Botanists work at colleges and universities, government agencies, and private companies.

HORTICULTURE

The study of horticulture includes growing plants, improving them, and developing new varieties, or cultivars, of plants. It's a broad field that includes many different kinds of **horticulturists.**

Research horticulturists may try to develop new plant cultivars that resist disease or stand up to drought or cold. They also study the ways in which a plant's handling and its environment—soil, climate, and other conditions—affect the way it grows. Other horticulturists are more involved in the ways plants are used. Some work with farmers to find ways to increase crop yields or quality—to produce crisper apples and sweeter corn, for example.

Plant lovers have a wide range of career choices. Above: Botanists are scientists who study different aspects of plant life. Some focus on roots, stems, and leaves. Right: A horticulturist specializes in growing and improving plants and developing new varieties.

Some horticulturists specialize in flowering plants or ornamental plants. Their focus is on plants that beautify the landscape. They cross plants to develop cultivars—perhaps a rose in a new shade of pink, or a dwarf variety of a shrub. They also collect plants from around the world, evaluate them, and introduce them to new areas.

Most horticulturists have four-year college degrees. Many have advanced degrees. College programs often combine science, agriculture, and business courses.

Horticulturists work for botanical gardens and for large commercial nurseries. Some work as agents for government agencies, such as the Cooperative Extension Service, which has branches all over the United States. They provide advice to farmers and gardeners. Government horticulturists may also direct the planting and care of trees, shrubs, and flowers along highways and in parks. Many horticulturists run their own businesses, growing plants for sale or acting as consultants for growers.

Up on the Rooftop

A career with plants could take you to high places—the roofs of buildings! Green roofs, sometimes called eco-roofs, are the latest trend in building design. These roofs are covered with plants.

People have enjoyed rooftop gardens for centuries. But the green roof is a new idea, meant to benefit the environment. A green roof can provide a habitat for insects, birds, and other animals. The plants and soil soak up rain, reducing stormwater runoff from the roof. And the plants soak up airborne pollutants and carbon dioxide, one of the "greenhouse" gases blamed for global warming. Green roofs are good insulators, so they save energy. Because they stay cooler than traditional roofs, they also help to reduce the "heat island" effect in cities. This effect occurs when asphalt and concrete bake in the sun and then radiate heat into the air.

They are usually planted in a lightweight growing medium made up of soil and gravel and other materials.

Green roofs are turning up in cities across North America. About 7 million square feet (650,300 square meters) of rooftops were planted in 2007. Ten acres of succulents cover the roof of a Ford truck plant in Dearborn, Michigan. Grasses and sedum top the Ballard Library in Seattle, Washington. On top of Chicago's City Hall, grasses and wild rye wave in the breeze. Flowering chives and dianthus grow on the Bronx County Hall of Justice

A "living roof" of native plants is being installed on the new California Academy of Sciences in San Francisco, set to open in 2008. Green roofs provide many environmental benefits.

Designing a green roof is usually a group effort. Architects and engineers design the roof to be extra strong, to support the weight of plants and soil, with good drainage and a waterproof membrane as protection from water. Landscape architects and contractors design the plantings and choose and install the plants. Growing plants on top of a roof is challenging because rooftops are usually dry and windy. Grasses and succulents, which need little water, often work well.

in New York City, and native savannah plants top the Gap office building in San Bruno, California. Native plants are also being installed on the new California Academy of Sciences building in San Francisco's Golden Gate Park.

Besides their environmental benefits, green roofs have another advantage. They provide park space where people can relax high above the city streets. As the green-roof movement spreads, there will be a growing need for specialists who can design, install, and maintain these special places.

Above: A landscape architect begins by studying and analyzing the site. On large projects, these architects usually work with building architects and engineers. Left: A landscape designer is creating teddy-bear topiaries for a client.

Nursery managers don't all have degrees in horticulture, but some training helps. Nursery managers grow plants—trees, shrubs, flowering plants, and vegetable plants—for sale to landscapers and individual gardeners. Most also sell garden supplies and equipment. A nursery manager needs a good head for business, an ability to manage workers and deal with customers—and, of course, a green thumb. Nursery managers and horticulturists alike can expect to get their hands dirty and do some physical labor in the course of their work.

LANDSCAPE DESIGN AND MAINTENANCE

Plants are raw materials for **landscape architects** and **landscape designers.** These specialists design parks and grounds to make them beautiful and useful, all in keeping with the natural environment. Some are specialists in certain types of design, such as historical gardens.

Landscape architects usually work alongside building architects and engineers on large projects, such as public parks and highways, shopping malls and housing develop-

Working with flowers isn't always a bed of roses. The demanding job of a floral designer requires a good eye for color, a flair for design, and plenty of expertise to produce lovely floral arrangements.

ments, or corporate and industrial parks. They begin by studying the site to learn all they can about the soil, the way the land is formed, and the existing plants and buildings.

Back in the office, the landscape architect prepares plans showing how the site will be graded; how buildings, roadways, walks, terraces, and plantings will be placed; and details such as drainage pipes and utility lines. The plans specify materials and types of plants. The landscape architect may also use models or computer simulations to show clients what the project will look like. When construction begins, the landscape architect inspects and sometimes directs the work.

Most states require landscape architects to be licensed. For this, they must pass a test. But before they can take the test, applicants must have a four- or five-year degree in the field and one to four years of experience working with a licensed landscape architect. College pro-

grams in landscape architecture include courses in science, horticulture, landscape design, engineering, surveying, and graphics.

Landscape designers do some of the same work as landscape architects. But they usually work on smaller projects, for individual homes or small businesses. No license is required, and many landscape designers complete two-year degree programs rather than the four- or five-year programs required for landscape architects.

Landscape contractors carry out the plans of architects and designers. They plan the steps in the operation, obtain the materials, and schedule the work. The contractor's own crew of landscapers may do some of the work, perhaps planting shrubs or sodding lawns. Subcontractors may handle other aspects, such as grading and paving.

Because plants are living, they grow and change. Sometimes they are attacked by diseases or pests and die. So finished projects must be maintained. Parks, college campuses, botanical gardens, golf courses, and other places with a lot of landscaping employ **grounds managers** for this. The grounds manager sets up a schedule for mowing, pruning, fertilizing, raking, and other regular jobs. Managers also choose plants to replace plants that die. They may do the maintenance work themselves or direct a crew of landscapers.

Landscapers get their training on the job. But landscape contractors and grounds managers often have two-year or four-year degrees. Courses in plant science, landscape design and engineering, and business are helpful. Many states require landscapers and grounds managers who use pesticides to be certified. For this, they must pass a test to show that they know how to use these chemicals safely.

Gary Strobel: Plant Biologist

Plant biologist Gary Strobel has traveled the world to collect clippings and cuttings from plants. But his most exciting discoveries have been made after returning to his laboratory at Montana State University. His work there has led to the development of important new drugs and other useful compounds.

Strobel's work was featured in a documentary, *Jewels of the Jungle,* shown on public television in 2007. The film showed him at work in the forests of Australia, Peru, and Bolivia as he searched for plants that might yield new "wonder drugs."

Much of Strobel's research has focused on the relationships between plants and microscopic organisms called endophytes. Endophytes are microbes—bacteria and fungi—that live inside plants. This research has uncovered new sources for medicines, including the drug taxol, which fights cancer. Taxol was originally discovered in the Pacific yew tree. Pacific yews are rare and slow-growing, so the drug was scarce at first. Then Strobel found that a fungus inside yew needles produced taxol. When scientists grew the fungus in the lab, they had a ready supply of the drug.

Strobel has also discovered new antibiotics and other substances useful in medicine, farming, and industry. For example, in 1999 he collected samples of about a dozen different fungi from a Central American rain forest. But when he placed them together in a container in his lab, all but one type died. Strobel named the survivor *Muscodor albus,* which means "stinky white fungus" in Latin. This fungus produced a gas that killed the others. Strobel and his co-researchers analyzed the gas and identified the different chemical compounds in it. Then they re-created it, using those chemicals, and tested it against lots of different microbes. The gas killed nearly all of them. Now it's being developed as a pesticide to protect crops from some common kinds of fungal pests. It may also be used as a safe and natural way to kill microbes that cause decay in fruits and vegetables when they are shipped or stored.

Thousands of other kinds of fungi may be waiting to be discovered. Some may hold cures for AIDS, malaria, or other major diseases. Gary Strobel is hunting for them.

Many large flower nurseries are located in parts of South America and other areas where the conditions are right for flowers year-round. **Flower importers** buy the flowers and bring them to the United States and Canada. They make sure that you can buy roses in December—no matter where you live. Wholesalers, brokers, and importers need good knowledge of their market. They must know what flowers will be in demand when, where to find them, and how to transport them undamaged to florists.

Florists, or floral designers, sell cut flowers to the public. They also design arrangements using fresh, dried, and artificial flowers and sometimes potted plants. A florist may put together a simple bouquet or design elaborate floral decorations for a wedding or some other occasion. Many florists run their own shops. Others work for large shops that employ several designers.

Florists need a good eye for color and design. Flower-arranging skills are often learned on the job, but courses in biology, art, and business help. Some two-year colleges and commercial schools offer training in flower-shop management, floral design, and related subjects.

Arborists are tree specialists, and sometimes tree care can be dangerous. If arborists need to climb a tree to inspect and trim branches, they use special climbing ropes and shoes with sharp cleats.

WORKING WITH FLOWERS

Growing, arranging, and selling cut and dried flowers are other possibilities for people who love plants, especially those with a flair for design. **Floriculturists**—flower growers—operate commercial nurseries that produce cut flowers. Their work and training is like that of other horticulturists and nursery managers. At just the right moment, the flowers they grow are cut, sorted, bunched, boxed, and shipped in refrigerated containers to wholesalers and brokers, who in turn sell them to flower shops and other retail outlets.

WORKING WITH TREES

Arborists are tree specialists. They plant trees, transplant them, and remove them when that's necessary. Arborists also care for trees—which can involve many different jobs. Trees may need pruning and trimming. Heavy branches may need to be braced with cables. A tree may need to be fertilized or treated for diseases and pests.

Some of this work is hard and dangerous. Climbing 50 feet (15 meters) into a tree to inspect or trim a branch requires good balance, strength, and steady nerves. Arborists work in crews of three or four, with those on the ground helping climbers in the tree. The climbers use special equipment, such as climbing ropes and belts and shoes with sharp cleats.

Many arborists learn on the job. But those who supervise crews or run their own businesses often have more formal education. They may take a two-year vocational program or study a related field, such as grounds management or landscape design. Like landscapers, those who handle pesticides generally must be certified.

OTHER CAREERS WITH PLANTS

Farming is the oldest career that involves plants. Farmers grow food crops, such as wheat, corn, and vegetables; and other types of crops, such as cotton and hay. Today many farms are big businesses, and farmers have degrees from agricultural colleges.

Interiorscaping is one of the newest plant careers. Interiorscapers choose and place plants in offices, hotels, and other buildings. They may sell the plants or lease them and maintain them while they are in place.

If you have a knack for writing or photography, you might consider combining that skill with your love of plants. Many publications cover gardening and landscape design, and they need **writers** and **photographers** to prepare material.

Forestry, soil conservation, and many other careers also involve plants. If your green thumb is itching, you have plenty of choices!

Getting Started

If you are interested in a career with plants, learn all you can about them, and get some experience in caring for plants. Plant a garden. Ask friends and neighbors if they need a plant-sitter—someone to care for houseplants and gardens when they go on vacation. Ask local florists or nurseries if they could use part-time help.

Here are some organizations that can give you more information:

Botanical Society of America—P.O. Box 299, St. Louis, MO 63166-0299 (*www.botany.org/bsa/careers*)

Royal Botanical Gardens—680 Plains Road West, Hamilton/Burlington, Ontario L7T 4H4 (*www.rbg.ca*)

American Nursery & Landscape Association—1000 Vermont Avenue, NW, Suite 300, Washington, D.C. 20005-4914 (*www.anla.org*)

Canadian Nursery Landscape Association— R.R.#4, Stn. Main, 7856 Fifth Line South, Milton, Ontario L9T 2X8 (*www.canadanursery.com*)

American Institute of Floral Designers—20 Light Street, Baltimore, MD 21230-3816 (*www.aifd.org*)

Canadian Horticultural Council—9 Corvus Court, Ottawa, Ontario K2E 7Z4 (*www.hortcouncil.ca/chc-main.htm*)

American Society of Landscape Architects—636 Eye Street, NW, Washington, DC 20001-3736 (*www.asla.org*)

Canadian Society of Landscape Architects—P.O. Box 13594, Ottawa, Ontario K2K 1X6 (*www.csla.ca/contactus.php*)

2007 KIDS' CHOICE AWARDS

Oscars are awarded to movie stars. Emmys go to TV stars. Grammys are won by singers and musicians. And ESPY's go to star athletes. But who can get an "Orange Blimp" award? All of the above. The Blimp is a special award that goes to people in all these fields.

The 2007 Blimps were awarded on March 31 by Nickelodeon, the children's network, during its 20th annual Kids' Choice Awards. The awards were presented in Los Angeles, in a star-studded ceremony that was telecast live. The show was seen in more than 205 million households in the United States, Europe,

Justin Timberlake (top) hosted the 2007 Kids' Choice Awards. Numerous celebs were super-slimed throughout the wacky funfest—including Tobey Maguire and Steve Carell (above).

Asia, Latin America, Australia, and Israel. And the winners were picked by a record-breaking 40 million kids who voted online and on their cell phones (via text messaging).

Dakota Fanning *(Charlotte's Web)* accepts the Blimp for Favorite Movie Actress.

As always, the show was part spoof and part audience scream-fest. Winners in 16 categories received Blimps—and the really lucky ones went home covered in green slime. In fact, slime flew in all directions during the event—dousing Mandy Moore, Jackie Chan, Steve Carell, and Tobey Maguire, to name just a few. Show host Justin Timberlake got the green goo, too, as did daredevil stuntman Ron Jones, who bungee-jumped 23 stories into a giant tank of green slime. And in the first-ever interactive sliming, viewers voted to bring the show to an end with a geyser of slime erupting from beneath the stage and drenching actor Vince Vaughn.

Burping was more thunderous than ever, as two-time Burp Award winner Justin Timberlake held a belch-off with all 12,000 people in the audience. It was no contest! And actor and comedian Ben Stiller won the "Wannabe Award" as the celebrity role model kids most "want to be."

THE WINNERS

Category	Winner
Favorite Movie	*Pirates of the Caribbean: Dead Man's Chest*
Favorite Movie Actress	Dakota Fanning *(Charlotte's Web)*
Favorite Movie Actor	Adam Sandler *(Click)*
Favorite Animated Movie	*Happy Feet*
Favorite Voice from an Animated Movie	Queen Latifah *(Ice Age: The Meltdown)*
Favorite Music Group	Black Eyed Peas
Favorite Female Singer	Beyoncé
Favorite Male Singer	Justin Timberlake
Favorite Song	"Irreplaceable" (Beyoncé)
Favorite TV Show	*American Idol*
Favorite TV Actress	Miley Cyrus *(Hannah Montana)*
Favorite TV Actor	Drake Bell *(Drake & Josh)*
Favorite Cartoon	*SpongeBob SquarePants*
Favorite Athlete	Shaquille O'Neal
Favorite Video Game	"SpongeBob SquarePants: Creature from the Krusty Krab"
Favorite Book	*Harry Potter* series by J. K. Rowling

KID STUFF

What makes you happy? Polltakers asked that question of 1,280 young people ages 13 to 24 in April 2007. And the answers were a surprise to anyone who thinks young people can't wait to get out on their own. Spending time with family ranked first with about 20 percent of the young people in the poll, more than any other answer. Closely following on the happiness scale was spending time with friends or with a significant other.

The poll was sponsored by the Associated Press and MTV. More than 100 questions were asked. Here are some findings:

- About 65 percent of the young people surveyed said they were happy with the way their lives were going.
- Almost 75 percent said their relationship with their parents made them happy. And more than half listed a parent as one of their heroes.
- Young people who were in a romantic relationship weren't always happier than those who weren't. But 92 percent of those polled said they wanted to get married someday.
- More than half said that religion was important in their lives.
- Almost no one said that money made them happiest. But almost half said that having more money would make them happier.

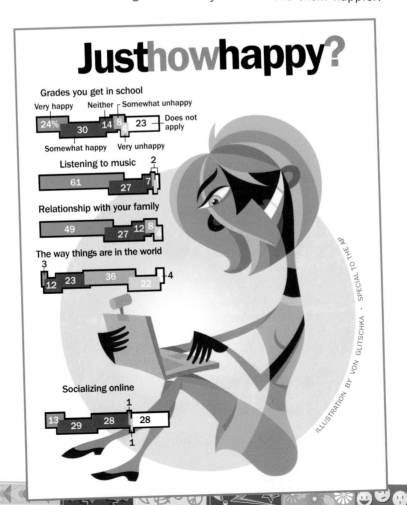

Just how happy?

Grades you get in school

Very happy — Neither — Somewhat unhappy
24% | 30 | 14 | 8 | 4 | 23 — Does not apply
Somewhat happy — Very unhappy

Listening to music
61 | 27 | 7 | 2

Relationship with your family
49 | 27 | 12 | 8

The way things are in the world
3
12 | 23 | 36 | 22 | 4

Socializing online
13 | 29 | 28 | 1 | 28 | 1

ILLUSTRATION BY VON GLITSCHKA · SPECIAL TO THE AP

CAITLIN SNARING
WASHINGTON

Caitlin Snaring, 14, of Redmond, Washington, won the 2007 National Geographic Bee. She was the second girl ever to win the contest, run by the National Geographic Society. More than five million kids in grades 4 to 8 took part in local geo bees in 2007. Fifty-five state and territorial champions went to Washington, D.C., for the national contest on May 22-23. Ten advanced to the finals, moderated by TV game-show host Alex Trebek. Caitlin, a home-schooled eighth-grader, studied 60 hours a week to prepare. "I saw every answer in my head," she said. She aced this final question: "What city, divided by a river of the same name, was the imperial capital of Vietnam for more than a century?" Her answer (Hue) brought her the top award, a $25,000 college scholarship.

America's top teen star? In 2007 that might well have been **Zac Efron.** The star of the hugely successful TV movie *High School Musical* (2006) thrilled fans with two new movies during the year. In his first big-screen role, he played teen heartthrob Link Larkin in the movie *Hairspray.* And he returned as Troy Bolton, basketball star and most popular guy at East High School, in *High School Musical 2.* Some 17.2 million viewers tuned in when the sequel aired on the Disney and Family channels in August, making it the most watched basic cable program ever. Zac, who turned 20 in October, is from Arroyo Grande, California. He got his start in musical theater and later had roles on *Summerland* and other television shows. But *High School Musical* made him a star.

Most 8-year-olds don't play with pythons. But for **Bindi Irwin,** snuggling with snakes is perfectly normal. Bindi is the daughter of Australian naturalist Steve Irwin, who became famous through his TV show *The Crocodile Hunter.* He died in an encounter with a stingray while filming an episode of the show in 2006. But Bindi and her mom, Terri Irwin, decided to carry on his work of teaching people about wild animals. Bindi's own TV show, *Bindi: The Jungle Girl,* premiered on the Discovery Kids cable network in June 2007. On the show, Bindi had fun with all sorts of creatures, from koalas to elephants, while explaining how animals need respect and protection. She had started work on the show with her dad before his death, and he appeared in some scenes.

Her parents named her Destiny Hope because they hoped she would accomplish great things. They gave her the nickname Smiley, which was soon shortened to Miley, because she was always smiling. And in 2007, **Miley Cyrus,** 15, was the star that tweens most wanted to see. Miley was a huge hit on her Disney Channel series *Hannah Montana,* which premiered in 2006. She played Miley Stewart, an ordinary girl who has a secret career as a pop star named Hannah Montana. On the show, Hannah's career is guided by her dad—played by Miley's real dad, country singer Billy Ray Cyrus. Miley has also released two hit albums as Hannah Montana. And her 2007 Hannah Montana concert tour sold out as soon as tickets were available.

She was just 11 in 2007, but **Abigail Breslin** had credits that many adult film stars would envy. She was nominated for an Academy Award as best supporting actress for her role as a beauty-pageant hopeful in the 2006 movie *Little Miss Sunshine*. (Right: Abigail in that film.) She appeared in a new movie, *No Reservations,* and finished work on another, *Definitely, Maybe.* And she landed the title role in *Kit Kittredge: An American Girl Mystery,* a movie based on the popular American Girls dolls. Her character is a girl growing up during the Great Depression of the 1930's. Abigail, who is from New York, collects the dolls. She's been acting in films since 2002. Her older brother Spencer is also an actor, and they have appeared together in several movies.

What if the world were full of people who looked normal but were really mutants with amazing superpowers? That was the idea behind one of 2007's hit TV series, *Heroes.* And the show launched the career of a new star—**Hayden Panettiere,** who played Claire Bennett, a cheerleader with self-healing powers. "She constantly has body parts falling off, getting chewed up or popped out—so it's been fun," said the 18-year-old actress. Hayden, originally from Palisades, New York, is a show-business pro. She started appearing in commercials before she was 1 year old. Later she acted in soap operas, prime-time TV shows, and more than a dozen movies. She also did voice-overs in *A Bug's Life* and other films. And her first album is set for release in 2008.

Mary Masterman, 17, won the top award—a $100,000 scholarship—in the 2007 Intel Science Talent Search (STS). STS is considered the top high-school science contest in the United States. It's sometimes called the "junior Nobel Prize." Past winners include six Nobel laureates.

A senior at Westmoore High School in Oklahoma City, Oklahoma, Mary won the award by building a low-cost spectrograph. A spectrograph is an instrument that analyzes light to detect the characteristics or "fingerprints" of different materials. Spectrographs are widely used in research and industry. They can identify the elements that make up distant stars, detect the presence of explosives or drugs, and even help determine the age of a piece of artwork. Accurate spectrographs can cost as much as $100,000.

Mary set out to design one that would be more affordable. She built hers for about $300, using an inexpensive laser, lenses, a camera, and aluminum tubing. "I had to keep coming up with creative ways to adjust or change something," she said. "It took three months to build and another three months before it actually functioned properly." She plans a career as a physicist or a chemist.

More than 1,700 high-school seniors nationwide entered the 2007 Intel STS. Of those, 40 finalists were invited to Washington, D.C., where they presented their projects at the National Institute of Science in March. In all, 10 students took home awards that included laptop computers and cash prizes.

"S-E-R-R-E-F-I-N-E." **Evan O'Dorney**, 13, rattled off those letters to win the 2007 Scripps National Spelling Bee in Washington, D.C, on May 31. By correctly spelling his final word (a term for a type of small forceps) in the contest, he won $35,000 in cash, a $5,000 scholarship, and a $2,500 savings bond. This was the third appearance in the national finals for Evan, an eighth-grader from Danville, California, who is home schooled. In 2006 he tied for 14th place. But in 2007 he outspelled 286 other contestants over two days of competition. (Nate Gartke, 13, of Canada, placed second.) Although Evan is a spelling whiz, he prefers math and music. "The spelling is just a bunch of memorization," he said after his victory.

First it was a family joke. Then it was a low-budget movie. And in 2007 *The Naked Brothers Band* was a hit cable television show, propelling brothers **Nat and Alex Wolff** to stardom. On the show, Nat, 12, and Alex, 9, played brothers who belong to a kids' rock group—and in real life, that's what they actually are. Their mom, actress and producer Polly Draper, made a "mockumentary" (a spoof documentary) about them in 2004. The cable network Nickelodeon aired the film and decided to base a sitcom on it. There has also been a TV movie, *The Naked Brothers Band: Battle of the Bands.* Nat and Alex write their own songs. Their dad, Michael Wolff, plays their on-screen father and doubles as the show's music director. And mom writes and directs most of the episodes.

WWW.COOLSITES

Put on your explorer's hat and visit the Dzanga-Sangha rain forest, the ancient city of Petra, or a dinosaur dig in Mongolia. . . .Find out what makes your hands prune up when soaked in water. . . .Mix together chemicals and build rockets. . . .Follow the adventures of a city girl who reluctantly goes off to camp. You can do all these things on the Internet's World Wide Web—one of the coolest places to be these days. If your computer is connected to an online service, visit the four Web sites described on these pages. Type in the address exactly as shown, and in seconds you'll be at the site.

Ology
http://ology.amnh.org/index.html

Follow your curiosity as you explore topics ranging from ancient stardust to the deep blue sea to the world's #1 genius. Discover what's in your cold medicine, how chocolate gets its flavor, and why the cookie-cutter shark has a weird green belly. Meet ichthyologists, paleontologists, and other "ologists." You too can become an Ologist, which will allow you to collect hundreds of colorful, informative cards; create a project using your collection; and then enter your project into the Hall of Fame. Under "Stuff to Do" you'll learn how to mint coins, create a make-believe fossil dig site, and bake some cosmic cookies!

Ask Dr. Universe
http://www.wsu.edu/DrUniverse/

Have you ever wondered how we take the Earth's temperature, why hair turns gray, or why we don't just print enough money to pay off the national debt? If you've got a question, about anything from cow belching to crystal glasses, ask Dr. Universe. This curious cat has a whole university campus of experts to call on. In addition to submitting questions, you can read answers to questions posed by others—or by Dr. Universe herself. There are also links to lots of other great sites on the Web.

The Hobby Shop
http://www.knowitall.org/hobbyshop/siteAgentMain.html

Cursor your way into a laboratory and do some experimenting. Find out what happens when you mix the liquids sodium carbonate and calcium nitrate. Build a conductivity tester and use it to test the ability of cooking oil, salt water, and other common substances to conduct electricity. Look through dissecting and compound microscopes at fruit flies and various kinds of human tissue. Then head outdoors with a catapult and some rockets that you've designed. How high will your rockets rise? Can you correctly adjust the catapult to hit five different targets?

Fun Brain
http://www.funbrain.com/kidscenter.html

Put your reading, memory, and math skills to use as you play games, create Mad Libs, and follow the adventures of a city girl who is more interested in fresh sushi than in fresh air: Will she survive eight weeks at a lakeside camp with moldy shower stalls and gross spiders? You'll need some quick reflexes when you enter the Math Arcade and Funbrain Arcade. Choose your skill level, then beat the current game to unlock the next game and advance. Can you win all the games in a series? Or perhaps you would rather just relax and read "The Diary of a Wimpy Boy," about his adventures at school and at home.

Kids of all ages are the stars at Circus Smirkus. They learn circus skills at a special camp, and some go on to perform in an actual traveling circus show!

CIRCUS SMIRKUS

Every summer a few hundred lucky young people "run away" to a special circus. They share the fun of Circus Smirkus. Kids have always been the biggest fans of the circus, but at Circus Smirkus they are also the stars!

Kids learn circus skills at Smirkus Camp, in Vermont. Those with solid skills can become Smirkus Troupers, touring and performing in many towns. In all, about 375 kids take part in the camp and show each summer. During the rest of the year, Circus Smirkus often sends artists-in-residence to elementary schools, where they introduce kids to basic circus skills.

Circus Smirkus celebrated its 20th birthday in 2007. It was founded in 1987 in Greensboro, Vermont, by Rob Mermin, a former circus performer and an instructor of mime, clowning, and other circus skills. Since then, 32 Smirkus graduates have gone on to professional circus careers.

SMIRKUS CAMP

★ Smirkling Camp is a two-day session for children 6 to 8 years old. They get to try basic circus skills like spinning plates, tumbling, and clowning, and can even "pie" the coaches!

★ Young people ages 8 to 15 can attend one- and two-week sleepaway sessions. The campers in these sessions learn acrobatics, juggling, and balance skills. They are also introduced to aerial equipment such as the trapeze, and they learn clowning, dancing, and mime.

★ Advanced camp is for teens 14 to 18 who already have good circus skills. They must audition for this camp—there are only 45 places.

Each camp session ends with a show in which campers demonstrate the skills they have learned for family and friends.

UNDER THE BIG TOP

Kids with excellent skills can try out to become Smirkus Troupers. Each year, the Troupers tour in a real circus show. For two months, they live the circus life, sometimes putting on more than 70 shows in some 15 towns, in a 750-seat Big Top tent. Usually there are about 25 Troupers in the show, backed by about 50 coaches, crew, and staff. They range in age from 10 to 18 years old. The younger Troupers are the stars, while the older Troupers take on supporting roles. Circus pros perform alongside the kids.

The Troupers do everything you would expect to see in a circus. They are acrobats and jugglers. They perform on the trapeze and

Skilled Smirkus performers: At right, the kids perform an aerial act high above the ring. Below, a youngster twirls 21 hula hoops!

RINGLING BROS. AND BARNUM & BAILEY COMBINED SHOWS

THE GREATEST ACTS FROM EVERY COUNTRY IN THE WORLD ASSEMBLED FOR THIS YEAR

History of the Circus

Circus shows have entertained people for more than 200 years. But the name "circus" goes back even further than that. Circus is a Latin word meaning "circle" or "ring." In ancient Rome, the Circus Maximus was an arena where chariot races and other exciting events were held.

The modern circus began in England. In 1768, Philip Astley, an English riding instructor, figured out how to ride standing on his horse's back while the horse cantered around a circle at a steady pace. He developed a show that featured this and other feats of skill and daring on horseback, performed in a circus ring. When he added clowning to the show, the modern circus was born. Before long, acts of all kinds joined the mix.

The first American circus was put on in Philadelphia, Pennsylvania, in 1785. George Washington, the nation's first president, became a circus fan. He was often in the audience at the Philadelphia circus of John Bill Ricketts. In 1797 he even sold his white horse, Jack, to Ricketts. Placed in a special stall, Jack became the first circus sideshow exhibit.

Circus shows grew in popularity and soon began to tour the country, traveling by wagon and, later, train. At each town, the circus put up its tent and put on its show. Often the circus announced its arrival with a colorful parade down the town's main street, led by a brass band or a steam calliope.

P. T. Barnum was one of the greatest showmen in American history. In 1871 he started a traveling circus he called "The Greatest Show on Earth." Barnum's shows were renowned for daring acts and exhibits such as the elephant Jumbo, billed as the largest in the world. Barnum's circus later joined with other shows. It became the famous Ringling Bros. and Barnum & Bailey Circus.

It takes many hours of practice (right) to learn how to properly perform the circus art of aerial silks. But for the circus performers who master the intricate acrobatics, the result is graceful aerial ballet (below).

vans, trucks, and trailers of the circus caravan. They look after props and even wash dishes.

Each year's show has a different theme. Superheroes, pirates, and the Wild West have been themes in the past. Many shows have been built around stories. The 2007 show, for example, presented a comical mystery, *The Zoot Suit Caper.* All the acts related to the theme and helped tell the story. There were colorful costumes and live music, too.

Kids who want to be in the show have to work hard on their skills. And even kids who have been Troupers before have to audition each year, to show that they have been improving and learning new skills. Only the best performers get to be part of the Big Top Tour.

other aerial equipment. And of course, they are clowns. All the kids in the Big Top Tour have chores outside the ring as well. They help raise the tent and set up bleachers before the show. After the show, they help take down the tent and pack everything into the

Many young people who take part in Circus Smirkus fall in love with the circus. A few may even think about becoming circus pros. But for most kids, their time at Circus Smirkus is a memory of great excitement and fun!

CREATIVITY

Like millions of young people around the world, two avid readers in Mesa, Arizona, grabbed their copies of Harry Potter and the Deathly Hallows *the moment it came out on July 21, 2007. The final book in J. K. Rowling's wildly popular series about a young wizard set sales records on its first day.*

"Bye, Harry!" Millions of fans around the world could barely wait to read the seventh and final book in the record-setting Harry Potter series.

THE MAGIC OF HARRY

On July 21, 2007, young people around the world flooded bookstores to grab copies of *Harry Potter and the Deathly Hallows,* the seventh and final volume in the wildly popular Harry Potter series. Millions of people had followed J. K. Rowling's tale of a young wizard since the first Harry Potter book came out in 1997. Now it was all coming to an end.

The series had become a phenomenon. More than 325 million copies of the previous six Harry Potter books had been sold worldwide. The books had outsold adult novels—a rarity in children's literature. They had been translated into 65 languages and sold in some 200 different countries and territories. Five had been made into movies. And *Harry Potter and the Deathly Hallows* set sales records on its first day out. In the United States alone, readers snapped up 8.3 million copies in the first 24 hours—about 5,700 books a minute!

UNDER A SPELL

What accounts for the magic of the Harry Potter books? Fantasy has always been popular with kids, and these books present a complete fantasy world—a magical society of witches and wizards that exists alongside the everyday world of Muggles (nonmagical folks). The wizarding world has its own government (the Ministry of Magic), shops (along Diagon Alley), and much more. Harry's school, the Hogwarts School of Witchcraft and Wizardry, is a magical version of an English boarding school. Students learn to cast spells, mix potions, and play Quidditch—a complicated sport played in the air, on broomsticks.

The series also has memorable characters and themes that young readers can relate to. It's the story of a battle between good and evil—Harry and his friends, on the side of good, against the evil Lord Voldemort and his

Rupert Grint, Daniel Radcliffe, and Emma Watson are honored at the Harry Potter Hand- , Foot- , and Wand-Print ceremony, in Hollywood, California, on July 9.

Phoenix, opened in theaters on July 11, 2007. It was a big event for fans—but it was soon overshadowed by the release of *Harry Potter and the Deathly Hallows.*

THE SERIES ENDS

The final Harry Potter book was the biggest publishing event of the year. Publishers and booksellers went to great lengths trying to keep the final plot a secret. There were a few last-minute "spoilers," but for the most part they succeeded.

Death Eaters. Harry is an orphan and, at first, an outcast who doesn't realize that he's a wizard. His magical abilities grow throughout the series, along with his knowledge of the role he must play in the fight. Voldemort's strength also grows, until he seems unstoppable.

J. K. Rowling, who wove these exciting tales, was unknown before the first book appeared. She wrote much of that book in cafes near her home in Edinburgh, Scotland, to escape her cold apartment and keep her newborn daughter warm. Several publishers rejected the manuscript. But once the book was published, it was an instant hit. The sales of the books, and the movies and merchandise based on them, have made Rowling one of Britain's wealthiest people—reportedly richer than Queen Elizabeth II.

The first movie came out in 2001. Daniel Radcliffe, a young British actor, starred as Harry. Two kids with little acting experience, Emma Watson and Rupert Grint, played his best friends, Hermione Granger and Ron Weasley. The young actors were 10 and 11 years old when they auditioned for their parts. They have stayed with the roles through the following movies, growing up just as their characters do in the films. In adult roles, the movies have featured major stars, including Ralph Fiennes as Voldemort and Alan Rickman as Snape.

The movie version of the fifth book in the series, *Harry Potter and the Order of the*

J. K. Rowling, author of the series, signs books for Potter fans at the premiere of *Harry Potter and the Order of the Phoenix* in London, England.

Many bookstores opened at midnight on July 21 to handle the rush of buyers they knew would appear. Fans lined up outside, many dressed as favorite characters from the series. Stores entertained the waiting buyers with special wizard-themed events, parties, and door prizes.

In some cities, there were even Potter-themed festivals before the book's release. Naperville, Illinois, staged a Harry Potter Weekend with costume contests, concerts, and outdoor screenings of the new Harry Potter

Seven Years at Hogwarts

Each book in J. K. Rowling's series follows Harry Potter through a year at school.

Year 1. *Harry Potter and the Sorcerer's Stone.* Harry is an unhappy 11-year-old orphan, living with his mean Muggle relatives, the Dursleys. Then he receives a letter inviting him to Hogwarts—a school unlike any other. Before long, Harry is learning to fly a broom and cast spells. He also has his first brush with the evil Lord Voldemort, who killed Harry's parents when he was an infant and then disappeared.

Harry Potter and the Chamber of Secrets

Harry Potter and the Sorcerer's Stone

Year 2. *Harry Potter and the Chamber of Secrets.* In their second year at school, Harry and his friends Ron and Hermione study Herbology and other magical musts. Harry struggles to please his Potions teacher, Professor Snape, who seems to have it in for him. But something worse than Snape is roaming the halls of Hogwarts—a monster, let loose by Voldemort, that is turning students to stone. Harry must find the mysterious Chamber of Secrets to stop it.

Year 3. *Harry Potter and the Prisoner of Azkaban.* The wizarding world is in an uproar over Sirius Black, an escaped convict said to have killed 13 people with one curse. Black is

Harry Potter and the Prisoner of Azkaban

movie. The public library held a "pin the scar on Harry" contest. The University of Pennsylvania, in Philadelphia, held a festival called Enlightening 2007. Potter fans could watch a screening of the new movie, stay in gothic-style dorm rooms, and try their hands at activities such as mixing potions, casting spells, and designing magic wands. Portland, Maine, had a Mugglefest. Fans rode an antique train disguised as the Hogwarts Express (which takes Harry and his friends to school) to a former locomotive factory that housed a re-creation of Diagon Alley.

Why so much excitement over a book? For one thing, the Harry Potter series has introduced many kids to the joys of reading for pleasure. In

hunting for Harry. But Harry is more afraid of the Dementors, the terrifying prison guards searching for Black. He learns to defend himself with the help of a new professor, Remus Lupin. And he learns that Black is actually his godfather, in a surprising twist that reveals the full story of his parents' death.

Harry Potter and the Goblet of Fire

Year 4. *Harry Potter and the Goblet of Fire.* Harry's fourth year at Hogwarts holds plenty of excitement. There's the Quidditch World Cup, a Yule Ball, and the Triwizard Tournament, in which Hogwarts faces two other wizardry schools. Someone enters Harry in the competition, and he must battle a dragon and other dangers. But the biggest threat is not part of the tournament. Harry must fight for his life against Voldemort, who takes human form for the first time in the series.

Year 5. *Harry Potter and the Order of the Phoenix.* Now 15, Harry is haunted by mysterious dreams. A cold-hearted new professor, Dolores Umbridge, takes away his broom and kicks him off the Quidditch team. Worst of all, he faces growing danger as Voldemort gathers strength. His fate seems to be bound up with Voldemort's, and he and his enemy both search for a mysterious prophecy that reveals how. Far darker in mood than the early novels, this book brings the death of Sirius Black.

Year 6. *Harry Potter and the Half-Blood Prince.* Harry is captain of his Quidditch team. He is even passing Potions, thanks to old notes from someone called the Half-Blood Prince. Who was the Prince? No one seems to know, and Harry has bigger worries. Hogwarts headmaster Albus Dumbledore has learned that Voldemort has transferred bits of his soul into six magical objects called Horcruxes. He can be defeated only if they are destroyed. But Voldemort hatches a plot, and Dumbledore dies before he and Harry can begin that task.

Year 7. *Harry Potter and the Deathly Hallows.* Harry continues the hunt for the Horcruxes, but the whole wizarding world is hunting for him. Even Hogwarts and the Ministry of Magic are under Voldemort's control. Harry's friends are with him, but in the end only he can face his enemy. Who will survive? As the series reaches its exciting finish, readers finally learn the answer to this question and others: Is Snape really evil? Is Dumbledore really dead? Will Ron and Hermione get together?

Harry Potter and the Order of the Phoenix

a survey of 500 kids ages 5 to 17 (sponsored in part by Scholastic, the Potter series' U.S. publisher), more than half said they had started to read books for fun only after picking up a Harry Potter book. And 65 percent said that they had done better in school since reading the books in the series. Some kids had started reading the series just because others were reading and talking about the books. But they were soon under Harry's spell.

Many young readers who had grown up with this series were sorry to see it come to an end. But that didn't stop them from diving into the final book and reading it cover to cover—all 700-plus pages. And as Harry's story reached its exciting climax, they were not disappointed.

2007

Leonardo DiCaprio and Jack Nicholson in *The Departed* (best motion picture).

ACADEMY AWARDS

CATEGORY	WINNER
Motion Picture	*The Departed*
Actor	Forest Whitaker *(The Last King of Scotland)*
Actress	Helen Mirren *(The Queen)*
Supporting Actor	Alan Arkin *(Little Miss Sunshine)*
Supporting Actress	Jennifer Hudson *(Dreamgirls)*
Director	Martin Scorsese *(The Departed)*
Cinematography	*Pan's Labyrinth*
Visual Effects	*Pirates of the Caribbean: Dead Man's Chest*
Song	"I Need to Wake Up" *(An Inconvenient Truth)*
Costume Design	*Marie Antoinette*
Animated Feature Film	*Happy Feet*
Foreign–Language Film	*The Lives of Others* (Germany)
Documentary Feature	*An Inconvenient Truth*
Documentary Short	*The Blood of Yingzhou District*

Left: Helen Mirren (best actress) in *The Queen*. Above: Forest Whitaker (best actor) in *The Last King of Scotland*. Below: Beyoncé, Anika Noni Rose, and Jennifer Hudson (best supporting actress) in *Dreamgirls*.

Tobey Maguire starred in the 2007 hit movie *Spider-Man 3*, the third in the series about the comic-book superhero.

IT'S MOVIE TIME!

"The third time's a charm," says an old proverb. Movie producers seemed to think that was true in 2007. Some of the year's biggest hits were "three-quels"—sequels to sequels of movies from past years. But there were plenty of original films, too. Moviegoers had their pick of animated films, fantasies filled with special effects, comedies, and gripping dramas.

SEEING TRIPLE

Each summer, movie producers try to come up with "blockbusters" that draw people to theaters. In 2007 the season led off with *Spider-Man 3,* the third in a series starring Tobey Maguire as the comic-book superhero. The movie lived up to its makers' hopes, setting box-office records on its opening day. This time Spiderman—the nerdy Peter Parker in everyday life—confronts multiple villains, including Flint Marko (Thomas Haden Church). And, infected by a blob of black goop from outer space, he develops a second personality. Of course, that leads to trouble with his true love, Mary Jane Watson (Kirsten Dunst).

An animated film, *Shrek the Third,* was another summer three-quel. In this episode, the green ogre Shrek (voiced by Mike Myers) suddenly finds that he is heir to the kingdom of Far, Far Away—and he doesn't want the job. Helped by his pals Donkey (Eddie Murphy) and Puss in Boots (Antonio Banderas), he sets out to find a replacement. But behind his back, the scheming Prince Charming (Rupert Everett) starts a rebellion.

Pirates of the Caribbean: At World's End was the third film loosely based on Disney's Pirates of the Caribbean amusement park ride. Johnny Depp returned as the eccentric pirate Captain Jack Sparrow, who was banished to Davy Jones's Locker at the end of the second film. To rescue him, his friends Will Turner (Orlando Bloom) and Elizabeth Swann (Keira Knightley) join forces with a pack of disreputable buccaneers. That sets in motion a wild tale full of double-dealing and special effects.

Another successful "three-quel" was *The Bourne Ultimatum,* with Matt Damon returning as Jason Bourne.

near their homes. Their friendship—and imagination—helps them come to terms with reality.

Other movies based on popular children's books included *Nancy Drew,* starring Emma Roberts as the girl detective; and *Harry Potter and the Order of the Phoenix,* the fifth in the Harry Potter series. *The Golden Compass* was based on the first book in Philip Pullman's trilogy *His Dark Materials.* In this fast-paced fantasy, the young heroine, Lyra (Dakota Blue Richards), is pursued across unknown worlds by an icy villain, Mrs. Coulter (Nicole Kidman).

In *Eragon,* based on Christopher Paolini's fantasy novel, the title character (Edward Speleers) finds a dragon's egg and discovers his destiny as a dragon-rider who must defend his homeland against an evil king. The dragon that carries him, Saphira, comes to life through amazing special effects.

The Golden Compass was an exciting fantasy adventure, starring Dakota Blue Richards.

Ocean's Thirteen was the third in a series of films about a team of sophisticated thieves. This time ringleader Danny Ocean (George Clooney) brings the band together in Las Vegas, Nevada, to get back at a casino owner who has cheated one of their group. Rounding out the summer was another suspenseful three-quel, *The Bourne Ultimatum.* Matt Damon returned as Jason Bourne, a spy who has lost his memory and is searching for the secret of his identity.

IMAGINARY WORLDS

Magical special effects brought imaginary worlds to the screen in 2007. *Bridge to Terabithia,* based on Katherine Paterson's classic novel for children, was the story of two gifted kids who are outsiders at their school. Jess (Joss Hutcherson) and Leslie (AnnaSophia Robb) strike up a friendship and create an imaginary kingdom on an island in a stream

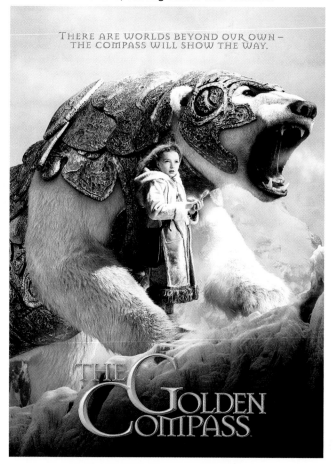

THERE ARE WORLDS BEYOND OUR OWN—
THE COMPASS WILL SHOW THE WAY.

THE GOLDEN COMPASS

One of the year's most imaginative animated films was *Ratatouille*, about a young French rat who yearns to be a chef.

Dazzling effects were also on display in *Stardust*. In this tale Tristan (Charlie Cox), a poor village boy, hopes to win the heart of a local girl by bringing her a fallen star from the sky. His quest brings him to a magical kingdom where the star has landed and taken human form as the beautiful Yvaine (Claire Danes). Tristan must save her from Lamia (Michelle Pfeiffer), a terrifying witch who plans to kill Yvaine in order to revive her own youth.

The Transformers—robots that turn into cars, trucks, and planes—started out as toys in the 1980's. Next came comic books, TV cartoons, and video games. And in 2007 they were on screen in a live-action film. The movie starred Shia LaBeouf as Sam Witwicky, a teenager whose car is a robot named Bumblebee. Bumblebee is one of a band of alien robots—the good Autobots—on a mission to Earth. Sam is soon caught up in a war between the Autobots and their evil counterparts, the Decepticons.

ANIMATED ACTION

No one wants a rat in a restaurant. But what if the rat has a passion for fine cooking? In *Ratatouille,* one of the year's top animated films, Remy (voiced by Patton Oswalt) is a young French rat who goes to Paris in hopes of becoming a chef. Of course, no restaurant will allow a rat to work in its kitchen. But Remy finds a partner at a top restaurant, a kitchen worker named Linguini (Lou Romano). With the rat hiding under his hat, Linguini carries out Remy's instructions and prepares elegant recipes, including the vegetable dish that gives the movie its name.

Comedian Jerry Seinfeld provided the voice for the lead character in *Bee Movie.* He's a young bee named Barry B. Benson who isn't satisfied with his future—a life of endless work inside the hive. Instead, he leaves the hive, explores New York City, and falls in love with a human florist (Renée Zellweger). He even files a lawsuit against the human race, for taking honey from bees.

In *Meet the Robinsons,* Lewis (Daniel Hansen and Jordan Fry) is a young orphan and a budding inventor who is menaced by a mysterious villain. He escapes to the future, where the eccentric Robinson family helps him. This animated film was shown in 3-D in selected theaters.

Filmmakers used another high-tech method to bring the Old English epic *Beowulf* to the screen. This tale is about a hero, Beowulf, who battles a dreadful monster and the monster's equally dreadful mother. The movie version used motion-capture technology. Actors performed the roles, and their movements were recorded and used to create computerized animated figures. Ray Winstone portrayed the hero. Crispin Glover was the monster, Grendel, and Angelina Jolie was Grendel's mother.

COMEDY AND ROMANCE

Fantasy met reality in the movie *Enchanted,* and the result was comedy. The story starts in an animated fairy-tale world. A princess named Giselle (Amy Adams) is about to marry her Prince Charming when his wicked stepmother, Queen Narissa (Susan Sarandon), sends her spinning through a magic portal. Giselle lands in modern New

Enchanted was an enchanting 21st-century fairy tale, starring Amy Adams and Patrick Dempsey.

The Simpsons Movie

After 18 seasons as a hit animated TV sitcom, The Simpsons came to theaters in 2007. Fans lined up to see America's funniest family—Homer, Marge, and their kids Bart, Lisa, and Maggie—in *The Simpsons Movie.* Eleven writers from the show helped write the script for this summer hit. Most of the series' regular characters appeared, along with the rock group Green Day, Tom Hanks, and other celebrities in cameo roles.

Homer sets the gag-packed plot in motion by doing something dumb, of course. He dumps his pet pig's waste into a local lake. D'oh! It's an environmental disaster, and the Environmental Protection Agency (EPA) puts a dome over Springfield, the Simpsons' hometown. The family flees to Alaska. Marge fumes. Lisa makes an environmental documentary. Bart gets in trouble. And Homer manages to save the day in spite of himself.

Sixteen U.S. cities named Springfield entered a contest to host the movie's premiere. The winner was Springfield, Vermont, and the movie opened there on July 21. Businesses jumped on the Simpsons bandwagon, too. Some 7-Eleven stores transformed into Simpsons-style "Kwik-E-Marts" and sold pink donuts, Buzz Cola, and other items seen in the movie. And an ice-cream maker came out with a new beer-and-donut-flavored ice cream. Homer would have loved it!

Jane Austen at the Movies

Jane Austen's novels are classics of English literature. Written about 200 years ago, these insightful stories of romance, manners, and misunderstandings are still enjoyed by readers today. And over the years her most popular books—*Pride and Prejudice, Sense and Sensibility, Emma,* and others—have been adapted for the big screen, some several times. In 2007, Jane Austen was back at the movies. Two films took new approaches to her life and work.

The Jane Austen Book Club was based on a modern novel by Karen Joy Fowler. It's the story of five women and one man who meet each month to discuss a different Austen novel. The books turn out to mirror their lives, and they begin to see themselves in Austen's characters.

John Travolta and Nikki Blonsky had the lead roles in the toe-tapping, bouncy film *Hairspray*, based on the award-winning Broadway musical.

Becoming Jane, starring Anne Hathaway, was one of two 2007 movies about the popular British novelist Jane Austen.

Also based on a recent novel, *Becoming Jane* was a fictional story about Jane Austen at age 20. Like one of her own heroines, Jane (Anne Hathaway) is a young woman determined to marry for love. Her family insists that money is more important. Will she run off with Tom Lefroy (James McAvoy), the dashing young Irishman who captures her heart?

In real life, Jane Austen never married. But she left the world a lasting legacy in her novels.

York City, and the movie switches to live action. She's taken in by a lawyer and single dad (Patrick Dempsey). And before long, other characters from the fairy-tale world show up, with hilarious results.

Based on a hit Broadway musical, the movie *Hairspray* was set in Baltimore, Maryland, in 1962. Tracy Turnblad (Nikki Blonsky), a bubbly plus-size teen, lands a part on the local dance-party TV show, horrifying the show's snooty star dancer, Amber Von Tussle (Brittany Snow). Soon Tracy also lands Amber's boyfriend, Link Larkin (Zac Efron). She becomes a leader for other teenage outsiders—including blacks, who are allowed on the show just once a month on "Negro Day." Backed by her mother (John Travolta, in makeup, wig, and lots of padding), she sets out to integrate the show.

In *Music and Lyrics,* Alex Fletcher (Hugh Grant) is a one-time pop star reduced to lip-synching his old hits at country fairs. He'll make a comeback if he can write a hit for a new teen star, Cora Corman (Haley Bennett)—but he can't come up with the lyrics. Enter Sophie Fisher (Drew Barrymore), a hopeful writer who tends plants for a living. She has a way with words, and she soon finds a way into Alex's heart.

Hilary Swank starred in the highly acclaimed *Freedom Writers,* the true story of a dedicated high-school teacher.

The characters in *No Reservations* cook up a romance in the kitchen of a high-priced New York City restaurant. Kate (Catherine Zeta-Jones) is a talented chef with no time for anything but her job. That changes after her niece Zoe (Abigail Breslin) comes to stay—and handsome Nick (Aaron Eckhart) comes to work at her restaurant.

Year of the Dog, a bittersweet comedy, was about a woman who gains happiness not through romance but through a love of ani-

No Reservations, starring Catherine Zeta-Jones and Aaron Eckhart, was a delightful romantic comedy about two chefs.

mals. Peggy (Molly Shannon) has a drab office job and lives alone, except for her beloved beagle, Pencil. When Pencil unexpectedly dies, she's shattered. She begins to adopt strays. She becomes a vegetarian. And she makes a new beginning as an animal-rights activist.

DRAMA

Among the many dramas that came to the screen in 2007 was *Freedom Writers,* the true story of a dedicated teacher (Hilary Swank) assigned to a high school in a rough part of Long Beach, California. She struggles to reach the kids in her freshman English class, who are poor, black and Hispanic, and surrounded by violence. And when she gets them to write journals, she begins to break through. Some of the students' stories are presented in flashbacks and voiceovers in this moving film.

The musical drama *Dreamgirls* was based on a hit Broadway musical of the same title. Set in the 1960's, the story follows the lives of three female singers, Effie White (Jennifer Hudson), Deena Jones (Beyoncé Knowles), and Lorrell Robinson (Anika Noni Rose). Under the wing of a manipulative manager (Jamie Foxx), they form a successful R&B group. Hudson won an Oscar as best supporting actress for her portrayal of Effie, who is pushed out of the lead singer's position as the group gains fame.

A fairytale landscape is portrayed in shimmering stained glass in a window by Louis Comfort Tiffany. Tiffany made his mark as an artist and craftsman with unique creations such as this.

LOUIS COMFORT TIFFANY: MASTER DESIGNER

"Those of us in America who began to experiment in glass were moved solely by a desire to produce a thing of beauty, irrespective of any rule, doctrine or theory. Color, and color only, was the end sought."

Louis Comfort Tiffany, 1893

Glowing, gemlike colors—sapphire blues, ruby reds, emerald greens—are the mark of Louis Comfort Tiffany's glass creations. In the late 1800's and early 1900's, the stained-glass lamps and windows, delicate vases, and other beautiful objects turned out by his New York studios made him world-famous.

Copies of Tiffany's works are very popular today, and the originals are sought out by collectors. During 2007, two important exhibitions focused on his work. Tiffany was remarkable not only for his designs but also for his technical breakthroughs in glassmaking.

A YOUNG ARTIST

Louis Comfort Tiffany was born on February 18, 1848, in New York City. His father, Charles Lewis Tiffany, was a successful jeweler and the founder of Tiffany & Company, New York's renowned jewelry store. Charles Tiffany hoped his son would enter the family business, but young Louis was more interested in drawing and painting. He was a rebellious teenager, and his parents sent him to a military academy in New Jersey for a disciplined education. The academy didn't shake his interest in fine art, and in 1865 he traveled to Europe to absorb the art and culture there.

Back in New York the next year, Tiffany began to seriously study drawing and painting. He met several artists, including the landscape painter George Inness, who had a strong influence on his painting style. On later trips abroad, he painted scenes in Europe and North

half of the 19th century. Artists of the Aesthetic Movement, for example, believed that art should be enjoyed for its beauty, not used to present a moral or a message. Artists and designers alike looked to other times and other cultures, including Japan and the Islamic world, for inspiration.

Tiffany was especially interested in the Aesthetic idea of bringing all the arts together to create beautiful home interiors.

The glass shades of Tiffany lamps turned the glare of electric lights into glowing colors. The lamps often featured stylized flowers, vines, fruits, and other subjects from nature.

Africa. He was impressed with the brilliant colors he saw everywhere in his travels, especially in the stained-glass windows of Europe's great cathedrals. (Stained glass is decorative glass that has been colored by mixing pigments into the glass.)

He also became familiar with the new ideas that were shaping the art world in the second

Although he had become a skillful painter, he began to focus more and more on the decorative arts.

In 1879 he founded Louis C. Tiffany and Associated Artists, a partnership with painters, textile designers, and furniture designers. Tiffany was in charge of the overall design process. The firm created interiors for a number of famous clients, including the author Mark Twain and the wealthy industrialist

Laurelton Hall: An Artist's Country Estate

In 1902, Tiffany began to build a new country estate, called Laurelton Hall, on Long Island. It became his crowning work of art. Sadly, fire destroyed the mansion in 1957. But bits and pieces of its fabulous decorations have survived. From November 2006 through May 2007, Laurelton Hall was the focus of a special exhibition at the Metropolitan Museum of Art in New York City.

Tiffany's magnificent estate covered 580 acres (235 hectares) overlooking Long Island Sound. It was surrounded by beautiful landscaping and gardens as colorful as the glass that made its owner famous. There were fountains, pools, stables, tennis courts, greenhouses, a chapel, and a studio on the grounds. Tiffany oversaw the design of every detail—even the smokestack for the estate's steam plant. (It looked like an Islamic minaret.)

The mansion itself had 84 rooms and eight levels. Tiffany diverted a stream on the property to travel under the house and come up in a fountain in a central court. The rooms were filled with hundreds of pieces of Tiffany's work, including stunning stained-glass windows. He also displayed his collections of Asian and Native American art. Most of the objects were auctioned off after his death, so they weren't destroyed in the fire.

Some elements from the house also survived the fire. One was the Daffodil Terrace, an outdoor room that led from the dining room to the gardens. Its ceiling was paneled with Favrile glass, and it was supported by columns with crowns styled to look like bunches of daffodils. The Daffodil Terrace and many other Tiffany creations (such as the "Rose Window" above) were on view in the Metropolitan Museum exhibit.

Cornelius Vanderbilt. President Chester A. Arthur hired the company to redecorate the public rooms at the White House, and Tiffany designed a large stained-glass screen for the entry.

A MASTER OF GLASS

Tiffany was increasingly fascinated with glass. He had begun experimenting with stained glass in 1875, establishing his own glassmaking studio. He wanted to reproduce the glowing colors of the medieval stained glass that he had seen in European cathedrals, and his inventory eventually grew to more than 5,000 colors. He found new ways to build color, shading, and texture into the glass itself, rather than painting the effects on the surface. He also developed a new technique that gave glass a metallic luster. He called this iridescent glass Favrile, but it soon became widely known as "Tiffany glass."

Tiffany used Favrile and other stunning glass effects in hand-blown bowls and vases, stained-glass windows and screens, and lamps with blown-glass and stained-glass shades. The glowing colors of the glass shades helped soften the glare of the new electric lights, which were just coming into use. The effect was stunning—as if a stained-glass window had been draped over the lamp. And Tiffany's glass designs were exotic and beautiful. He became a leader of the design movement known as Art Nouveau (from the

French words for "new art"), which featured flowing, natural forms with touches of Asian and African influences.

Like other Art Nouveau designers, Tiffany often presented stylized subjects from nature—grasses, vines, lilies, peacock feathers, and insects. A hand-blown vase might take the form of an onion or another plant, with a slender stem rising from a bulblike base. In leaded-glass works, each piece of glass was carefully selected and shaped for its part in the picture. Even the leading between the glass pieces was part of the design. If a window or a lamp showed a flower, each petal of the flower would be a separate piece of glass, outlined in dark leading.

Favrile glass had a metallic sheen. Tiffany used it in objects such as this two-part vase (left), "spider-web" lamp (above), and vase shaped like a jack-in-the-pulpit (right).

Tiffany didn't do the work himself, and he created only some of the designs. Instead, he hired skilled artisans to create these handmade objects. Eventually, he opened his own factory in Queens, New York.

THE GILDED AGE

While Tiffany was establishing his reputation as a master of glass, his business and his personal life went through a series of ups and downs. In 1884, Mary, his wife of 12 years, died, leaving him with three young children. Then some poor business decisions brought him to the brink of bankruptcy. His father helped him reorganize his business as the Tiffany Glass Company. His father also gave him a new project—building a mansion in New York City where the whole Tiffany family could live together. Before long, Tiffany remarried and settled down with his new wife, Louise.

Tiffany's business continued to grow. Only the wealthy could afford his creations. But this was the era known as the Gilded Age, when financiers and industrialists such as the railroad magnate Cornelius Vanderbilt accumulated enormous fortunes. They spent lavishly, building huge mansions and stuffing them with costly furnishings and works of art. And Tiffany creations were all the rage in Gilded Age society.

The "Tiffany Girls" in 1904. Clara Driscoll (far left, in white blouse) was one of Tiffany's top designers. The dragonfly lamp above was probably her work.

Clara Driscoll and the Tiffany Girls

To produce his fabulous glass windows and other pieces, Tiffany hired skilled craftsmen—but they weren't all men. Some 50 women were among his most valued employees. They created some of his most famous pieces. In 2007 the New York Historical Society featured their work in an exhibit called "A New Light on Tiffany: Clara Driscoll and the Tiffany Girls."

Clara Driscoll was a native of Ohio who had moved to New York City to attend art school. By 1888 she was working at the Tiffany Studios in Manhattan. A few years later, she became head of the women's glass-cutting department. Tiffany set up this department in 1892. The all-male glasscutters' union had gone on strike, and he hired women from art schools to replace the striking workers. The women were so skilled that he kept them on when the strike ended.

It was a painstaking craft. Working in pairs, the women selected an area of a sheet of glass with just the right color and pattern to suit one detail of a lamp, window, or mosaic. Then they carefully cut the piece to fit that detail and wrapped the edges with a strip of copper foil. Male workers at Tiffany's Queens factory would then join the pieces with leading to assemble the finished object.

Women and men earned the same salaries—$7 weekly for novice glasscutters and up to $12 a week for skilled artisans. Clara Driscoll made $35 a week. It was a high salary for a woman in those days. But she would have had to spend about two months' pay to buy one of the lamps that she made.

Driscoll worked for Tiffany for more than 20 years. She was not only a skilled artisan, she was also one of Tiffany's top designers. One of her lamps won a prize at the Paris World's Fair in 1900. But like the other "Tiffany Girls," she rarely received credit. The exhibit at the New York Historical Society put a long-overdue spotlight on their work.

In time, Tiffany began to branch out in new directions. He experimented with glass mosaics, designs created with bits of colored glass. As in the stained-glass creations, the glass pieces were chosen carefully for their color and shading. Tiffany backed them with metallic foil, for extra luster. He began to use mosaics on walls, floors, and many small objects. For one New York City mansion, he created a pillared hall covered with glittering mosaic designs in gold, white, and pale green glass. For the 1893 World's Columbian Exposition, in Chicago, Illinois, he combined mosaic panels and stained-glass windows to create a beautiful chapel. Millions of people visited the fair, and the chapel made Tiffany famous. (The

Tiffany made jewelry and accessories in the Art Nouveau style, such as this peacock table mirror (above) and necklace of enamel and precious stones (right).

chapel has been reconstructed at the Charles Hosmer Morse Museum of American Art in Winter Park, Florida.)

In the following years, the lamps and other glass creations turned out by Tiffany's studios won top awards at several other international expositions. Art museums displayed his blown-glass vases. And he continued to experiment with new techniques, including enameling. His studio began to create exotic "cameo-cut" glass vases, made of layers of glass in different colors. Designs were carved into the layers, revealing the colors below.

LATE CAREER

Tiffany was at the peak of his career in 1902, when his father died. He then became president of the jewelry firm that his father had founded. This took him in yet another direction. While continuing his glass business (now known as the Tiffany Studios), he also began to design jewelry. His necklaces, pins, and other pieces were unlike anything his father had made. They reflected the Art Nouveau style, with informal shapes and themes taken from nature or from Asian art. He exhibited some of his first pieces at the 1904 Louisiana Purchase Exposition in St. Louis, Missouri.

Late in life, Tiffany became something of a patron of the arts. He established a foundation to further art appreciation and production. He also staged several theatrical festivals. At these events, invited guests were treated to dance and music performances in elaborate settings that he designed. The festivals were a return to his early ideal of bringing all the arts together.

But Tiffany's business declined with the start of World War I. After the war, in 1919, he retired. By the time of his death in 1933, the Tiffany Studios had gone bankrupt. Tastes were changing. People wanted a sleeker, more modern look. Tiffany designs were seen as gaudy and excessive. Most of the interiors he created were destroyed as people redecorated. Tiffany lamps and vases were stashed in attics or tossed in the trash.

Then, in the 1950's and 1960's, tastes changed once again. People took a fresh look at Louis Comfort Tiffany and the Art Nouveau style. Tiffany lamps and other objects were suddenly in great demand. When the genuine items were fished out of attics and put up for auction, they commanded huge prices. And mass-produced "Tiffany-style" lamps were suddenly everywhere. The copies lacked the beauty of the originals, but they sold at prices that most could afford.

Tiffany is still admired today for his innovations in glassmaking, his artistic eye, and for the beautiful objects he created.

Steven Van Zandt, James Gandolfini, and Tony Sirico in *The Sopranos* (best drama series).

2007

EMMY AWARDS

CATEGORY	WINNER
Comedy Series	*30 Rock*
Actor—Comedy Series	Ricky Gervais, *Extras*
Actress—Comedy Series	America Ferrera, *Ugly Betty*
Supporting Actor—Comedy Series	Jeremy Piven, *Entourage*
Supporting Actress—Comedy Series	Jaime Pressly, *My Name Is Earl*
Drama Series	*The Sopranos*
Actor—Drama Series	James Spader, *Boston Legal*
Actress—Drama Series	Sally Field, *Brothers & Sisters*
Supporting Actor—Drama Series	Terry O'Quinn, *Lost*
Supporting Actress—Drama Series	Katherine Heigl, *Grey's Anatomy*
Miniseries	*Broken Trail*
Variety, Music, or Comedy Series	*The Daily Show With Jon Stewart*
Reality-Competition Program	*The Amazing Race*

Left: America Ferrera (best actress, comedy series) in *Ugly Betty*. Above: James Spader (best actor, drama series) in *Boston Legal*. Below: Alec Baldwin and Tina Fey in *30 Rock* (best comedy series).

The rock group Fall Out Boy had a number-one album with *Infinity on High* in 2007. The band also performed at the Live Earth concerts and at the MTV Video Music Awards during the year.

THE MUSIC SCENE

The year 2007 offered plenty of proof that the music world is changing. The growing practice of downloading music from the Internet led established stars to release new works through unconventional routes. New artists were gathering fans online even before landing contracts with big recording companies. And with worldwide access over the Internet, performers and trends were flowing across national boundaries. Music lovers had access to a growing range of fresh sounds in every musical style.

POP POWER

California singer-songwriter Colbie Caillat's first big-label album, *Coco,* went right to the top five when it was released in July. But Caillat's acoustic pop sound wasn't new to fans. Her song "Bubbly" had already received more than 10 million plays on the social-networking Web site MySpace—and it was the popularity of her MySpace page that convinced the Universal Republic label to sign her. "Bubbly" stayed on the charts as one of the year's top downloads.

Little Voice, a top-album download, was the debut effort from singer-songwriter Sara Bareilles. It included the single "Love Song" along with other folk-flavored tracks. Another newcomer, 17-year-old Sean Kingston, featured reggae-flavored pop on his debut album. The album, titled simply *Sean Kingston,* included one of the summer's catchiest singles, "Beautiful Girls."

There was plenty of star power on the pop charts during the year, as established artists came out with new releases. Jennifer Lopez packed her new release, *Brave,* with dance-worthy tracks such as "Do It Well" and "Stay Together." Singer-songwriter Ben Harper and his backup band, the Innocent Criminals, had a hot download with "In the Colors," from their new album *Lifeline.* Maroon 5 followed up their hit 2002 album *Songs About Jane* with a new release, *It Won't Be Soon Before Long.* It included the number-one single "Makes Me Wonder."

Three was a magic number for several top stars. Kelly Clarkson, the 2002 winner on

TV's *American Idol,* cemented her star status with her third album, *My December.* Norah Jones delivered more of her trademark jazzy sounds on her third collection, *Not Too Late.* And two Canadian singer-songwriters had best-selling third albums. Avril Lavigne served up a collection of punchy, up-tempo songs on *The Best Damn Thing,* including the hit single "Girlfriend." And Feist mixed jazzy pop and folk on *The Reminder.*

Hilary Duff featured danceable tunes on *Dignity,* her 2007 release. The title track and another song on the album, "No Work, All Play," took aim at Hollywood party girls. Britney Spears also had a new album, *Blackout,* and a hit single, "Gimme More." A number of pop artists reflected concerns about world events and the environment in their new works. Among them was Prince, whose 2007 album was titled *Planet Earth.*

British singer-songwriter James Blunt's second U.S. release, *All the Lost Souls,* featured haunting ballads and folk flavors. And the debut album from London singer-songwriter Mika, *Life in Cartoon Motion,* had a very different sound—perky pop fizz.

ROCKERS NEW AND OLD

One of the biggest rock releases of the year came from the band Linkin Park. *Minutes to Midnight* offered fans a more melodic sound than the group's two previous studio albums. It sold an estimated 625,000 copies in its first week. The sixth album from the Texas group Spoon, titled *Ga Ga Ga Ga Ga,* featured ten stripped-down rock tunes with the taut guitar-and-piano sound that's this band's trademark.

Live Earth

Live Earth, a series of concerts spanning 24 hours and seven continents, was staged on July 7, 2007. It may have been the largest worldwide music event ever. More than 150 of the world's top musical artists performed on stage in eight countries—Australia, Brazil, Britain, China, Germany, Japan, South Africa, and the United States. Hundreds of thousands of music fans attended, and millions more tuned in through TV, radio, and Internet links.

The event's goal was to draw attention to the problem of global warming. Former U.S. Vice President Al Gore, a leader on the climate issue, helped organize it. The performers included legendary groups such as the Police and current headliners like Kanye West, Kelly Clarkson, the Black Eyed Peas, and Jon Bon Jovi (right). Joined by other celebrities, they called on fans to fight global warming by saving energy and by pressuring public officials to take action. Profits went to the Alliance for Climate Protection, led by Gore, and other environmental groups.

Twenty-two-year-old Colbie Caillat scored one of the year's top pop hits with "Bubbly," a single off her album *Coco*.

Also returning was Fall Out Boy, with *Infinity on High*. Filled with catchy guitar rock, it debuted at number-one in February. The Foo Fighters were back with *Echoes, Silence, Patience & Grace*, featuring the hard-driving single "The Pretender." New faces included Chris Daughtry, a former *American Idol* contestant. His debut album, *Daughtry*, topped the rock charts early in the year.

The Canadian band Arcade Fire followed up their 2004 debut, *Funeral*, with *Neon Bible*. The new album was recorded in a church near Montreal, the hometown of this independent seven-member group. Like their first, it featured dark, moody, and original music. Trent Reznor's band Nine Inch Nails had a chart-topping album with *Year Zero*. The band's "industrial" sound blended hard beats with electronic distortion and static in tracks like the hit single "Survivalism." And the White Stripes released *Icky Thump*, a new album that—like much of this inventive duo's work—was hard to classify.

The British indie band Arctic Monkeys, who took the United States by storm in 2006, were back with a hard-rocking second album, *Favourite Worst Nightmare*. They weren't the only band to hop the Atlantic in 2007. Aqualung's second U.S. release, *Memory Man*, included some soul-flavored songs. Klaxons, a London trio, released *Myths of the Near Future*,

Arcade Fire, the indie rock band from Canada, received critical acclaim for its second album, *Neon Bible*.

a high-energy debut. The Fratellis, from Scotland, had a hot download with "Flathead" off their 2006 debut, *Costello Music.* And *Twelve Stops and Home,* from The Feeling, featured peppy pop sounds that brought the Beatles to mind.

Bruce Springsteen teamed up with the E Street Band for the first time in five years, and the result was *Magic,* Springsteen's eighth number-one album. Spirited tracks like "Radio Nowhere" and "Livin' in the Future" showed why he has become a rock icon. Other veterans with new releases included Neil Young and John Mellencamp. And Sting reunited with The Police for a worldwide tour.

R&B AND HIP-HOP

Mary J. Blige, the reigning queen of hip-hop and soul, scooped up Grammy awards in 2007 for her album *The Breakthrough* and single "Be Without You." She also released a collection of some of her best-loved songs, titled *Reflections—A Retrospective.*

Introducing Joss Stone was actually the third album from the sultry British singer of the title, who was just 20 years old. Hip-hop flavored sev-

eral tracks, including "Music," with guest artist Lauryn Hill. Keyshia Cole was joined by Lil' Kim and Missy Elliott in "Let It Go," a hot summer download from her second album, *Just Like You.* Rihanna had a hit single with "Umbrella," featuring Jay-Z. And British singer Amy Winehouse echoed the soul sounds of the 1960's on her hot-selling album *Back to Black.*

Newcomer Soulja Boy's single "Crank That" was the top-selling single for seven weeks. It was finally overtaken by Chris Brown's "Kiss Kiss" (featuring T-Pain), from his new album *Exclusive.* T-Pain had his own chart-topper with "Buy U a Drank (Shawty Snappin')." And Robin Thicke became the first white male singer to top the R&B charts in 20 years with his single "Lost Without U."

The talented leader of the Black Eyed Peas, will.i.am, came out with a solo album titled *Songs About Girls.* He also helped produce a new album from Macy Gray, *Big,* bringing a fresh sound to Gray's unique stylings. The

The CD Slump

Is the CD dead? With more and more fans downloading music from the Internet, many people were asking that question. Record stores were closing. Sales of new CD's were down by more than 20 percent. Sales of legal digital downloads from services such as iTunes weren't enough to make up for the decline.

Some people blamed high CD prices. Some blamed mediocre music. But file sharing was clearly part of the problem. The music industry has gone after people who share music files illegally over the Internet, taking them to court. But a lot of file sharing takes place among friends and is impossible to police. File sharing and CD burning accounted for 37 percent of the music Americans obtained in 2006.

To make up for lost income, some recording artists have started to rely more on concerts. And some are experimenting with new outlets for their music. In 2007, former Beatle Paul McCartney released his latest album, *Memory Almost Full,* through the Starbucks coffee-

house chain. And the British rock group Radiohead (Thom Yorke shown above) offered a ten-song online version of their new album, *In Rainbows,* for whatever price downloaders chose to pay. While some chose to pay nothing, the average was about $8. A version of the album with better sound quality was also available on CD, at a fixed price.

Top-rated *Introducing Joss Stone* was the 20-year-old British singer's third album and included the hit single "Tell Me 'Bout It."

COUNTRY

Carrie Underwood went from complete unknown to national celebrity as winner of 2005's *American Idol* talent search. In 2007 she was on top of the country-music world, with a shelf full of awards for her debut album *Some Hearts* and a second album, *Carnival Ride* climbing the charts. Underwood co-wrote many of the songs on her new album and had a hit with the first single from it, "So Small."

Newcomer Taylor Swift, 17, scored with her self-titled debut album and its first single, titled "Tim McGraw." Meanwhile, the real Tim McGraw released *Let It Go,* the first collection of new material from this country superstar since 2004. He and his country-singer wife, Faith Hill, were also guest artists on singer-songwriter Lori McKenna's first major-label album, *Unglamorous.*

Kenny Chesney, Toby Keith, and Reba McEntire were among other big names with new albums. The country-pop trio Rascal Flatts released *Still Feels Good,* and rising star Jason

Composer, producer, and rapper Timbaland came out with his second album, *Timbaland Presents Shock Value,* featuring big-name guest artists.

Peas' Fergie stayed on the charts with her single "Glamorous," featuring Ludacris, from her solo debut album *The Dutchess.* And British rapper-singer M.I.A. returned to the charts with a new album, *Kala.*

Singer, songwriter, and producer Ne-Yo opened a recording studio and came out with his own label in 2007. He also came out with his second number-one album, *Because of You.* Timbaland, who has helped to produced hits for everyone from Aaliya to Jay-Z, also put together his second album in 2007. *Timbaland Presents Shock Value* featured a list of big-name guest artists, including Justin Timberlake and Nelly Furtado in "Give It to Me."

Hip-hop's big names also lined up to work with R. Kelly on his new release, *Double Up;* with the New York rapper Fabolous on *From Nothin' to Somethin';* and with Miami mix-tape king DJ Khaled on *We the Best.* Rapper Kanye West brought out *Graduation,* the third of three albums with titles linked to education.

Aldean topped the country charts with his single "Johnny Cash." Honky-tonk singer Gretchen Wilson extended her winning streak with *One of the Boys.*

Country, blues, or rock? Several artists blurred the lines in 2007. Lucinda Williams explored failed relationships and family losses on *West,* her eighth studio album. The 1980's rock group Bon Jovi, which topped the country charts in 2006 with "Who Says You Can't Go Home," blended country flavors into the tracks on their new album, *Lost Highway.*

MUSIC NOTES

Rock or hip-hop? The Rock and Roll Hall of Fame saw no need to draw that line in 2007. It inducted its first hip-hop group—Grandmaster Flash and the Furious Five, who broke new ground with "The Message" in 1982. Featuring rapper Melle Mel, that single described the tensions of inner-city life.

Also welcomed into the Hall were the 1960's girl group the Ronettes; punk-rock pioneer Patti Smith; the 1980's hard-rock band Van Halen; and R.E.M., a group that paved the way for alternative rock.

Carrie Underwood captured two 2007 Grammys—for Best New Artist and Best Country Female Vocal Performance.

2007 Grammy Awards

Record of the Year	"Not Ready to Make Nice"	Dixie Chicks, artists
Album of the Year	*Taking the Long Way*	Dixie Chicks, artists
Song of the Year	"Not Ready to Make Nice"	Dixie Chicks, Dan Wilson, songwriters
New Artist of the Year	Carrie Underwood, artist	
Pop Vocal Album	*Continuum*	John Mayer, artist
Pop Performance, Female	"Ain't No Other Man"	Christina Aguilera, artist
Pop Performance, Male	"Waiting on the World to Change"	John Mayer, artist
Pop Performance, Group	"My Humps"	Black Eyed Peas, artists
Rock Album	*Stadium Arcadium*	Red Hot Chili Peppers, artists
Rock Song	"Dani California"	Red Hot Chili Peppers, artists
Rock Vocal Performance	"Someday Baby"	Bob Dylan, artist
Rock Performance, Group	"Dani California"	Red Hot Chili Peppers, artists
Rhythm and Blues, Album	*The Breakthrough*	Mary J. Blige, artist
Rhythm and Blues Performance, Female	"Be Without You"	Mary J. Blige, artist
Rhythm and Blues Performance, Male	"Heaven"	John Legend, artist
Rhythm and Blues Performance, Group	"Family Affair"	Sly and the Family Stone, artists
Rap Album	*Release Therapy*	Ludacris, artist
Rap Solo Performance	"What You Know"	T.I., artist
Rap Performance, Group	"Ridin"	Chamillionaire featuring Krayzie Bone, artists
Score for a Motion Picture	*Memoirs of a Geisha*	John Williams, composer
Musical Show Album	*Jersey Boys*	Bob Gaudio, producer/composer

PEOPLE, PLACES, EVENTS

Dinosaurs ruled the Earth for 200 million years. And in 2007 they were back, stomping and roaring across North America in an amazing show. **"Walking With Dinosaurs—The Live Experience!"** featured life-size animatronic dinosaurs interacting with each other and with human actors. They were so large that the show could be presented only in arenas! Ten species were featured, including the terrifying *Tyrannosaurus rex* (above), *Stegosaurus* (right), and a *Brachiosaurus* standing 43 feet (13 meters) tall. The show depicted the dinosaurs' development and the changes that took place on Earth during their time, including the impact of the massive comet that is thought to have led to their extinction. Audiences saw how meat-eating dinosaurs evolved to walk on two legs and how plant-eaters fended off predators, all ex-

plained by an actor portraying a paleontologist. Based on a British TV series, the show was developed in Australia, where it was a huge hit. Its two-year North American tour began in the summer of 2007.

Rarely does a sequel top the hit it follows, but that was the case for **High School Musical 2**. This made-for-TV movie, a follow-up to the 2006 hit *High School Musical,* drew the largest audience in cable-TV history when it aired on the Disney Channel on August 17, 2007. In *HSM2,* the kids are on summer vacation. But Sharpay (Ashley Tisdale) is still trying to get Troy (Zac Efron) away from his girlfriend Gabriella (Vanessa Hudgens). The action unfolds with plenty of singing and dancing.

Dramatic new skyscrapers are changing the skylines of many world cities. One of the most dramatic is being built in La Défense, a business district on the edge of Paris, France. The design, by the Los Angeles architect Thom Mayne, was chosen in an international competition. Called the **Phare Tower** (from the French word for lighthouse), the curving building looks different from every angle. It will stand on huge steel legs and soar 985 feet (300 meters). People will ride giant glass-enclosed escalators up to the lobby, which will have gardens, cafes, and shops. The building is designed to be energy efficient, too. It will have an outer "skin" that looks like draped fabric but is actually pierced metal. And it will be topped by a "wind farm" that will power its ventilation system. It won't use outside energy for heating and cooling for five months of the year. The Phare Tower is scheduled to be completed in 2012.

The year 2007 marked the 25th anniversary of the **Vietnam Veterans Memorial** in Washington, D.C. This simple but powerful memorial consists of two polished black granite walls that meet to form a V. The names of more than 58,000 Americans who died or were missing in action in Vietnam are carved on the walls. The monument was controversial when it was built, in 1982. A traditional bronze statue of three soldiers was even placed nearby to satisfy critics. But "the Wall," as the memorial is known today, has become one of the most-visited places in the capital. In 2007 it received the Twenty-Five Year Award from the American Institute of Architects, as a work that has stood the test of time.

The Wall was designed by Maya Lin (left). Lin is a well-known architect today, but at the time she was a senior in college. She heard about a national competition to design a memorial honoring soldiers who had died in the Vietnam War, and she entered. The competition was "blind," so the judges didn't know who had entered the designs. They chose Lin's. Lin has since designed other large-scale works, including the Civil Rights Memorial in Montgomery, Alabama. She has also created sculptures and designed houses and furniture. But the Wall remains her best-known work.

Have you ever imagined a face in the clouds? **Giuseppe Arcimboldo** must have done that. He created some of the oddest paintings in the history of art, and in 2007 people lined up to see them at an exhibition in Paris.

Arcimboldo was born in Milan, Italy, in 1527. He began his career as a traditional painter. But in the 1560's, as a court painter to the Habsburg rulers of Austria, he began to paint bizarre caricatures. The paintings showed people in formal portrait poses. But the figures and faces were made up entirely of fruits, flowers, animals, fish, household articles, and whatever else the artist found appropriate. For example, *The Spring* (above) shows a reclining figure of a person made up of flowers, fruits, and vegetables—including cherries, peas, and lettuce. *Spring* (right) is a portrait of a young man made up of flowers, leaves, and shoots.

Kids had a chance to outsmart adults on ***Are You Smarter Than a 5th Grader?***, a hit TV game show that premiered in February 2007 with comedian Jeff Foxworthy (center) as host. Adults tried to answer 5th-grade-level questions, revealing how much they had forgotten since grade school. For help, they could turn to some real 5th graders. These "classmates" had a chance to study before the show. They answered the questions secretly by writing their answers. When contestants were stumped, they could ask a classmate for up to two "cheats" (copying or peeking at the classmate's answer). Contestants who answered wrong were out of the game, but they were allowed one "save" if their classmate answered correctly.

Shrunken heads. George Washington's hair. A giant meteorite. These objects and more went on view at the **Ripley's Believe It or Not! Odditorium** in New York City's Times Square in 2007. (Below: An acrobat performs at the opening.) The Odditorium, one of 30 worldwide, was inspired by Robert Ripley. Born in 1890, Ripley became a collector of oddities. He featured his finds in the long-running cartoon strip *Ripley's Believe It or Not*.

Fans of the classic children's books *Alice's Adventures in Wonderland* and *Through the Looking-Glass* celebrated the 175th anniversary of the birth of their author in 2007. Charles Lutwidge Dodgson (right) wrote the books under the pen name **Lewis Carroll**. He was born in 1832, in the village of Daresbury in England. The eldest son in a family of eleven children, he often wrote stories and drew pictures to entertain his brothers and sisters. But in school he stammered and was shy, which made him a target for bullying.

Dodgson went to Oxford University and stayed on there, teaching mathematics. He also wrote humorous poems and articles for magazines, signing them Lewis Carroll. And he took up the new art of photography. Among his favorite photography subjects was Alice Liddell, daughter of an Oxford dean. *Alice's Adventures in Wonderland* began as a story he made up for her when she was 10. In 1865, the book was published with illustrations by John Tenniel. (Above: Two of Tenniel's pictures.) It was a hit, and the sequel *Through the Looking-Glass* was published seven years later. Both books have been delighting readers around the world ever since.

FUN TO READ

Wherever you are, a book is a great companion! Reading keeps you smiling, whether you like fantasy, true-life stories, or poetry. Check out the following pages for some favorite stories and poems, and for news about the top books of 2007.

⊶ THE PLOT TO KILL HITLER ⊷

From 1933 until 1945, Germany was ruled by Adolf Hitler and his National Socialist (Nazi) Party. Hitler was a power-hungry dictator. Under his leadership, the Nazis turned Germany into a police state. And they prepared for aggressive war against Germany's European neighbors.

At first, many Germans supported Hitler and the Nazis because conditions were so bad after Germany's defeat in World War I in 1917. The collapse of the German economy during the Great Depression of the 1930's and violent confrontations between Communists and extremist right-wing groups led to a sense of despair.

After coming to power, Hitler and the Nazis took steps to rebuild the German economy. Jobs were now available; the army was expanded and reorganized; order and stability replaced chaos and confusion.

But the price paid for this "New Order"—the Nazis' term for their reorganization of society—was the loss of individual rights and democratic principles. Labor unions were abolished. Opposition newspapers were closed down. And all aspects of life were closely regulated. State security forces, including the much-feared Gestapo (secret police), hunted down political opponents. They tortured and killed many and imprisoned others in concentration camps.

At the core of Nazi policy was a belief in the racial superiority of the Germanic peoples

(Aryan race). Another aspect of German policy was the right of Germans to conquer so-called inferior races (such as Russians, Poles, and other Slavic people). Nazi racial policy led to the murder of some six million Jews in "death camps," and millions of other people in slave-labor camps. Aggressive war policies led to the German invasion of Poland in 1939 and the conquest of much of Europe during the early years of World War II.

From the beginning of Hitler's rule, there were many Germans who actively opposed the Nazi dictator. Groups consisting of students, intellectuals, and even civilian and military officials tried to oust Hitler. But these efforts failed.

Individual Germans, outraged by Nazi atrocities, took action on their own. The most serious effort to get rid of Hitler occurred in 1944. In July of that year, a group of German officers led by Colonel Claus von Stauffenberg planted a bomb in Hitler's East Prussian headquarters. The 100th anniversary of von Stauffenberg's birth was marked in 2007.

In the following dramatized account (in which some characters and events are fictionalized), we see the action unfolding on that fateful 1944 summer day through the eyes of Carl Ludwig Beck, a fictitious young German officer who is a participant in the plot to kill Hitler.

In the early morning hours of July 20, 1944, a young German Army officer sat stiffly behind the wheel of a staff car, anxiously awaiting the arrival of another officer. It was a warm summer day in Berlin, Germany's capital, and Lieutenant Carl Ludwig Beck nervously tugged at the collar of his tunic where little beads of sweat had formed.

But it wasn't just the balmy weather that caused the 24-year-old officer to perspire. Tucked under the front seat was a leather briefcase containing an explosive device. In just a few hours, if all went well, the bomb now concealed in the car would be set off right next to Adolf Hitler, Führer (leader) of Nazi Germany and the most powerful and ruthless dictator of modern times. For this young officer was part of "Operation Valkyrie"—a plot to kill Hitler organized by anti-Nazi German officers and civilians.

Beck glanced at his watch: 5:45 A.M. "I hope he comes soon," he muttered softly to himself. "All this waiting is getting to me." His eyes darted across the tree-lined *Bendlerstrasse* to the drab building that housed the War Office. Although the first rays of light had appeared, dark shadows still shrouded much of the building. As a precaution against enemy air raids, thick curtains covered the windows, adding to the gloomy atmosphere.

Less than two months earlier, on June 6, Allied forces—American, British, Canadian, and French—had stormed ashore at Normandy on the French coast. Now, as the Allied troops battled their way toward Germany, bombing raids on German cities had increased.

Beck strained for a glimpse of his commanding officer. Still no sign. Suddenly he was aware of footsteps behind him. Looking into the rearview mirror, he saw a uniformed figure approaching the driver's side of the car.

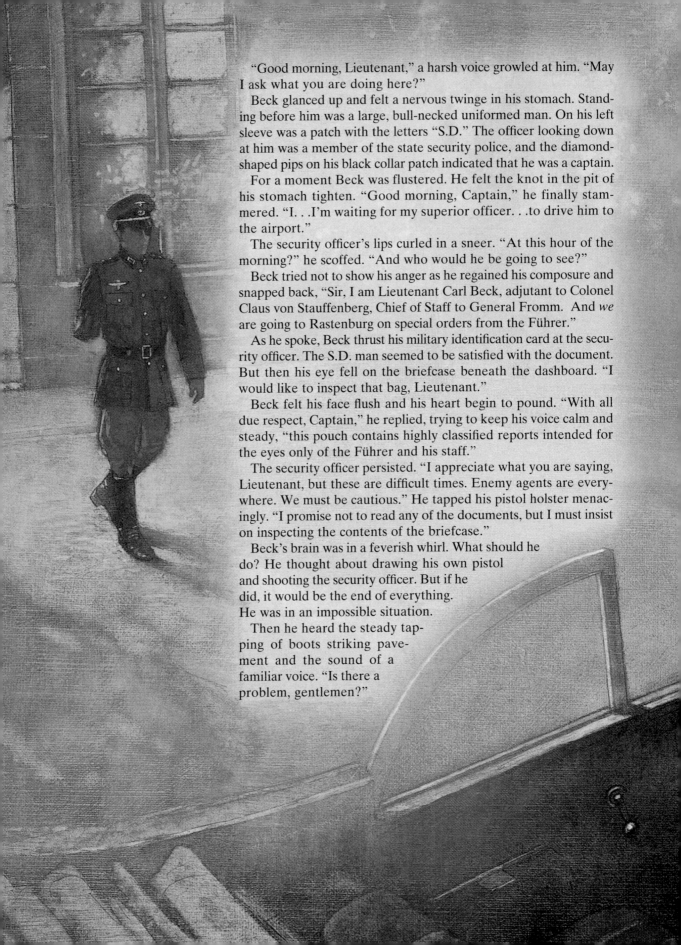

"Good morning, Lieutenant," a harsh voice growled at him. "May I ask what you are doing here?"

Beck glanced up and felt a nervous twinge in his stomach. Standing before him was a large, bull-necked uniformed man. On his left sleeve was a patch with the letters "S.D." The officer looking down at him was a member of the state security police, and the diamond-shaped pips on his black collar patch indicated that he was a captain.

For a moment Beck was flustered. He felt the knot in the pit of his stomach tighten. "Good morning, Captain," he finally stammered. "I. . .I'm waiting for my superior officer. . .to drive him to the airport."

The security officer's lips curled in a sneer. "At this hour of the morning?" he scoffed. "And who would he be going to see?"

Beck tried not to show his anger as he regained his composure and snapped back, "Sir, I am Lieutenant Carl Beck, adjutant to Colonel Claus von Stauffenberg, Chief of Staff to General Fromm. And *we* are going to Rastenburg on special orders from the Führer."

As he spoke, Beck thrust his military identification card at the security officer. The S.D. man seemed to be satisfied with the document. But then his eye fell on the briefcase beneath the dashboard. "I would like to inspect that bag, Lieutenant."

Beck felt his face flush and his heart begin to pound. "With all due respect, Captain," he replied, trying to keep his voice calm and steady, "this pouch contains highly classified reports intended for the eyes only of the Führer and his staff."

The security officer persisted. "I appreciate what you are saying, Lieutenant, but these are difficult times. Enemy agents are everywhere. We must be cautious." He tapped his pistol holster menacingly. "I promise not to read any of the documents, but I must insist on inspecting the contents of the briefcase."

Beck's brain was in a feverish whirl. What should he do? He thought about drawing his own pistol and shooting the security officer. But if he did, it would be the end of everything. He was in an impossible situation.

Then he heard the steady tapping of boots striking pavement and the sound of a familiar voice. "Is there a problem, gentlemen?"

Coming toward them, his step jaunty and his bearing erect and military, was Colonel Claus von Stauffenberg. The lower right sleeve of his tunic was pinned up, since he had lost most of his right arm—as well as two fingers of his left hand—during the fighting in North Africa a year earlier. In addition, he wore a black eye patch, for he had also lost his left eye.

When he reached the car, Stauffenberg repeated the question. "Do we have a problem here, gentlemen?"

The security policeman snapped to attention and clicked his heels loudly. "Good morning, Colonel," he said, raising his arm in the Nazi salute.

"Sir," Beck said. "This officer insists on inspecting your briefcase."

Stauffenberg seemed only mildly annoyed. "Didn't you explain that we are under orders to report to the Führer's headquarters by noon today and that the briefcase contains a report on the Reserve Army that the Führer has personally requested?"

Before either of the officers could respond, Stauffenberg went on, "And I don't think the Führer or Field Marshal Keitel will be pleased if we are delayed."

He smiled as he spoke, but his tone was crisp and commanding.

"But if this officer wishes to inspect the briefcase, then let him do so," Stauffenberg added. "Give it to him, Lieutenant."

Stunned, Beck slowly lifted the briefcase. But before he could hand it over, Stauffenberg continued, a hard edge in his voice.

"Of course, if we are late to the staff conference in Rastenburg, I shall have to inform the Führer of the *reason* for our delay."

Stauffenberg's one eye focused on the security officer as he said this. Now it was the turn of the police official to stammer. "Please, Colonel. . . I didn't fully understand the nature of your mission."

Beck could barely conceal a grin as the security officer ran around to the passenger side of the car and grabbed the door handle. "Allow me, Colonel," he said as he opened the door for Stauffenberg.

"Thank you, Captain—very kind of you," Stauffenberg replied with a haughty air. "By the way, what is your name, Captain?" Stauffenberg inquired as he eased into the passenger seat.

"Mueller, sir," the security man replied, clicking his heels with such force Beck thought the soles would pop out of his leather boots.

"Make a note of that name, Lieutenant Beck," Stauffenberg ordered with mock seriousness. "I shall certainly want to commend Captain Mueller for his diligence."

Once again Mueller snapped to attention.

"Thank you, sir," he said, and then added a quick "Heil Hitler."

Stauffenberg touched his cap, then ordered Beck to proceed. "Let's be off, Lieutenant. We don't want to be late for the meeting."

The car roared off, leaving the security officer standing in a cloud of exhaust fumes. When they were safely on the road to Rangsdorf Airport, Beck expressed his admiration for the way Stauffenberg had handled the situation.

Stauffenberg laughed. "Boldness, my young friend, is an important quality for a successful officer. Remember, I come from a long line of soldiers."

The drive to the airport took them past the imposing Reich Chancellery, the heart of the Nazi German government, with its columned entrance adorned by an enormous Nazi eagle. A few years earlier, the showcase building would have been lit up by floodlights. But the wartime blackout had put an end to that.

Farther on they came to a part of the city that had been bombed out by American and British aircraft. As Beck surveyed the shattered buildings, he thought back to when he had first entered the army in 1940. In those days, the German war machine had seemed unbeatable, conquering most of Western Europe in a matter of months. And it

was the German Air Force—the *Luftwaffe*—that had unleashed devastating air attacks on cities in Belgium, Holland, and Great Britain.

"Look around you, Beck," Stauffenberg remarked, as if reading the lieutenant's mind. "You see before you the real monument to Adolf Hitler. Not pompous statues and gaudy buildings, but bombed-out homes and freshly dug graves."

They arrived at the airport just after 7 A.M. An old Heinkel twin-engine bomber, converted into a staff plane, was waiting for them. As soon as the two officers had boarded, the plane took off.

The flight to Rastenburg, in East Prussia, took three hours, giving Stauffenberg and Beck plenty of time to review the plan. Inside Stauffenberg's briefcase, wrapped in a spare shirt, was a small slab of hexite, a plastic explosive. Inserted into the hexite was a simple fuse and detonator. By using a pair of small pliers, Stauffenberg could nip the fuse, releasing an acid that would eat through the wire and trigger the bomb. The fuse had a short setting—only ten minutes. So everything would have to be done quickly and efficiently.

Out of earshot of the pilot and crew, the two officers went over the sequence of events that would follow Hitler's death. A temporary government had been organized to replace the Nazis. At its head was Beck's uncle, General Ludwig Beck, the former Army Chief of Staff who had resigned in 1938 to protest Hitler's aggressive war plans.

General Beck would serve as Regent and temporary commander-in-chief of the armed forces. Colonel Stauffenberg would be Secretary of State for War. Other members of the new government would be a mix of many political parties. Only Nazi and Communist Party members would be barred.

As soon as Hitler was dead, word would be flashed from the Führer's headquarters to Berlin. There, commanders and troops who were part of

Operation Valkyrie would arrest key Nazi officials and seize important installations. Similar action would be taken by conspirators throughout German-occupied Europe.

Stauffenberg was confident that once Hitler was out of the way, they would be able to negotiate a decent peace settlement with the Allies. Beck nodded his head in agreement. But as he gazed out the window, a troubled expression hardened his youthful features.

Stauffenberg sensed something was wrong and asked, "What's bothering you, Lieutenant?"

Beck faltered momentarily, then replied, "I just wonder if what we're doing is right. After all, we are about to become assassins. Do we have to kill Hitler? Couldn't we take him prisoner instead, hold him hostage—then force the government to start peace talks?"

The colonel shook his head. "No, Beck, we can't do it any other way. We're dealing with a devil, and you can't reason with a devil. Either we destroy Hitler, or the monster will destroy us—and Germany."

"You know, most of us were awed by Hitler in the early days," Stauffenberg continued. "He pulled us out of bad economic times, rebuilt the army, provided jobs for everyone. He seemed like a miracle man. But then came the war and things changed."

Stauffenberg paused, pointing to his empty sleeve and the eye patch. "When I was in the hospital recovering from my wounds, I had plenty of time to think. My eyes were bandaged and it seemed as if I might lose my sight completely. I thought of our soldiers dying in the snow around Stalingrad. About the Russian villages our troops destroyed, the civilians who were massacred. About the slave-labor camps, and those other camps we're not supposed to know about. You know, the camps where they are killing Jews. . ."

Beck interrupted him. "Yes, of course, Colonel, I know. I served on the Eastern Front. But we took an oath—an oath of loyalty to Hitler."

Stauffenberg nodded. "You're right, Beck; we all took the oath. And it was an oath we should never have taken. Our loyalty as soldiers should always be to the nation and not to any one man. Now we have taken an oath to work together to save Germany."

He paused, then added, "Yesterday I spoke with your uncle, General Beck, and he told me, 'For a good man, what is right is always clear. The problem is to find the strength to do it.'"

Stauffenberg reached over and gently touched Beck on the arm. "We must stand together. Our cause is just. Can I count on you?"

Beck smiled weakly. "Of course, Colonel. Our cause *is* just. You can count on me."

The plane landed at the small Rastenburg airstrip at 10 A.M. A staff car was waiting to shuttle them to Hitler's forest headquarters—the *Wolfsschanze,* or "Wolf's Lair"—a few miles away.

As the car made its way through a gloomy forest of birch and pine trees, Stauffenberg whispered to Beck, "We are about to enter the Wolf's Lair, my friend. Getting in will be no problem. The trick will be to get out without being devoured by the wolves."

Beck shuddered at the words. Up ahead loomed a guard post manned by soldiers of the S.S., the Nazi Elite

Guard. A sentry inspected their passes, then waved them through. The staff car continued along a narrow road that cut through a network of minefields.

A couple of miles up the road they came to another checkpoint—an electrified barbed-wire fence. Once again, S.S. guards with automatic weapons checked their passes, then phoned ahead to announce their arrival. Beck felt his stomach knotting as they approached and entered the heavily guarded inner compound. The staff car slowly cruised along a U-shaped

road, finally coming to a halt in a parking area not far from Hitler's underground bunker and the wooden conference building where most of the staff meetings were held.

An officer from the camp commandant's office greeted them and informed the visitors that the staff meeting originally scheduled for 1 P.M. had been pushed up to 12:30. When Stauffenberg asked why, the officer explained that Benito Mussolini, the ousted Italian fascist dictator, was scheduled to meet with Hitler at 2:30 P.M.

"The Führer wants the staff meeting out of the way before Mussolini's arrival," the officer explained. "However, there's plenty of time for you to freshen up and have some breakfast."

Stauffenberg and Beck exchanged glances.

The time change meant that they would have to work faster than they had planned.

Beck, Stauffenberg, and the camp commandant's adjutant breakfasted at the officers' mess hall. Finishing quickly, Stauffenberg left the two junior officers and went to speak with the camp's chief signal officer, a fellow conspirator. It would be this officer's job to send word to Berlin that Hitler was dead and then to cut communications between Rastenburg and the outside world.

It was a few minutes past noon when Stauffenberg returned. "We must report to Field Marshal Keitel now," Stauffenberg told Beck.

Field Marshal Wilhelm Keitel, chief of the Army General Staff, greeted Stauffenberg in a formal but friendly manner. Beck saw before him a large man in a bemedaled uniform.

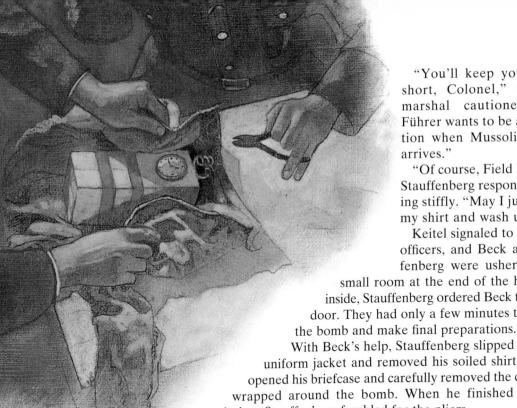

"You'll keep your report short, Colonel," the field marshal cautioned. "The Führer wants to be at the station when Mussolini's train arrives."

"Of course, Field Marshal," Stauffenberg responded, bowing stiffly. "May I just change my shirt and wash up?"

Keitel signaled to one of his officers, and Beck and Stauffenberg were ushered into a small room at the end of the hall. Once inside, Stauffenberg ordered Beck to lock the door. They had only a few minutes to activate the bomb and make final preparations.

With Beck's help, Stauffenberg slipped out of his uniform jacket and removed his soiled shirt. Then he opened his briefcase and carefully removed the clean shirt wrapped around the bomb. When he finished changing clothes, Stauffenberg fumbled for the pliers.

"I see them, Colonel," Beck offered, reaching in and pulling out the rubber-handled pliers. "Shall I nip the fuse?"

"No," said Stauffenberg firmly. "That's my responsibility." He took the pliers and quickly snipped the end of the fuse, releasing the acid.

"There—it's done," the colonel said with a heavy sigh. "We have exactly ten minutes before this thing goes off."

A rapping at the door jolted them. It was Field Marshal Keitel, bellowing his annoyance at the delay. "Come on, Stauffenberg, we're already late for the conference."

Beck glanced at his watch: 12:32 P.M. Quickly wrapping the bomb in the soiled shirt, Beck placed it back in the briefcase, covering the shirt with some papers.

Then they left the room and joined Keitel for the short walk to the one-story conference building. As they proceeded down the corridor to the map room where the conference was being held, Stauffenberg called out to the sergeant in charge of the telephone room, "I'm expecting an important call from Berlin. Send someone to fetch me as soon as it comes." This was a ploy designed to give Stauffenberg an excuse for leaving the room after he had planted the bomb.

Seconds later they were at the entrance to the conference room. The door was opened, and as Keitel and the colonel entered the room, Stauffenberg said to Beck, "Take care of those matters we discussed, Lieutenant." Then the door closed abruptly.

Following his instructions, Beck went to the telephone exchange and called the airport, alerting their pilot to be ready to take off at a moment's notice. Then he went directly to the car park. After informing the driver of the staff car that he wouldn't be needed on the trip back to the airstrip, Beck slid behind the wheel and waited.

Minutes ticked by slowly. Finally, after what seemed like an hour, he saw Stauffenberg walking quickly toward him. As the colonel neared the car, Beck checked his watch. It was 12:42 P.M.

"It should go off any second now," Stauffenberg said anxiously as he got into the front seat next to Beck. "I placed the briefcase no more than twelve feet from where Hitler was standing."

The two men looked toward the building as more seconds slowly ticked by. And then, with an ear-shattering roar that shook the ground and made them both duck instinctively, the bomb exploded.

When the two officers looked up, they saw debris raining down on the shattered building. Cries for help could be heard from the wounded men.

"My God," Beck heard himself saying in amazement, "nobody could survive that blast!"

"You're right, Beck," Stauffenberg said jubilantly. "We've done it! Hitler is dead! Come on, let's get out of here."

Beck stepped on the gas. In the confusion after the explosion, they raced quickly through the first checkpoint without being stopped.

At the second checkpoint, S.S. guards confronted them. The one-armed colonel jumped out of the car and grabbed the guard post phone. He appeared to speak briefly to someone in authority, then told the guards, "It's all right, I'm allowed to pass."

Before the startled S.S. men could question him further, Stauffenberg got back in the car and the two officers roared off.

"Who did you speak to?" Beck asked.

"No one," Stauffenberg replied with a laugh. "It was just a bluff."

By the time they reached the last checkpoint, however, word had been flashed to the guards that no one was to pass through without special clearance. Wooden barriers with sharpened stakes had been pulled across the road, and a squad of S.S. men barred the way.

Beck slammed on the brakes and the car screeched to a halt. A sergeant with a machine pistol dangling from a shoulder strap approached the car.

"You must have a special pass to leave the area, Colonel," the sergeant informed the two officers.

"I have orders to meet General Fromm at the airstrip," Stauffenberg lied. "I'm allowed through."

The sergeant lowered his machine pistol menacingly. "I'm sorry, sir, but you must have clearance."

Beck felt his heart pumping furiously, and he was certain that the S.S. men could hear the heavy pounding.

But Stauffenberg remained calm as usual. Getting out of the car, he insisted on speaking directly to the camp commandant's adjutant. The sergeant glared at the colonel, then pointed to the phone.

Beck caught fragments of the conversation. "Captain. . .It's Stauffenberg. . . We had just had breakfast. . .I need clearance. . .Urgent orders."

When he had finished, Stauffenberg handed the phone curtly to the sergeant. After speaking with the camp adjutant, the sergeant allowed them to pass.

Moments later, they were racing along the twisting forest road. At times Beck thought the car would surely slam into a tree. Finally, they arrived at the airstrip where their plane was already on the tarmac, engines whining. Shortly after 1 P.M. they were airborne again, and three hours later they landed in Berlin.

Arriving at the War Ministry building in *Bendlerstrasse* at around 5 P.M., Beck and Stauffenberg found a scene of confusion. The plan to seize key installations and prominent Nazi officials hadn't been put into effect. A shocked Stauffenberg was told that the conspirators had hesitated because the message that flashed from Rastenburg after the bomb went off seemed to indicate that Hitler was still alive.

"That's impossible!" Stauffenberg exclaimed. "I saw the explosion. It looked like a hundred-and-fifty-millimeter shell had scored a direct hit on the building. No one could have survived."

Stauffenberg quickly took command and began issuing orders. The elite Guard Battalion was ordered to move into the center of Berlin. Troops and police loyal to the conspirators were sent to arrest leading Nazi officials and disarm S.S. units.

But in the midst of the flurry of activity, a white-faced officer rushed in with shocking news. He informed them that Nazi Propaganda Minister Joseph Goebbels had just issued a statement, broadcast on the radio, that Hitler was alive.

"It could be a trick," Stauffenberg responded.

The messenger shook his head. "No, Colonel, the commander of the Guard Battalion was summoned to Goebbels's office and allowed to speak by phone with Hitler. He has reaffirmed his loyalty to the Führer and is now leading his troops here to arrest us."

Standing off to the side, Beck was stunned by the developments. He watched as a visibly shaken Stauffenberg conferred with other key plotters, including his uncle General Beck. When the conference was over, Stauffenberg spoke to the young lieutenant.

"It's finished, Beck; the whole plan has fallen apart," the colonel told him. "In a little while the S.S. will be here and we will all be arrested. I must see this thing through to the end. It's my duty."

Then he clutched Beck's arm. "Your uncle and I agree that someone must tell the world that there were decent Germans—soldiers and civilians—who stood up to Hitler and nearly toppled the whole rotten Nazi regime. You are the one we have selected."

Beck protested, "I'm no coward—I'm not going to run away!"

But Stauffenberg insisted that Beck make his escape. "Change into civilian clothes. Make your way to the address on this paper—destroy it after you've memorized it. The people there will help you reach the Allied lines. God be with you."

Ten minutes later, Lieutenant Carl Beck, now dressed as an ordinary civilian, made his way along the darkened streets of Berlin, his head still reeling from the day's events. Overhead he could hear the drone of B-17 bombers making their nightly bombing run over the German capital. As he listened to the distant explosions, Beck hoped that each of the bombs would be another nail in the coffin of Adolf Hitler and the Nazi empire he had created.

⌒EPILOGUE⌒

Adolf Hitler had survived the bomb blast at his Rastenburg headquarters by sheer luck. After Stauffenberg left the map room, another officer had jostled the briefcase containing the bomb. Because it was in his way, the officer placed it behind one of the heavy wooden beams supporting the map table. That simple act shielded Hitler from the full effect of the blast. He emerged from the wrecked building with only minor burns and bruises and damaged eardrums.

In the wake of the assassination attempt, thousands of Germans believed to have been involved in the plot were rounded up and brutally tortured and killed. After a failed suicide attempt, General Beck was shot to death by a Nazi soldier. Colonel Claus von Stauffenberg and several fellow officers were shot by a firing squad that very evening in the courtyard of the War Ministry.

Less than one year after the failure of "Operation Valkyrie," Adolf Hitler was dead, and the Nazi regime was in shambles. On April 30, 1945, with Russian troops less than a mile from his underground Berlin bunker, the Nazi dictator committed suicide.

Summing up the July 20th plot, one British historian has written: "Operation Valkyrie failed, but it was boldly, brilliantly conceived. Those who took part in it set an example of moral courage which will live on for countless generations of Germans down the ages."

A monument to Colonel von Stauffenberg and his co-conspirators now stands at the spot where they were executed. There are no monuments to Adolf Hitler.

HENRY I. KURTZ
Author, *The U.S. Army*

BEST BOOKS, 2007

The John Newbery Medal and the Randolph Caldecott Medal are important children's book awards. They are sometimes considered the "Academy Awards" of U.S. children's book publishing.

The American Library Association gives both awards annually. The Newbery Medal is given to the author of the best American literary work for young children. The Caldecott Medal is given to the illustrator of the best American picture book for children. Here are the 2007 winners.

NEWBERY MEDAL

The Higher Power of Lucky, by Susan Patron, is a novel about a 10-year-old girl who struggles to get control of her life after her mother's accidental death. Lucky is being raised in Hard Pan, California, a run-down collection of shacks and trailers, smack in the middle of the desert, with a population of 43. There, Lucky tries to adjust to her new life and find a "higher power" that will help her with her difficulties. Lucky and her friends, her trusty dog HMS Beagle, and the quirky residents of Hard Pan combine to make this an outstanding story.

Newbery Honor Books. *Rules,* by Cynthia Lord, tells the story of 12-year-old Catherine, whose younger brother, David, is autistic. Catherine doesn't like taking care of him and is embarrassed by his behavior—so she creates rules for him. Catherine is especially unhappy about the fact that her brother's needs come first in her family. She loves David, but she resents him nevertheless. Her growing friendship with Jason, a 14-year-old paraplegic, helps Catherine understand her feelings.

In *Penny From Heaven,* by Jennifer L. Holm, preteen Penny Falucci lives with her "plain old American" mother and maternal

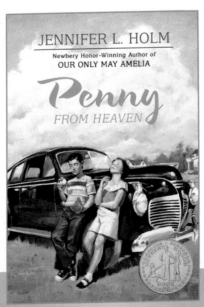

grandparents. She is spending the summer of her twelfth birthday with her deceased father's family. But she is disappointed that both her mother and her father's large Italian family refuse to discuss how her father died. The secret of his death is eventually revealed in this gently paced novel, which takes place in 1953. The story is partly based on real events in the author's life.

Sixteen-year-old orphan Hattie Brooks is the courageous title character in *Hattie Big Sky*, by Kirby Larson. Bounced from one relative to another, Hattie leaves Iowa to take over her late uncle's homestead in Montana—Big Sky Country. Her adventures there highlight the hardships faced by many Montana homesteaders in the early 1900's.

CALDECOTT MEDAL

In *Flotsam*, illustrated and written by David Wiesner, a curious boy goes to the beach to look for bottles, toys, and other bits of flotsam that have washed up on the beach. He finds a very old underwater camera with film in it. When he develops the film, he discovers some fantastical pictures. In one, a mechanical windup fish swims along with a school of real fish. In another, a blown-up puffer fish floats above the water like a hot-air balloon. At the end of the book, there's a portrait of a girl holding photos of other children from around the world and from times past. Using the old camera, the boy takes a photo of himself holding the other photos. He

then tosses the camera back into the sea, to be picked up by someone else somewhere else.

Caldecott Honor Books. *Gone Wild: An Endangered Animal Alphabet,* by David McLimans, has 26 pages of bold and playful black-and-white illustrations of endangered animals, one for every letter of the alphabet. Each animal's shape—from Chinese Alligator to Grevy's Zebra—is formed from the letter of the alphabet that begins the animal's name. The Z, for example, is covered with the black-and-white stripes of a zebra.

Moses: When Harriet Tubman Led Her People to Freedom is illustrated by Kadir Nelson and written by Carole Boston Weatherford. The book relates how Harriet Tubman's religious faith helped her escape from slavery and then guide other African-American slaves from the South to freedom in the North along the Underground Railroad.

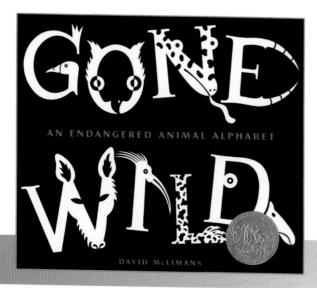

The Arabian Nights is one of the best-known pieces of Arabic literature in the West. It's a collection of stories within a story—tales that are told by a princess to save her life.

The heroine of the stories is Princess Scheherazade. She marries Sultan Shahriyar, who has killed his first wife for being unfaithful. Every night since then, he has married a new wife, and then had her beheaded the next morning. Scheherazade avoids the same fate by entertaining him each night with a story—stopping just before she reaches the end. The following night she finishes the tale and begins a new story. After a thousand and one nights, the Sultan realizes that she is a good and faithful wife.

The true origins of the stories aren't known. But many of them are thought to be based on old tales told by Indian, Persian, and Arab storytellers. They are believed to have been first written down in Egypt, in the 1400's. In the 1700's, a French translation called A Thousand and One Nights appeared, and several English translations followed. Along the way new tales were added, and different versions of the older stories were given.

One of the most famous tales, "Aladdin and the Wonderful Lamp," follows. This was one of the stories that were added to the collection, and its origin is unknown. Like many of the other tales, it has appeared in many different versions.

 # Aladdin and the Wonderful Lamp

Long, long ago there lived a tailor named Mustapha. He was so poor that he could barely support his wife and son. Now, his son, whose name was Aladdin, was very lazy and didn't obey his parents, and he played all day in the streets with other lazy boys. His father was so upset with his son that he became ill and died in a few months. Aladdin and his mother were now poorer than ever.

One day, as Aladdin was playing with his friends, a stranger passed by and stopped and stared at Aladdin. This stranger was a magician. Taking Aladdin aside, he said, "Boy, isn't your father Mustapha the tailor?" "Yes," replied the boy. "But he is now dead."

At these words, the magician kissed him and cried, "I am your uncle. I have been in Africa for many years and have just come home." Then he gave the boy some money and said, "Go and tell your mother that I will visit her tomorrow."

As soon as the magician had gone, Aladdin ran to his mother overjoyed. "Mother," he said, "I have met my uncle!" "No, my son," answered his mother, "you have no uncle on your father's side or mine." But the next day, as Aladdin's mother was preparing dinner, the magician entered, his arms filled with meats and various fruits. He greeted Aladdin's mother and told her how upset he was that he hadn't arrived in time to see his brother.

Then he turned to Aladdin and asked him what trade he intended to work at. At this question Aladdin hung down his head, embarrassed, while his mother replied that he was just a lazy boy, who spent much of the day living on the streets.

"This is not good," said the magician. "If you have no desire to learn a craft, then I will purchase a shop for you and furnish it with the finest merchandise." Aladdin's mother, who until then hadn't believed that the magician was really her husband's brother, now could no longer doubt it. She gratefully thanked him for all his kindness.

The next day the magician took Aladdin to a merchant who provided the boy with a handsome suit of clothes. Together they went to the richest shops, the largest mosques, and the most well-known inns. The magician then led Aladdin out of the city, and they traveled many miles until they reached a valley between two great mountains.

"We will go no farther," said the magician. "I will now show you some extraordinary things. First, gather some loose sticks." When Aladdin had done that, the magician set fire to them. At the same time, he muttered several magical words and cast incense upon the flames. Immediately, a great smoke arose and the ground began to shake. Then the ground opened up, revealing a great stone slab with a brass ring in the middle.

Aladdin was so frightened that he started to run away, but the magician caught hold of him and knocked him to the ground. Aladdin stood up, trembling, and with tears in his eyes he asked what he had done to deserve such a punishment. "I have my reasons," answered the magician harshly. "Now, my boy," he continued, softening his tone, "under this stone is hidden a treasure that is destined to be yours. And fate decrees that no one but you may lift the stone or enter the cave, but to do so, you must obey my instructions."

Aladdin promised that he would. The magician told him to take hold of the ring and lift the stone, and to say at the same time the names of his father and grandfather. Aladdin followed the instructions and raised the heavy stone with ease. When the stone was pulled up, there appeared a cave with steps leading down.

"Listen, my boy, to what I tell you," said the magician. "Go down the steps, and at the bottom you will find an open door. Beyond the door are three great halls. Pass through them without stopping. At the end of the third hall you will find a door that opens out into a garden filled with fine fruit trees. Walk across the garden to a terrace, where you will see a lighted lamp in a niche in the terrace wall. Take down the lamp, pour out the oil, and bring it to me." The magician then took a ring from his finger and placed it on Aladdin's finger, telling him that it would protect him from all evil.

Aladdin went into the cave, descended the steps, and found the three halls just as the magician had described. He passed through each one, crossed the garden, took down the lamp, poured out the oil, and started to leave with it. But as he came down from the terrace, he stopped for a moment to look around. He saw that all the trees were filled with what seemed to be glass fruits of different colors. Actually,

the white fruits were pearls, the transparent ones were diamonds, the red were rubies, the green were emeralds, the blue were sapphires, and the purple were amethysts. Aladdin didn't realize how valuable the fruits were, but he was so pleased with their beauty that he gathered some of every kind.

Aladdin returned the way he had come and found the magician waiting impatiently for him. Now, the lamp that Aladdin was holding had magical powers. The magician was planning to take it from Aladdin before the boy got out of the cave. He then intended to push Aladdin down the steps so there would be no witness to what had occurred. But Aladdin wisely refused to give up the lamp until he was out of the cave. This so enraged the magician that he moved the stone that had covered the cave back into place. And, having lost all hope of getting the wonderful lamp, the magician returned to Africa.

Of course, the magician wasn't Aladdin's uncle at all. He had just needed the boy to get the magic lamp.

When Aladdin found himself thus buried alive, he sat down on the steps, without any hope of ever again seeing the sun. He remained like this for two days, without eating or drinking. On the third day, clasping his hands in despair, he accidentally rubbed the ring that the magician had forgotten to take back. Immediately, an enormous genie appeared, and said, "I am the slave of any who may possess the ring and will grant you two wishes. What would you have me do?"

Aladdin answered without hesitation. "Whoever you are, deliver me from this place immediately!" He had no sooner spoken these words than he found himself outside the cave. He quickly made his way home and joyfully greeted his mother. Aladdin related to her all that had happened and showed her the transparent fruits of different colors. The mother, too, was unaware of their value and laid them carelessly aside.

Aladdin slept soundly until the next morning, but upon waking he found that there was no food in the house, nor any money. "Alas, my son," said his mother, "I haven't a bit of bread to give you." "Mother," replied Aladdin, "give me the lamp I brought home with me yesterday. I will go and sell it."

Aladdin's mother brought the lamp, and because it was very dirty, she took some fine sand and water to clean it. But as soon as she began to rub it, a hideous genie appeared before her and said in a voice like thunder, "I am the slave of any who may possess the lamp. What would you have me do?"

Aladdin said, "We are hungry. Bring us something to eat." The genie disappeared and in an instant returned with a silver tray on which were twelve silver dishes containing the most delicious foods. These he placed on a table and disappeared.

Mother and son had enough food for two days. On the third day, Aladdin went to the silver market and sold one of the silver dishes and bought enough food to last for some time. When all the silver dishes had been sold, Aladdin brought out the lamp once again. In this way, he and his mother continued to live for some time. And although they had an incredible treasure in their copper lamp, they lived quietly and frugally.

In the meantime, Aladdin and his mother learned that the fruits he had gathered in the garden were very valuable and not just brightly colored pieces of glass.

One day, a royal order proclaimed that the Princess Badroul-boudour, the Sultan's daughter, would be passing through the city. When Aladdin saw her, he immediately fell in love. Upon returning home, he announced to his mother, "I love the Princess, and I have decided to ask the Sultan for her hand in marriage."

Aladdin's mother burst out laughing. "My son," she said, "you must be mad to talk thus!" "I assure you, my mother," replied Aladdin, "that I am not mad, and I expect you to use your persuasion with the Sultan." "I, go to the Sultan?" answered his mother, amazed. "I cannot undertake such an errand. And who are you, my son," she continued, "to think of the Sultan's daughter? Have you forgotten that your father was one of the poorest tailors in the city? Besides, no one ever goes to the Sultan without taking him a fitting present." Aladdin replied, "Wouldn't those jewels that I brought home from the garden make an acceptable present?" And he arranged the brilliant stones in a large porcelain dish.

The next morning, Aladdin's mother took the precious gift and set out for the Sultan's palace. She entered the audience chamber and placed herself before the Sultan, the Grand Vizier, and the great lords of the court. She saluted the Sultan, and he said to her, "My good woman, what business brings you here?"

Aladdin's mother told him about her son's love for the Princess and his desire to marry her. She ended by presenting the porcelain dish to the Sultan. The Sultan stared in amazement at the many beautiful and valuable jewels. He turned to his Grand Vizier and said, "Is not such a present worthy of the Princess?"

These words upset the Grand Vizier because he had hoped that the Princess would marry his son. So he whispered to the Sultan, "The present is certainly worthy of the Princess, but I beg you to grant me three months. In that time I hope that my son will have a richer present than Aladdin, who is a complete stranger to his majesty."

The Sultan agreed and, turning to Aladdin's mother, said to her, "My good woman, go home and tell your son that I agree to his proposal, but that my daughter cannot marry until the end of three months." Aladdin's mother, overjoyed, rushed home to tell her son, who thought himself the most happy of all men.

When the three-month period had passed, the Grand Vizier had not come up with a richer present. But the Sultan was now having doubts about giving his daughter to a stranger, and he thought of putting Aladdin off by issuing an order that would be impossible to fulfill. So when Aladdin's mother went to the Sultan to remind him of his promise, he said, "My good woman, it is true that Sultans should keep their promises, and I will do so as soon as your son sends me forty trays of gold, each filled with stunning jewels, carried by forty magnificently dressed slaves."

When Aladdin heard of the Sultan's request, he took the lamp and rubbed it and ordered the genie to fetch the desired present as quickly as possible. In a short time the genie returned with forty slaves, each bearing on his head a heavy gold tray filled with pearls, diamonds, rubies, and emeralds, all larger and more beautiful than those already presented to the Sultan.

The forty slaves and the humble mother walked through the streets to the palace. There, the Sultan cast his eyes on what was before him and hesitated no longer. At the sight of such immense riches and Aladdin's quickness in satisfying his demand, he was persuaded that the young man would make a most desirable son-in-law. Therefore he said to Aladdin's mother, "Go and tell your son that I wait with open arms to embrace him."

When Aladdin heard the joyous news, he again summoned the obedient genie. "Genie, provide me with the finest clothing, a magnificent and swift steed, richly clothed slaves to walk by my side, and ten thousand pieces of gold, half of which I will give to the people in the streets. Bring my mother six female attendants, as richly dressed as those of any princess. I would also have you build me a palace near the Sultan's. Build it of the finest marble of various colors. Let the walls be of gold and silver, and the windows studded with brilliant gems. Let there be a spacious park separating the two palaces. And let there be a carpet of the plushest velvet for the Princess to walk upon, between the two palaces."

And so the genie granted Aladdin all his wishes, and the marriage between the two young people took place the next day.

For several years, the Princess and Aladdin lived happily in peace and contentment. But one day, the African magician became curious—he wondered what had befallen Aladdin after he had left him in the cave. When he learned that Aladdin, instead of having perished miserably, had escaped, had married a beautiful princess, was living splendidly, and was in possession of the wonderful lamp, he became enraged.

In less than a day, the magician was at Aladdin's palace, where he was told that Aladdin was on a hunting trip. The magician then went to a coppersmith's and bought a dozen copper lamps. He placed these in a basket and returned to Aladdin's palace. As he approached, he began crying out, "Who will change old lamps for new ones?"

Now the Princess, who was in the palace, heard him and remembered the old lamp that Aladdin had. Not knowing the value of the lamp, she had a slave take it and make the exchange.

The magician left the palace grounds. As soon as he was alone, he rubbed the lamp and the genie appeared, saying, "What would you have me do? I will obey you as your slave, and the slave of any who may possess the lamp."

"I command you," replied the magician, "to transport me and also the palace that you have built in this city, with all the people in it, to Africa." The genie disappeared, and so too did the magician and the palace.

When the Sultan awoke the next morning, he went to his window to admire Aladdin's palace. But to his great amazement, all he saw was an empty space. He called for his Grand Vizier and demanded, "Tell me, what has become of Aladdin's palace?" "His palace!" exclaimed the Vizier. "Is it not in its usual place?" And when the Vizier went to the window, he too was struck with amazement. "Alas," said the Grand Vizier, "it has vanished completely. I always thought that the building, with all its magnificent riches, was the work of magic and a magician!"

At these words the Sultan flew into a great passion. "Where is that impostor, that wicked wretch?" he cried. "Go and bring him to me in chains!" A detachment of troops met Aladdin as he was returning from the hunt and arrested him.

When Aladdin was brought before the Sultan, he said, "I don't know what I have done to lose your favor. What crime have I committed?" "Your crime, you wretch," yelled the Sultan. "Do you not know it? Where is your palace? What has become of my daughter?" Aladdin looked from the window and, seeing the empty spot where his palace had stood, was thrown into confusion.

Finally, he said, "I know not where my palace has vanished. Grant me forty days in which to find out." "Go," said the Sultan. "I give you the forty days you ask for, but if you do not find my daughter, you shall not escape my wrath!"

For many days, Aladdin roamed about the city making inquiries, but all in vain. Finally he wandered into the country and sat down by the bank of a river to rest. Clasping his hands in despair, he accidentally rubbed the ring that the magician had placed upon his finger before he went into the cave. Immediately the same genie appeared who had helped him escape.

Aladdin remembered that the genie of the ring would grant him one more wish, and said, "Genie, I command you to transport my palace back to where it stood." "What you command is not in my power," answered the genie. "I am only the slave of the ring. You must summon the slave of the lamp." "If that is the case," said Aladdin, "I command you to transport me to the spot where my palace now stands."

Instantly Aladdin found himself in Africa, in his wife's room in the palace. When the Princess saw him standing there, she couldn't believe her eyes. After they had embraced, Aladdin said, "I beg you, dear Princess, tell me what became of an old lamp that I left in my dressing room when I left for the hunt." "Alas, dear husband," answered the Princess, "I was afraid our misfortune might be owing to that lamp, and what grieves me most is that I have been the cause of it." "Princess," replied Aladdin, "do not blame yourself, but tell me into whose hands it has fallen."

The Princess related just what had happened. She further went on to say that the wicked magician visited her each night and tried to persuade her to take him for a husband in place of Aladdin. "And," she added, "he carries the wonderful lamp with him at all times. He never lets it out of his sight."

"Princess," said Aladdin, "I think I have a plan to free ourselves from this terrible wretch. When he comes to see you tonight, place this powder in a cup of wine and offer it to him. He will esteem it so great a favor from you that he will not refuse." With those words Aladdin left her room.

When evening arrived, the magician came at the usual hour. As Aladdin had predicted, he readily drank the wine the Princess offered—and fell to the floor dead. Aladdin then entered and took the lamp and rubbed it. "Genie," said Aladdin, "transport this palace instantly to where it came from."

The following morning, the Sultan awoke and wandered over to his window, absorbed in grief. As he cast his eyes toward the spot he expected to find empty, he now saw Aladdin's palace in all its grandeur. He quickly rushed to his daughter's side, and with tears of joy they embraced.

The Sultan was so happy that he held a ten-day festival for the entire city to honor the return of the Princess and Aladdin.

POETRY

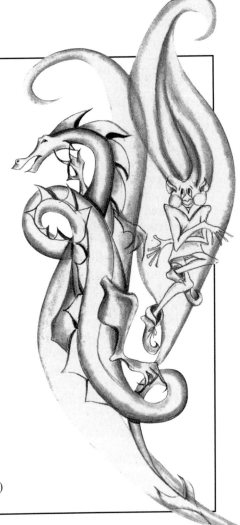

FLAME FAIRIES

Knights on golden prancing steeds,
　Elves and goblins leaping higher,
I can see the finest things
　In the dancing fire!

Sometimes dragons twist and curl
　Tails of red and purple light,
Sometimes giants, sometimes gnomes,
　Meet in fearsome fight!

Banners stream above the wood,
　Gaily-painted ships sail past
With a green or yellow flag
　Flying from the mast.

Then they change from this to that,
　Steeds to castles, ships to kings,
And a dragon vanishes
　Into golden rings.

Flames are fairies prisoned fast,
　Long within the logs they lie;
Once they're free they gaily leap
　Upward to the sky!

Rupert Sargent Holland (1878–1952)

THINKING OF EAST MOUNTAIN

It's been so long since I headed for East Mountain—
how many times have the roses bloomed?
White clouds have scattered themselves away—
and this bright moon—whose house is it setting on?

Li Po (8th Century)

THE CAT

Within that porch, across the way,
　I see two naked eyes this night;
Two eyes that neither shut nor blink,
　Searching my face with a green light.

But cats to me are strange, so strange—
　I cannot sleep if one is near;
And though I'm sure I see those eyes
　I'm not so sure a body's there.

William Henry Davies (1871–1940)

THE STARGAZER

A stargazer out late at night,
With eyes and thoughts turned both upright,
Tumbled by chance into a well
(A dismal story this to tell);
He roared and sobbed, and roared again,
And cursed the "Bear" and "Charles's Wain."

His woeful cries a neighbour brought,
Less learned, but wiser far in thought;
"My friend," quoth he, "you're much misled,
With stars to trouble thus your head;
Since you with these misfortunes meet,
For want of looking to your feet."

UNKNOWN

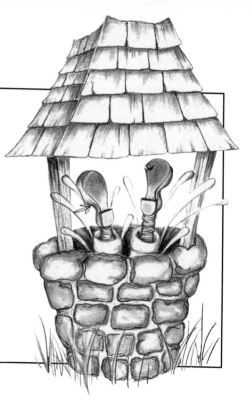

AS THE WORLD TURNS

I'm up and down and round about,
Yet all the world can't find me out,
Though hundreds have employed their leisure,
They never yet could take my measure,
I'm found in almost every garden,
Nay, in the compass of a farthing;
There's not a chariot, coach, nor mill,
Can move an inch except I will.
(A circle)

JONATHAN SWIFT (1667–1745)

THE DAISY'S SONG

The sun, with his great eye,
Sees not so much as I;
And the moon, all silver-proud
Might as well be in a cloud.

And O the spring—the spring!
I lead the life of a king!
Couch'd in the teeming grass,
I spy each pretty lass.

I look where no one dares,
And I stare where no one stares,
And when the night is nigh
Lambs bleat my lullaby.

JOHN KEATS (1795–1821)

In medieval England, stories say, lived the most famous outlaw of all time—a robber who stole from the rich to give to the poor and whose skill with a longbow was legendary. He was Robin Hood, who lived deep in Sherwood Forest with his band of merry men. But no one knows if the tales of Robin Hood are true—or if the famous bandit even existed.

Some historians have said that Robin Hood was really Robert Fitzooth, Earl of Huntingdon, who lived in the 1100's. Others have thought that he was Roger Godberd, a notorious bandit of the 1200's. Old records of that time also refer to a fugitive named Robert Hood. But there is no firm evidence that any of these people were the source of the Robin Hood tales.

One thing is certain: By the end of the 1300's, legends about Robin Hood were widespread in England. And over the following centuries, in songs, plays, and stories, new versions of the tales appeared. In them, Robin was a bold and cheerful soul who always acted on the side of right. Members of his band—Friar Tuck, Will Stutely, Little John, Allen-a-Dale, and others—also became well-known characters. Dressed in green, they drove their chief enemy, the Sheriff of Nottingham, to distraction. The stories even gave Robin Hood a sweetheart, Maid Marian.

Collections of Robin Hood tales especially for children began to appear in the 1800's. Among them was The Merry Adventures of Robin Hood, by the American author and illustrator Howard Pyle, which appeared in 1883. The story that follows is based on a tale in that book about how Robin Hood fools the Sheriff and wins a prize.

Robin Hood
and the Shooting Match

The Sheriff was extremely angry because of his failure to take jolly Robin, for it came to his ears, as ill news always does, that the people laughed at him and made a jest of his thinking to serve a warrant upon such a one as the bold outlaw; and a man hates nothing so much as being made a jest of. So he said, "Our gracious Lord and Sovereign King shall know of this, and how his laws are despised by this band of rebel outlaws."

Then he bade all his servants and retainers to make ready to go to London Town, to see and speak with the King.

At this there was bustling at the Sheriff's castle, and men ran hither and thither on this business and that. The forge fires of Nottingham glowed red far into the night like twinkling stars, for all the smiths of the town were busy making or mending armor for the Sheriff's troop of escort. For two days this labor lasted. Then, on the third, all was ready for the journey. So forth they started in the bright sunlight, and they journeyed for two days, until they saw at last the spires and towers of great London Town. And many folks stopped and gazed at the show they made riding along the highways with their flashing armor, and gay plumes and trappings.

In London, King Henry and his fair Queen Eleanor held their court, gay with ladies in silks and satins and velvets and cloth of gold, and also brave knights and gallant courtiers.

Thither came the Sheriff and was brought to the King.

"Now what would you have?" said the King. "Let us hear what may be your desires."

"O good my Lord and Sovereign," said the Sheriff, as he knelt upon the ground, "in Sherwood Forest in our own good shire of Nottingham, lives a bold outlaw whose name is Robin Hood."

"In good sooth," said the King, "his doings have reached even our own royal ears. He is a saucy, rebellious varlet, yet, I am glad to own, a right merry soul nevertheless."

"But hearken, O my most gracious Sovereign," said the Sheriff. "I sent a warrant to him with your own royal seal attached, by a right lusty knave, but he beat the messenger and stole the warrant. And he kills your deer and robs your own subjects even on the great highways."

"Why, how now," said the King, wrathfully. "What would you have me do? Come you not to me with a great array of men-at-arms and retainers, and yet you are not able to take a single band of lusty knaves without armor, in your own county! Are you not my Sheriff? Are not my laws in force in Nottinghamshire? Can you not take your own course against those that break the laws? Go, and think well. Devise some plan of your own but trouble me no further. But look well to it, master Sheriff, for I will have my laws obeyed by all men within my kingdom, and if you are not able to enforce them, you are no sheriff for me. So look well to yourself, or ill may befall you as well as all the thieving knaves in Nottinghamshire. When the flood comes it sweeps away grain as well as chaff."

Then the Sheriff turned away with a sore and troubled heart, and sadly he rued his fine show of retainers, for he saw that the King was angry because he had so many men about him and yet could not enforce the laws. So, as they all rode slowly back to Nottingham, the Sheriff was thoughtful and full of care. Not a word did he speak to anyone, and not one of his men spoke to him, but all the time he was busy devising some plan to take Robin Hood.

"Aha!" cried he suddenly, smiting his hand upon his thigh, "I have it now! Ride on, my merry men all, and let us get back to Nottingham Town as speedily as we may. And mark well my words: Before a fortnight is passed, that evil knave, Robin Hood, will be safely clapped into Nottingham jail."

But what was the Sheriff's plan?

As a trader takes each coin in a bag of silver coins, feeling each to find whether it is clipped or not, so the Sheriff took up thought after thought in turn, feeling around the edges of each but finding in every one some flaw. At last he thought of the daring soul of jolly Robin and how he often came even within the walls of Nottingham.

"Now," thought the Sheriff, "could I but persuade Robin nigh to Nottingham Town so that I could find him, I warrant I would lay hands on him so stoutly that he would never get away again." Then of a sudden it came to him like a flash that were he to proclaim a great shooting match and offer some grand prize, Robin Hood might be persuaded by his spirit to come to the competition. It was this thought that had caused him to cry "Aha!" and smite his palm upon his thigh.

So, as soon as he had returned to Nottingham, he sent messengers north and south, east and west, to proclaim through town, hamlet, and countryside, this grand shooting match. Everyone was bidden that could draw a long bow, and the prize was to be an arrow of pure gold.

When Robin Hood first heard the news of this, he called all his merry men about him in Sherwood Forest and said to them:

"Now hearken, my merry men all, to the news that I have heard today. Our friend the Sheriff has proclaimed a shooting match and has sent messengers to tell of it through all the countryside, and the prize is to be a bright golden arrow. Now I would gladly have one of us win it, both because of the grandness of the prize and because our sweet friend the Sheriff has offered it. So we will take our bows and shafts and go there to shoot, for I know right well that merriment will be a-going. What say you, lads?"

Then young David of Doncaster spoke up and said, "Now listen, I pray, good master, to what I say. I, too, have heard news of this same match. But, master, I have heard that this knavish Sheriff has laid a trap for you in this shooting match and wishes nothing so much as to see you there. So go not, good master."

"Now," said Robin, "you are a wise lad and keep your ears open and your mouth shut, as becomes a wise and crafty woodsman. But shall we let it be said that the Sheriff of Nottingham did cow bold Robin Hood and a band of the best archers in all merry England? Nay, good David, what you tell me makes me desire the prize even more. But we must meet guile with guile. Now some of you clothe yourselves as friars, and some as rustic peasants, and some as tinkers, or as beggars, but see that each man takes a good bow, in case need should arise. As for myself, I will shoot for this same golden arrow, and should I win it, we will hang it from the branches of our good greenwood tree for the joy of all the band. How like you the plan, my merry men all?"

Then "good, good!" cried all the band right heartily.

A fair sight was Nottingham Town on the day of the shooting match. All along the green meadow beneath the town wall stretched a row of benches, one above the other, which were for knight and lady, squire and dame, and rich burghers and their wives; for none but rank and quality were to sit there. At the end of the range, near the target, was a canopied grandstand with a raised seat, for the Sheriff of Nottingham and his dame. The range was twoscore paces broad. At one end stood the target; at the other a tent of striped canvas, from the pole of which fluttered many-colored flags and streamers. In this booth were casks of ale, free to the archers who might wish to quench their thirst.

Across the range from where the seats for the better folk were was a railing to keep the poorer people from crowding in front of the target. Already, while it was early, the benches were beginning to fill with people of quality, who kept constantly arriving in little carts. With them came also the poorer folk, who sat or lay upon the green grass near the railing. In the great tent the archers were gathering by twos and threes. Some talked loudly of the fair shots each man had made in his day. Some looked well to their bows, drawing a string betwixt the fingers to see that there was no fray upon it, or inspecting arrows, shutting one eye and peering down a shaft to see that it was not warped, but straight and true, for neither bow nor shaft should fail at such a time and for such a prize. And never was there such a company of yeomen as were gathered at Nottingham Town that day, for the very best archers of merry England had come to this shooting match. There was Gilbert o' the Red Cap, the Sheriff's own head archer, and Diccon Cruikshank of Lincoln Town. There was Adam o' the Dell, a man of Tamworth, of threescore years and more, yet hale and lusty still, who in his time had shot in the famous match at Woodstock and had there beaten that renowned archer, Clym o' the Clough. And many more famous men of the longbow were there, whose names have been handed down to us in goodly ballads of the olden time.

But now all the benches were filled with guests, when at last the Sheriff himself came with his lady, he riding with stately mien on his milk-white horse and she on her brown filly. He wore a robe of royal blue and a cape of rich, dark fur; his jerkin and hose were of sea-green silk, and his shoes of black velvet, the pointed toes fastened to his garters with golden chains. A golden chain hung about his neck, and at his

collar was a great ruby set in red gold. His lady was dressed in blue velvet, all trimmed with swan's down. They made a gallant sight as they rode along side by side, and so they came to their place, where men-at-arms stood about, waiting for them.

Then when the Sheriff and his dame had sat down, he bade his herald wind upon his silver horn; who thereupon sounded three blasts that came echoing cheerily back from the gray walls of Nottingham. Then the archers stepped forth to their places. All the folks shouted with a mighty voice, each man calling upon his favorite archer while ladies waved silken scarves to urge each yeoman to do his best.

Then the herald stood forth and loudly proclaimed the rules of the game as follows:

"Shoot each man from yon mark, which is sevenscore yards and ten from the target. Each man will shoot one arrow first, and from all the archers the ten that shoot the truest shafts shall be chosen to shoot again. Each of these ten shall shoot two arrows; then the three that shoot the truest shafts shall be chosen to shoot again. Each of those three shall shoot three arrows, and to him that shoots the truest shafts shall the prize be given."

Then the Sheriff leaned forward, looking keenly among the press of archers to find whether Robin Hood was among them; but no one was there clad in Lincoln green, such as was worn by Robin and his band. "Nevertheless," said the Sheriff to himself, "he may still be there, and I miss him among the crowd."

And now the archers shot, each man in turn, and the good folk never saw such archery as was done that day. All the people shouted aloud, for it was noble shooting.

And now but ten men were left of all those that had shot before, and of these ten, six were famous throughout the land, and most of the folk gathered there knew them. These six men were Gilbert o' the Red Cap, Adam o' the Dell, Diccon Cruikshank, William o' Leslie, Hubert o' Cloud, and Swithin o' Hertford. Two others were yeomen of merry Yorkshire, another was a tall stranger in blue who said he came from London Town, and the last was a tattered stranger in scarlet who wore a patch over one eye.

"Now," said the Sheriff to a man-at-arms who stood near him, "see you Robin Hood among those ten?"

"Nay, that do I not, your worship," answered the man. "Six of them I know right well. Of those Yorkshire yeomen, one is too tall and the other too short for that bold knave. Robin's beard is as yellow as gold, while yon tattered beggar in scarlet hath a beard of brown, besides being blind in one eye. As for the stranger in blue, Robin's shoulders, I ween, are three inches broader than his."

"Then," said the Sheriff, smiting his thigh angrily, "yon knave is a coward, as well as a rogue, and dares not show his face among good men and true."

Then, after they had rested a short time, those ten stout men stepped forth to shoot again. Each man shot two arrows, and as they shot not a word was spoken, but all the crowd watched with scarce a breath of sound. But when the last had shot his arrow another great shout arose, while many cast their caps aloft for joy of such marvelous shooting.

And now but three men were left. One was Gill o' the Red Cap, one the tattered stranger in scarlet, and one Adam o' the Dell of Tamworth Town. Then all the people called aloud, some crying, "Ho for Gilbert o' the Red Cap!" and some, "Hey for stout Adam o' Tamworth!" But not a single man called upon the stranger in scarlet.

"Now, shoot well, Gilbert," cried the Sheriff, "and if yours is the best shaft, fivescore silver pennies will I give you besides the prize."

"Truly I will do my best," said Gilbert, right sturdily. "A man cannot do aught but his best, but that I will strive to do this day."

So saying, he drew forth a fair smooth arrow with a broad feather and fitted it deftly to the string. Then, drawing his bow with care, he sped the shaft. Straight flew the arrow and lit easily in the target, a finger breadth from the center. "Gilbert, Gilbert!" shouted all the crowd. "Now, by my faith," cried the Sheriff, clapping his hands together, "that is a shrewd shot."

Then the tattered stranger stepped forth, and all the people laughed to see him aim with but one eye. He drew the good yew bow quickly, and quickly loosed a shaft; so short was the time that no man could draw a breath betwixt the drawing and the shooting. Yet his arrow lodged nearer the center than the other by twice the length of a barleycorn.

"Now by all the saints in paradise!" cried the Sheriff, "that is a lovely shaft in very truth!"

Then Adam o' the Dell shot, carefully and cautiously, and his arrow lodged close beside the stranger's. After a short space they all shot again, and once more each arrow lodged within the target, but this time Adam o' the Dell's was farthest from the center, and again the tattered stranger's shot was the best. Then, after another time of rest, they all shot for the third time. This time Gilbert took great heed to his aim, keenly measuring the distance and shooting with shrewdest care. Straight flew the arrow, and all shouted until the very flags that waved in the breeze shook with the sound, and the rooks and daws flew clamoring about the roof of the old gray tower, for the shaft had lodged close beside the spot that marked the very center.

"Well done, Gilbert!" cried the Sheriff, right joyously. "Glad I am to believe the prize is yours, and right fairly won. Now, knave, let me see you shoot a better shaft than that."

The stranger said naught but took his place. All was hushed, and no one spoke or even seemed to breathe, so great was the silence for wonder what he would do. Quite still stood the stranger, holding his bow in his hand, while one could count five. Then he drew his trusty yew, holding it drawn but a moment, and loosed the string. Straight flew the arrow, and so true that it smote a gray goose feather from off Gilbert's shaft, which fell fluttering through the sunlit air. The stranger's arrow lodged close beside his of the Red Cap—and in the very center. No one spoke and no one shouted, but everyone looked amazed.

"Nay," quoth old Adam o' the Dell presently, drawing a long breath and shaking his head as he spoke; "twoscore years and more have I shot shaft, and maybe not all times bad, but I shoot no more this day, for no man can match with yon stranger, whosoe'er he may be." Then he thrust his shaft into his quiver, rattling, and unstrung his bow without another word.

Then the Sheriff came down from his dais and drew near, in all his silks and velvets, to where the tattered stranger stood leaning upon his stout bow, while the good folk crowded around to see the man who shot so wondrously well. "Here, good fellow," said the Sheriff, "take the prize, and well and fairly have you won it, I trow. What may be your name, and whence come you?"

"Men do call me Jock o' Teviotdale, and thence am I come," said the stranger.

"Then, by Our Lady, Jock, you are the best archer that e'er my eyes beheld, and if you will join my service I will clothe you with a better coat than that you have on your back. You will eat and drink of the best, and at every Christmastide fourscore marks shall be your wage. I vow you draw better bow than that coward knave, Robin Hood, who dared not show his face here this day. Say, good fellow, will you join my service?"

"Nay, that I will not," said the stranger, roughly. "I will be my own, and no man in all merry England shall be my master."

"Then get you gone!" cried the Sheriff, and his voice trembled with anger. "And by my faith I have a good mind to have you beaten for your insolence!" Then he quickly strode away.

It was a right motley company that gathered about the noble greenwood tree in Sherwood's depths that same day. A score and more of barefoot friars were there, and some that looked like tinkers, and some that seemed to be sturdy beggars. And seated upon a mossy couch was one all clad in tattered scarlet, with a patch over one eye; and in his hand he held the golden arrow that was the prize of the great shooting match. Then, amid a noise of talking and laughter, he took the patch from his eye and stripped away the scarlet rags from his body and showed himself all clothed in fair Lincoln green, and said he: "Easy come these things away, but walnut stain comes not so speedily from yellow hair." Then all laughed louder than before, for it was Robin Hood himself who had won the prize from the Sheriff's very hands.

Then all sat down to the woodland feast and talked among themselves of the merry jest that had been played upon the Sheriff. But when the feast was done, Robin Hood took Little John apart and said, "Truly am I vexed, for I heard the Sheriff say today, 'You shoot better than that coward knave, Robin Hood, who dared not show his face here this day.' I would gladly let him know who it was who won the golden arrow from out of his hand, and also that I am no coward such as he takes me to be."

Then Little John said, "Good master, take me and Will Stutely, and we will send yon fat Sheriff news of all this by a messenger such as he does not expect."

That day the Sheriff sat down to his meal in the great hall of his house at Nottingham Town. Long tables stood down the hall, at which sat men-at-arms and household servants and good stout villeins, in all fourscore and more. There they talked of the day's shooting as they ate their meat and quaffed their ale. The Sheriff sat at the head of the table upon a raised seat under a canopy, and beside him sat his dame.

"By my troth," said he, "I did reckon fully roundly that that knave, Robin Hood, would be at the game today. I did not think that he was such a coward. But who could that saucy knave be who answered me to my beard so bravely? I wonder that I did not have him beaten; but there was something about him that spoke of other things than rags and tatters."

Then, just as he finished speaking, something came flying through the window and fell rattling among the dishes on the table. Those who sat near were startled, wondering what it might be. After a while one of the men-at-arms gathered courage enough to pick it up and bring it to the Sheriff. Then everyone saw that it was a blunted gray goose shaft, with a fine scroll tied near to its head. The Sheriff opened the scroll and glanced at it, while the veins upon his forehead swelled and his cheeks grew ruddy with rage as he read, for this was what he saw:

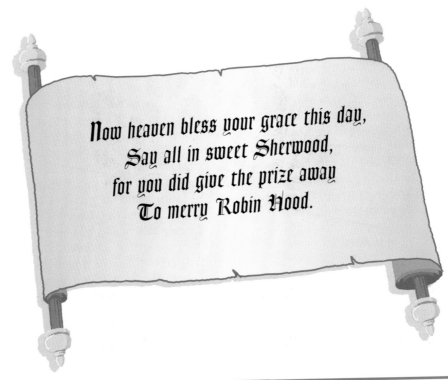

Now heaven bless your grace this day,
Say all in sweet Sherwood,
For you did give the prize away
To merry Robin Hood.

THE NEW BOOK OF KNOWLEDGE
2008

The following articles are from the 2008 edition of *The New Book of Knowledge*. They are included here to help you keep your encyclopedia up to date. Cross-references appearing in these articles refer to the 2008 edition of the set. Some of the articles referenced may not be found in older editions.

Above: A group of Adélie penguins toboggan across the frozen Arctic landscape. *Left:* Emperor penguins are the largest species of penguins. *Below:* The little blue, or fairy, penguin is the smallest. *Opposite page:* Crested penguins, such as the macaroni, have yellow and black plumes above their eyes.

PENGUINS

When early explorers first saw penguins, they thought these strange animals were some combination of fish, mammal, and bird. In fact, penguins are a kind of bird. But they began evolving from flying birds about 60 million years ago. Eventually they lost their ability to fly. And they became better swimmers and divers than any other bird on Earth. There are seventeen species of penguins. They belong to the family Spheniscidae.

A common myth about penguins is that they live only in cold, snowy places like Antarctica. But penguins live in habitats ranging from the warm tropics along the equator to the freezing ice cover of Antarctica. They are found only in the Southern Hemisphere, along the coastlines of South America, southern Africa, southern Australia, New Zealand, Antarctica, and many sub-Antarctic islands.

▶ CHARACTERISTICS OF PENGUINS

Like all birds, penguins lay eggs and have wings, feathers, and beaks. Their bodies have a thick layer of blubber (fat) and are shaped like a football, which makes them streamlined for swimming. They spend most of their lives at sea. There, they use their short, stiff wings to propel them through the water at speeds up to 15 miles (24 kilometers) per hour. Penguins cannot fly because their wings are too short and their bodies are too heavy. In addition, their bones are solid. The bones of most other birds are hollow, which aids in flight. Solid bones make penguins less buoyant. This enables the birds to dive and swim underwater more easily.

Penguins have webbed feet that are used like a rudder for steering, not paddling. Their feet are placed far back on their bodies, which gives them their upright posture while on land.

A penguin's body is covered with thousands of small feathers. In fact, penguins have more feathers than any other bird—approximately 70 per square inch. Their feathers lie over each other like shingles on a roof. They form a protective barrier against the cold water and wind. Penguins spend a

lot of time straightening out their feathers in a process called **preening**. Penguins coat their feathers with a light oily substance that they get from a gland located at the base of the tail. This oily surface helps keep the cold ocean water from reaching their skin.

The feathers on a penguin's back are black or dark gray. The feathers on its belly are whitish. This coloration, called **counter-shading**, is a form of camouflage. It protects the birds from predators. When a predator swimming above a penguin looks down, the penguins' dark back blends in with the dark ocean below. When a predator swimming below a penguin looks up, the penguins' light belly blends in with the ice or sunlight coming through the ocean surface above.

Penguins have slightly hooked beaks, which are used for eating, preening, and defense. They do not have teeth. Instead, penguins have fleshy projections, called papillae, on the top of their tongues and the roof of their mouths. The papillae point backward toward their throats and help penguins hold on to their slippery food, which they swallow whole.

When traveling long distances or trying to escape from predators, penguins swim by leaping in and out of the water like a dolphin

or a porpoise. This behavior, called **porpoising**, allows them to swim faster. Penguins are air breathers, so they take a breath on each leap above the ocean surface. When traveling across snow or ice, penguins sometimes flop down on their bellies and push themselves along using their wings and feet. This behavior is called **tobogganing**. It allows them to slide across the snow and ice faster than they can walk across it.

Emperor penguins are the largest penguins. They stand approximately 3½ feet (1 meter) tall and weigh between 65 and 95 pounds (29 and 43 kilograms). They live exclusively in Antarctica. The smallest penguin is the little blue, or fairy, penguin. This tiny bird with dark blue feathers weighs just 2 to 3 pounds (0.9 kilogram to 1.3 kilograms) and stands about 8 inches (20.3 centimeters) tall. It is found in New Zealand and along the

Although penguins cannot fly, they are expert swimmers. They use their stiff wings to propel them through the water and their webbed feet for steering.

southern coast of Australia. Even though it is the smallest penguin, it is one of the loudest.

▶ **LIVES OF PENGUINS**

Penguins eat fish, squid, and krill (shrimplike animals). But their diet varies depending on their species and where they live. Krill make up a large part of the diet for many of the penguins living in Antarctica and the sub-Antarctic region.

Penguins breed in huge groups called **colonies**. The birds are very territorial and will aggressively defend their

nests from other penguins. Breeding habits vary depending on the species. Some penguins mate for life. But species living in colder climates tend to have more than one mate during their lifetime. Most species lay two eggs, and the parents take turns incubating them. The chicks typically hatch after 30 or 45 days.

The two largest penguins, the emperor and the king, lay only one egg. They incubate the egg by placing it on top of their feet and covering it with a loose flap of skin on their belly. They stand on their heels and raise their toes so they do not drop the egg. Of all the penguin species, only the male emperor penguin incubates the egg completely by himself. This is done for about 65 days during the middle of the Antarctic winter, when temperatures reach as low as –100°F (–74°C) and winds blow up to 100 miles (161 kilometers) per hour.

When penguin chicks hatch, the parents take turns sitting on them to keep them warm and feeding them by regurgitating (throwing up) food. When returning from the sea, penguins call loudly to locate their mate or chicks. When the mate or chicks hear the other penguin's voice, they call back to help guide the returning penguin.

Newborn penguins are covered with a soft, fluffy down that is typically gray or brown. These downy feathers do not provide any protection from the cold or the rain. In addition, chicks cannot regulate their body temperature. So

Left: Penguins, such as these king penguins, breed in huge groups called colonies. *Above:* A gentoo penguin incubates its egg. Most species of penguins lay two eggs, which the parents take turns incubating.

A king penguin preens its chick. Penguin chicks are covered with a thick layer of downy feathers before they grow their first set of waterproof feathers.

Within three or four months (for most penguin species), the chicks are ready to leave their parents and head off to sea on their own. Before doing so, however, they must grow their first set of waterproof feathers. This process is called **fledging**. When the chicks have finished fledging, they are called juveniles.

The feathers of juveniles have the same structure as those of the adults, but they are different in color and pattern. So juvenile penguins look distinctly different from their parents. The only exception to this is the little blue penguin. The juveniles and adults of this species look exactly the same. When they are just over a year old, all juvenile penguins go through their first true **molt**. This means they lose all of their juvenile plumage and grow in their first set of feathers that have the adult pattern and coloration. After this molt, they are finally considered adults.

they must remain snugly under their parents to stay warm and dry. When the chicks grow too large to fit under their parents' bellies, they sometimes gather with other chicks to form **crèches**, or small huddles. By this time, the chicks have grown a second, thicker layer of downy feathers. They are also able to regulate their body temperature. So both parents can leave them for short periods to go to sea to hunt for food.

Penguins are often thought of as birds that live only in cold, snowy places. However, most species spend at least part of the year in places that are warm. Only two species, the Adélie and the emperor, live in the cold Antarctic year-round. The pink-shaded areas on this map show where penguins live.

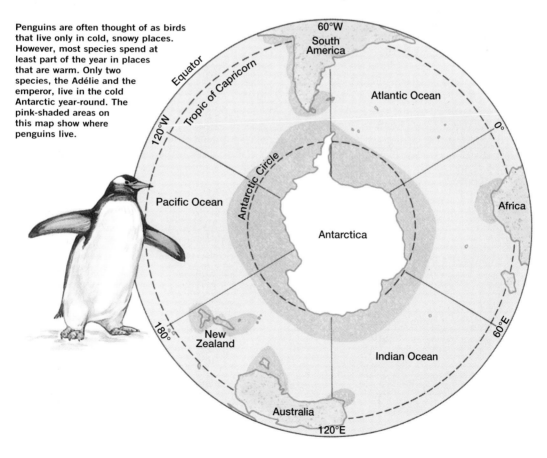

PENGUIN CONSERVATION

Every species of penguin is protected by law. But penguins still need help to survive. So most zoos and aquariums participate in a Species Survival Plan (SSP). This kind of plan is designed to maintain a healthy breeding population of various penguin species. If the number of birds in the wild declines significantly, the animals in the SSP's can be used to replenish the populations.

Contamination by spilled oil is a major threat to many species of penguins. Unfortunately, there are only a few rehabilitation centers capable of rescuing penguins that have become covered in oil. One of the best known is the South African Foundation for the Conservation of Coastal Birds (SANCCOB), located in Cape Town, South Africa. In June 2000 SANCCOB oversaw the rescue and rehabilitation of

Oil spills are a major threat to penguins. When the birds become covered with oil, they must be thoroughly cleaned if they are to survive.

20,000 African penguins that were covered in oil when a ship sank near their breeding grounds. Thousands of volunteers from around the world flew to South Africa to help rescue the oiled penguins, ultimately saving over 91 percent of them. This was the largest and most successful rescue of sea birds in history.

The average life span of penguins in the wild ranges from about ten to fifteen years. But larger species generally have longer lives. Emperor penguins live about twenty years in the wild. Little blues live about ten years.

▶ PENGUINS AND THEIR ENVIRONMENT

Penguins are a source of food for many animals. These include seals, sea lions, sharks, killer whales (orcas), and even the occasional octopus. Other birds also pose a danger to penguins. Skuas, caracaras, sea eagles, kelp gulls, and giant petrels will steal eggs and small chicks. Non-native animals, such as dogs, rats, and foxes, introduced into penguins' environments also prey on the birds.

Did you know that...

penguins can dive deeper than any other bird on Earth? The deepest recorded penguin dive was made by an emperor penguin that dove 1,695 feet (517 meters) deep. It held its breath for an astonishing 22 minutes. This is deeper than a typical dive. Most penguin species routinely dive between 200 and 500 feet (60 and 150 meters) deep.

But the greatest threats penguins face come from people. In the past, people collected and ate penguin eggs. They also used penguin guano (droppings) as fertilizer. Some penguin species make their nests out of dried guano. When it is removed they are forced to nest in the open, where they are vulnerable to land predators and overheating in the sun. Today penguins become entangled in fishing nets and drown. Commercial fishing has depleted the supply of fish and krill that they eat. Oil spills, other kinds of pollution, and warmer ocean temperatures (due to global warming) also take their toll on penguin populations. And coastal development has encroached on many nesting sites.

Over the last hundred years, penguin populations have declined drastically because of the activities of people. The populations of many species have dropped 90 percent. And 12 of the 17 penguin species are currently classified as threatened or endangered. All species of penguins are now protected by law.

DYAN deNAPOLI
Former Senior Penguin Aquarist
New England Aquarium
Founder, THE PENGUIN LADY Educational
Programming

EGYPT

Egypt is a nation located at the northeastern corner of Africa, where Africa and Asia meet. It links the Muslim countries of southwest Asia with those of North Africa. The country is bordered by Libya on the west and by Sudan on the south. It is bounded on the north by the Mediterranean Sea and on the east by Israel and the Red Sea. With over 80 million people, Egypt is the world's most populous Arab country. It is the second most populous nation in Africa, after Nigeria.

Egypt has lengthy coasts on both the Mediterranean and Red seas. So it has long been an important center of trade and communication for Asia, Africa, and Europe. Its location became even more important when the Suez Canal was opened in 1869. The canal makes the long voyage around the southern tip of Africa unnecessary.

Egypt has one of the longest histories of any nation. It came into being about 3200 B.C. King Menes (also called Narmer) united the cities of northern and southern Egypt under one government. During his time, the giant statue known as the Sphinx was built. It appears part human and part beast and has fascinated travelers for centuries. For more information, see EGYPT, ANCIENT in this volume.

Beginning about 1000 B.C., Egypt's power declined and different peoples ruled it. In 331 B.C., Alexander the Great conquered Egypt. Other rulers followed, including Roman and Byzantine emperors. And Egypt became mostly Christian. This changed in A.D. 640, when Muslims from the Arabian Peninsula conquered Egypt. (The Muslims were members of the newly formed religion of Islam.) Egypt has remained Muslim since that time. Britain took control of Egypt in 1882 and then granted the country independence in 1922.

In the 21st century, Egypt is modernizing its economy to better serve a growing population. Egypt still depends on its traditional cotton growing and tourist industries. But resources such as oil and natural gas are growing in importance. To make further progress, the government must ensure that many more new and better jobs are created each year. Other priorities include reducing poverty and improving education, especially in rural areas.

The Nile River (*right*) was the cradle of a great civilization 5,000 years ago. The Pharaoh (king) Tutankhamen (*above*) came to power more than 3,000 years ago. Today the Nile is at the center of modern Egypt, providing water for crops and serving as a highway for traders and travelers.

▶ PEOPLE

Most Egyptians are descended from the Arab settlers who followed the Muslim conquest in 640 and from the descendants of the ancient Egyptian pre-Islamic population. The typical Egyptian reflects a mixture of the two heritages. The Egyptian Copts, a sizeable minority, date back to pre-Islamic times. They are members of one of the earliest Christian churches. There are also some people of Armenian, French, Greek, and Italian ancestry.

Language. Arabic is the official language of Egypt. Classical Arabic is the written language. It is used for conducting official business. Colloquial (informal) Arabic is the spoken language of the street. Both forms are used by the media, for business transactions, and in schools. Colloquial Arabic is widely used on television, which is very popular, and in the film industry. It is also used in songs and folk literature and popular poetry.

English and French are spoken among the more highly educated and by those who work in the tourism sector, where Italian and German are also heard.

The Coptic language developed from ancient Egyptian. It was spoken in Egypt until the 1100's but is now used only in ceremonies of the Coptic Church.

Religion. Most Egyptians are Sunni Muslims. (Muslims are followers of Islam, a religion based on the teachings of the prophet Muhammad.) Coptic Christians are the second largest religious group. There are also small groups of Roman Catholics, Greek Orthodox, and Protestants. Egypt's cities are filled with mosques (Muslim houses of worship). Five times a day, the voice of the muezzin (prayer-caller) calls the faithful to prayer.

Education. Egypt has two systems of education. One is public and the other is private. All levels of public education in Egypt are

Egypt's cities are growing rapidly, as people from villages arrive to find jobs. Cairo (*above* and *right*) is Egypt's capital, its largest city, and its economic and cultural center. Founded by Arab conquerors in the A.D. 900's, it is the largest city in Africa.

free. Five years of primary and three years of secondary school are required for all children. Three additional years of secondary school are needed for college or university. With over 200,000 students, Cairo University offers a wide range of studies.

One of Egypt's major challenges is its low level of literacy (the ability to read and write). Although eight years of education are required, girls and women tend to receive less education than boys and men. The government is working to enroll more children—both boys and girls—in primary school and some progress has been made in recent years.

Rural Life. About half of Egypt's people live in the countryside. The rest live in cities, which are rapidly growing in population.

The country people, or fellahin, live in thousands of small villages. Each village has a mosque, a few shops, a religious school, and sometimes a church. The villages lie along the Nile River or near irrigation canals. The fellahin farm the land that they own or rent. The staple foods are bread made from corn flour and a dish made of beans, called ful. Meat is usually reserved for special holidays.

City Life. Life in Egyptian cities has been strongly influenced by modern European culture. There are broad, paved streets and well-tended parks. Many cities, particularly Cairo, are overcrowded and housing is in short supply.

Egyptian city-dwellers live in modern apartment buildings as well as crowded tenement districts. Or they live in private homes in the suburbs, an extension of the city. City dwellers dress mostly in Western-style clothing. However, traditional Islamic dress has become more common among women.

Sports and Recreation. Soccer is the favorite sport of most Egyptians. Others include tennis and squash. Because of the temperate climate, swimming is also popular.

▶ **LAND**

Land Regions. The ancient Greek historian Herodotus called Egypt "the gift of the Nile." He was referring to the life-giving water and rich silt that the river carries from equatorial Africa to the desert of Egypt. Almost all of Egypt's people live on less than 5 percent of the land, on the fertile soil that borders the Nile River. Most of the rest of Egypt is desert inhabited largely by nomadic Bedouin.

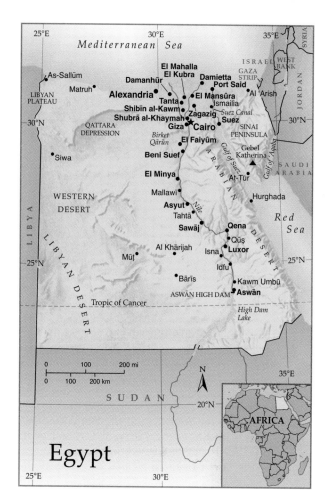

Egypt

Egypt consists of four geographical regions: the Nile River valley and its delta (the fan-shaped plain at its mouth); the Libyan, or Western, Desert in the west and south; the Arabian, or Eastern, Desert in the east; and the Sinai Peninsula. The Sinai Peninsula lies in southwest Asia. It is the site of Egypt's highest mountain, Gebel Katherina. Gebel Katherina rises to 8,651 feet (2,737 meters).

The Libyan Desert is a great arid plain. Most of it lies below 1,000 feet (300 meters). The southern part of the Libyan Desert has no oases or settlements. To the north, the Qattara Depression covers about 7,000 square miles (18,100 square kilometers). It is 436 feet (133 meters) below sea level.

Rivers. The Nile is the world's longest river. It travels over 3,000 miles (4,800 kilometers) through Africa before it enters Egypt. Then it flows northward through Egypt for over 900 miles (1448 kilometers) before it empties into the Mediterranean Sea.

Egypt's growing economy includes the production of petroleum (*far left*). Agriculture, once the most important sector of the economy, now employs only 30 percent of the workforce. Cotton (*left*) is the main commercial crop.

foxes, jackals, boars, and hyenas. And crocodiles inhabit the Upper Nile. Egypt has more than 300 species of birds and 100 species of fish.

In Upper, or southern, Egypt, the Nile River flows between high sandstone cliffs. The mammoth Aswan High Dam was opened in 1971. It doubled Egypt's power capacity and expanded the land used for farming by providing water for irrigation. From Aswan the Nile flows north to Cairo. Just below Cairo the river splits into two major branches, the Rosetta and the Damietta. This area is known as the Delta, or Lower Egypt. See the article NILE RIVER in Volume N.

The Suez Canal. The canal links the Mediterranean Sea with the Gulf of Suez, an arm of the Red Sea. Because it shortens travel time between Europe and Asia, the canal is one of the world's chief commercial waterways. The canal and the Isthmus of Suez are the traditional boundary between Africa and Asia. For more information, see the article SUEZ CANAL in Volume S.

Climate. Egypt has a generally warm, dry climate. Summers are hot. In the south, daytime temperatures may reach 107°F (42°C), but nights are cool. Winters are usually mild. Rainfall is limited and is heaviest on the Mediterranean coast.

Natural Resources. Egypt has deposits of petroleum, natural gas, iron ore, phosphates, manganese, limestone, gypsum, talc, asbestos, lead, and zinc.

Vegetation and Animal Life. Egypt's desert climate limits most vegetation to the Nile Valley and Delta and the oases. The most widespread native tree is the date palm. Others include the carob, tamarisk, and sycamore. The lack of forest and grazing areas limits wild animal life. But Egypt has

▶ **ECONOMY**

Egypt's economy has several strong resources to draw upon. These include energy resources, including oil; income from the Suez Canal; and a profitable tourist industry. But for many years the country's economy performed well below potential. In 2004 the Egyptian government began to reduce the state's role in the economy. It sold some state firms to private investors and made it easier for private firms to invest. These and other factors helped the economy grow.

Many challenges remain, however. Higher growth is needed to provide jobs for the over 1 million Egyptians who enter the economy each year. Poverty is a problem, especially in rural areas. The government has made progress in reducing poverty among the poorest Egyptians. But 20 percent of Egyptians still fall below the poverty line. That means that they earn or consume less than they need to achieve adequate nutrition, shelter, medical care, and other necessities. Better jobs will require better education for Egypt's young people, especially women.

Services. Service industries contribute over 50 percent of Egypt's yearly gross domestic product (GDP). (GDP is the total market value of all final goods and services produced in a country in one year.) Over half of Egypt's workers are engaged in service industries, including government and tourism.

Manufacturing. Egypt's manufacturing sector contributes about one-third to GDP each year. It includes firms that produce textiles, food products, chemicals, pharmaceuticals, cement, metals, and light manufactures.

Agriculture. The Nile Valley is one of the most intensively cultivated and productive farming regions in the world. Agriculture contributes less than 20 percent to GDP. But it employs about 30 percent of Egypt's workers. Cotton is the major export crop. Egypt is also an important producer of rice, wheat, corn, beans, fruits, and vegetables. Livestock raising includes cattle, water buffalo, sheep, and goats.

Mining. Mining is increasingly important to Egypt's economy. Crude oil and petroleum products are among the country's top exports. Egypt also produces natural gas, salt, phosphates, iron ore, and coal.

Energy. Egypt relies mostly on fossil fuels, such as oil, to meet its energy needs. Its energy sector produces oil and natural gas. And the country is a rapidly growing supplier of liquefied natural gas, which is exported. Hydroelectric power is supplied by the Aswan High Dam.

Trade. Egypt exports crude oil and petroleum products, cotton, textiles, metal products, and chemicals. Its major imports are machinery and equipment, foodstuffs, chemicals, wood products, and fuels.

Transportation. The Nile River and the Suez Canal are Egypt's major transportation arteries. The Suez Canal and Sumed Pipeline are important routes for Persian Gulf oil shipments. Egypt's railroad system is state controlled. Egyptair, the state-owned airline, flies locally and abroad.

Communication. Egypt's large telephone system was upgraded in the 1990's. It offers land-based as well as cellular service. There are several million Internet users.

The Bibliotheca Alexandrina, which opened in 2002, is a modern replica of the great library that existed in Alexandria in ancient times. It also features a planetarium.

▶ **MAJOR CITIES**

Cairo (Al-Qahirah, in Arabic) is Egypt's capital and largest city. It is also a major commercial and cultural center. With nearly 7 million people, it is the largest city in Africa. For more information, see the separate article CAIRO in Volume C.

Alexandria, with over 3 million people, is Egypt's second largest city. It is a busy port on the Mediterranean Sea. Founded by Alexander the Great in the 300's B.C., it was long a cultural center of the Mediterranean region. It was famed in ancient times for its Pharos, or lighthouse, and for its great library. Opened in 2002, the Bibliotheca Alexandrina is a modern replica of that library. It also features museums and a planetarium.

Giza is a suburb of Cairo. It is the site of Cairo University. The Great Pyramid and the statue of the Sphinx sit on the Plateau of Giza. (The pyramids served as tombs for the early Egyptian kings.)

Port Said is one of Egypt's principal ports. It is located at the northern (Mediterranean) end of the Suez Canal.

The ancient city of **Luxor** is one of the country's major tourist attractions. Its historical sites include the Temple of Luxor, the Temple of Karnak, and the Valley of the Kings. For more information on the Pharos and the pyramids, see the articles PYRAMIDS in Volume P and WONDERS OF THE WORLD in Volume WXYZ.

▶ **CULTURAL HERITAGE**

Arabic literature traces its roots to the A.D. 500's. Poetry, novels, and plays are the offshoots of this rich legacy. From the mid-1800's to the present, Arabic literature interacted with Western influences. Muhammad Husayn Haykal wrote one of the earliest novels in modern Arabic, *Zaynab* (1914). One of the first Egyptian writers to be known outside of the Middle East was Taha Hussein. He wrote *Al-Ayyam* (1929–30), which was translated into English in 1943 as *The Stream of Days*. The novelist and playwright Tawfiq al-Hakim is known as the father of modern Arabic drama.

Other famous modern Egyptian writers include the playwright and short story writer Yusuf Idris and the poet Salah Abd al-Sabur. The novelist Naguib Mahfouz was the first Arab author to win (1988) the Nobel Prize

Pharaoh Ramses II built a tomb for his favorite queen, Nefertari. The walls are decorated with figures of Egyptian gods.

for literature. His works, most notably the *Cairo Trilogy* (1956–57), have been translated into hundreds of languages.

Egypt is also one of the region's main filmmaking and publishing centers.

▶ GOVERNMENT

The constitution was amended in 2005 to allow the president to be elected by popular vote. The president serves a 6-year term. There are no limits to the number of terms the president may serve. The legislature consists of the People's Assembly and the Advisory Council.

▶ HISTORY

Ancient Egypt. There is disagreement about early Egyptian dates. But it is thought that Egypt came into being about 3200 B.C. At that time a king named Menes united Egypt. Some of the most impressive structures known were built before 2200 B.C. The Great Pyramid was constructed by King Khufu, or Cheops, perhaps about 2600 B.C.

The Hyksos were an eastern people about whom little is known. Around 1675 B.C., they conquered Egypt, bringing the first horses and chariots ever seen in Egypt. By about 1500 B.C. the Egyptians had driven the invaders out.

About 1375 B.C., Amenhotep IV, later Akhenaten, became king of Egypt. He abolished the worship of the many ancient Egyptian gods. He introduced the worship of only one god. But after Akhenaten's death the believers in the old gods regained power, and Akhenaten's ways were discarded. Ramses II (1292–1225 B.C.) is best known for his monuments and temples at Karnak and for the temple he carved out of the cliffs on the bank of the Nile at Abu Simbel.

Around 1000 B.C., Egyptian power declined. Between this time and 331 B.C., Egypt was ruled in turn by the Libyans, Nubians, Assyrians, and Persians. In 331 B.C., Egypt was conquered by Alexander the Great. On Alexander's death one of his generals became ruler of Egypt, as Ptolemy I. The dynasty (ruling family) of the Ptolemies ended in 30 B.C. Cleopatra was the last of the Ptolemies. She was famous for her love for the Roman Marcus Antonius (Mark Antony). When the Romans defeated her armies, she took her own life. Egypt then became a Roman province.

For the next 670 years Egypt had a succession of rulers appointed by Roman and Byzantine emperors. The Persians also ruled it briefly.

The Arab Conquest: Muslim Egypt. In A.D. 640, Muslims came from the Arabian Peninsula and conquered Egypt. They founded the city of Cairo in 969 and made it their capital. One of the most famous of the rulers of Egypt in this era was Saladin (Salah El Dine). He fought the Christian Crusaders at the end of the 1000's.

Mameluk and Turkish Rule. Egypt was ruled by the Mameluks from 1250 until 1517. That year it came under the domination of the Ottoman Turks. In 1798 the French general Napoleon Bonaparte invaded Egypt. And it led to the discovery of the Rosetta stone, which provided a long-sought key to ancient Egyptian hieroglyphic writing. (For more information, see HIEROGLYPHIC WRITING SYSTEMS in Volume H.)

Napoleon's troops were forced to withdraw from Egypt in 1801 by British and Turkish forces. In 1805, Mehemet Ali was made viceroy, or royal governor, of Egypt by the Ottoman sultan. Seizing power for himself, Mehemet Ali ruled until 1848. He undertook a remarkable program of reforms, modernization, and military conquest.

British Colonization. Egypt's prosperity declined under Mehemet Ali's hereditary successors. They borrowed large sums of money from the British and French. In 1875 the British government bought Egypt's shares in the Suez Canal. The canal had been built by the French and opened in 1869. To collect their debts, the British and French set up a commission to oversee Egyptian finances. A nationalist revolt in 1881–82 was put down by British troops, who occupied the country. In 1914, Egypt was officially declared a British protectorate.

Britain granted Egypt independence in 1922. But during World War II (1939–45), Egypt and the Suez Canal served as vital links in Britain's empire and as the gateway to India.

The 1952 Revolution: Nasser.

After World War II, discontent and resistance to the British colonizers grew. The Egyptians resented Britain's continued control of the Suez Canal. The government of King Farouk, who had come to the throne in 1936, was corrupt and inefficient. The military blamed the government for losing a 1948–49 war with the new nation of Israel. In 1952 a group of army officers began a revolt that overthrew the king, and in 1953, they set up a republic. A leader of the revolution, Colonel Gamal Abdel Nasser, became Egypt's president in 1956.

In 1956, Nasser nationalized (took state control of) the Suez Canal. When Israel was denied use of the canal, its forces attacked. They occupied most of Egypt's Sinai Peninsula and the Gaza Strip. At the same time, British and French troops landed in the canal area. After the United Nations (UN) intervened, the three nations withdrew. The support of the United States for the UN intervention earned appreciation for the United States in Egypt.

Arab unity was one of Nasser's main goals, and in 1958 he merged Egypt with Syria in a federation called the United Arab Republic.

But Syria withdrew in 1961 because of political differences.

The removal of UN forces in the Sinai at Egypt's request and Egypt's closing of the Gulf of Aqaba to Israeli ships led to war with Israel in 1967. Israel again invaded the Sinai, reaching the Suez Canal itself, and retook the Gaza Strip.

Sadat: War and Peace.

In 1970, Nasser died and was succeeded as president by Anwar el-Sadat. In 1971, Egypt changed its name to the Arab Republic of Egypt. Determined to regain the lost Sinai, Sadat, in 1973, launched an attack on Israeli positions on the east bank of the canal. Following a cease-fire, UN forces were again stationed in the area. Israel withdrew from the canal, which was reopened to shipping in 1975. Israel was allowed to use the canal for nonmilitary cargoes.

In 1977, Sadat visited Israel to discuss the question of peace in the region. His historic journey led to a peace treaty between Egypt and Israel. Israel agreed to a gradual withdrawal of its forces from the Sinai Peninsula. A formal peace treaty was signed in 1979.

Mubarak as President.

In 1981, Sadat was assassinated by members of a group that opposed his peace policies. His successor as president, Hosni Mubarak, supported the peace treaty. The last Israeli forces withdrew from the Sinai in 1982, and the area was returned to Egypt.

Mubarak was re-elected several times. As president, he restored Egypt to its position as one of the leaders of the Arab world. Egypt was formally welcomed back into the Arab League in 1989. This was ten years after it had been suspended for signing the peace treaty with Israel. During the Persian Gulf War (1990–91), Egypt provided one of the largest forces to the U.S.-led military coalition against Iraq.

In 2005, the People's Assembly amended Egypt's constitution to allow multiple candidates to run for president. In September 2005, Mubarak was re-elected to a fifth term as president.

RUTH WARREN
Author, *First Book of the Arab World*
Reviewed by MONA N. MIKHAIL
New York University

See also EGYPTIAN ART AND ARCHITECTURE; NASSER, GAMAL ABDEL; SADAT, ANWAR EL-; SUEZ CANAL.

Hosni Mubarak became president of Egypt in 1981 and was re-elected to a fifth term in 2005. He is one of the longest-serving leaders in the Arab world.

FERDINAND (1452–1516) AND ISABELLA (1451–1504)

King Ferdinand and Queen Isabella were the first monarchs to rule a united Spain. They are remembered for sponsoring Christopher Columbus' voyage across the Atlantic in 1492. But the importance of their reign was even more far-reaching. With their marriage, Ferdinand and Isabella united Aragón and Castile, Spain's two most powerful kingdoms. This union laid the foundation of a mighty empire. It dominated Europe and the New World for well over 100 years.

Isabella I of Castile was born on April 22, 1451. Her cousin Ferdinand II of Aragón was born on March 10, 1452. They married in 1469, the year Isabella became queen of Castile. Their two kingdoms were formally united when Ferdinand became king of Aragón in 1479.

In the 1400's, Spain was made up of several kingdoms. Aragón, Castile, and Navarre were controlled by Christians. But another kingdom, Granada, was ruled by the Moors (Muslims from North Africa).

Ferdinand and Isabella were called the Catholic Monarchs. They wanted Spain to be inhabited only by Christians. In 1483, with the cooperation of Pope Sixtus IV, they revived a brutal organization called the Inquisition. It was first organized in the 1100's to root out heretics (people who did not believe in the teachings of the Catholic Church). Ferdinand and Isabella hoped a new Inquisition would unite the Spanish people under one religion and make them loyal subjects. Many heretics were burned at the stake.

At the same time, Ferdinand and Isabella fought to drive the Moors from Spain. In 1492 they captured the kingdom of Granada.

Ferdinand and Isabella were the first rulers of a united Spain. In 1492 they sponsored the voyage that led to Christopher Columbus' discovery of the New World.

Then they ordered the Moors—and also the Jews—to either convert to Christianity or leave Spain. Thousands fled.

That same year, the monarchs sponsored Christopher Columbus on a voyage to find a new route to Asia by sailing westward across the Atlantic Ocean. Ferdinand and Isabella supplied Columbus with money and ships. But instead of finding Asia, Columbus discovered what came to be known as the New World. He claimed the land and all of its wealth for Spain.

Meanwhile, Ferdinand and Isabella further extended their influence in Europe. Isabella gained the support of the Castilian nobles. Ferdinand, a strong military leader and a clever diplomat, brought stability to Aragón. He also conquered Naples, much of southern Italy, and part of the kingdom of Navarre. Those victories brought all of the territory south of the Pyrenees mountains (except Portugal) under Spanish control. Ferdinand and Isabella also made powerful foreign alliances. Each of their five children married the heirs of other European kingdoms.

Isabella died on November 26, 1504. Ferdinand died on January 23, 1516. They are buried together in the Royal Chapel at Granada Cathedral.

Reviewed by WILLIAM D. PHILLIPS, JR.
University of Minnesota

Did you know that...

Catherine of Aragón, the youngest of Ferdinand and Isabella's five children, was the first of the six wives of England's King Henry VIII?

HANDBALL

Handball is a fast-paced, exciting sport. It is usually played by two or four people. When two people play against each other, it is called singles. When four people play—two teams of two players—it is called doubles. The object of the game is for a player to strike a small rubber ball with his or her hand and bounce it off a wall in such a way that an opposing player cannot return it to the front wall before it hits the floor twice.

Handball is a fast-paced, exciting sport. Players take turns hitting a small rubber ball with their hands and bouncing it off a wall. Courts have one, three, or four walls.

▶ HANDBALL GAMES

Handball can be played on three kinds of courts: One-wall, three-wall, and four-wall. These can be found at parks, playgrounds, resorts, fitness clubs, and recreation centers.

One-Wall Courts

One-wall handball is an American game. It developed chiefly around the New York City area.

The wall is 20 feet (6.1 meters) wide and 16 feet (4.9 meters) high. The floor is 20 feet wide and 34 feet (10.3 meters) long from the wall to the back edge of the long line. The long line, which runs across the rear of the court, marks the back boundary. Sidelines extend 3 feet (0.9 meter) beyond the long line. A line called the short line is drawn across the court 16 feet from the front wall. After the ball is served against the front wall, it must bounce in the receiving zone, which is bounded by the short line, the long line, and the two sidelines.

Three-Wall Courts

Three-wall handball is played on a court with a front wall and two side walls, but no back wall. It measures 40 feet (12.2 meters) by 20 feet by 20 feet. A partial ceiling extends about 20 feet back from the front wall. It is also used in play.

Three-wall is played outdoors in parks and recreation centers all over the United States. A national three-wall tournament is held every Labor Day weekend. It is conducted by the United States Handball Association, the sport's governing body in the United States.

Four-Wall Courts

The four-wall court measures 20 feet wide and 40 feet long. The height of the front wall is 20 feet. The height of the back wall is 14 feet (4.2 meters). The short line is exactly halfway between the front wall and the back wall, 20 feet from each. In four-wall handball, the ball may be hit off the front wall, both side walls, the back wall, or the ceiling.

▶ EQUIPMENT

The official handball measures about $1\frac{7}{8}$ inches (5 centimeters) in diameter and weighs about $2\frac{5}{32}$ ounces (61 grams). Lighter and larger balls may be used if a specific tournament permits.

Gloves must be worn at all times during play. They may or may not be padded.

Since handball requires quick starts, stops, and fast footwork, strong, well-fitting suction or crepe-soled shoes should be worn.

▶ THE STROKES

There are three basic strokes used in handball. They are the underhand stroke, the sidearm stroke, and the overhand stroke. In the underhand, most of the power comes from the wrist and forearm. The sidearm stroke gets most of its power the same way. But it is usually faster than the underhand, and the ball can be hit harder. The overhand stroke is for hitting balls when they bounce high or before they hit the ground.

▶ RULES AND SCORING

The United States Handball Association Rules are the official handball rules of the

United States. The basic rules are the same in other countries.

The basic rules that apply to both one-and four-wall games are as follows:

1. Only one hand can be used in striking the ball.
2. A player attempting to return a ball must hit it before it bounces twice.
3. A match consists of the best two out of three games.
4. A game is won by the side first scoring 21 points, or 11 points in a tie-breaking game.
5. Only the side serving can score.
6. Service changes when the side serving fails to return the ball legally.

Illegal Serves

The following serves are illegal in four-wall handball. Any two in succession put the server out, except for the last three serves, which call for the serve to be transferred to the opponent:

- if during a serve any part of the foot extends beyond the serving zone
- if the partner is not in the service box while waiting for service
- if the ball hits the front wall and the back wall or the ceiling before hitting the floor behind the short line
- if the ball hits the front wall and any two other walls before hitting the floor
- if the ball hits the floor and the front wall at the same time (this would be where floor and wall join)
- if a legally served ball touches the server before hitting the floor

▶ HISTORY

Games with balls have been around for thousands of years. Records indicate that the ancient Egyptians, as well as the Aztecs, Incas, and Maya, played some form of handball. Handball as it is played today is Celtic in origin. About 1880, when many young men went from Ireland to the United States, they brought the game of four-wall handball with them.

The first championship court was built in Brooklyn, New York, in the late 1880's. Handball is played today, sometimes in slightly different forms, in many countries. A sport called team handball, or fieldball, is popular in Europe. But it is quite different from the handball played against walls.

CHARLES J. O'CONNELL
Former Chairman
National Handball Committee
Amateur Athletic Union

Reviewed by United States Handball Association

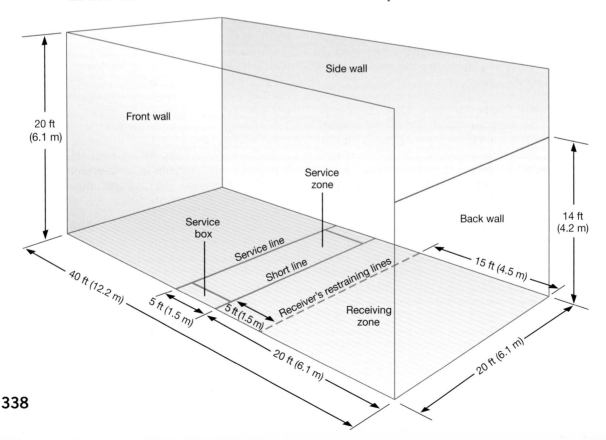

FEET AND HANDS

At first glance, an eagle's foot, a horse's hoof, a turtle's foot, and your foot look very different. Yet all these feet have the same basic pattern of bones. In fact, so do the feet of most other four-limbed **vertebrates**. Vertebrates are animals with backbones.

Vertebrates with four limbs are called **tetrapods**. In general, all limbs do the same work. They support the body and move it from place to place. Many animals have limbs that help them do certain kinds of work especially well. Some animals have limbs that enhance their ability to crawl, walk, run, jump, and climb. Others have limbs adapted for swimming or flying. Only a few vertebrates, such as snakes, have lost their limbs and move without legs.

Most four-limbed vertebrates move on all four legs. The structures at the ends of the legs are called feet. Some four-limbed vertebrates are **bipedal**. This means they move on two feet at least some of the time. Humans are true bipeds. This means we stand, walk, and run only on two feet.

In some four-limbed vertebrates, the front limbs, or forelimbs, have been modified for functions other than walking. If they have

Different kinds of limbed animals display a wide variety of feet and hands. Although these feet and hands look very different, they have a lot in common, too. In fact, the similarities and differences provide clues to how limbed animals are related.

been modified for grasping, the forelimbs are often called arms. The structures at the ends of the arms are called hands. In bipeds with arms, the arms and hands are free to lift or pick things up, carry young, or bring food to the mouth. The animals that most consistently use their hands for grasping are the primates. This group includes humans. In some four-limbed vertebrates, the forelimbs have been modified for other functions. For example, the forelimbs of birds and bats are wings.

▶ **THE BASIC PATTERN**

In the early four-limbed vertebrates, a basic pattern of bones was established in the limbs. It was passed on to four-limbed vertebrates that evolved later. In some of these animals, the pattern stayed much the same. In others, it became highly modified.

In the basic pattern, the limb is divided into three segments—an upper part, a middle part, and a lower part. The upper part typically has one bone. (In the human arm, this bone is the humerus. In the human leg, it is the femur.) The middle part typically has two bones. (In the human arm, these bones are the radius and ulna. In the human leg, they are called the tibia and fibula.)

The lower part is the hand or foot. It is made up of many bones. The block-like or rounded sets of bones in the wrist are called carpals. (The ones in the ankle are called tarsals.) They are followed by a set of long, thin bones that form the base of the palm (or sole). These are called metacarpals (or metatarsals). Beyond these bones are the bones of the digits, or fingers (or toes). These are called phalanges. The fingers and toes of humans consist of a line of three phalanges.

In the four-limbed vertebrates, a pattern can be seen in the bones of the hand or foot. This pattern was inherited from a common ancestor that had a hand or foot with five digits (fingers or toes). The limb is often said to be **pentadactyl** ("penta" means five, and "dactyl" means digit).

The pentadactyl limb goes back more than 300 million years. This is when four-limbed vertebrates first came out of the water and started living on land. Since then, the pentadactyl limb has been passed down in modified form to many different animals. For example, it can be seen in the limbs of the salamander, mouse, dog, cat, monkey, lizard, alligator, and turtle—and in your own hand and arm.

Origin of the Limb

Most limbed vertebrates use their limbs for walking on land. But the ancestors of the earliest limbed vertebrates were swimmers. In fact, they were fish. Unlike other fish, they had fleshy, limb-like fins supported by simple skeletons. The bones even fit together to form a kind of segmented limb. Because of their unusual fins, these fish are called lobe-finned fish. At first, the limb-like fin had only two segments. Eventually a three-part limb evolved. Earlier, lungs capable of breathing air had developed.

Fossils of the extinct *Tiktaalik* show that limbs developed as early as 380 million years ago. *Tiktaalik* could swim in water and walk on land.

Most lobe-finned fish are extinct. But a few relatives survive. These include coelocanths and lungfishes. When they move their fins to swim, they do so in a step-cycle. They move one fin, then the other, the way limbed animals move their limbs when they walk.

Step-cycle swimming would have been helpful to the early lobe-finned fish, which lived in shallow water environments choked with vegetation and other obstacles. They would have been able to escape predators and catch food more easily.

Fossils of the first limbed animals show that these creatures were very fish-like. They had gills, finned tails, and skulls like those of fishes. Some had many fingers, seven or more, much like the rays of a fin. Eventually they moved onto land.

Fossils of one animal, *Tiktaalik*, show that the three-part limb developed as early as 380 million years ago. Other fossils show another important modification: distinct fingers. Eventually the number of digits was reduced to the basic five of the pentadactyl limb.

In some animals, the bones of the pentadactyl limb have been fused to increase strength. In others, bones have been eliminated. Or they have been duplicated to increase function. Modifications are especially common in the bones of the hand and wrist.

Different Kinds of Early Tetrapods

The first limbed vertebrates can be divided into two groups. The first included amphibian-like animals that lived in or close to the water. They probably hunted like alligators and crocodiles do today. They grew to be very large, but generally had short limbs that ex-

Homologous Structures

In many kinds of animals, limbs share structural similarities because the animals are closely related to a common ancestor. The limbs of these animals are said to be homologous structures.

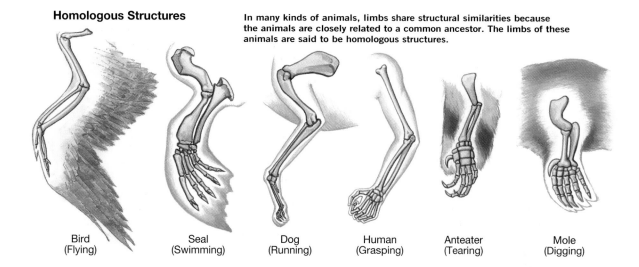

Bird
(Flying)

Seal
(Swimming)

Dog
(Running)

Human
(Grasping)

Anteater
(Tearing)

Mole
(Digging)

tended from the sides of their bodies. Living amphibians are descendents of this group. They are very different from their large ancestors. All are small. They include the limbless, worm-like caecelians, the salamanders, and the frogs. They have four fingers on the forelimbs and five toes on their hind limbs.

The second group of early limbed vertebrates included animals that usually stayed on dry land. Their limbs were positioned underneath their bodies. This helped them walk more efficiently and bear more weight. Better lungs and thicker skins developed. Another key change was the ability to produce eggs that could be laid on dry land. Animals in this group are the ancestors of all other living limbed vertebrates (mammals and reptiles).

▶ REPTILES

Reptiles are a highly diverse group. They include crocodiles, lizards, snakes, turtles, and birds. Extinct members of this group include flying forms (the pterosaurs) and marine forms (such as the ichthyosaurs and plesiosaurs). Extinct members also include the dinosaurs from which birds descended.

Most reptiles have the basic pentadactyl limb. Examples include turtles, most lizards, alligators, and some dinosaurs. During the Mesozoic Era, which lasted from about 240 to 65 million years ago, many reptiles evolved highly modified pentadactyl limbs. This happened because many reptile species explored new habitats. The diverse conditions led to many new adaptations.

In some groups of reptiles, the modifications were extreme. For example, marine reptiles such as ichthyosaurs and plesiosaurs had shortened upper limb segments. And the lowest segment of each limb was a rigid paddle. The digit bones were duplicated, resulting in many flat, interlocking segments. Some of these reptiles had five fingers. Others had additional fingers that broadened and stiffened the paddle.

In reptiles from one group, the archosaurs, an ankle developed that can be seen in today's crocodiles. These animals have archosaur ancestors. The ankle can twist so that the feet may face forward. Crocodiles can use it to bring their limbs under their bodies and lift their bellies off the ground.

Other archosaurs led to the pterosaurs and dinosaurs. In these archosaurs, a hinged ankle developed. This ankle was better at supporting an erect walking style. Some of these animals walked erect on four feet. And some were bipedal, like today's birds, which evolved from the dinosaurs.

In the flying pterosaurs, the limb was elongated into a wing. Wingspans of pterosaurs got to be longer than 36 feet (12 meters)— the size of a small plane. The span of each wing was mostly due to a very long fourth finger. From the tip of this finger, a wing membrane stretched to the edge of the body and parts of the hind limb.

The ancestors of the dinosaurs had five fingers. But in most dinosaurs, the number was reduced to four or three. Some dinosaurs had

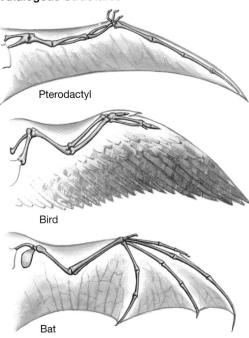

Pterodactyl

Bird

Bat

Some animals have structures that serve similar functions even though the animals are not closely related to a common ancestor. Such structures are analogous forms.

heavy, solid limbs and broad feet. These modifications helped support the weight of heavy dinosaurs, such as the long-necked sauropods.

Most dinosaurs were bipeds. Theropods are a good example. They stood on their hind limbs, which had modifications to support fast running. The tibia and fibula were fused together, the foot was lengthened, and the number of weight-bearing toes was reduced to three. Modifications in the forelimb included a flexible wrist, which allowed the hand to be part of a motion similar to the flapping of a bird's wing. This motion allowed the theropods to close their hands and arms around prey.

▶ **BIRDS**

Birds have limbs that are modified versions of theropod limbs. Theropods had three-fingered hands, and birds have three fingers that help support their wings. (In birds, the central finger is the longest.) Birds can move their wings the way theropods moved their forelimbs. But birds use the flapping motion to power flight instead of seizing prey. The entire arm, from the shoulder to the tips of the fingers, is long and tapering.

The bones of the wing that correspond to the bones of the hand form the manus. In the manus, some bones have been fused, and others have been reduced. The result is a light and strong wing support. When the wing is outstretched, the outer half of the wing is supported by the manus.

Birds, like humans, are bipeds. They walk on their hind legs and stand on two feet. Just like their dinosaurian ancestors, they have four toes. Three are weight-bearing. And the fourth is modified for other functions. In perching birds, this toe points backward and allows the foot to hang on to branches easily.

On the ground the two feet provide steady support. Birds also use their feet to hold food, make nests, and seize prey.

The ability to fly has been lost in some birds. They have become too large, or their wings have become too small. Many flightless birds have long, strong hind limbs for running. Such birds include the ostrich, emu, rhea, and cassowary. Some flightless birds are extinct. One such group, the "terror birds," included large predators. One group of birds, the penguins, became great swimmers. Their wings became smaller, and their feathers came to be used for insulation. However, penguins still "fly," as they flap their wings to propel themselves through the water.

▶ **MAMMALS**

The ancestors of the mammals are as old as the reptiles. These creatures led to the mammals and several mammal-like groups. Of all these creatures, only the mammals survive. Mammals now make up the dominant group of four-limbed vertebrates.

Mammals exhibit a wide range of limb forms. In all mammals, both the hind limbs and the forelimbs are under the body. As a result, mammals do not have limbs that sprawl upon the ground. They can use their limbs to keep their bodies off the ground. Mammals can put one foot in front of the other when they walk, instead of swinging their limbs outward from their sides. Many also have forelimb modifications that reflect their different habitats and lifestyles.

Form and Function. Specialized limbs are found in dolphins, bats, birds, horses, and many other mammals. Other mammals such as mice, rats, cats, and dogs do not have extensively modified limbs. When these animals walk or run, their heels and soles do not touch the ground. This makes their legs functionally longer and thus capable of running faster. These quick-moving animals travel lightly on their toes.

Some mammals walk on the flats of their feet. A bear, for example, has the regular mammal foot except that the sole is large and stays fairly flat against the ground. Bears walk on the soles of their feet, as humans do. Many mammals that move on their toes or soles have large claws on their feet for defense, capturing prey, or digging.

When an animal is very large and heavy, its limbs must be adapted to bear that weight. The limbs are thickened, and the toes are largely held together by flesh. The result is a column-like limb. This sturdy, weight-bearing structure appeared in many large extinct animals. Today it is seen in the elephant, rhinoceros, and hippopotamus.

Many mammals, some fairly large, rely on their running ability to escape predators. They may also travel long distances for food. These mammals typically have hooves. They walk and run on the tips of their toes—actually their toenails. Animals with hooves are divided into two groups. One has an odd number of toes, and the other has an even number of toes.

Hoofed Mammals. Many of the hoofed mammals live on wide, grassy plains or on open, rocky hillsides. When alarmed, they run away suddenly and rapidly. Running speed is so important that their limbs are shaped for sprinting. Their heels never touch the ground. The toes are encased in hooves, which consist of horn-like material and grow out of the last bones of the toes of the animal's foot. The term "hoof" may be used to refer to the entire foot. But it is really just the tip of the toe.

The five-toed pattern can no longer be seen in most of today's hoofed mammals. But fossils show that it existed in the ancestors of these animals. Gradually the bones in the feet and legs became longer. The weight-bearing bones became thicker. And the non-weight-bearing bones disappeared or combined with other bones. These changes resulted in a foot better suited for running.

Animals with two toes are often called **cloven-hoofed**. The reason is that each hoof looks like one hoof that has been cloven, or split, in half. But there are really two hooves,

each covering a separate toe. The weight of the body spreads the two toes apart. This spread gives the foot a firm hold on the ground. It helps goats, for example, keep a firm and steady footing when they climb steep, rocky slopes.

Still other animals, such as the heavy rhinoceros, walk on three toes while the horse, donkey, and zebra walk on one. These hoofed mammals are odd-toed. In the odd-toed hoofed mammals, like their even-toed hoofed relatives, the toes that were not used gradually disappeared.

Aquatic Mammals. Some mammals left the land and began to live in the water. As time passed, the feet and legs of these mammals were modified for swimming. Generally, they became fins. Even so, the five-toed pattern can still be seen inside the fins. It reminds us that the ancestors of whales, porpoises, walruses, and seals walked on the land.

The whales are the most modified of these. Whales and dolphins are the descendants of a group of even-toed hoofed mammals that adapted to the water. The front legs and feet turned into paddles for swimming. The hind legs disappeared almost completely. Only traces of the bones are found in the skeleton. Their tails turned into large tail fins to propel them in the water.

Mammals with Hands. Most animals that climb trees dig their claws into the bark. But some mammals grasp the branches with their fingers. The mammals that climb by grasping are primates. This is a group that includes lemurs, tarsiers, monkeys, apes, and humans.

Lemurs, tarsiers, and the smaller monkeys have hands and feet that can grasp and cling very easily. On the ground, these primates walk on all fours. But when these animals are

Hands

Orangutan

Chimpanzee

Human

Feet

Orangutan

Chimpanzee

Human

Of all animals, apes are most closely related to humans. Like humans, apes such as orangutans and chimpanzees have opposable thumbs. These apes also have opposable big toes, but humans do not.

in the trees, they use their hands and feet to cling to branches. In this manner, they can run along branches and leap from tree to tree swiftly and safely. Many larger primates, including some apes, travel very easily in the trees. But some apes are too heavy to run along branches. Instead, gibbons, orangutans, and chimpanzees swing from branch to branch. They reach their long arms upward until their long fingers can grasp the branch above. Their thumbs are short and are not used in grasping. But the big toes are long, and they help the hind feet grasp the branch on which the animal is standing. The arms are very strong and much longer than the legs.

The gorilla is too large and heavy to travel through the trees, even by swinging from branch to branch. These apes usually climb trees only to get fruit or to sleep.

They live on the ground and walk on their hind feet and the knuckles of their hands. This is called **knuckle walking**.

Humans have a much stronger walking foot than any ape. A human's toes are shorter and do not move as freely when separated from the others. The big toe is in line with the other toes. And the heel provides firmer support. The sole of the foot is arched. And the muscles are better arranged. With these advantages, humans can stand upright and balance on two legs, the arms hanging freely.

In structure the human hand is much like the hand of an ape. The fingers can move from side to side or up and down like a hinge. The wrist can turn in almost any direction. The thumb can cross the palm to oppose (be placed against) the fingers. A thumb or toe that moves this way is called **opposable**. A human's big toes are not opposable like an ape's. But human thumbs are much more so. A human's thumb, which is longer than an ape's, can move easily and at greater distances from the index finger and can touch the tips of each finger.

Flying Mammals. The limbs of one group of mammals are used for flight. Like birds and pterosaurs, bats have had their arms modified to serve as wings. The wing is a membrane of skin. It stretches between the fingers and down the side of the body to the hind legs. The bones of the bat's fingers are extremely long and slender, except the thumb. This finger is separate and clawed. The bat's hind legs are almost useless for walking. When it is on the ground, the bat uses its forelimbs and hind limbs to scramble over surfaces, or hang upside down from branches.

▶ **EVOLUTIONARY HISTORY**

Studies of feet and hands help scientists understand how animals evolved over time. But these studies yield just one set of data. Scientists examine other body structures— skulls, rib cages, hips, and so on. They also consider things besides body parts. For example, they study genetics, geology, and climate. All these studies produce different kinds of clues that can be fit together like puzzle pieces. They can be combined to form a picture of evolutionary history.

ALAN D. GISHLICK
Gustavus Adolphus College

DISARMAMENT

Disarmament means controlling, limiting, or reducing the size of armed forces and the number and type of weapons. By disarming, governments hope to prevent wars or limit the damage to lives and property when wars occur. The efforts to disarm have been many. The successes have been few.

Some historians have estimated that since 3600 B.C. the world has had only about 300 years of peace. During this time there probably have been over 14,000 wars. These wars took the lives of more than 1 billion people.

Efforts toward disarmament grew in the 1900's. After World War I (1914–18), there was a burst of hope for worldwide disarmament. In 1919 the Treaty of Versailles was signed, ending the war. The treaty required Germany to disarm. This would have allowed other nations of the world to disarm, too. But Germany rearmed when Adolf Hitler came to power in the 1930's. Twenty years after the Treaty of Versailles was signed, the world was at war again.

After the end of World War II in 1945, disarmament became more important than ever before. This was because the United States and the Soviet Union, as well as other nations, built up enormous stores of nuclear weapons. These weapons were capable of destroying entire countries.

▶ NUCLEAR DISARMAMENT

The first plan to control nuclear weapons was proposed in 1946 by the United States at the United Nations. It was called the Baruch Plan in honor of Bernard Baruch. He was the U.S. representative to the United Nations Atomic Energy Commission. At the time,

only the United States had atomic weapons. The Baruch Plan called for these weapons to be destroyed. American atomic secrets would be turned over to an international atomic control agency. The agency would then be in charge of all activities involving atomic energy in peacetime as well as wartime. But the plan was rejected by the Soviet Union.

The United States made other disarmament proposals. It proposed to reduce the size of armed forces and the number of weapons, both nuclear and non-nuclear. It also proposed to ban nuclear testing; stop production of nuclear materials; and use nuclear materials only for peaceful purposes, such as generating electricity.

During the Cold War (1945–90) the Soviet Union put forward its own disarmament plans. These generally dealt with matters similar to those contained in the U.S. plans. But the two sides could not agree on one basic question: How could each nation make sure the other kept its end of the agreement? The United States insisted that inspectors be allowed on Russian and U.S. soil to verify that there was no cheating. The Soviet Union argued that inspection and control would merely be cover-ups for American spying.

No disarmament came out of these long years of discussion. But the United States did have some success with the Atoms for Peace Plan presented in 1953. Four years later this led to the creation of an International Atomic Energy Agency. It is still operating.

▶ TWO APPROACHES TO DISARMAMENT

Generally two approaches have been taken to the problem of disarmament. One approach is to try to work out a total disarmament program. The other is to attempt to agree on any single measure or group of measures that would add to world peace and security.

Total Disarmament

Total disarmament means reducing the number of weapons step by step until there are none (or almost none) left. The differences between the United States and many other nations on achieving total disarmament center on three issues. These are balance, inspection (monitoring), and methods of keeping the peace during disarmament and after.

Balance means disarming in a way that neither side ever gains a military advantage. The United States and the Soviet Union agreed that there ought to be balance. But until the early 1970's each believed that the other side's proposals would give that side an advantage.

The United States believes in unlimited inspections, so that each side can be sure the other is disarming. Closed societies such as Iran want to limit what inspectors can see.

Finally, there is the disagreement about keeping the peace during and after disarmament. The United States wants a permanent organization to make sure that world peace and security are protected as weapons are reduced. Other states agree with the idea of some international control. But they dislike the idea of a permanent organization.

Limited Disarmament

Agreement among the world's nations on total disarmament will be difficult to accomplish. However, since the 1960's there has been considerable progress in agreements to greatly limit nuclear, chemical, and biological weapons. These are referred to as weapons of mass destruction, or WMD.

In 1968, after years of negotiations, the Nuclear Nonproliferation Treaty was signed. (**Nonproliferation** means controlling the spread of something.) More than 150 countries have ratified this treaty. It seeks to prohibit the spread of nuclear weapons to countries that do not have them. The treaty also requires countries with nuclear weapons to try to reduce the numbers they have.

Beginning in 1969, the Soviet Union and the United States held *Strategic Arms Limitation Talks* (SALT). These were aimed at limiting and eventually reducing the numbers of their strategic nuclear arms. The talks focused on those arms that could travel very long distances, even across continents, to reach targets in the enemy's territory.

A strategic arms limitation treaty was finally agreed upon. It was signed in 1972. The pact limited the numbers of nuclear weapons each nation could maintain. In 1979 the two nations agreed upon a second SALT pact. It imposed further limitations. In 1987 improved relations between the United States

and the Soviet Union led to the signing of the INF treaty. It banned all *i*ntermediate-range *n*uclear *f*orces capable of reaching targets in Europe. For the first time, both sides agreed to permit inspections of military facilities to verify that the terms of the treaty were being carried out.

In 1990, with the end of the Cold War, the United States and the Soviet Union agreed to several additional disarmament treaties on reducing conventional weapons based in Europe. A *St*rategic *A*rms *R*eduction *T*reaty (START), cutting long-range nuclear missiles, was signed by the United States and the Soviet Union in 1991. A second START treaty was signed between the state that replaced the Soviet Union, the Russian Federation, and the United States in 1993. In 2002, the United States and Russia signed the Treaty of Moscow, pledging to eliminate two-thirds of their long-range nuclear warheads by 2012.

In 1996 the United Nations General Assembly approved the Comprehensive Test Ban Treaty, banning all nuclear testing. But it was rejected by the U.S. Senate in 1999.

Biological and Chemical Warfare. Infecting the enemy with diseases is called biological warfare. A 1975 treaty prohibiting the production of biological weapons has been ratified by over 100 nations.

Chemical warfare is the military use of chemicals that kill people or destroy food supplies. In 1997, 165 nations signed the Chemical Weapon Convention Treaty, prohibiting the use or sale of poison gas weapons.

▶ THE FUTURE

When the Cold War ended with the collapse of the Soviet Union in 1991, there was great hope that weapons of mass destruction might be eliminated and funds diverted to peaceful causes. But since then India, Pakistan, and North Korea have tested nuclear weapons and Iran continues to develop them. Moreover, Russia has threatened to withdraw from some of the treaties enacted by the former Soviet Union. And the United States has considered developing new nuclear weapons.

WILLIAM C. FOSTER
Former Director, United States Arms Control and Disarmament Agency

Reviewed by LAWRENCE KORB
Former Assistant U.S. Secretary of Defense
Senior Fellow, Center for American Progress

GERBILS

Gerbils are rodents belonging to the family Muridae. This family also includes rats, mice, voles, lemmings, hamsters, and muskrats. There are about 85 species of gerbils. They live in deserts throughout Africa and the Middle East and in arid (dry) parts of Asia.

Characteristics of Gerbils. Gerbils have short front legs with small feet. They use their long hind legs and large hind feet to hop about. Their coats are usually tan, brown, or dark red on top, with lighter fur underneath. The tips of their tails often end in a tuft of longer fur. This tuft may be a different color from the body. Like all rodents, gerbils have special front teeth called incisors, which are used for gnawing.

The smallest species is the pygmy gerbil. It can be as small as about 2½ inches (6 centimeters) long, with a 3-inch (8-centimeter) tail. It weighs less than an ounce. Larger species, such as the Indian gerbil, can be up to 8 inches (20 centimeters) long and have a 9½-inch (24-centimeter) tail. They can weigh as much as 8 ounces (226 grams). Gerbils generally live for only a few years in the wild.

Lives of Gerbils. Gerbils usually avoid the sun during the day by resting in cool, moist underground burrows. They come out at night and gather seeds, which they carry in their cheeks back to their burrows to eat. Some gerbils will eat other animals such as snails. Gerbils receive almost all the water they need from their food.

Gerbils that live in cooler climates are often social. There are sometimes several

Gerbils are a kind of rodent related to rats and voles. They live in dry habitats throughout Africa, the Middle East, and in parts of Asia.

families living in the same burrow system. But gerbils that inhabit hot deserts are usually solitary. Baby gerbils (called pups) are born hairless and helpless with their eyes closed. A typical litter has three to five young.

Gerbils and Their Environment. Wild gerbils are sometimes considered pests. They can spread diseases and eat large quantities of grain. Their burrowing can also damage irrigation canals and pastures. For these reasons, people sometimes kill them or destroy their burrows. Gerbils are also a source of food for many animals, including owls and snakes. Thirty-four species of gerbils are currently on the endangered list.

DOROTHY HINSHAW PATENT
Author, science and nature books for children
See also RODENTS.

GERBILS AS PETS

Gerbils are popular pets. The species usually found in pet stores is the Mongolian gerbil. They are social animals, so it is best to keep more than one. Their social nature also makes them relatively easy to tame.

A glass aquarium with a fine wire mesh cover makes the best gerbil home. The animals need a 2- to 3-inch (5- to 8-centimeter) layer of bedding, such as grass or hay, or torn paper towels or tissues. (Do not use newspaper or pine or cedar wood shavings. These can harm your pet.) The bedding should be changed at least once a week. Empty tissue boxes can provide your pets with a safe nesting place. They will also appreciate cardboard tubes from rolls of toilet paper or paper towels. They will crawl through these and chew on them. Gerbils will eat store-bought food. But they can also be fed seeds, small amounts of fresh fruits and vegetables, raisins, mealworms, and bits of hard-boiled egg. A water bottle should also be provided.

Pet gerbils can live as long as five years.

GERMANY

Germany is a nation located in Central Europe. It is wedged between eight countries and bordered on the north by the North Sea and the Baltic Sea. To Germany's east are Poland and the Czech Republic. To its west are France, Luxembourg, Belgium, and the Netherlands. And to its south are Austria and Switzerland.

Germany has the largest population of any European country. It is Europe's largest economy, producing close to 2 trillion dollars in goods and services each year. It is also one of the world's leading industrial economies and top exporters. Germany is a member of the European Union (EU), a powerful economic group of more than two dozen countries. In addition, it is a member of the Group of Eight (G8), a political forum of some of the most powerful countries in the world.

Germany's strength today reflects an upward climb. Many of its cities and other economic assets were destroyed during World War II (1939–45). In 1949 the country was divided into two parts. One became East Germany (the German Democratic Republic), which was aligned with the Soviet Union. It had a communist form of government and a centrally planned economy controlled by the state. The other part became West Germany (the Federal Republic of Germany). It had a democratic government and a capitalist economy. The artificial division created great economic and personal hardships.

For several decades the "two Germanys" developed separately. Then, in 1990, East Germany reunited with West Germany as the Federal Republic of Germany and adopted its democratic form of government. By that

Looking like a castle from a fairy tale, Neuschwanstein is set high in the Bavarian mountains. It was built for King Ludwig II of Bavaria but remained unfinished at his death in 1886.

time, West Germany had rebuilt much of its economy, and its people were living better than those in East Germany. When the new government took office in 1991, it began a long process of raising living standards in the former East Germany. But gaps still exist in income, health care, and education, leaving some Germans with the sense that the country remains divided. The problem is expected to resolve in time as the economies come together.

Germany's challenges include an aging population, a growing number of immigrants and would-be entrants, and new global competitors, such

Faces of Germany. *From far left to below:* A young girl displays the German flag. A family in Bavarian costume celebrates *Oktoberfest*. This farmer is from Germany's Black Forest. A Turkish girl and her friend enjoy a meal of flat bread with cheese.

as China and India. It is equipped to deal with these challenges, which it shares with most of the world's highly industrialized countries. In its favor are a strong tradition of industrial quality, financial expertise, and well-educated, highly skilled workers.

▶ **PEOPLE**

Origins. Germanic peoples arrived in northern and central Europe at least 2,000 years ago. Their origin is unclear, but they are known to have formed tribes that migrated to the region over many centuries. They developed a common language and culture that set them apart from other peoples of Europe.

Ethnic Germans (people of German ancestry) make up over 90 percent of Germany's people. The country also has more than 7 million residents who are not of ethnic German ancestry. They include people who came from Turkey after World War II as guest workers and their descendents. Today there is a Turkish population of about 2 million people; over

one-fourth of them were born in Germany. In addition there are over 2 million residents from EU states and in excess of 1 million from other European states. Another 1 million come from Asia.

People of nonethnic German origin now make up less than 10 percent of the population. But they are growing faster in number than ethnic Germans and have a higher number of young people. Some ethnic Germans fear that these minorities will change German society and culture. Some say they are costing the country too much in terms of health care and other social benefits. But supporters see them as part of the solution to Germany's need for a younger workforce and a way to acquire workers with needed technical skills.

Language. The official spoken and written language is modern German, or High German (Hochdeutsch). However, the ordinary speech of most Germans is influenced by the country's many regional dialects. See the article on the German language in this volume.

Religion. Germany's constitution guarantees freedom of religion. Since the Reformation, which began in 1517, Germany has been divided between a generally Protestant north and a Roman Catholic south and west. Just over one-third of Germans are Protestants;

The Cologne Cathedral is Germany's largest cathedral. It took over 600 years to complete. The Hohenzollern Bridge (in the foreground) crosses the River Rhine.

About 500,000 Jews lived in Germany before World War II. But most of them either escaped Germany or were killed in concentration camps during the war. The Jewish population now stands at about 108,000.

Germany has no state church. But Christian and Jewish groups receive government financial support through a "church tax." Muslim organizations are seeking official status, which would allow them to receive government funds also.

most belong to the Evangelical Church. One-third are Roman Catholics. Another 25 percent, or over 20 million Germans, have no recorded religion. This is partly the legacy of the former East German government, which discouraged religious practice.

A much smaller but growing group of 3 million is Muslim, representing less than 4 percent of the total.

Education. Most German education operates on a three-track system. After four years (from age 6 to 10) of compulsory primary school (*Grundschule*), students are divided into three groups. Those in the first track enter a *Gymnasium*, which prepares them to enter a university. After nine years they earn a degree and the right to attend a university tuition free. Students entering a university present an *Abitur*, or certificate, showing successful completion of study at a *Gymnasium*, or at one of the few comprehensive schools (*Gesamtschule*). They do not take university entrance exams.

Students in the second track attend a general high school (*Realschule*) for up to six years. They receive both academic and technical training. If they qualify, *Realschule* graduates may transfer to a *Gymnasium* and go on to a university.

Those in the third track spend five to six years in a general school (*Hauptschule*). This is followed by three to four years of part-time vocational training and employment. Currently, most German students attend either the *Realschule* or the *Gymnasium*. Transfers from one track to another are possible although seldom done.

In addition to public schools, which most students attend, there are also many Roman Catholic private schools. For students with disabilities, there is an extensive network of special education schools.

Germany has more than 100 universities. Most are public. Famous universities were

FACTS and figures

FEDERAL REPUBLIC OF GERMANY (Bundesrepublik Deutschland) is the official name of the country.

LOCATION: North central Europe.

AREA: 137,803 sq mi (356,910 km²).

POPULATION: 82 million (estimate).

CAPITAL AND LARGEST CITY: Berlin.

MAJOR LANGUAGE: German.

MAJOR RELIGIOUS GROUPS: Protestant, Roman Catholic.

GOVERNMENT: Republic. **Head of state**—president. **Head of government**—chancellor. **Legislature**—federal parliament, consisting of the Bundesrat (Federal Council) and the Bundestag (Federal House of Representatives).

CHIEF PRODUCTS: Agricultural—wheat, rye, oats, barley, sugar beets, potatoes, hops, wine grapes, livestock. **Manufactured**—iron and steel, motor vehicles, electrical equipment, precision instruments, optical equipment, plastics, pharmaceuticals (medical drugs), china, glass, textiles, processed foods. **Mineral**—coal, potash, iron ore, petroleum, natural gas.

MONETARY UNIT: Euro (1 euro = 100 cents).

founded at Heidelberg (1386), Leipzig (1409), and Rostock (1419). They helped set standards that were used by universities worldwide.

Libraries and Museums. Germany has nearly 9,000 public libraries and over 200 science libraries.

There are close to 5,000 museums in Germany. These include over 500 art museums, nearly 600 science and technology museums, and over 250 natural history museums. Art museums such as the Pergamon in Berlin, the Alte Pinakothek and Neue Pinakothek in Munich, and the Zwinger galleries in Dresden are among the best in the world.

The Ludwig museum is one of Cologne's most important attractions. It displays art from the 20th century to the present, including works by Henri Matisse.

▶ **WAY OF LIFE**

The people of the former West Germany generally have a high standard of living. Workers tend to be better off than in other developed countries. Most enjoy an annual vacation of six weeks, comprehensive health care, and good pensions. The average age of retirement is 60, although it is being raised by the government to postpone retirement. Millions of Germans can afford to and do travel outside the country each year.

People living in the former East Germany tend to be less well off than those in the former West Germany. The sudden change from a planned to a free-market economy created severe problems. Unprofitable industries were closed and unemployment, which is still high, rose dramatically. This has contributed to the feeling among many easterners that they are "second-class" citizens. Thus the government continues to finance the modernization of the eastern German economy and its integration with western Germany.

Nearly all jobs are open to women, and women have full legal equality with men. In 2005, Germany elected its first woman chancellor. However, on average, women continue to earn less than men in production industries. The government is urging more women to enter the workforce. It is supporting this effort by helping finance child care, which is currently in short supply.

Food and Drink. Each region of Germany has its own specialties. Bavaria is famous for its *Knödel* (dumplings). The Hamburg area is known for its delicious seafood dishes. Westphalian pumpernickel and German rye bread are also popular in other countries.

In a famous Munich beer hall, people celebrate *Oktoberfest*, which occurs from mid-September until early October and attracts millions of visitors from around the world.

Favorite foods all over Germany include Wiener schnitzel (breaded veal cutlet), pork chops, herring, and sauerbraten. Sauerbraten is beef marinated in vinegar and spices before roasting. Sausages, in all their many varieties, are served everywhere, from little street stands to the finest restaurants. However, Germans have become more health conscious in recent years. They eat fewer fatty foods and prefer a more balanced diet.

Beer and wine are the favorite alcoholic drinks along with a variety of schnapps (liquors). The best-known German wines come from the Rhine and Moselle River regions. Non-alcoholic beverages, including mineral water and *Schorle* (juice and mineral water), are also popular.

Sports and Recreation. Soccer is the favorite German sport. Gymnastics, swimming, horseback riding, tennis, hiking, and handball are also popular. Winter sports, such as skiing and ice-skating, draw thousands of families to the Bavarian Alps and other winter resorts.

During the months of September and October, the Rhineland celebrates the wine harvest. There are weeks devoted to the music of Ludwig van Beethoven in Bonn and to Johann Sebastian Bach at Ansbach. In Munich, large amounts of food and beer are consumed during the *Oktoberfest*. The annual Children's Festival at Biberach always draws large crowds.

In addition, people living in Germany as well as tourists attend festivals staged at the country's many castles and palaces. There are outdoor concerts in castle courtyards, wine festivals, and medieval banquets complete with minstrels and knights in costumes. Many small medieval towns in the south present historical plays.

National Holidays. National holidays include January 1 (New Year's Day), May 1 (Labor Day), October 3 (Day of Unity), and December 25 and 26 (Christmas). The pre-Lenten season is celebrated with carnivals in Munich, Cologne, and other areas. *Fastnach* (Mardi Gras) is well known for its parades and carnival atmosphere. During the holidays, Christmas trees are decorated with silvery strands of "angel hair" and white candles. On Christmas Eve, carols are sung and gifts are exchanged.

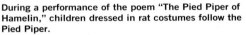

Soccer fans with hats the colors of the German flag watch a German player and a Latvian player battle for the ball during a European Championship game.

During a performance of the poem "The Pied Piper of Hamelin," children dressed in rat costumes follow the Pied Piper.

▶ LAND

Germany is in the heart of Europe. It has few natural frontiers to mark its borders. Its location and lack of natural barriers have led to many invasions and also to German invasions of its neighbors.

Landforms. Germany is a highly industrialized and urbanized nation, but over one-third of its land is suitable for agriculture. The country can be divided into three distinct regions. They are the northern lowlands, the central uplands, and the southern mountains.

The northern German lowlands slope toward the Baltic and North seas, Germany's only areas of seacoast. In the plains of the northern lowlands, forests alternate with meadows and marshy lakes.

In the central German uplands, deep river valleys alternate with forested hills. Many of the forests and hills, painted houses, and turreted castles of the region were used as settings for the Grimm brothers' fairy tales.

Southern Germany has more rugged mountains. It is the land of the Black Forest and the Bavarian Alps. The Black Forest is a region of low-level mountains running along the Rhine Valley to the Swiss border. The Black Forest is actually very dark green—the color of the dense fir trees that cover the slopes. It is a planted forest.

The Bavarian Alps in southeastern Germany are one of Europe's favorite winter playgrounds. Alpine lakes and steep slopes attract thousands of tourists. They come for the skiing and other sports. The Zugspitze, the highest peak in all Germany, at 9,720 feet (2,963 meters), is in the Bavarian Alps.

Rivers and Lakes. The Rhine River is about 820 miles (1,320 kilometers) long. It is Germany's chief river and the most important commercial waterway in western Europe. The Rhine rises in the mountains of Switzerland and empties into the North Sea. Other important German rivers—such as the Main, the Moselle, and the Neckar—flow into the Rhine. It was along the banks of the Rhine that the Romans planted the first vineyards in Germany. These now provide the grapes for the famed Rhine wine.

The Zugspitze is in the Bavarian Alps, in southeastern Germany. At 9,720 feet (2,963 meters), it is the highest peak in the country.

The Danube is one of Europe's major rivers. It rises in the Black Forest and flows through seven other countries before emptying into the Black Sea. This river is important for transportation and is a source of hydroelectric power. In the south, alpine lakes sparkle in deep valleys cut by glaciers. Germany's largest lake is Lake Constance.

Climate. Most of Germany has a fairly mild climate. Winter fogs and dark, cloudy days are common in the northern lowlands. Northern cities such as Hamburg and Berlin have average winter temperatures of around 36°F (2°C). Summer temperatures average 64°F (18°C) or more.

Rainfall generally increases to the south. There is usually more rain during the summer. More than 75 inches (1,900 millimeters) of rain or snow fall in the Bavarian Alps each year. From the Harz Mountains south, peaks are usually snowcapped all winter.

Mineral Resources. Germany's most important natural resources consist of reserves of coal and industrial salt. They are among the most important in Europe. Coal is the basis of Germany's steel industry and is also used to generate electric power.

A variety of salts, as well as local lignite, provide raw materials for a very important

353

Throughout the Rhineland, medieval castles as well as fortresses dot the steep, wooded hillsides.

chemical industry in the Halle-Leipzig area. Germany also produces much of the world's potash. There is some petroleum and natural gas in the northwest.

▶ ECONOMY

Germany has become one of the top five economic powers in the world. In the 1990's and first few years of the 21st century, the country as a whole struggled with low economic growth and high unemployment. These problems threatened Germany's way of life, which includes government health, unemployment, housing, retirement, and other social benefits. Labor market and other reforms started in the 1990's have helped the economy, including lowering unemployment.

But the government still faces the problem of an aging population, which requires more in social security payments than Germany's economy is generating. And it is still spending large sums of money to raise living standards in the former East Germany.

Services. Services contribute some 70 percent to Germany's gross domestic product (GDP). (GDP is the total amount of goods and services produced in a country, usually in one year.) Two-thirds of Germany's workers are in services, including trade, transportation, and tourism.

Manufacturing. Manufacturing contributes about one-third of GDP and employs about the same percentage of the workforce. The country is among the world's largest producers of chemicals, machinery, vehicles, machine tools, electronics, food and beverages, and ships. Germany is the world's third largest auto producer. German-made luxury cars, including BMW, Mercedes-Benz, and Porsche, are popular worldwide.

Germany also has a crafts industry that consists of hundreds of thousands of companies. They produce Hummel-brand statuary, porcelain (Dresden china), wood carvings (such as soldier nutcrackers for Christmas), quilts, and other items. About 98 percent of companies are small or medium-sized and employ fewer than 500 workers.

Agriculture. Agriculture contributes less than 1 percent to Germany's GDP and employs less than 3 percent of workers. The chief crops grown are potatoes, wheat, barley, sugar beets, fruit, and cabbages. Livestock raising includes cattle, pigs, sheep, and poultry.

Mining. The mining sector is not a major contributor to GDP and employs only a small portion of Germany's workforce. The rich coal mines of Germany's Ruhr district provide energy for factories in such industrial centers as Essen and Dortmund. Germany is also a world-class producer

A violin maker pursues his craft in the city of Munich. Germany has a thriving crafts industry.

Germany

NORTH FRISIAN ISLANDS

North Sea

Baltic Sea

DENMARK

RÜGEN

Flensburg

Kiel

Lübeck

Rostock

EAST FRISIAN IS.

Wilhelmshaven

Emden

Bremerhaven

Hamburg

Schwerin

Lake Müritz

Elbe River

Bremen

Oldenburg

NETHERLANDS

Ems River

Weser River

Osnabrück

Hannover

Braunschweig

Potsdam

Berlin

Spree

Frankfurt an der Oder

Oder River

POLAND

Münster

Bielefeld

Magdeburg

Wittenberg

Dessau

Cottbus

Neisse R.

Duisburg

Essen **Dortmund**

Rhine River

Ruhr R.

Düsseldorf

Cologne

Kassel

HARZ MTS.

Halle

Leipzig

Meissen

Elbe R.

Aachen

Bonn

Koblenz

Fulda R.

Erfurt

Weimar

Jena

Gera

Dresden

Chemnitz

ERZGEBIRGE

BELGIUM

Moselle R.

Werra R.

LUXEMBOURG

Wiesbaden

Mainz

Frankfurt am Main

Main River

Würzburg

Bayreuth

CZECH REPUBLIC

FRANCE

Mannheim

Heidelberg

Saarbrücken

Ansbach

Nuremberg

BOHEMIAN FOREST

Karlsruhe

Rhine River

Neckar R.

Stuttgart

Regensburg

Danube River

Passau

BLACK FOREST

Biberach

Ulm

Augsburg

Freiburg

Lake Constance

Munich

Inn River

AUSTRIA

SWITZERLAND

Oberammergau

BAVARIAN ALPS

Zugspitze ▲

54° N   51° N   48° N

3° E   6° E   9° E   12° E   15° E

EUROPE

AFRICA

0   50   100 mi
0   50   100 km

N

INDEX TO GERMANY POLITICAL MAP

Aachen............B4
Ansbach............D5
Augsburg............D6
Bayreuth............D4
Berlin............E2
Biberach............C6
Bielefeld............C3
Bonn............B4
Braunschweig............D3
Bremen............C2
Bremerhaven............C2
Chemnitz............E4
Cologne............C4
Cottbus............E3
Dessau............E3
Dortmund............C3
Dresden............E4
Duisburg............B3
Düsseldorf............B3
Emden............C2
Erfurt............D4
Essen............C3
Flensburg............D1
Frankfurt am Main............C4
Frankfurt an der Oder............F3
Freiburg............C6
Gera............E4
Halle............E3
Hamburg............D2
Hannover............D3
Heidelberg............C5

Jena............D4
Karlsruhe............C5
Kassel............C3
Kiel............D1
Koblenz............C4
Leipzig............E3
Lübeck............D1
Magdeburg............D3
Mainz............C4
Mannheim............C5
Meissen............E3
Munich............D6
Münster............C3
Nuremberg............D5
Oberammergau............D6
Oldenburg............C2
Osnabrück............C3
Passau............E5
Potsdam............E3
Regensburg............E5
Rostock............E1
Saarbrücken............B5
Schwerin............D2
Stuttgart............C5
Ulm............D6
Weimar............D4
Wiesbaden............C4
Wilhelmshaven............C2
Wittenberg............E3
Würzburg............D5

of potash, which is used in making chemical fertilizers.

Energy. Fossil fuels, such as coal and petroleum, provide nearly two-thirds of Germany's supply of energy. Germany produces coal in abundance but must rely on

Above: This high-speed train is part of the service offered by the Flughafen Fernbahnhof railway station in Frankfurt. *Left:* An autoworker puts some final touches on a BMW car.

imports of petroleum. Another major source is nuclear energy. But the government plans to phase out the use of nuclear power by 2021, as many Germans perceive it as dangerous. Other sources of energy include natural gas and hydroelectricity.

Trade. The EU is Germany's largest trading partner. The next largest is the United States. Among Germany's major exports are machinery, motor vehicles, chemicals, and manufactures. Its major imports include machinery, motor vehicles, chemicals, foodstuffs, textiles, and metals.

Transportation. Germany has extensive highway, railroad, and canal systems that link various parts of the country. Trucks compete with railroads in the transportation of goods. The German airline, Lufthansa, serves all international routes. The German national highways (Autobahn) have high-speed stretches and those with no speed limit.

Communications. Germany has advanced communications systems. These include highly developed telecommunications systems that offer land-based and cellular telephone service. The weekly newspapers *Die Zeit*, the *Frankfurter Allgemeine Zeitung*, and the *Süddeutsche Zeitung* are read throughout the nation and known internationally for

their high quality. *Bild* and *Bild am Sonntag* focus on everyday news and celebrities. Germany has over 30 million Internet users.

▶ **MAJOR CITIES**

German cities are both rooted in the past and very modern. Most lay in ruins at the end of World War II. But many have now been restored. The great majority of Germans live in urban areas (cities and large towns). Aside from Berlin, the capital and most populous city, the largest cities are in western Germany. It is the most densely populated part of the country and one of the most densely populated areas in Europe.

Berlin is Germany's largest city, with over 3 million people. It was the capital of Germany from 1871 to 1945. Between 1945 and 1990, Berlin, like Germany itself, was divided in two. The eastern part was the seat of government of East Germany. The western part was closely linked to West Germany. With reunification in 1990, Berlin again became the national capital. See BERLIN in this volume.

Hamburg is Germany's second largest city, with nearly 2 million people. It is one of Europe's leading seaports and an important shipbuilding and manufacturing city. Tourists are fond of Hamburg's Hagenbecks Tierpark, which is a park and a zoo. They also visit the Planten und Blumen botanical garden, which includes an open-air theater, children's playgrounds, and restaurants.

Munich, one of Germany's most visited cities, has over 1 million people. It offers world-famous art collections and historic treasures. It is home to the Frauenkirche (Cathedral of Our Lady). Tourists also visit the Alte Pinakothek, one of Europe's great museums, the National Theater, and the Cuvillies Theater. Outdoors, Munich offers botanical and zoological gardens.

For hundreds of years, Munich has had a reputation for fine beers. The Hofbräuhaus is the most famous of the beer halls, or *Bierhallen*. There are also many *Bierstuben* (beer rooms), *Biergarten* (beer gardens), and *Bierkellern* (beer cellars) serving every variety of beer. But the greatest festivities take place during the *Oktoberfest*. It is a 16-day holiday that begins at the end of September. Yodelers, music bands, folk dancers, mountains of food, and rivers of beer are all features of this festival

Frankfurt, located on the Main River, is a busy, modern city, with one of the largest airports in Europe. It has been an important banking center since the Middle Ages. Several of Germany's largest banks are headquartered there, along with the European Central Bank. The bank regulates monetary policy for EU members that share a common currency (the Euro).

The Brandenburg Gate, in the historic center of Berlin, is the city's best-known symbol.

▶ **CULTURAL HERITAGE**

Germany's contributions to culture are among the most significant in the world. It has produced literary masterpieces from writers such as Johann Wolfgang von Goethe, Herman Hesse, and Thomas Mann. It is also the birthplace of some of the world's most famous composers of classical music, including Wolfgang Amadeus Mozart, Johannes Brahms, Ludwig van Beethoven, and Wilhelm Richard Wagner.

To learn more, see these articles in Volume G: GERMANY, ART AND ARCHITECTURE OF; GERMANY, LANGUAGE OF; GERMANY, LITERATURE OF; and GERMANY, MUSIC OF.

▶ **GOVERNMENT**

The two Germanys had separate constitutions from 1949 to 1990. On October 3, 1990, when East Germany merged with West Germany, the united country retained the official name of West Germany—the Federal Republic of Germany. It also adopted its constitution and form of government, with slight changes.

Germany is a federal republic made up of 16 *Länder* (states). The legislature is a federal parliament. It is made up of the Bundestag (Federal House of Representatives) and the Bundesrat (Federal Council). The Bundestag is the major body, responsible for passing the country's laws. Its members are elected by the people for 4-year terms. The Bundesrat delegates, who essentially represent the *Länder*, are elected by the *Länder* cabinets.

The skyline of Frankfurt shows a modern city. It is the headquarters of several of Germany's largest banks.

The Reichstag building is the seat of the German parliament and a favorite place for tourists to visit. Its glass dome is open to the public.

The Bundestag elects a chancellor, who heads the government. The chancellor is usually the leader of the largest political party in the Bundestag. A president serves as head of state but has little political power. The president is elected for five years by members of the Bundestag and the state legislatures.

Each state has its own government, which administers national laws and provides for education, police, and internal security.

The major political parties consist of the Christian Democratic Union (center-right) and the Social Democratic Party (center-left). In Germany a party has to receive 5 percent of the vote in order to gain representation in the Bundestag. Thus, small parties with over 5 percent of the vote can gain entry into the legislative process. A few parties gain around 8 percent of the national vote and often are part of coalition governments at the national or state levels. The Greens (environmentalists and international peace activists) are an example of a successful small party. They were part of the ruling coalition with the Social Democratic Party during the 1990's.

▶ HISTORY

Early History. Germany was at the edge of European history until the year 58 B.C. That year, Julius Caesar led the Roman armies to the Rhine River. The Roman legions clashed with the German tribes, who fought back stubbornly. In A.D. 9 a Roman army was defeated by the Germans. Unable to conquer the German tribes north of the Rhine, the Romans built a line of forts and walls along the lower Rhine and other rivers. They founded many towns and brought Roman civilization to this region.

When the Western Roman Empire collapsed in the 400's, Germanic tribes moved across Europe in large numbers. As the tribes took Roman towns, they mixed with Romans and learned Roman ways. Many became Christians. One Christian tribe, the Franks, began to conquer and unite other tribes. They built up a large empire in Germany and Gaul (part of present-day France).

Charlemagne. Charlemagne, who is called Karl der Grosse (Charles the Great) in German, was the most powerful of the Frankish kings. Charlemagne brought most of western Europe under his control. As he conquered various tribes, he converted them to Chris-

LANDER (STATES) OF GERMANY

Baden-Württemberg

Bavaria

Berlin

Brandenburg

Bremen

Hamburg

Hesse

Lower Saxony

Mecklenburg-Western Pomerania

North Rhine-Westphalia

Rhineland-Palatinate

Saarland

Saxony

Saxony-Anhalt

Schleswig-Holstein

Thuringia

tianity. On Christmas Day, in the year 800, Pope Leo III crowned Charlemagne emperor of the lands that would become known as the Holy Roman Empire. The territories ruled by Charlemagne were also known as the First Reich (First Empire). See the article on Charlemagne in Volume C.

Treaty of Verdun. After Charlemagne died, the Treaty of Verdun (843) gave his grandson, Louis the German, the eastern part of the empire—from the Rhine to the Elbe (later Germany).

The Holy Roman Empire. The Holy Roman Empire was "neither Holy, nor Roman, nor an Empire," according to the French philosopher Voltaire. In the Middle Ages, it was a loose collection of many small states that were joined by large north German cities.

In 955 the Saxon king Otto I (Otto the Great) defeated the Magyars, whose raids had plagued Germany. In 962, Otto was crowned Holy Roman emperor by the pope.

Frederick I, known as Frederick Barbarossa ("Red Beard"), was crowned emperor in Rome in 1152. He succeeded in uniting the warring sections of Germany. Under him the empire reached the peak of its power. After Frederick I, local princes grew stronger again. During the reign of Frederick II, who died in 1250, the Holy Roman Empire declined in size and in importance.

See the articles on the Holy Roman Empire and the Habsburgs in Volume H.

The Hanseatic League. During the Middle Ages, some north German cities grew strong and their merchants rich. These large cities became free cities. The most important were Hamburg, Bremen, and Lübeck. To protect themselves and regulate trade, these cities and others formed an organization called the Hanseatic League. For centuries the league controlled trade on the Baltic Sea and with the Scandinavian countries.

The Reformation. Until the 1500's the rival German states were united by the Roman Catholic religion. But in 1517 a priest named

Frederick I, called Barbarossa ("Red Beard"), brought the Holy Roman Empire to the height of its power.

Martin Luther nailed a list of 95 theses—his disagreements with the church—on the door of a church in the town of Wittenberg. Luther criticized what he believed to be wrongdoing in the church and demanded reforms. The pope dismissed him from the church, so Luther's followers, called Protestants or Lutherans, split away from the Roman Catholic Church.

North Germans flocked to the Protestant banner. South Germans and Austrians continued to worship as Roman Catholics. In 1555 the Peace of Augsburg brought an uneasy truce between the two groups. But the peace did not last.

The Thirty Years' War. In 1618 the Protestant nobles of Bohemia rebelled when the emperor sought to re-establish Roman Catholicism. This touched off the Thirty Years' War (1618–48). Other countries were drawn in until most of Europe was involved. The war devastated Germany, where most of the fighting took place. One-third of the population may have died as a result of the war, which ended with the Peace of Westphalia. For more information, see the articles on the Reformation, Martin Luther, and the Thirty Years' War in volumes QR, L, and T, respectively.

The Rise of Prussia. The Peace of Westphalia had lessened the importance of the Holy Roman Empire. Under the rule (1640–88) of the "Great Elector," Frederick William, the state of Brandenburg took over the leadership of the alliance of northern states. Frederick William's son Frederick I took the title of king of Prussia in 1701. Prussia developed a strong army and an efficient government. Its royal family, the Hohenzollerns, were to become the first rulers of a united German nation.

Under Frederick II (the Great), who reigned from 1740 to 1786, Prussia became a major European power. See the article on Frederick the Great in Volume F.

Two Revolutions. The French Revolution, which broke out in 1789, and the rise of Napoleon drew Prussia into war again. Napoleon crushed Prussia in 1806–07. But an alliance of Prussia, Russia, Austria, and Britain eventually defeated Napoleon in

Germany from 1871 to the Present

1814. The Congress of Vienna (1815) made Germany a loose confederation of states. Prussia gained the Rhineland with the Ruhr coal deposits.

In 1848, revolutions aimed at establishing more representative government swept across much of Europe. German liberals drew up a constitution. They called for a German federal state with a constitutional monarchy under the king of Prussia. But the king rejected the Constitution.

Bismarck and Unification. Prince Otto von Bismarck, chancellor to King William I of Prussia, succeeded in unifying Germany by force of arms.

Under Bismarck, Prussia won quick victories over Denmark in 1864 and Austria in 1866. The defeat of Austria gave Prussia the leadership of the German states. In 1867, Bismarck organized the North German Confederation, uniting German states north of the Main River. The king of Prussia became president of the confederation.

In 1870, Bismarck turned Prussia's military against France, maneuvering the French emperor, Napoleon III, into war. In the Franco-Prussian War (1870–71), Prussia quickly defeated France. The south German states now joined Prussia's confederation. All of Germany was united in the Second Reich (Second Empire) when King William I was crowned kaiser (emperor) in 1871. This was the birth of the modern German state. See the article on the Franco-Prussian War in Volume F.

The Empire. Germany prospered under Bismarck's leadership, becoming the strongest power on the continent. As chancellor, Bismarck kept a balance of power in Europe. But William II, who became kaiser in 1888, was young and ambitious. In 1890 he forced Bismarck to resign and began running the empire in his own way.

William II speeded up Germany's overseas colonial growth, seizing several African lands and Pacific islands. He also made Germany a leading commercial and naval power. Britain and France, which already had powerful colonial empires, saw their interests threatened. As a result of two crises in the North African state of Morocco (in 1905–06 and 1911), Britain, France, and Russia formed an alliance, the Triple Entente, to counter the Central Powers—Germany and Austria-Hungary.

World War I (1914–18). In 1914 a Serbian nationalist assassinated Archduke Francis Ferdinand, the heir to the throne of Austria-Hungary. The assassination led to an explosive conflict between the rival European powers. Germany backed Austria-Hungary's declaration of war against Serbia. In turn, the nations of the Triple Entente declared war on the Central Powers. Japan, Italy, and the United States entered the war on the side of the Entente, or Allied, powers. The Turkish Ottoman Empire and Bulgaria sided with the Central Powers.

German armies advanced quickly into Belgium and France. But the conflict then settled into a military stalemate between the two sides, punctuated by fierce battles for a few miles or a few yards of ground. In November 1918 an exhausted Germany accepted the Allied armistice terms, ending the fighting. The war resulted in an estimated 2 million German military and civilian deaths. This death and destruction, along with defeat and the punishment of the victors, helped set the stage for the rise of the German leader Adolf Hitler and World War II.

The war also brought down the imperial government of Kaiser William. This resulted in the first democratic republic in Germany's history.

The Treaty of Versailles. The Treaty of Versailles, signed in 1919, imposed severe penalties on Germany. It stripped Germany of Alsace-Lorraine and of its overseas colonies. Part of the Rhineland was to be occupied for a number of years by Allied forces. The treaty created the Polish Corridor—a narrow strip of land that cut off East Prussia from the rest of Germany. This was done to give a restored Poland access to the sea. Many German-speaking people were left outside the newly drawn boundaries.

Germany was limited to an army of 100,000 soldiers. And it was forced to pay the Allies the equivalent of $33 billion in reparations (payments for damages). These severe penalties later supported Hitler's argument for a military build up in the 1930's.

For more information, see the article on World War I in Volume WXYZ.

The Weimar Republic. In 1919 a popularly elected national constituent assembly met in the city of Weimar. It drew up a constitution that made Germany a representative democracy called the Weimar Republic. Friedrich Ebert was named president.

Many Germans bitterly resented the harsh terms of the Treaty of Versailles. Democracy and the Weimar Republic became connected in their minds with Germany's defeat in World War I. Moreover, in the early 1920's, inflation made German money almost worthless. Many Germans were unemployed, hungry, and desperate. Some began to think that democratic government could never bring them prosperity.

In the mid-1920's, however, Germany experienced several years of normalcy. But hopes for economic recovery were dashed by the worldwide Great Depression. It began in 1929 and hit Germany especially hard. By 1933 more than 6 million people were out of work. Germans began to listen to the promises of Adolf Hitler. He was the leader of the National Socialist German Workers' Party, whose members were known as Nazis.

The Rise of Hitler and the Nazis. The Nazis promised to make Germany rich and great again. They demanded changes to the Treaty of Versailles and return of the lost territories. As conditions grew worse, they received more votes. In April 1932, the aging Paul von Hindenburg, a military hero of the war, was re-elected president. The National Socialists and their allies soon became the strongest party in the Reichstag, or parliament. Von Hindenburg was persuaded to name Hitler chancellor in January 1933. The Weimar Republic had ended and the Third Reich (The Third Empire) had begun.

In March 1933, the Reichstag granted Hitler dictatorial powers. He soon began to take charge of all aspects of German life. The Nazi party became the sole legal political party. Democratic organizations, such as trade unions, were crushed. Storm troopers and the Gestapo (the secret police) hunted down political opponents of the regime. They sent many of them to concentration camps, where they died. By 1934, with Von Hindenburg dead, Hitler was the unquestioned *Führer* (leader) of Germany.

Nazi ideology included the concept of Germans as a "master race." Under the Nuremberg Laws of 1935, German Jews became second-class persons. They lost their citizenship and were barred from many professions. Pre-war persecution of the Jews reached its

The Nazis, led by Adolf Hitler (with arm outstretched in the Nazi salute), came to power in the early 1930's. He promised to restore Germany's greatness. His invasion of Poland in 1939 set off World War II.

theless, in March 1939, German troops invaded what remained of Czechoslovakia.

World War II (1939–45). Britain and France, militarily weak, had tried to appease Hitler in order to maintain peace. However, when German armies invaded Poland in September 1939, the two countries declared war on Germany. In the first years of the conflict, Hitler's armies quickly conquered most of the European continent, from the English Channel to the borders of the Soviet Union. His armies occupied Austria, Belgium, France, Norway, Poland, and other countries.

But these successes led Hitler to overreach himself. In June 1941 he invaded the Soviet Union, in spite of a Soviet-German agreement not to go to war against each other. This action, together with the U.S. entry into the war in December 1941, marked the beginning of a slow but sure decline for Hitler. The Allied powers, or Allies, consisting mainly of France, the United Kingdom, the United States, and the Soviet Union, slowly turned the tide of the war.

In 1944, Germany came under attack from the west by U.S. and British forces and from the east in 1945 by Soviet armies. With many of its cities destroyed by bombing, Germany was forced to surrender. The signing of the surrender documents took place on May 7, 1945. Hitler did not live to see the surrender of his Third Reich. He had committed suicide a week earlier, along with other Nazi leaders.

For more information, see the articles on World War II and Adolf Hitler in volumes WXYZ and H, respectively.

The Nuremberg Trials. War-crimes trials of the surviving Nazi leaders were held in the city of Nuremberg between 1945 and 1946. The charges included crimes against humanity and violations of the established laws of war. Among other horrible crimes, the Nazi regime was charged with killing 6 million Jews, Romanies (formerly known as Gypsies), and members of other groups. Millions of people had died under German occupation. Many others had been deported to Germany and forced to work.

In the main trial, 12 out of 22 Nazi leaders were sentenced to death. Three were acquitted (that is, found not guilty). The remainder received prison terms.

Allied Occupation. The war left Germany in ruins, a land of bombed cities filled with

height in 1938 with the widespread destruction of synagogues (houses of worship) and Jewish properties. Many Jews, along with non-Jewish Germans, fled the country.

The Road to War. Hitler adopted an aggressive foreign policy aimed at expanding Germany's territory. He enlarged the German army and added to its weapons, something forbidden under the Versailles treaty. In 1936 he sent German troops into the Rhineland and formed an alliance with Italy and Japan. In 1938, German troops marched into Austria, which was annexed to Germany.

Hitler turned to Czechoslovakia, which had a considerable German minority. At the Munich conference of 1938, Hitler met with British, French, and Italian leaders and demanded territory from Czechoslovakia. This was agreed to by the Western leaders. Never-

starving, homeless people. The Allies divided Germany into four occupation zones. The British zone consisted of Northwest Germany. The United States took over southern Germany. France occupied southwestern Germany. The Soviet Union occupied the east and much of central Germany. Berlin, the seat of the Allied Control Council, lay deep inside the Soviet zone. Berlin was also divided into four occupation sectors.

The Allies had plans for creating a peaceful Germany. But a peace conference never took place, and a split developed between the Soviet Union and the Western Allies. Under the heavy influence of the Soviet Union, the Socialist Unity Party of Germany was created in 1946 out of the Communist Party of Germany and the Social Democratic Party in the Soviet controlled zone. This was to be the governing party of East Germany until 1990.

Britain and the United States combined their zones and in 1948 issued a new currency. The Soviet Union created a new currency for the eastern zone of Germany and Berlin. Germany was now effectively divided into West and East Germany, each with its own political administration and currency. Berlin was likewise divided.

Early in 1948, the Soviets withdrew from the Allied Control Council, which met in Berlin. This made cooperation between East and West on political and economic matters nearly impossible. In the summer of 1948, the Soviets blocked all roads into West Berlin.

By the war's end in 1945, a defeated Germany had been devastated, with many of its cities in ruins. Children play amid the rubble of Berlin.

For about a year the United States and Britain supplied Berlin with goods delivered by airplanes. This was known as the Berlin airlift. It was the start of the Cold War between the Soviet Union and the West.

Creation of West Germany. In 1949 the Allied military government ended. The Western zones of occupation were combined to form the Federal Republic of Germany (West Germany). But an Allied High Commission still had authority over political matters.

West Germany rapidly recovered from the war with economic aid from the United States through the Marshall Plan. It also helped about 10 million people from East Germany and the former German eastern territories. Under the leadership of Chancellor Konrad Adenauer, West Germany became a prosperous industrial nation.

In 1955, West Germany became fully independent. It then joined the North Atlantic Treaty Organization (NATO). NATO is an organization of states that support each other against military attack. In 1957, it was one of six nations to sign the Treaty of Rome, which created the European Economic Community (EEC). (The EEC evolved into today's EU.) Ludwig Erhard succeeded Adenauer as chancellor. Erhard strengthened West Germany's ties with Britain and the United States.

The first attempts to improve West Germany's relations with East Germany were made by Chancellor Kurt Kiesinger, who served from 1966 to 1969. This policy was continued by Willy Brandt, chancellor from 1969 to 1974, and by Chancellor Helmut Schmidt in 1974. Schmidt's government split apart in 1982, and Helmut Kohl became chancellor, serving until 1988.

Development of East Germany. The German Democratic Republic (East Germany) was also established in 1949. The leading figure in the new government was Walter Ulbricht. He became head of the Socialist Unity (Communist) Party in 1950 and chairman of the Council of State, or head of state, in 1960.

East Germany's economic recovery in the years immediately after World War II was slow. Many people fled the country, and there was a serious shortage of skilled labor. Ulbricht continued the Soviet policy of placing industry and agriculture under government control. In 1950, East Germany became a member of the Council for Mutual Economic

In 1990, in front of the Brandenburg Gate, Germans wave flags in celebration of the reunification of their country.

Assistance (COMECON). This linked its economic activities with those of the Soviet Union and its allies in Eastern Europe.

The Soviet Union proclaimed East Germany a fully sovereign state in 1954. The following year, it became a charter member of the Warsaw Pact. By 1961, as many as one thousand people a day were fleeing East Germany. To stop this, the East German government closed its border with West Germany in 1961 and built the Berlin Wall, dividing eastern and western Berlin.

In 1973 both East and West Germany were admitted to the United Nations. In 1976, Erich Honecker became the leader in East Germany and worked to normalize relations between East and West.

Reunification: One Germany. The political reforms begun in the Soviet Union in the late 1980's spread to Eastern European Communist nations in 1989. The critical element was the willingness of the Soviet Union to pull back its military and to loosen its hold on the Soviet bloc (the countries under its control). This led shortly to the disintegration of the Soviet bloc and then the Soviet Union.

In East Germany there were many demonstrations for greater freedom. Honecker was forced to resign, and the new leaders opened the Berlin Wall, permitting East Germans to cross freely again to the West. A non-Communist coalition government was elected in East Germany in March 1990. The merger of East Germany with West Germany on October 3, 1990, marked the birth of a new united Federal Republic of Germany. In December 1990, the first free, all-German election since 1932 was held.

The Christian Democratic Union (CDU) under Helmut Kohl continued as the party in power, now over a unified Germany. In the parliamentary elections of 1998, it was beaten by the Social Democratic Party (SPD), led by Gerhard Schröder, who became chancellor. The SPD then formed a coalition government with the Greens, Germany's environmentalist party.

In 1999, Schröder's popularity dropped when the soaring national debt forced him to cut government spending on social programs. Nevertheless he was re-elected by a narrow margin in 2002. This was due partly to his willingness to oppose U.S. military action in Iraq and to his effective handling of the 2002 flood in Germany. Schröder's cut in social programs aimed at reviving Germany's stagnant economy. But unemployment remained around 10 percent.

In the 2005 election, the vote count for the CDU and SPD was so close that the two parties were forced to negotiate a coalition cabinet and government. This meant that government decisions would require the agreement of both major parties. This was only the second time in postwar Germany that a coalition was needed. Parliament elected CDU leader Angela Merkel to succeed Schröder as chancellor. She was the first woman to head the German government.

GARY L. MARIS
Stetson University
Author, *International Law: An Introduction*

In 2005, Parliament elected CDU leader Angela Merkel as chancellor. She was the first woman to head the German government.

GUINEA PIGS

Guinea pigs are rodents belonging to the family Caviidae. The guinea pig is a domestic animal. It does not live in the wild. Wild guinea pigs, called cavies, are a different species. Guinea pigs came from South America, where all other members of the Caviidae family live today.

Characteristics of Guinea Pigs. Guinea pigs have short, stocky bodies with short, strong legs. They have a large head and little or no tail. Their bodies range from about 8 to 20 inches (20 to 50 centimeters) in length. They can weigh up to 2 pounds (1 kilogram). Other species in the Caviidae family can be as small as 9 inches (23 centimeters) long and weigh only 11 ounces (311 grams). The largest species in the family is the mara. It measures about 29 inches (74 centimeters) long and weighs up to 30 pounds (14 kilograms). Like all rodents, guinea pigs have large front teeth called incisors. They use these incisors for gnawing.

Guinea pigs are social animals that make excellent pets. They have short, stocky bodies and large heads, with soft fur in a variety of colors and lengths.

GUINEA PIGS AS PETS

Guinea pigs are very popular pets. They enjoy being handled and rarely bite. They need large cages with solid floors and bedding such as torn paper, cardboard, clean hay, or wood shavings. (Do not use cedar or pine wood shavings or newspaper for bedding. These can harm your pet.) Their cages should be cleaned once or twice a week. An empty cardboard tissue box makes an ideal sleeping den.

Guinea pigs are social animals, and they do better kept in pairs or small groups. It is best to have two or more females, as males may fight. Guinea pigs should be fed special guinea pig food, which has lots of vitamin C in it, not regular rodent food. Well-rinsed greens, fruits, and vegetables make good treats. Be careful not to give your guinea pigs too much food. They will overeat and get fat. Your pets should also be provided with a water bottle.

Although all guinea pigs are similar in shape and size, selective breeding has created a variety of appearances in their coats. They can be black, white, brown, red—or combinations of these colors. Abyssinian guinea pigs have short, swirly hair. The coat of Peruvians is long and straight. There are even hairless guinea pigs.

Lives of Guinea Pigs. Guinea pigs can be active both during the day and at night. They eat only plant foods, especially leafy ones.

Guinea pigs are able to mate at a young age and can breed year-round. A litter usually has two to five young, born with hair and open eyes. They can eat solid food the first day. Guinea pigs normally live four to seven years. They communicate with one another by a variety of whistles, squeaks, and chirps.

Guinea Pigs and Their Environment. Guinea pigs have been domesticated (tamed) for about 3,000 years. They were bred by the Incas in the 1400's and 1500's for food and for use in religious and healing rituals. They are still raised for food in Bolivia, Ecuador, and Peru. Guinea pigs have been important in medical and scientific research for many years. Two of the guinea pig's wild relatives are endangered.

DOROTHY HINSHAW PATENT
Author, science and nature books for children
See also RODENTS.

BERLIN

Berlin, the capital of the Federal Republic of Germany, lies in the northeastern part of the country. It is Germany's largest city and one of the ten largest in Europe. It has long been a center of German and European political, economic, cultural, and intellectual life.

Germany became a modern state in 1871 with Berlin as its capital. In 1949, after World War II (1939–45), Berlin—like Germany itself—was divided into two parts. East Berlin became the capital of East Germany (the German Democratic Republic). West Berlin became a federal state of West Germany (the Federal Republic of Germany).

In 1990, East and West Germany were reunited as the Federal Republic of Germany. East and West Berlin were reunified, and Berlin was restored as the country's capital.

With reunification, Berlin regained its status as a cultural center of Germany and the world. It is famous for its Philharmonic Orchestra, opera houses, theater groups, yearly cultural festival, and museums.

▶ LAND

Berlin lies on the great sandy plain of the North German lowlands. The city has an urban area of 347 square miles (892 square kilometers). It has many parks filled with trees, and water covers nearly 7 percent of its area. Average temperatures in Berlin range from 30°F (-1°C) in the winter to 67°F (20°C) in the summer.

▶ PEOPLE

Berlin has a population of about 3.5 million people. Most are of German ethnic origin, but over 13 percent are not. This includes a group of about 120,000 Turks (people from Turkey and their descendants). Many Turks originally came to Berlin as guest workers in the 1960's and 1970's.

Most Berliners are Protestant. Most Turks are Muslim. Berlin's rising Muslim population now exceeds 200,000. There are some 30 Muslim places of worship in the city. Berlin's Jewish population

Above: Joggers run through Berlin's Tiergarten park. ***Left:*** A tour boat cruises along Berlin's Spree River. Berlin Cathedral can be seen the background.

has fallen to a few thousand, from 160,000 in the 1930's. This is the result of emigration and of the persecution of the Jews by German Nazis during World War II.

Education and Libraries. Over 139,000 students study in Berlin's universities, colleges, and polytechnical schools. The city has three major universities: the Free University of Berlin, Humbolt University, and the Technical University of Berlin. The Berlin University of the Arts is also important. Some 4,500 students study there.

Among Berlin's famous libraries is the University Library. It has over 2 million volumes in its collection.

Museums and the Arts. There are more than 170 museums and collections in Berlin. The Pergamon Museum is noted for the large original Pergamon altar (100's B.C.) brought from Turkey. It also offers the famous Gate of Ishtar from the 500's B.C. city of Babylon. The Egyptian Museum holds the bust of the Egyptian queen Nerfertiti, who is known as the most beautiful woman in Berlin.

The Bode Museum features art and artifacts from ancient Egypt and Byzantium. The Old National Gallery (Altes Nationalgalerie) houses paintings from the late 1700's to the early 1900's. It also has a collection of Greek and Roman art. The Old Masters Gallery (Gemäldegalerie) contains European Art from the 1200's to the 1700's.

In addition, Berlin's Museum of German History traces 2,000 years of German civilization. The Museum of Jewish History is one of the finest of its kind. Even its architecture is designed to convey historical information.

Parks and Recreation. The Tiergarten is Berlin's central park and covers more than 630 acres (252 hectares). It has playgrounds and walking trails and is a favorite way for Berliners to get away from the city. There are also beautiful flower gardens, canals, a lake, and the world's oldest zoo. Berlin's Botanical Garden (Botanischer Garten) is spread over 108 acres (43 hectares). It is home to over 20,000 different species of plants from around the world.

Soccer is the most popular sport in Germany, which hosted the soccer World Cup in 2006. However, Germans have many sporting outlets. There are over 400,000 sporting clubs in Berlin. Skiing, bicycling, and swimming are among the favored activities.

Berlin has an extensive transportation system. The new Main Train Station (Hauptbahnhof) provides travelers with long-distance service.

▶ ECONOMY

Berlin had a strong economy before World War II but suffered massive destruction during the war. After the war, there was dramatic rebuilding. However, the city's reunification in 1990 brought many challenges. West Berlin's standard of living was considerably higher than that of East Berlin. There are still gaps in education, income levels, health care, and other areas of life in Berlin that have to be closed. In 2006 unemployment in Berlin was close to twice the national average.

Services. Berlin's service industry, with its large tourist, public service, finance, and retail sectors, is the major source of jobs. The city also has the largest number of scientific and technological research institutions in Germany.

Manufacturing. Industries in the greater Berlin area produce electrical and electronic equipment, machinery, and motor vehicles. They also manufacture engineering products, processed foods, chemicals, and clothing.

Transportation. Berlin has extensive bus, streetcar, subway (U-Bahn), and elevated train (S-Bahn) transportation. An auto expressway encircles the city completely. In 2006 a new Main Train Station (Hauptbahnhof) for long-distance trains was opened. It has sufficient capacity to meet Berlin's growth for decades. The city's three airports are being merged into one. By 2011 this new Berlin-Brandenburg International Airport will handle some 22 to 25 million people a year.

Communication. *Der Tagesspiegel, Berliner Morgenpost,* and *Berliner Zeitung* are the

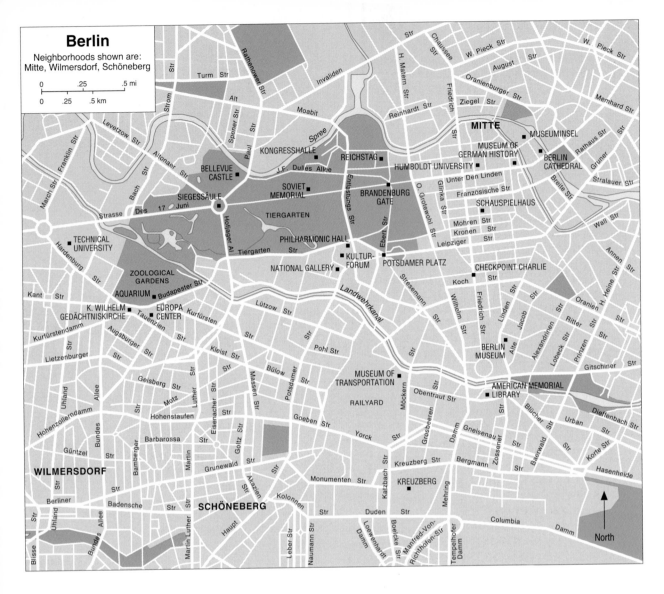

Berlin

Neighborhoods shown are:
Mitte, Wilmersdorf, Schöneberg

MITTE

WILMERSDORF

SCHÖNEBERG

city's major print newspapers. They can also be accessed online.

GOVERNMENT

Berlin is one of the 16 Länder (states) of the Federal Republic of Germany. Its legislative body is the House of Representatives with 130 members elected by popular vote. The Senate has a governing mayor and no more than eight senators. Each senator is responsible for a particular government department. Senators are nominated by the governing mayor and approved by the House. The governing mayor is elected by the House. Governing policy is proposed by the mayor and requires the approval of the Senate and consent of the House.

HISTORY

The city of Berlin developed out of the merger of two small trading settlements, Kölln and Berlin, in 1307. In 1486, Berlin became the seat of the electors (rulers) of what was then the small state of Brandenburg. The Thirty Years' War (1618–48) over whether Protestantism or Catholicism should dominate in German communities destroyed the city. About half its population was killed.

In 1701, Berlin became the capital of the kingdom of Prussia. In 1871 the German states united around Prussia to form the modern German state. Berlin became its capital. In 1920, 86 small communities around old Berlin were merged into greater Berlin (Gross Berlin, in German) as it now appears.

Places of Interest

Brandenburg Gate

Charlottenburg Palace

Berlin Cathedral, built in 1894–1904, is a beautiful example of neoclassical architecture. It is an Evangelical (Protestant) place of worship. It was built to be the final resting place for Prussian rulers.

Brandenburg Gate, Berlin's best-known symbol, is located in the historic center of the city. It is a triumphal arch some 85 feet (26 meters) high with the Goddess of Victory on the top. It was built in 1791 as a symbol of peace.

Charlottenburg Palace (Schloss Charlottenburg), on the outskirts of the city, is one of the oldest surviving Prussian palaces in Germany. The original construction was in 1695. Other buildings and a beautiful garden were added later. The palace offers spectacular collections of paintings and porcelains.

The **Friedrichstrasse** has become a landmark street for shopping, cultural activities, and doing business.

Kurfürstendamm features fashionable shops, restaurants, and theaters. Also located here is the bombed out tower of the Kaiser Wilhelm Memorial Church. It is meant to remind people of the destruction of war.

Museum Island (Museuminsel) holds several of Berlin's major art museums as well as the Berlin Cathedral.

Potsdamer Platz is one of the busiest squares in Europe. It has become a center of night life as well as shops and soaring high-rise buildings. Various museums and even a casino are located here.

Reichstag (1894), the old parliament building, burnt down in 1933 and was then reconstructed. It is a landmark of historical importance and home to the present German legislature. From its glass dome visitors have a spectacular view of the entire city.

▶ THE CITY DIVIDED

On May 2, 1945, Soviet armies captured Berlin. By agreement, forces from the United States, Britain, France, and the Soviet Union each occupied a sector of the city. They administered it jointly. In 1948, the Soviets withdrew from that arrangement. They cut off all land and water communications between western Germany and the three western sectors of the city. Their goal was to control the entire city. In response, Britain, France, and the United States launched a massive airlift. They flew over 2 million tons of food and other supplies to the isolated western sectors. Eleven months later, in May 1949, the Soviets, not having gained control of the city, lifted the blockade.

After the blockade, the city remained divided. The Soviet sector became East Berlin. The U.S., British, and French sectors were joined into one sector to form West Berlin.

▶ REUNIFICATION

In 1961, the East German authorities erected a fortified wall separating East and West Berlin. At least 125 people died trying to flee. The Berlin Wall was a symbol of a divided city and nation for nearly 30 years. Change came in November 1989 when the Soviet Union indicated that it would no longer interfere in East German politics. After widespread protests by East Germans, the East German government opened the guarded crossing points of the wall, and the division ended.

On October 3, 1990, East and West Germany were reunited to become the Federal Republic of Germany. And Berlin once again became the capital of a unified Germany.

GARY L. MARIS
Stetson University
Author, *International Law: An Introduction*

The Berlin Wall was a symbol of the divided city for nearly 30 years. Its destruction in November 1989 meant the end of the division of Berlin.

369

HAMSTERS

Hamsters are rodents belonging to the family Muridae. This family also includes rats and mice. There are about 20 species of hamsters. They live in dry, often rocky areas of Europe, the Middle East, and Central and Northern Asia.

Hamsters are rodents in the same family as rats and mice. They are easy to tame and make good pets. In the wild, they live in dry, rocky areas.

Characteristics of Hamsters. Hamsters have compact bodies and short legs. Their fur is thick, and their ears and eyes are large. Most hamsters have coats in shades of gray and brown. But the common, or black-bellied, hamster can be black with lighter patches. The smallest species is the Roborovski hamster. It weighs about half an ounce (14 grams) and is about 2 inches (5 centimeters) long. The common hamster is the largest species. It can measure from about 8 to 13 inches (20 to 33 centimeters) long and weigh up to 2 pounds (1 kilogram).

Lives of Hamsters. Hamsters are burrowing animals that generally spend the daytime underground. They come out at night to gather food, which consists mostly of plants. Some species will eat insects, frogs, young birds, and other small animals. Hamsters have cheek pouches in which they carry food back to their burrow for storage. And like all rodents, hamsters have large front teeth called incisors. They use these to gnaw.

Hamsters are usually solitary. During mating season, males and females find each other by making high-pitched sounds and by smell.

Soon after mating, the female makes a soft nest in her burrow. There she gives birth to six or seven blind and hairless young, called pups. The pups are weaned in about three weeks. Hamsters live about two years.

Hamsters and Their Environment. Because they eat grain and can multipy very fast, wild hamsters are considered agricultural pests in many countries. As humans have cultivated more and more land, some species of hamsters have become endangered.

DOROTHY HINSHAW PATENT
Author, science and nature books for children

See also RODENTS.

HAMSTERS AS PETS

Hamsters are easy to tame. The species commonly kept as a pet is the Syrian hamster. Because they tend to be solitary in the wild, they should be kept in separate cages. Some dwarf hamsters are more social. Several can be kept together in the same cage as long as they get to know each other when they are young.

An aquarium or a wire cage with a solid bottom makes the best hamster home. Provide your pet with lots of wood shavings for bedding, which should be changed weekly. (Do not use cedar or pine, which can harm your pet.) Place the cage in an area that is quiet during the day, when your pet sleeps. But remember to interact with it in the evening when it is awake.

Special hamster food is available at pet shops. Place the food in a shallow bowl that cannot tip over. Your pet should also have a water bottle. Replace the water daily.

Hamsters need a nest box. You can either buy one from a store or make one from cardboard. An empty tissue box also works well. Provide your hamster with strips of paper towels or tissues for nesting material. Occasionally check the nest box for stored food, which should be removed. The nest box should be cleaned only about once a month unless it becomes very soiled. Hamsters will use an exercise wheel, and they enjoy crawling through cardboard tubes from rolls of toilet paper or paper towels. Your pet will also appreciate blocks of wood or fresh tree branches to gnaw on (again, not cedar or pine).

FRUITS AND FRUIT GROWING

The name "fruit" is usually given to any fleshy part of a plant that has developed from a flower and has seeds. Fruits are one way nature ensures that new plants will grow from the old. The fruits we enjoy include apples and plums, lemons and oranges, and bananas and mangoes. These fruits are varied in shape, color, and taste. Eating fruits gives people a boost of healthy nutrition. Fruits provide vitamins, fiber, and special chemicals that ward off cancer.

▶ HISTORY OF FRUIT GROWING

Early people gathered fruits from wild plants long before crops were grown for food. Fruit was eaten fresh. Or it was dried in the sun to provide food for the winter.

People eventually realized that crops could be **cultivated**. This means that crops could be grown where people wanted them. And the quality of plants could be improved. People probably started by selecting the seeds from the tastiest and most satisfying of the wild fruits. Fruits gradually became better—sweeter, juicier, or larger than the wild varieties.

The cultivation of fruit plants goes back thousands of years. Fragments of apples dating back about 8,500 years have been discovered in present-day Turkey. And people around the world started cultivating grapes. One popular species was cultivated about 7,000 years ago in present-day Iran.

Many cultivated varieties were brought to new places from the places they originated. The practice goes back to ancient times. Persian traders carried peaches from China to what is today Iran. Arab merchants carried the Chinese sour orange and tart lemon to North Africa and southern Spain.

Fruits stacked side by side in the grocery store may have been grown far away from each other. Some fruits grow well in tropical climates. Others grow best where it is cooler.

For many fruits, spreading a cultivated variety was easy. If a plant could be grown from seeds, merchants, soldiers, and sailors could simply carry the seeds from place to place. But if a plant had to be grown from cuttings, or pieces cut from a plant, spreading a variety could be difficult. This lesson was learned by the soldiers of Alexander the Great. They encountered the banana in the Indus Valley. But they had difficulty getting the fruit home to Greece before it rotted.

▶ CLASSIFYING FRUIT

Fruit growers classify fruits according to the climates in which they grow best. They group fruits into three main classes.

Tropical fruits thrive in tropical regions, which lie along an invisible ribbon that wraps around the Earth near the equator. Tropical conditions are ideal for fruits that cannot stand cold.

In the warm, rainy areas of South America, Asia, Africa, and northern Australia, people

WONDER QUESTION

What are the oldest and newest fruits?

One of the oldest fruits, the fig, may in fact be the oldest domesticated crop in the world, dating back over 11,000 years, well before people began growing grains. One of the newest, the grapefruit, is probably not even 300 years old.

Fruit growers divide the many kinds of fruit into three groups—tropical, subtropical, and temperate. Tropical fruits grow best in warm, rainy areas. Bananas are often considered tropical (*left*). Subtropical fruits, such as oranges (*far left*), thrive in mild climates. Temperate fruits, such as cherries (*below*), do well in cooler regions.

grow fruits such as mangoes and papayas. Many tropical fruits are best when ripened on the plant, rather than picked early. Some do not ship well, and so are found only locally. But other tropical fruits considered exotic to people in northern areas are being shipped longer distances. These include mangosteen, durian, carombola, rambutan, and rollinia.

Some fruits, such as avocados and bananas, may be considered either tropical or **subtropical fruits**. This is because they are grown in both tropical and subtropical climates. In subtropical parts of the world such as southern Florida, winters are usually mild. These areas are good for growing citrus fruits such as oranges, limes, lemons, and grapefruit. These fruits, which grow on evergreen trees, can endure light frosts. But they are injured by temperatures of about 27°F (−3°C) or lower.

Temperate fruits need a climate that is relatively cool. The most successful temperate fruits are grown on trees, vines, or shrubs that shed their leaves in the fall. These plants need a dormant (or resting) period over the winter. Without a period of cold weather, they will not thrive.

Temperate fruits include apples, pears, peaches, plums, prunes, cherries, apricots, grapes, figs, and many kinds of berries. Most of these fruits will stand temperatures below 0°F (−18°C) without injury. But figs and some kinds of grapes are not as hardy. They may be injured by temperatures of about 14°F (−10°C).

▶ **THE FRUIT INDUSTRY**

Bringing fruit to market is a process with many steps. Each step involves special tasks. But each step is also part of a larger system called an industry.

Site Selection

Locations for fruit growing are selected carefully. This is true even for relatively hardy fruits, including those that grow in temperate climates. They resist cold in the winter. But new growth is tender in the spring. Open blossoms may be killed by temperatures below 27°F.

In citrus groves, growers go to extreme lengths to protect their trees from cold. An entire expensively raised crop can be lost in freezing conditions. Growers use oil-burning smudge pots when temperatures fall near the danger point. They operate wind machines that repeatedly push warm air down into the trees. Both overhead and ground-level sprinkler irrigation systems are used to keep temperatures a bit higher during a freeze. Water applied from above releases heat as it turns to ice on the tree's leaves. Another tool is freeze-protection fabric. It can be draped over shorter trees.

Irrigation

Where rainfall is not dependable, fruit growers need sources of irrigation water.

Sources include rivers, lakes, wells, rainwater cisterns, and recycled wastewater. For thousands of years, farmers have brought water to their fields from rivers via canals. Gravity then brings the canal water into fields of crops through furrows. Sometimes irrigation water is pumped through pipes to large sprinklers. Or it is distributed through drip or microjet irrigation. Both types of irrigation provide water at or near ground level to individual plants or trees. Drip systems deliver water drop by drop. Microjet systems produce a fine spray.

Fertilizers

Fruit growers often enrich soil by adding substances called fertilizers. Fertilizers can be natural or artificial. Usually soil is most in need of nitrogen. But significant amounts of

magnesium and potash may be required as well. When substances are needed in quantity, they are added directly to soil.

Some substances are needed in small amounts. These substances include iron, zinc, manganese, boron, and copper. They can be absorbed easily through the leaves of plants. They are usually sprayed on.

Controlling Pests

Insects and diseases can damage fruit crops. There are natural controls that help keep certain pests and diseases at bay. These controls include climate, geographic location, and temperature range. Biological controls can be helpful, too. They include creatures that eat insects. Birds, toads, predatory insects, and domestic chickens, ducks, and geese help eliminate pests.

But fruit growers rely mostly on synthetic, or non-natural, controls. These include pesticides or chemical sprays. Depending on the fruit and the climate, sprays are applied during each growing season. But people are realizing that chemical spraying has drawbacks. Spraying is expensive. And it can be harmful to the air, the soil, the water, and human health. Pesticides also kill beneficial insects. And predatory insects adjust to them.

Other controls include crop rotation and the development of resistant plants. For centuries, plants have been modified through traditional breeding techniques. These are still used, but genetic engineering is also being used to create new plants. This newer technique is still controversial.

Pollination

A fruit forms from a pollinated, or fertilized, flower. And it usually has seeds. Pollen itself is the microscopic grain that surrounds the sperm cells, or male reproductive cells, of seed plants. Pollination is the transfer of

Most fruit is picked by hand as soon as it is ripe. Apples must be harvested within two weeks in order to keep well in storage.

373

pollen from the stamen, or male part, to the pistil, or female part, of flowers. Without pollination, fruit will not develop.

Some fruit plants are pollinated naturally by the wind or living creatures. These include bees, butterflies, and even bats. Other fruit plants need help from people. Growers may use hand, or mechanical, pollination.

Many apple varieties need a different variety for cross-pollination. If none is growing nearby, a farmer may place large bouquets of the blossoms of suitable varieties in the orchard. Growers around the world bring hives full of bees into their orchards when the blossoms begin to open. Sweet cherries, pears, and some plums also need cross-pollination. But some fruit trees are self-pollinators. For example, there are certain nectarines and peaches that pollinate themselves.

Oranges do not require cross-pollination. In fact most orange growers try to prevent cross-pollination. This is because cross-pollination increases the number of seeds in the fruit.

Pruning Trees

Pruning, or cutting back branches, is done to give a tree a convenient size and shape. The goal is to make spraying and harvesting easier. On young trees, the short tips of upright branches are often removed. This forces new side branches to grow. Growers prefer branches that form wide angles with the trunk. Such branches can support heavy loads of fruit well. Removing limbs also helps to increase the amount of light that reaches the inner and lower parts of the tree. Trees that are kept open to sunlight and air produce more fruit of better size and color.

Growing

Farmers patiently tend their new plantings with care. Some fruit plants, like strawberry plants, produce a crop after the first year of growth. Banana and pineapple plants produce their first crops after one or two years. Grape vines produce some fruit the third year after planting. And peach trees produce fruit three or four years after planting. Many other fruit trees, such as apple trees and orange trees, need five to eight years after planting before they bear much fruit.

HOW BOTANISTS CLASSIFY FRUIT

Scientists who study plants are called **botanists**. Botanists decide how to classify a fruit by looking at how it develops from a flower. They also consider how the mature fruit is structured.

According to botanists, the two main types of fruit are simple and compound. A simple fruit develops from a flower with a single ovary. (This is the seed-bearing part of the flower.)

Simple fruits can be dry or fleshy. Dry fruits include things you may not think of as fruit: beans, peas, wheat grains, and nuts such as acorns and chestnuts. Fleshy fruits include apples, cherries, and grapes. In fact, each of these fleshy fruits represents a botanical subgroup.

Apples are **pomes**, which have a thin outer skin and a fleshy middle layer that surrounds hollow, seed-bearing cavities. Another familiar pome is the pear.

Cherries are **drupes**, which have a thin outer skin, a soft and juicy middle layer, and a single hard-shelled seed in the center. This seed is so hard that drupes are also called stone fruits. Besides cherries, drupes include apricots, peaches, and plums.

Grapes are **true berries**. This kind of fruit has a firm or leathery skin and is usually soft inside with many seeds. True berries include bananas, oranges, and tomatoes.

There are two kinds of compound fruit. One kind develops from a flower with many ovaries. Examples include strawberries and blackberries. The other kind of compound fruit develops from a cluster of flowers on a single stem. Examples include figs and pineapples.

Fruit that is to be sold fresh must be packed and shipped soon after it is harvested. Some fruits, such as strawberries, spoil quickly.

Harvesting

Most fruits must be picked as soon as they are ripe. Berries, peaches and plums must be picked from one to three times a week. To keep well in storage, apples are harvested within ten days or two weeks. But citrus fruits, as well as avocados, can remain on the trees for two to four months after they ripen.

Most fruit is picked by hand. Finding enough workers for this hot, difficult work has become a problem around the world. For decades, growers in the United States were able to rely on migrant workers. These workers moved from place to place, following the fruit harvests. Often accompanied by their families, many workers lived in substandard housing.

In recent years, however, fewer workers coming from Mexico and Central and South America have decided to work in the fields. They are finding better-paying, more stable jobs in other industries.

Handling, Storage, and Packing

Once fruit is harvested, it may be shipped at once and sold fresh. Or it may be put into cold storage. Or it may be processed. In the processing plant, it may be canned, frozen, dried, or squeezed for juice.

Governmental rules require that fruit be sorted into grades. A fruit's grade depends on its color and size, as well as the condition of its skin. After sorting, fruit is washed and placed in wrappers, in breathable or mesh bags, or in pint or quart boxes. Fruit is then packed in larger boxes that can be placed on pallets (movable platforms).

Products that will be shipped are loaded directly into large standardized containers. These containers are put on trucks, trains, planes, or ships.

Shipping

Fruits are transported all over the world by air, by sea, and by truck, as well as by people carrying baskets to market. But bringing fruit to the consumer has never been simple.

Fruit going long distances is often picked early and sent off unripe. But fresh, ripe fruit may be shipped, too, even though it bruises easily. When ripe peaches are shipped, they must be kept cool and moved to market quickly. But they may be sent in an unrefrigerated truck, provided the shipper delivers them to the market the morning after they are picked. If two or three days are needed for shipping, the peaches are picked while they are still firm. And then they are sent in refrigerated cars or trucks. Specially designed computer programs regulate humidity and temperature during transport.

▶ NEW USES FOR FRUIT

The main use of fruits is to provide food. But fruits have other uses. Peach pits, for instance, are being burned as fuel. Citrus peels are being used as sources of essential oils. These oils are used in medicines and pharmaceuticals, as well as in industrial cleaners. And some fruits, such as apples and the tropical guarana, are being used instead of artificial ingredients to make antioxidants. (These are chemical compounds that extend the shelf life of packaged foods.)

Wastes from fruit processing are proving useful, too. Materials left over from processing apples, pineapples, grapes, and citrus fruits are routinely added to animal feed. And citrus waste generated in both Florida and Brazil is being turned into liquid fuel for use in cars.

Reviewed by MEREDITH SAYLES HUGHES
The FOOD Museum

See also APPLE; BANANAS; DATE; FIG; GRAPES AND BERRIES; LEMONS AND LIMES; MELONS; ORANGES AND GRAPEFRUIT; PEACH, PLUM, AND CHERRY; PEAR; PINEAPPLE; TROPICAL FRUIT.

ORANGUTANS

Orangutans belong to a group of mammals called primates. Orangutans are among our closest relatives. They are members of the same family as human beings, Hominidae, which also includes gorillas, bonobos, and chimpanzees. In fact, their name comes from the Malaysian words for "person of the forest."

Orangutans are the only great ape native to Asia. They are found only on the islands of Sumatra and Borneo. All other great apes live in Africa. There are two species of orangutans, Sumatran and Bornean. Bornean orangutans are subdivided into three subspecies.

Characteristics of Orangutans. Orangutans prefer to live in lowland forests where fruit, their favorite food, is abundant. They spend most of their time in the trees, and they are the largest **arboreal**, or tree-dwelling, animal on Earth. Orangutans are uniquely adapted for this kind of life. Their long arms, elongated hands and feet, and remarkable

Orangutans are among our closest relatives. They are found only on the islands of Borneo and Sumatra, in Asia. All other great apes live in Africa.

strength help them climb easily among the high branches. Orangutan hair varies from a rusty brown to bright orange. Wild adult males weigh about 190 pounds (86 kilograms). Wild adult females may be half that size, weighing about 88 pounds (40 kilograms).

There are two forms of adult males, usually termed flanged and unflanged. Flanged males have cheekpads (flanges), a throat sac, long hair, and a long beard. They also produce calls that travel through the forest. These calls attract females and warn away rival males. Unflanged males do not have these physical traits and do not make calls. Both forms of males can father offspring.

Lives of Orangutans. Orangutans are the least social of the great apes. Except for when a mother is raising her offspring, orangutans spend most of their time alone.

Female orangutans have the slowest reproduction rate of any land mammal. They begin having babies when they are about 15 years old. They have only one baby every 6 to 9 years. That baby stays with its mother until her next offspring is born. Orangutans can live to about 60 years old.

Orangutans are very intelligent. They learn from each other, invent ways to solve problems, and make and use tools. Captive orangutans have even been able to learn a form of language, choosing symbols on a computer screen to express their thoughts.

Orangutans and Their Environment. Orangutans are currently threatened with extinction. Their greatest threat comes from the destruction of their forest home by commercial activities such as logging and agriculture. Unless the current trend is reversed, conservationists predict that some orangutan populations may be extinct within the next 20 years.

ROBERT SHUMAKER
Great Ape Trust of Iowa

Did you know that...

orangutan groups living in different forests have developed their own special behaviors?

Scientists compared the behavior of orangutan populations from different areas. And they found some significant differences. For example, different groups of orangutans have developed different ways of making a "kissing" noise that signals annoyance. Orangutans in one group press leaves to their mouths to make the sound, while orangutans in another group use their hands.

Some scientists see such differences as evidence that orangutans have developed cultures. "Culture" can be generally defined as behavior that is learned and passed on by individuals within a social group. Culture has been thought to be strictly a human trait.

SUPPLEMENT

Deaths

Independent Nations of the World

The United States

    Senate

    House of Representatives

    Cabinet

    Supreme Court

    State Governors

Canada and Its Provinces and Territories

James Brown

DEATHS

Antonioni, Michelangelo. Italian movie director; died on July 30, at the age of 94. Antonioni was one of the most influential Italian film directors of the 1960's. He gained international recognition for *L'Avventura* (*"The Adventure,"* 1960), *La Notte* (*"The Night,"* 1961), *Blow-Up* (1966), and *The Passenger* (1975).

Astor, Brooke. American philanthropist, civic leader, and socialite; died on August 13, at the age of 105. In 1953 she married Vincent Astor of the famously wealthy Astor family. Upon his death six years later, she proceeded to put her husband's fortune to good use by helping others. She gave tens of millions to many charities, and especially to New York City's great cultural institutions. She received a Presidential Medal of Freedom in 1998—America's highest civilian honor.

Bergman, Ingmar. Swedish movie director; died on July 30, at the age of 89. Bergman, who directed more than 60 films, was considered one of the greatest filmmakers in motion-picture history. His most famous movies included *Smiles of a Summer Night* (1955), *The Seventh Seal* (1957), *Wild Strawberries* (1957), and *Cries and Whispers* (1972). Three of his films won Academy Awards for Best Foreign Language Film: *The Virgin Spring* (1960), *Through a Glass Darkly* (1961), and *Fanny and Alexander* (1982).

Bishop, Joey. American comedian and actor; died on October 17, at the age of 89. Bishop began his career as a standup comedian. He had two popular television shows in the 1960's, both named *The Joey Bishop Show*. The first (1961–65) was a sitcom; the second (1967–69) a talk show. Bishop was a member of the Rat Pack, a group of talented, wisecracking entertainers that included Frank Sinatra, Dean Martin, Sammy Davis, Jr., and Peter Lawford.

Brown, James. American singer and songwriter; died on December 25, 2006, at the age of 73. Brown was one of the most important figures in 20th-century American music and was known as "The Godfather of Soul." He began his career in the 1950's, and was the force behind the evolution of gospel and rhythm and blues into soul and funk. He also made his mark on rock, jazz, disco, reggae, and hip hop. Among Brown's notable hit songs were "Please, Please, Please," "Papa's Got a Brand New Bag," and "I Got You (I Feel Good)."

Browne, Roscoe Lee. American actor; died on April 11, at the age of 81. With his rich baritone voice and dignified bearing, Browne was a

Liz Claiborne

Merv Griffin

sought-after actor on the stage, screen, and television. He also did narrations and voice-overs. Browne excelled at Shakespearean roles as well as comedic ones. He won an Emmy Award for a guest appearance on the 1980's series *The Cosby Show*.

Buchwald, Art. American humorist, columnist, and author; died on January 17, at the age of 81. For 40 years, beginning in the early 1960's, Buchwald wrote a column that was published in *The Washington Post* and 500 other newspapers. The column won him the 1982 Pulitzer Prize for Commentary. Called "The Wit of Washington," he was known for poking fun at politicians, government leaders, and the wealthy.

Claiborne, Liz. Pioneering American fashion designer; died on June 26, at the age of 78. Claiborne started her own line of women's clothes in 1976. Within ten years her company, Liz Claiborne, Inc., had retail sales of more than $1 billion. She became the first woman to have a company on the Fortune 500 list. By 2007, her company designed and sold not only women's clothes but men's clothing, fashion accessories, and fragrances as well.

Fossett, Steve. American record-setting adventurer; disappeared and was presumed dead on September 3, at the age of 63, while flying a small plane over the Nevada desert. Fossett had set more than 110 records in airplanes, balloons, gliders, and ships. His most recent record, set in 2006, was for the longest non-stop, unrefueled flight of a plane. He flew the *GlobalFlyer*, a lightweight experimental plane, from Florida to England, a distance of 25,766 miles (41,467 kilometers).

Goulet, Robert. American entertainer; died on October 30, at the age of 73. With his rich baritone voice and dark, good looks, Goulet became a Broadway, movie, and television star. He made his Broadway debut in 1960 in the musical *Camelot*. "If Ever I Would Leave You," from that show, became his signature song. Goulet won a 1962 Grammy Award, and a 1968 Tony Award (for *The Happy Time*).

Griffin, Merv. American talk-show host, game-show host, and entertainment-industry show-man; died on August 12, at the age of 82. Griffin started out in show business as a singer. He appeared in movies and on the stage before hosting *The Merv Griffin Show* on television (1962–86). He also created and produced the highly successful and still-running shows *Jeopardy!* and *Wheel of Fortune*.

Lady Bird Johnson

Deborah Kerr (with Burt Lancaster)

Ho, Don. Hawaiian-American musician and entertainer; died on April 14, at the age of 76. Ho rose to nationwide fame in the 1960's with such hit songs as "I'll Remember You," "Pearly Shells," and "Tiny Bubbles," which became his signature song. In the mid-1970's, he hosted *The Don Ho Show* on television. He remained popular into the 2000's, singing his laid-back style of music while accompanying himself on the ukulele or organ.

Johnson, Lady Bird. Former First Lady of the United States; died on July 11, at the age of 94. Born Claudia Alta Taylor, she married Texan Lyndon B. Johnson, helping him to thrive politically and to become the 36th president of the United States after the assassination of President John F. Kennedy in 1963. While First Lady, she championed a campaign to beautify the nation's parks and highways. After her husband's death in 1973, she became a member of the National Park Service Advisory Board and founded the National Wildflower Research Center (later, the Lady Bird Johnson Wildflower Center), in Austin, Texas.

Kerr, Deborah. Scottish actress; died on October 16, at the age of 86. Kerr's career spanned 40 years, and she was one of Hollywood's most versatile actresses. From 1949 to 1960 Kerr was nominated six times for Best Actress Academy Awards; she won a Golden Globe Award for her role in the musical *The King and I* (1956). Her other memorable films include *From Here to Eternity* (1953), *Tea and Sympathy* (1956), *An Affair to Remember* (1957), *Heaven Knows, Mr. Allison* (1957), *Separate Tables* (1958), and *The Sundowners* (1960).

Kirkpatrick, Jeane. U.S. ambassador to the United Nations from 1981 to 1985; died on December 7, 2006, at the age of 80. A professor of political science at Georgetown University in Washington, D.C., Kirkpatrick served as Ronald Reagan's foreign-policy adviser during the 1980 election campaign. When Reagan, the Republican candidate, won the presidency, he appointed Kirkpatrick U.N. ambassador. She was the first American woman to hold that position.

Knievel, Evel. American motorcycle stuntman; died on November 30, at the age of 69. Dubbed "America's Legendary Daredevil," Knievel often wore a dazzling red-white-and-blue costume. He made 300 motorcycle jumps and broke nearly 40 bones during his 15-year career, which

Evel Knievel

he ended at the age of 42. One of Knievel's most famous stunts was a record-setting 151-foot (46-meter) jump across the fountains in front of a casino in Las Vegas, Nevada. He later tried to jump the 1,700-foot- (518-meter-) wide Snake River Canyon in Idaho in a rocket-powered "Skycycle." That attempt failed, but it brought him even more fame and popularity.

L'Engle, Madeleine. American writer; died on September 6, at the age of 88. The author of dozens of works of fiction, poetry, and essays, L'Engle is best known for her children's classic *A Wrinkle in Time*. The science-fantasy story won the 1963 Newbery Medal as the best American literary work for young readers. Her other books include *A Wind in the Door, A Ring of Endless Light,* and *A Swiftly Tilting Planet.*

Mailer, Norman. American writer; died on November 10, at the age of 84. Mailer, who wrote more than 40 fiction and nonfiction books, was also a journalist, playwright, and screenwriter. His first book, *The Naked and the Dead,* was published in 1948. *The Armies of*

Luciano Pavarotti

Norman Mailer

the Night (1968), about the anti-Vietnam War march on the Pentagon, won a Pulitzer Prize and the National Book Award. *The Executioner's Song* (1979) also won a Pulitzer Prize.

Menotti, Gian Carlo. Italian-born American composer and librettist of operas; died on February 1, at the age of 95. Menotti wrote his first opera when he was 11. He wrote 25 more, two of which—*The Consul* and *The Saint of Bleeker Street*—won Pulitzer Prizes in the 1950's. Menotti's Christmas opera, *Amahl and the Night Visitors,* has been staged more than 600 times. He founded two popular summer musical festivals—Festival of the Two Worlds in Spoleto, Italy; and the Spoleto Festival in Charleston, South Carolina.

Pavarotti, Luciano. Italian opera star; died on September 6, at the age of 71. Pavarotti, a lyric tenor with great personal charm, first achieved operatic stardom in the 1960's. He went on to become a world-renowned superstar with a huge, diversified audience. His televised concerts and TV appearances brought opera to people who had never visited an opera house. Pavarotti was often referred to as one of the Three Tenors—along with Plácido Domingo and José Carreras.

Phil Rizzuto

Schirra, Walter (Wally), Jr. American astronaut; died on May 3, at the age of 84. A U.S. Navy pilot, Schirra flew in 90 combat missions during the Korean War, earning a Distinguished Flying Cross. In 1959, he became an astronaut with the National Aeronautics and Space Administration (NASA). Schirra flew on missions during NASA's first three space programs—Mercury, Gemini, and Apollo—and logged more than 295 hours in space. He was the fifth astronaut to be sent into space, and the third to orbit Earth.

Schlesinger, Arthur M., Jr. American historian; died on February 28, at the age of 89. Schlesinger was special assistant to President John F. Kennedy from 1961 to 1963. His many books on American political history include *The Age of Jackson* (1945) and *A Thousand Days* (1965), on Kennedy's presidency; both won Pulitzer Prizes. In 2004, Schlesinger wrote *War and the American Presidency,* his perspective on the George W. Bush presidency during the Iraq War.

Sills, Beverly. American opera singer; died on July 2, at the age of 78. Sills began singing professionally when she was 4 years old. She made her operatic stage debut while still in her teens. Over the years, she performed with the San Francisco Opera, the New York City Opera, the

Rizzuto, Phil. New York Yankee Hall of Fame shortstop and baseball announcer; died on August 13, at the age of 89. Known as "the Scooter," Rizzuto played 13 seasons with the Yankees during the 1940's and 50's. During that time, he helped the Yankees win seven World Series. Rizzuto was named the American League's most valuable player in 1950. In 1956, he joined the Yankees' radio and television broadcast team. During his 40 years in that job, fans would eagerly await any exciting play and Rizzuto's inevitable response: "Holy Cow!"

Rostropovich, Mstislav. Russian cellist and conductor; died on April 27, at the age of 80. Rostropovich, who started playing the cello when he was 10, was one of the greatest cellists of the 20th century. Many of his works were written for him by the world's great composers. Rostropovich supported anti-Soviet dissidents and championed artistic freedom in his homeland, the Soviet Union. Because of this, his citizenship was revoked. He moved to the United States, where he was the musical director and conductor of the U.S. National Symphony Orchestra from 1977 to 1994.

Wally Schirra, Jr.

Beverly Sills

Boston Symphony, La Scala, and the Metropolitan Opera, becoming an international star. She was known for her beautiful coloratura soprano voice, and for making opera a part of popular culture. Sills retired from singing in 1980. She then became director of the New York City Opera and later, chairman of Lincoln Center and the Metropolitan Opera.

Vonnegut, Kurt. American novelist; died April 11, at the age of 84. Vonnegut wrote short stories, plays, and novels. His best-selling novel, *Slaughterhouse-Five* (1969), drew on his World War II experience. Captured by the Germans, Vonnegut witnessed the firebombing of Dresden, Germany, which killed tens of thousands. He and other captured Americans were kept in a cell in an underground meat locker known as *Schlachthof Fünf*—"Slaughterhouse Five." His satirical and darkly humorous works made him a counterculture hero.

Waldheim, Kurt. Austrian diplomat and politician; died on June 14, at the age of 88. Waldheim was elected United Nations Secretary-General in 1972 and held that position for ten years. He then returned to Austria, where he ran for the presidency in 1986. During the election campaign, it was revealed that he had lied about his ties to Nazi organizations and war crimes during World War II. Waldheim won the presidential election, serving until 1992. But he was shunned by Western countries and banned from entering the United States.

Wyman, Jane. Movie and television star; died September 10, at the age of 90. Wyman began her acting career in the 1930's. Her best-known films were *Johnny Belinda* (1948), which earned her an Academy Award; and *Magnificent Obsession* (1954). In the 1980's, she played a leading role on the TV soap opera *Falcon Crest.* From 1940 to 1948, Wyman was married to Ronald Reagan, an actor who later became president of the United States.

Yeltsin, Boris. First president of the Russian Federation; died on April 23, at the age of 76. Yeltsin was elected president of Russia, the largest of the 15 republics making up the Soviet Union, in June 1991. He was the first political leader in Soviet history to be directly elected by the people. In December 1991, he played the chief role in forcing Mikhail Gorbachev (the last president of the Soviet Union) to resign, and in bringing about the final collapse of the Soviet Union. Yeltsin became president of the Russian Federation (the official name of Russia), and served until 1999. He helped to convert the former Communist country to a free-market economy and develop a new foreign policy.

Boris Yeltsin

INDEPENDENT NATIONS OF THE WORLD

NATION	CAPITAL	AREA (in sq mi)	POPULATION (estimate)	GOVERNMENT
Afghanistan	Kabul	250,000	31,900,000	Hamid Karzai—president
Albania	Tirana	11,100	3,200,000	Bamir Topi—president Sali Berisha—premier
Algeria	Algiers	919,595	34,100,000	Abdelaziz Bouteflika—president
Andorra	Andorra la Vella	175	100,000	Albert Pintat—premier
Angola	Luanda	481,354	16,300,000	José Eduardo dos Santos—president
Antigua and Barbuda	St. John's	171	100,000	Baldwin Spencer—prime minister
Argentina	Buenos Aires	1,068,297	39,400,000	Cristina Fernández de Kirchner—president
Armenia	Yerevan	11,500	3,000,000	Robert Kocharyan—president
Australia	Canberra	2,967,895	21,000,000	Kevin Rudd—prime minister
Austria	Vienna	32,374	8,300,000	Heinz Fischer—president Alfred Gusenbauer—chancellor
Azerbaijan	Baku	33,500	8,600,000	Ilham Aliyev—president
Bahamas	Nassau	5,380	300,000	Hubert Ingraham—prime minister
Bahrain	Manama	240	800,000	Hamad bin Isa al-Khalifa—king
Bangladesh	Dhaka	55,598	149,000,000	Iajuddin Ahmed—president
Barbados	Bridgetown	168	300,000	Owen Arthur—prime minister
Belarus	Minsk	80,154	9,700,000	Aleksandr Lukashenko—president
Belgium	Brussels	11,781	10,600,000	Albert II—king Guy Verhofstadt—premier
Belize	Belmopan	8,867	300,000	Said Musa—prime minister
Benin	Porto-Novo	43,484	9,000,000	Thomas Yayi Boni—president
Bhutan	Thimbu	18,147	900,000	Jigme Khesar Namgyel Wangchuck—king
Bolivia	La Paz Sucre	424,165	9,800,000	Juan Evo Morales—president
Bosnia and Herzegovina	Sarajevo	19,800	3,800,000	3-member presidency
Botswana	Gaborone	231,804	1,800,000	Festus Mogae—president
Brazil	Brasília	3,286,478	189,300,000	Luiz Inacio Lula da Silva—president
Brunei Darussalam	Bandar Seri Begawan	2,226	400,000	Hassanal Bolkiah—head of state
Bulgaria	Sofia	42,823	7,700,000	Georgi Parvanov—president Sergei Stanishev—premier
Burkina Faso	Ouagadougou	105,869	14,800,000	Blaise Compaoré—president
Burundi	Bujumbura	10,747	8,500,000	Pierre Nkurunziza—president
Cambodia	Phnom Penh	69,898	14,400,000	Norodom Sihamoni—king Hun Sen—prime minister
Cameroon	Yaoundé	183,569	18,100,000	Paul Biya—president
Canada	Ottawa	3,851,809	32,900,000	Stephen Harper—prime minister
Cape Verde	Praia	1,557	500,000	Pedro Pires—president

NATION	CAPITAL	AREA (in sq mi)	POPULATION (estimate)	GOVERNMENT
Central African Republic	Bangui	240,535	4,300,000	François Bozizé—president
Chad	N'Djamena	495,754	10,800,000	Idriss Deby—president
Chile	Santiago	292,257	16,600,000	Michelle Bachelet—president
China	Beijing	3,705,390	1,318,000,000	Hu Jintao—president Wen Jiabao—premier
Colombia	Bogotá	439,736	46,200,000	Alvaro Uribe Vélez—president
Comoros	Moroni	838	700,000	Ahmed Abdallah Mohamed Sambi—president
Congo (Zaire)	Kinshasa	905,565	62,600,000	Joseph Kabila—president
Congo Republic	Brazzaville	132,047	3,800,000	Denis Sassou-Nguesso—president
Costa Rica	San José	19,575	4,500,000	Oscar Arias Sánchez—president
Croatia	Zagreb	21,829	4,400,000	Stipe Mesic—president
Cuba	Havana	44,218	11,200,000	Fidel Castro—president (incapacitated) Raúl Castro—acting president
Cyprus	Nicosia	3,572	1,000,000	Tassos Papadopoulos—president
Czech Republic	Prague	30,469	10,300,000	Vaclav Klaus—president Mirek Topolanek—premier
Denmark	Copenhagen	16,629	5,500,000	Margrethe II—queen Anders Fogh Rasmussen—premier
Djibouti	Djibouti	8,494	800,000	Ismail Omar Guelleh—president
Dominica	Roseau	290	100,000	Roosevelt Skerrit—prime minister
Dominican Republic	Santo Domingo	18,816	9,400,000	Leonel Fernández Reyna—president
East Timor	Dili	5,743	1,000,000	José Ramos-Horta—president
Ecuador	Quito	109,483	13,500,000	Rafael Correa—president
Egypt	Cairo	386,660	73,400,000	Mohammed Hosni Mubarak—president Ahmed Nazif—premier
El Salvador	San Salvador	8,124	6,900,000	Elias Antonio Saca—president
Equatorial Guinea	Malabo	10,831	500,000	Teodoro Obiang Nguema Mbasogo—president
Eritrea	Asmara	45,405	4,900,000	Isaias Afworki—president
Estonia	Tallinn	17,413	1,300,000	Toomas Hendrik Ilves—president
Ethiopia	Addis Ababa	426,372	77,100,000	Girma Woldegiorgis—president
Fiji	Suva	7,055	900,000	Ratu Josefa Iloilo—president
Finland	Helsinki	130,120	5,300,000	Tarja Halonen—president Matti Vanhanen—premier
France	Paris	213,000	61,700,000	Nicolas Sarkozy—president François Fillon—premier
Gabon	Libreville	103,346	1,300,000	Omar Bongo—president
Gambia	Banjul	4,361	1,500,000	Yahya Jammeh—head of state
Georgia	Tbilisi	27,000	4,500,000	Mikhail Saakashvili—president
Germany	Berlin	137,744	82,300,000	Horst Köhler—president Angela Merkel—chancellor
Ghana	Accra	92,099	23,000,000	John Kufuor—president

NATION	CAPITAL	AREA (in sq mi)	POPULATION (estimate)	GOVERNMENT
Greece	Athens	50,944	11,200,000	Karolos Papoulias—president Costas Caramanlis—premier
Grenada	St. George's	133	100,000	Keith Mitchell—prime minister
Guatemala	Guatemala City	42,042	13,400,000	Álvaro Colom Caballeros—president-elect
Guinea	Conakry	94,926	10,100,000	Lansana Conté—president
Guinea-Bissau	Bissau	13,948	1,700,000	João Bernardo Vieira—president
Guyana	Georgetown	83,000	800,000	Bharrat Jagdeo—president
Haiti	Port-au-Prince	10,714	9,000,000	René Garcia Préval—president
Honduras	Tegucigalpa	43,277	7,100,000	Manuel Zelaya—president
Hungary	Budapest	35,919	10,100,000	László Sólyom—president Ferenc Gyurcsany—premier
Iceland	Reykjavik	39,768	300,000	Olafur Grimsson—president Geir H. Haarde—premier
India	New Delhi	1,269,340	1,131,900,000	Pratibha Patil—president Manmohan Singh—prime minister
Indonesia	Jakarta	735,358	231,600,000	Susilo Bambang Yudhoyono—president
Iran	Tehran	636,293	71,200,000	Ayatollah Ali Khamenei—religious leader Mahmoud Ahmadinejad—president
Iraq	Baghdad	167,925	29,000,000	Jalal Talabani—president Nouri Kamel al-Maliki—premier
Ireland	Dublin	27,136	4,400,000	Mary McAleese—president Bertie Ahern—prime minister
Israel	Jerusalem	8,019	7,300,000	Shimon Peres—president Ehud Olmert—prime minister
Italy	Rome	116,303	59,300,000	Giorgio Napolitano—president Romano Prodi—premier
Ivory Coast	Yamoussoukro	124,503	20,200,000	Laurent Gbagbo—president
Jamaica	Kingston	4,244	2,700,000	Bruce Golding—prime minister
Japan	Tokyo	143,751	127,700,000	Akihito—emperor Yasuo Fukuda—premier
Jordan	Amman	35,475	5,700,000	Abdullah II—king Nader al-Dahabi—prime minister
Kazakhstan	Almaty	1,049,000	15,500,000	Nursultan A. Nazarbayev—president
Kenya	Nairobi	224,959	36,900,000	Mwai Kibaki—president
Kiribati	Tarawa	264	100,000	Anote Tong—president
Korea (North)	Pyongyang	46,540	23,300,000	Kim Jong Il—president Kim Yong Il—premier
Korea (South)	Seoul	38,025	48,500,000	Lee Myung Bak—president-elect Han Duck Soo—premier
Kuwait	Kuwait	6,880	2,800,000	Sabah al-Ahmad al-Jabir al-Sabah— head of state
Kyrgyzstan	Bishkek	76,641	5,200,000	Kurmanbek Bakiyev—president
Laos	Vientiane	91,429	5,900,000	Choummali Saignason—president Bouasone Bouphavanh—premier
Latvia	Riga	24,600	2,300,000	Valdis Zatlers—president

NATION	CAPITAL	AREA (in sq mi)	POPULATION (estimate)	GOVERNMENT
Lebanon	Beirut	4,015	3,900,000	Fouad Siniora—prime minister
Lesotho	Maseru	11,720	1,800,000	Letsie III—king Pakalitha Bethuel Mosisili—premier
Liberia	Monrovia	43,000	3,800,000	Ellen Johnson-Sirleaf—president
Libya	Tripoli	679,362	6,200,000	Muammar el-Qaddafi—head of government
Liechtenstein	Vaduz	61	40,000	Hans Adam II—prince
Lithuania	Vilnius	25,174	3,400,000	Valdas Adamkus—president
Luxembourg	Luxembourg	998	500,000	Henri—grand duke Jean-Claude Juncker—premier
Macedonia	Skopje	9,928	2,000,000	Branko Crvenkovski—president
Madagascar	Antananarivo	226,657	18,300,000	Marc Ravalomanana—president
Malawi	Lilongwe	45,747	13,100,000	Bingu wa Mutharika—president
Malaysia	Kuala Lumpur	127,317	27,200,000	Sultan Mizan Zainal Abidin—king Abdullah Badawi—prime minister
Maldives	Male	115	300,000	Maumoon Abdul Gayoom—president
Mali	Bamako	478,765	12,300,000	Amadou Toumani Touré—president
Malta	Valletta	122	400,000	Eddie Fenech Adami—president Lawrence Gonzi—prime minister
Marshall Islands	Majuro	70	100,000	Kessai Note—president
Mauritania	Nouakchott	397,954	3,100,000	Sidi Ould Cheikh Abdallahi—president
Mauritius	Port Louis	790	1,300,000	Anerood Jugnauth—president Navinchandra Ramgoolam—premier
Mexico	Mexico City	761,602	106,500,000	Felipe Calderón—president
Micronesia	Colonia	271	100,000	Joseph J. Urusemal—president
Moldova	Chisinau	13,000	4,000,000	Vladimir Voronin—president
Monaco	Monaco-Ville	0.6	30,000	Albert II—prince
Mongolia	Ulan Bator	604,248	2,600,000	Nambaryn Enkhbayar—president
Montenegro	Podgorica	5,415	600,000	Filip Vujanovic—president
Morocco	Rabat	172,413	31,700,000	Mohammed VI—king Abbas el Fassi—premier
Mozambique	Maputo	309,494	20,400,000	Armando Guebuza—president
Myanmar (Burma)	Naypyidaw	261,218	49,800,000	Than Shwe—head of government
Namibia	Windhoek	318,260	2,100,000	Hifikepunye Pohamba—president
Nauru	Yaren District	8	10,000	Ludwig Scotty—president
Nepal	Katmandu	54,362	27,800,000	Gyanendra Bir Bikram Shah—king
Netherlands	Amsterdam	15,770	16,400,000	Beatrix—queen Jan Peter Balkenende—premier
New Zealand	Wellington	103,736	4,200,000	Helen Clark—prime minister
Nicaragua	Managua	50,193	5,600,000	Daniel Ortega—president
Niger	Niamey	489,190	14,200,000	Mamadou Tandja—president
Nigeria	Abuja	356,667	144,400,000	Umaru Musa Yar'Adua—president

NATION	CAPITAL	AREA (in sq mi)	POPULATION (estimate)	GOVERNMENT
Norway	Oslo	125,056	4,700,000	Harold V—king Jens Stoltenberg—premier
Oman	Muscat	82,030	2,700,000	Qaboos bin Said al-Said—sultan
Pakistan	Islamabad	310,404	169,300,000	Pervez Musharraf—president
Palau	Koror	192	20,000	Tommy Remengesau—president
Panama	Panama City	29,761	3,300,000	Martín Torrijos Espino—president
Papua New Guinea	Port Moresby	178,260	6,300,000	Michael Somare—prime minister
Paraguay	Asunción	157,047	6,100,000	Nicanor Duarte Frutos—president
Peru	Lima	496,222	27,900,000	Alan García—president
Philippines	Manila	115,830	88,700,000	Gloria Macapagal-Arroyo—president Noli de Castro—vice-president
Poland	Warsaw	120,725	38,100,000	Lech Kaczynski—president Donald Tusk—premier
Portugal	Lisbon	35,553	10,700,000	Anibal António Cavaco Silva—president José Sócrates Carvalho Pinto de Sousa—premier
Qatar	Doha	4,247	900,000	Hamad bin Khalifa al-Thani—head of state
Romania	Bucharest	91,700	21,600,000	Traian Basescu—president Calin Popescu-Tariceanu—premier
Russia	Moscow	6,600,000	141,700,000	Vladimir V. Putin—president
Rwanda	Kigali	10,169	9,300,000	Paul Kagame—president
St. Kitts and Nevis	Basseterre	105	50,000	Denzil Douglas—prime minister
St. Lucia	Castries	238	200,000	Stephenson King—prime minister
St. Vincent and the Grenadines	Kingstown	150	100,000	Ralph Gonsalves—prime minister
Samoa	Apia	1,097	200,000	Tuiatua Tupua Tamasese Efi—head of state
San Marino	San Marino	24	30,000	Fiorenzo Stolfi—head of government
São Tomé and Príncipe	São Tomé	372	200,000	Fradique de Menezes—president
Saudi Arabia	Riyadh	830,000	27,600,000	Abdullah bin Abdul-Aziz al Saud—king
Senegal	Dakar	75,750	12,400,000	Abdoulaye Wade—president
Serbia	Belgrade	34,116	9,500,000	Boris Tadic—president
Seychelles	Victoria	107	100,000	James Michel—president
Sierra Leone	Freetown	27,700	5,300,000	Ernest Bai Koroma—president
Singapore	Singapore	224	4,600,000	S. R. Nathan—president Lee Hsien Loong—prime minister
Slovakia	Bratislava	18,933	5,400,000	Ivan Gasparovic—president
Slovenia	Ljubljana	7,819	2,000,000	Danilo Türk—president
Solomon Islands	Honiara	10,983	500,000	Manasseh Sogavare—prime minister
Somalia	Mogadishu	246,200	9,100,000	Abdullahi Yusuf Ahmed—president
South Africa	Pretoria Cape Town Bloemfontein	471,444	47,900,000	Thabo Mbeki—president
Spain	Madrid	194,896	45,300,000	Juan Carlos I—king José Luis Rodríguez Zapatero—premier

NATION	CAPITAL	AREA (in sq mi)	POPULATION (estimate)	GOVERNMENT
Sri Lanka	Colombo	25,332	20,100,000	Mahinda Rajapaksa—president
Sudan	Khartoum	967,500	38,600,000	O. Hassan Ahmed al-Bashir—president
Suriname	Paramaribo	63,037	500,000	Ronald Venetiaan—president
Swaziland	Mbabane	6,704	1,100,000	Mswati III—king
Sweden	Stockholm	173,731	9,100,000	Carl XVI Gustaf—king Fredrik Reinfeldt—premier
Switzerland	Bern	15,941	7,500,000	Pascal Couchepin—president
Syria	Damascus	71,498	19,900,000	Bashar al-Assad—president Naji Otari—premier
Taiwan	Taipei	13,885	22,900,000	Chen Shui-bian—president Chang Chun-hsiung—premier
Tajikistan	Dushanbe	55,250	7,100,000	Oqil Oqilov—premier
Tanzania	Dar es Salaam	364,898	38,700,000	Jakaya Kikwete—president
Thailand	Bangkok	198,457	65,700,000	Bhumibol Adulyadej—king Surayud Chulanont—premier
Togo	Lomé	21,622	6,600,000	Faure Gnassingbe—president
Tonga	Nuku'alofa	270	100,000	Siaosi Tupou V—king Feleti Sevele—premier
Trinidad & Tobago	Port of Spain	1,980	1,400,000	George Maxwell Richards—president Patrick Manning—prime minister
Tunisia	Tunis	63,170	10,200,000	Zine el-Abidine Ben Ali—president
Turkey	Ankara	301,381	74,000,000	Abdullah Gül—president Recep Tayyip Erdogan—prime minister
Turkmenistan	Ashkhabad	188,455	5,400,000	K. Berdymukhamedov—president
Tuvalu	Funafuti	10	10,000	Apisai Ielemia—prime minister
Uganda	Kampala	91,134	28,500,000	Yoweri Museveni—president
Ukraine	Kiev	231,990	46,500,000	Viktor A. Yushchenko—president
United Arab Emirates	Abu Dhabi	32,278	4,400,000	Khalifa bin Zayed al-Nahayan—president
United Kingdom	London	94,226	61,000,000	Elizabeth II—queen Gordon Brown—prime minister
United States	Washington, D.C.	3,618,467	302,200,000	George W. Bush—president Richard Cheney—vice-president
Uruguay	Montevideo	68,037	3,300,000	Tabaré Vázquez—president
Uzbekistan	Tashkent	172,750	26,500,000	Islam A. Karimov—president
Vanuatu	Vila	5,700	200,000	Kalkot Matas Kelekele—president
Vatican City	Vatican City	0.17	800	Benedict XVI—pope
Venezuela	Caracas	352,143	27,500,000	Hugo Chávez—president
Vietnam	Hanoi	128,402	85,100,000	Nong Duc Manh—Communist Party secretary Nguyen Tan Dung—premier
Yemen	Sana	203,849	22,400,000	Ali Abdullah Saleh—president Ali Muhammad Mujawwar—premier
Zambia	Lusaka	290,585	11,500,000	Levy Mwanawasa—president
Zimbabwe	Harare	150,333	13,300,000	Robert Mugabe—president

THE CONGRESS OF THE UNITED STATES

UNITED STATES SENATE
(49 Democrats, 49 Republicans, 2 Independents)

Alabama
Richard C. Shelby (R)
Jeff Sessions (R)

Alaska
Ted Stevens (R)
Lisa Murkowski (R)

Arizona
John S. McCain III (R)
Jon Kyl (R)

Arkansas
Blanche L. Lincoln (D)
Mark Pryor (D)

California
Barbara Boxer (D)
Dianne Feinstein (D)

Colorado
Wayne Allard (R)
Ken Salazar (D)

Connecticut
Christopher J. Dodd (D)
Joseph I. Lieberman (I)

Delaware
Joseph R. Biden, Jr. (D)
Thomas Carper (D)

Florida
Mel Martinez (R)
Bill Nelson (D)

Georgia
Johnny Isakson (R)
Saxby Chambliss (R)

Hawaii
Daniel K. Inouye (D)
Daniel K. Akaka (D)

Idaho
Larry Craig (R)
Michael Crapo (R)

Illinois
Richard J. Durbin (D)
Barack Obama (D)

Indiana
Richard G. Lugar (R)
Evan Bayh (D)

Iowa
Chuck Grassley (R)
Tom Harkin (D)

Kansas
Sam Brownback (R)
Pat Roberts (R)

Kentucky
Mitch McConnell (R)
Jim Bunning (R)

Louisiana
David Vitter (R)
Mary Landrieu (D)

Maine
Olympia J. Snowe (R)
Susan Collins (R)

Maryland
Barbara A. Mikulski (D)
Ben Cardin (D)

Massachusetts
Edward M. Kennedy (D)
John Kerry (D)

Michigan
Carl Levin (D)
Debbie Stabenow (D)

Minnesota
Norm Coleman (R)
Amy Klobuchar (D)

Mississippi
Thad Cochran (R)
Trent Lott (R)

Missouri
Christopher Bond (R)
Claire McCaskill (D)

Montana
Max Baucus (D)
Jon Tester (D)

Nebraska
Chuck Hagel (R)
Ben Nelson (D)

Nevada
Harry Reid (D)
John Ensign (R)

New Hampshire
Judd Gregg (R)
John E. Sununu (R)

New Jersey
Frank Lautenberg (D)
Robert Menendez (D)

New Mexico
Pete V. Domenici (R)
Jeff Bingaman (D)

New York
Charles E. Schumer (D)
Hillary Rodham Clinton (D)

North Carolina
Richard Burr (R)
Elizabeth Dole (R)

North Dakota
Kent Conrad (D)
Byron L. Dorgan (D)

Ohio
George Voinovich (R)
Sherrod Brown (D)

Oklahoma
Tom Coburn (R)
James M. Inhofe (R)

Oregon
Gordon Smith (R)
Ron Wyden (D)

Pennsylvania
Arlen Specter (R)
Robert P. Casey, Jr. (D)

Rhode Island
Jack Reed (D)
Sheldon Whitehouse (D)

South Carolina
Jim DeMint (R)
Lindsey Graham (R)

South Dakota
John Thune (R)
Tim Johnson (D)

Tennessee
Lamar Alexander (R)
Bob Corker (R)

Texas
Kay Bailey Hutchison (R)
John Cornyn (R)

Utah
Orrin G. Hatch (R)
Robert F. Bennett (R)

Vermont
Patrick J. Leahy (D)
Bernie Sanders (I)

Virginia
John W. Warner (R)
Jim Webb (D)

Washington
Patty Murray (D)
Maria Cantwell (D)

West Virginia
Robert C. Byrd (D)
John D. Rockefeller IV (D)

Wisconsin
Herb Kohl (D)
Russell D. Feingold (D)

Wyoming
Michael Enzi (R)
John Barrasso (R)*

*named to fill vacancy in 2007

(D) Democrat
(R) Republican
(I) Independent

UNITED STATES HOUSE OF REPRESENTATIVES
(232 Democrats, 200 Republicans, 3 vacancies)

Alabama
1. J. Bonner (R)
2. T. Everett (R)
3. M. Rogers (R)
4. R. B. Aderholt (R)
5. R. E. Cramer, Jr. (D)
6. S. Bachus (R)
7. A. Davis (D)

Alaska
   D. Young (R)

Arizona
1. R. Renzi (R)
2. T. Franks (R)
3. J. B. Shadegg (R)
4. E. Pastor (D)
5. H. Mitchell (D)
6. J. Flake (R)
7. R. M. Grijalva (D)
8. G. Giffords (D)

Arkansas
1. M. Berry (D)
2. V. Snyder (D)
3. J. Boozman (R)
4. M. Ross (D)

California
1. M. Thompson (D)
2. W. Herger (R)
3. D. Lungren (R)
4. J. T. Doolittle (R)
5. D. O. Matsui (D)
6. L. C. Woolsey (D)
7. G. Miller (D)
8. N. Pelosi (D)
9. B. Lee (D)
10. E. O. Tauscher (D)
11. J. McNerney (D)
12. T. Lantos (D)
13. F. P. Stark (D)
14. A. G. Eshoo (D)
15. M. M. Honda (D)
16. Z. Lofgren (D)
17. S. Farr (D)
18. D. A. Cardoza (D)
19. G. Radanovich (R)
20. J. Costa (D)
21. D. Nunes (R)
22. K. McCarthy (R)
23. L. Capps (D)
24. E. Gallegly (R)
25. H. P. McKeon (R)
26. D. Dreier (R)
27. B. Sherman (D)
28. H. L. Berman (D)
29. A. B. Schiff (D)
30. H. A. Waxman (D)
31. X. Becerra (D)
32. H. L. Solis (D)
33. D. E. Watson (D)
34. L. Roybal-Allard (D)
35. M. Waters (D)
36. J. Harman (D)
37. L. Richardson (D)*
38. G. F. Napolitano (D)
39. L. T. Sanchez (D)

40. E. R. Royce (R)
41. J. Lewis (R)
42. G. G. Miller (R)
43. J. Baca (D)
44. K. Calvert (R)
45. M. Bono (R)
46. D. Rohrabacher (R)
47. L. Sanchez (D)
48. J. Campbell (R)
49. D. E. Issa (R)
50. B. Bilbray (R)
51. B. Filner (D)
52. D. Hunter (R)
53. S. A. Davis (D)

Colorado
1. D. DeGette (D)
2. M. Udall (D)
3. J. Salazar (D)
4. M. N. Musgrave (R)
5. D. Lamborn (R)
6. T. G. Tancredo (R)
7. E. Perlmutter (D)

Connecticut
1. J. B. Larson (D)
2. J. Courtney (D)
3. R. L. DeLauro (D)
4. C. Shays (R)
5. C. Murphy (D)

Delaware
   M. N. Castle (R)

Florida
1. J. Miller (R)
2. A. Boyd (D)
3. C. Brown (D)
4. A. Crenshaw (R)
5. G. Brown-Waite (R)
6. C. Stearns (R)
7. J. L. Mica (R)
8. R. Keller (R)
9. G. M. Bilirakis (R)
10. C. W. Young (R)
11. K. Castor (D)
12. A. H. Putnam (R)
13. V. Buchanan (R)
14. C. Mack (R)
15. D. Weldon (R)
16. T. Mahoney (D)
17. K. B. Meek (D)
18. I. Ros-Lehtinen (R)
19. R. Wexler (D)
20. D. Wasserman Schultz (D)
21. L. Diaz-Balart (R)
22. R. Klein (D)
23. A. L. Hastings (D)
24. T. Feeney (R)
25. M. Diaz-Balart (R)

Georgia
1. J. Kingston (R)
2. S. D. Bishop, Jr. (D)
3. L. A. Westmoreland (R)
4. H. Johnson (D)
5. J. Lewis (D)

6. T. Price (R)
7. J. Linder (R)
8. J. Marshall (D)
9. N. Deal (R)
10. P. C. Broun (R)*
11. P. Gingrey (R)
12. J. Barrow (D)
13. D. Scott (D)

Hawaii
1. N. Abercrombie (D)
2. M. Hirono (D)

Idaho
1. B. Sali (R)
2. M. K. Simpson (R)

Illinois
1. B. L. Rush (D)
2. J. L. Jackson, Jr. (D)
3. D. Lipinski (D)
4. L. V. Gutierrez (D)
5. R. Emanuel (D)
6. P. Roskam (R)
7. D. K. Davis (D)
8. M. L. Bean (D)
9. J. D. Schakowsky (D)
10. M. S. Kirk (R)
11. J. Weller (R)
12. J. F. Costello (D)
13. J. Biggert (R)
14. vacant
15. T. V. Johnson (R)
16. D. A. Manzullo (R)
17. P. Hare (D)
18. R. LaHood (R)
19. J. Shimkus (R)

Indiana
1. P. J. Visclosky (D)
2. J. Donnelly (D)
3. M. E. Souder (R)
4. S. Buyer (R)
5. D. Burton (R)
6. M. Pence (R)
7. vacant
8. B. Ellsworth (D)
9. B. Hill (D)

Iowa
1. B. Braley (D)
2. D. Loebsack (D)
3. L. L. Boswell (D)
4. T. Latham (R)
5. S. King (R)

Kansas
1. J. Moran (R)
2. N. Boyda (D)
3. D. Moore (D)
4. T. Tiahrt (R)

Kentucky
1. E. Whitfield (R)
2. R. Lewis (R)

3. J. Yarmuth (D)
4. G. Davis (R)
5. H. Rogers (R)
6. B. Chandler (D)

Louisiana
1. vacant
2. W. J. Jefferson (D)
3. C. Melancon (D)
4. J. McCrery (R)
5. R. Alexander (R)
6. R. H. Baker (R)
7. C. W. Boustany, Jr. (R)

Maine
1. T. H. Allen (D)
2. M. H. Michaud (D)

Maryland
1. W. T. Gilchrest (R)
2. C. A. Ruppersberger (D)
3. J. Sarbanes (D)
4. A. R. Wynn (D)
5. S. H. Hoyer (D)
6. R. G. Bartlett (R)
7. E. E. Cummings (D)
8. C. Van Hollen (D)

Massachusetts
1. J. W. Olver (D)
2. R. E. Neal (D)
3. J. P. McGovern (D)
4. B. Frank (D)
5. N. Tsongas (D)*
6. J. F. Tierney (D)
7. E. J. Markey (D)
8. M. E. Capuano (D)
9. S. F. Lynch (D)
10. W. D. Delahunt (D)

Michigan
1. B. Stupak (D)
2. P. Hoekstra (R)
3. V. J. Ehlers (R)
4. D. Camp (R)
5. D. E. Kildee (D)
6. F. Upton (R)
7. T. Walberg (R)
8. M. Rogers (R)
9. J. Knollenberg (R)
10. C. S. Miller (R)
11. T. G. McCotter (R)
12. S. M. Levin (D)
13. C. C. Kilpatrick (D)
14. J. Conyers, Jr. (D)
15. J. D. Dingell (D)

Minnesota
1. T. Walz (D)
2. J. Kline (R)
3. J. Ramstad (R)
4. B. McCollum (D)

5. K. Ellison (D)
6. M. Bachmann (R)
7. C. C. Peterson (D)
8. J. L. Oberstar (D)

Mississippi
1. R. F. Wicker (R)
2. B. G. Thompson (D)
3. C. W. Pickering (R)
4. G. Taylor (D)

Missouri
1. W. L. Clay (D)
2. W. T. Akin (R)
3. R. Carnahan (D)
4. I. Skelton (D)
5. E. Cleaver (D)
6. S. Graves (R)
7. R. Blunt (R)
8. J. A. Emerson (R)
9. K. C. Hulshof (R)

Montana
   D. R. Rehberg (R)

Nebraska
1. J. Fortenberry (R)
2. L. Terry (R)
3. A. Smith (R)

Nevada
1. S. Berkley (D)
2. D. Heller (R)
3. J. C. Porter (R)

New Hampshire
1. C. Shea-Porter (D)
2. P. Hodes (D)

New Jersey
1. R. E. Andrews (D)
2. F. A. LoBiondo (R)
3. J. Saxton (R)
4. C. H. Smith (R)
5. S. Garrett (R)
6. F. Pallone, Jr. (D)
7. M. Ferguson (R)
8. B. Pascrell, Jr. (D)
9. S. R. Rothman (D)
10. D. M. Payne (D)
11. R. P. Frelinghuysen (R)
12. R. D. Holt (D)
13. A. Sires (D)

New Mexico
1. H. Wilson (R)
2. S. Pearce (R)
3. T. Udall (D)

New York
1. T. H. Bishop (D)
2. S. Israel (D)
3. P. T. King (R)
4. C. McCarthy (D)
5. G. L. Ackerman (D)
6. G. W. Meeks (D)

7. J. Crowley (D)
8. J. Nadler (D)
9. A. D. Weiner (D)
10. E. Towns (D)
11. Y. D. Clarke (D)
12. N. M. Velázquez (D)
13. V. Fossella (R)
14. C. B. Maloney (D)
15. C. B. Rangel (D)
16. J. E. Serrano (D)
17. E. L. Engel (D)
18. N. M. Lowey (D)
19. J. Hall (D)
20. K.E. Gillibrand (D)
21. M. R. McNulty (D)
22. M. D. Hinchey (D)
23. J. M. McHugh (R)
24. M.A. Arcuri (D)
25. J. T. Walsh (R)
26. T. M. Reynolds (R)
27. B. Higgins (D)
28. L. M. Slaughter (D)
29. J. R. Kuhl, Jr. (R)

North Carolina
1. D. K. Butterfield (D)
2. B. Etheridge (D)
3. W. B. Jones (R)
4. D. E. Price (D)
5. V. Foxx (R)
6. H. Coble (R)
7. M. McIntyre (D)
8. R. Hayes (R)
9. S. W. Myrick (R)
10. P. T. McHenry (R)
11. H. Shuler (D)
12. M. L. Watt (D)
13. B. Miller (D)

North Dakota
   E. Pomeroy (D)

Ohio
1. S. Chabot (R)
2. J. Schmidt (R)
3. M. R. Turner (R)
4. J. Jordan (R)
5. R. E. Latta (R)*
6. C. Wilson (D)
7. D. L. Hobson (R)
8. J. A. Boehner (R)
9. M. Kaptur (D)
10. D. J. Kucinich (D)
11. S. T. Jones (D)
12. P. J. Tiberi (R)
13. B. Sutton (D)
14. S. C. LaTourette (R)
15. D. Pryce (R)
16. R. Regula (R)
17. T. Ryan (D)
18. Z. Space (D)

Oklahoma
1. J. Sullivan (R)
2. D. Boren (D)
3. F. D. Lucas (R)
4. T. Cole (R)
5. M. Fallin (R)

Oregon
1. D. Wu (D)
2. G. Walden (R)

3. E. Blumenauer (D)
4. P. A. DeFazio (D)
5. D. Hooley (D)

Pennsylvania
1. R. A. Brady (D)
2. C. Fattah (D)
3. P. English (R)
4. J. Altmire (D)
5. J. E. Peterson (R)
6. J. Gerlach (R)
7. J. Sestak (D)
8. P. Murphy (D)
9. B. Shuster (R)
10. C. Carney (D)
11. P. E. Kanjorski (D)
12. J. P. Murtha (D)
13. A. Y. Schwartz (D)
14. M. F. Doyle (D)
15. C. W. Dent (R)
16. J. R. Pitts (R)
17. T. Holden (D)
18. T. Murphy (R)
19. T. R. Platts (R)

Rhode Island
1. P. J. Kennedy (D)
2. J. R. Langevin (D)

South Carolina
1. H. E. Brown, Jr. (R)
2. J. Wilson (R)
3. J. G. Barrett (R)
4. B. Inglis (R)
5. J. M. Spratt, Jr. (D)
6. J. E. Clyburn (D)

South Dakota
   S. Herseth Sandlin (D)

Tennessee
1. D. Davis (R)
2. J. J. Duncan, Jr. (R)
3. Z. Wamp (R)
4. L. Davis (D)
5. J. Cooper (D)
6. B. Gordon (D)
7. M. Blackburn (R)
8. J. S. Tanner (D)
9. S. Cohen (D)

Texas
1. L. Gohmert (R)
2. T. Poe (R)
3. S. Johnson (R)
4. R. M. Hall (R)
5. J. Hensarling (R)
6. J. Barton (R)
7. J. A. Culberson (R)
8. K. Brady (R)
9. A. Green (D)
10. M. T. McCaul (R)
11. K. M. Conaway (R)
12. K. Granger (R)
13. M. Thornberry (R)
14. R. Paul (R)
15. R. Hinojosa (D)
16. S. Reyes (D)
17. C. Edwards (D)
18. S. Jackson-Lee (D)

19. R. Neugebauer (R)
20. C. A. Gonzalez (D)
21. L. Smith (R)
22. N. Lampson (D)
23. C. D. Rodriguez (D)
24. K. Marchant (R)
25. L. Doggett (D)
26. M. C. Burgess (R)
27. S. P. Ortiz (D)
28. H. Cuellar (D)
29. G. Green (D)
30. E. B. Johnson (D)
31. J. R. Carter (R)
32. P. Sessions (R)

Utah
1. R. Bishop (R)
2. J. Matheson (D)
3. C. Cannon (R)

Vermont
   P. Welch (D)

Virginia
1. R. J. Wittman (R)*
2. T. D. Drake (R)
3. R. C. Scott (D)
4. J. R. Forbes (R)
5. V. H. Goode, Jr. (R)
6. B. Goodlatte (R)
7. E. Cantor (R)
8. J. P. Moran (D)
9. R. Boucher (D)
10. F. R. Wolf (R)
11. T. Davis (R)

Washington
1. J. Inslee (D)
2. R. Larsen (D)
3. B. Baird (D)
4. D. Hastings (R)
5. C. McMorris Rodgers (R)
6. N. D. Dicks (D)
7. J. McDermott (D)
8. D. G. Reichert (R)
9. A. Smith (D)

West Virginia
1. A. B. Mollohan (D)
2. S. M. Capito (R)
3. N. J. Rahall II (D)

Wisconsin
1. P. Ryan (R)
2. T. Baldwin (D)
3. R. Kind (D)
4. G. Moore (D)
5. F. J. Sensenbrenner, Jr. (R)
6. T. E. Petri (R)
7. D. R. Obey (D)
8. S. Kagen (D)

Wyoming
   B. Cubin (R)

*elected in special election in 2007

(D) Democrat
(R) Republican

UNITED STATES SUPREME COURT

Chief Justice: John G. Roberts, Jr. (2005)
Associate Justices:
John Paul Stevens (1975)
Antonin Scalia (1986)
Anthony M. Kennedy (1988)
David H. Souter (1990)
Clarence Thomas (1991)
Ruth Bader Ginsburg (1993)
Stephen G. Breyer (1994)
Samuel A. Alito, Jr. (2006)

UNITED STATES CABINET

Secretary of Agriculture: Edward T. Schafer*
Attorney General: Michael B. Mukasey
Secretary of Commerce: Carlos M. Gutierrez
Secretary of Defense: Robert M. Gates
Secretary of Education: Margaret Spellings
Secretary of Energy: Samuel W. Bodman
Secretary of Health and Human Services: Michael O. Leavitt
Secretary of Homeland Security: Michael Chertoff
Secretary of Housing and Urban Development: Alphonso Jackson
Secretary of the Interior: Dirk Kempthorne
Secretary of Labor: Elaine L. Chao
Secretary of State: Condoleezza Rice
Secretary of Transportation: Mary E. Peters
Secretary of the Treasury: Henry M. Paulson, Jr.
Secretary of Veterans Affairs: James B. Peake

*nominated but not confirmed

Michael B. Mukasey, a retired federal court judge, became U.S. Attorney General in 2007.

STATE GOVERNORS

Alabama	Bob Riley (R)	Montana	Brian Schweitzer (D)
Alaska	Sarah Palin (R)	Nebraska	Dave Heineman (R)
Arizona	Janet Napolitano (D)	Nevada	Jim Gibbons (R)
Arkansas	Mike Beebe (D)	New Hampshire	John Lynch (D)
California	Arnold Schwarzenegger (R)	New Jersey	Jon S. Corzine (D)
Colorado	Bill Ritter (D)	New Mexico	Bill Richardson (D)
Connecticut	M. Jodi Rell (R)	New York	Eliot Spitzer (D)
Delaware	Ruth Ann Minner (D)	North Carolina	Michael F. Easley (D)
Florida	Charlie Crist (R)	North Dakota	John Hoeven (R)
Georgia	Sonny Perdue (R)	Ohio	Ted Strickland (D)
Hawaii	Linda Lingle (R)	Oklahoma	Brad Henry (D)
Idaho	C.L."Butch" Otter (R)	Oregon	Ted Kulongoski (D)
Illinois	Rod Blagojevich (D)	Pennsylvania	Edward G. Rendell (D)
Indiana	Mitch Daniels (R)	Rhode Island	Don Carcieri (R)
Iowa	Chet Culver (D)	South Carolina	Mark Sanford (R)
Kansas	Kathleen Sebelius (D)	South Dakota	Mike Rounds (R)
Kentucky	Steve Beshear (D)*	Tennessee	Phil Bredesen (D)
Louisiana	Bobby Jindal (R)*	Texas	Rick Perry (R)
Maine	John Baldacci (D)	Utah	Jon Huntsman, Jr. (R)
Maryland	Martin O'Malley (D)	Vermont	Jim Douglas (R)
Massachusetts	Deval Patrick (D)	Virginia	Timothy M. Kaine (D)
Michigan	Jennifer Granholm (D)	Washington	Christine Gregoire (D)
Minnesota	Tim Pawlenty (R)	West Virginia	Joseph Manchin III (D)
Mississippi	Haley Barbour (R)**	Wisconsin	Jim Doyle (D)
Missouri	Matt Blunt (R)	Wyoming	Dave Freudenthal (D)

*elected in 2007   **re-elected in 2007   all others, incumbents   (D) Democrat   (R) Republican

CANADA

Capital: Ottawa
Head of State: Queen Elizabeth II
Governor General: Michaëlle Jean
Prime Minister: Stephen Harper (Conservative)
Leader of the Opposition: Stéphane Dion (Liberal)
Population: 32,976,026
Area: 3,851,809 sq mi (9,976,185 km²)

PROVINCES AND TERRITORIES

Alberta
Capital: Edmonton
Lieutenant Governor: Norman L. Kwong
Premier: Ed Stelmach (Progressive Conservative)
Leader of the Opposition: Kevin Taft (Liberal)
Entered Confederation: Sept. 1, 1905
Population: 3,473,984
Area: 255,285 sq mi (661,188 km²)

British Columbia
Capital: Victoria
Lieutenant Governor: Steve L. Point
Premier: Gordon Campbell (Liberal)
Leader of the Opposition: Carole James
   (New Democratic Party)
Entered Confederation: July 20, 1871
Population: 4,380,256
Area: 366,255 sq mi (948,600 km²)

Manitoba
Capital: Winnipeg
Lieutenant Governor: John Harvard
Premier: Gary Albert Doer (New Democratic Party)
Leader of the Opposition: Hugh McFayden
   (Progressive Conservative)
Entered Confederation: July 15, 1870
Population: 1,186,679
Area: 251,000 sq mi (650,090 km²)

New Brunswick
Capital: Fredericton
Lieutenant Governor: Herménégilde Chiasson
Premier: Shawn M. Graham (Liberal)
Leader of the Opposition: Jeannot Volpé
   (Progressive Conservative)
Entered Confederation: July 1, 1867
Population: 749,782
Area: 28,354 sq mi (73,436 km²)

Newfoundland and Labrador
Capital: St. John's
Lieutenant Governor: Edward M. Roberts
Premier: Danny Williams (Progressive Conservative)
Leader of the Opposition: Yvonne Jones (Liberal)
Entered Confederation: March 31, 1949
Population: 506,275
Area: 156,185 sq mi (404,517 km²)

Nova Scotia
Capital: Halifax
Lieutenant Governor: Mayann E. Francis
Premier: Rodney Macdonald (Progressive Conservative)
Leader of the Opposition: Darrell Dexter (New
   Democratic Party)
Entered Confederation: July 1, 1867
Population: 934,147
Area: 21,425 sq mi (55,491 km²)

Ontario
Capital: Toronto
Lieutenant Governor: David C. Onley
Premier: Dalton McGuinty (Liberal)
Leader of the Opposition: Robert W. Runciman
   (Progressive Conservative)
Entered Confederation: July 1, 1867
Population: 12,803,861
Area: 412,582 sq mi (1,068,582 km²)

Prince Edward Island
Capital: Charlottetown
Lieutenant Governor: Barbara A. Hagerman
Premier: Robert W. J. Ghiz (Liberal)
Leader of the Opposition: Olive Crane (Progressive
   Conservative)
Entered Confederation: July 1, 1873
Population: 138,627
Area: 2,184 sq mi (5,657 km²)

Quebec
Capital: Quebec City
Lieutenant Governor: Pierre Duchesne
Premier: Jean Charest (Liberal)
Leader of the Opposition: Mario Dumont
    (Action démocratique du Québec)
Entered Confederation: July 1, 1867
Population: 7,700,807
Area: 594,860 sq mi (1,540,700 km^2)

Saskatchewan
Capital: Regina
Lieutenant Governor: Gordon Barnhart
Premier: Brad Wall (Saskatchewan Party)
Leader of the Opposition: Lorne Calvert
    (New Democratic Party)
Entered Confederation: Sept. 1, 1905
Population: 996,869
Area: 251,700 sq mi (651,900 km^2)

Yukon
Capital: Whitehorse
Commissioner: Geraldine Van Bibber

Premier: Dennis Fentie (Yukon Party)
Leader of the Opposition: Arthur Mitchell (Liberal)
Organized as a Territory: June 13, 1898
Population: 30,989
Area: 186,299 sq mi (482,515 km^2)

Northwest Territories
Capital: Yellowknife
Commissioner: Antony W.J. (Tony) Whitford
Premier: Floyd Roland
Reconstituted as a Territory: Sept. 1, 1905
Population: 42,637
Area: 468,000 sq mi (1,170,000 km^2)

Nunavut
Capital: Iqaluit
Commissioner: Ann Meekitjuk Hanson
Government Leader: Paul Okalik
Organized as a Territory: April 1, 1999
Population: 31,113
Area: 797,600 sq mi (1,994,000 km^2)

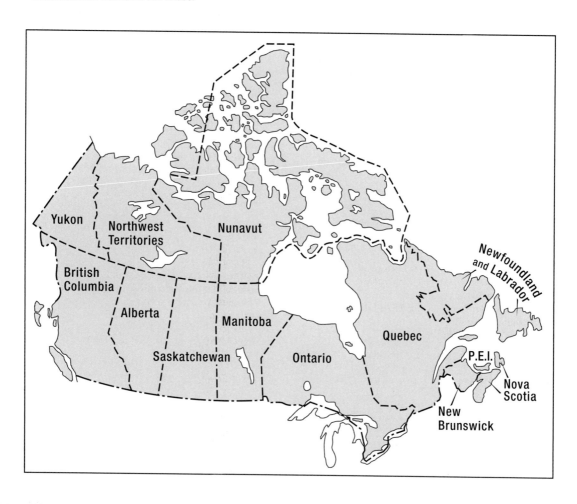

INDEX

A

Abbas, Mahmoud (Palestinian president) 39, 66, *picture* 66

Abdallahi, Sidi Ould Cheikh (president of Mauritania) 22

Abdullah II (king of Jordan) 66

Abe, Shinzo (premier of Japan) 35, 72

Academy Awards 260–61, *pictures* 260, 261

Accidents and disasters
bridge collapse (Minnesota) 32, *picture* 32
cyclone (Bangladesh) 38
drought (southeastern U.S.) 36
earthquake (Peru) 32
oil spills 39
tornado (Kansas) 26
tornadoes (Florida) 20
Virginia Tech mass shooting 25
wildfires (California) 38
wildfires (Greece) 33, *pictures* 33

Adams, Amy (American actress) 265, *picture* 265

Adams, Gerry (Northern Ireland political leader) 22

Aesthetic Movement (in art) 269

Afghanistan 42–43, 384

Africa 29 *see also* names of countries

African Americans
Brown, James, death of 378
Browne, Roscoe Lee, death of 378–79
Jamestown 200, 203
Little Rock desegregation, 50th anniversary of 169
Robinson, Jackie 192
Winfrey, Oprah 68

African Union (AU) 67

Agriculture 84–85, 107, 232, 239, 371–75

Agriculture, Department of (United States) 36

Ahmadinejad, Mahmoud (president of Iran) 46, 47, *picture* 47

Airplanes *see* Aviation

Alabama 36

"Aladdin and the Wonderful Lamp" (story) 304–11

Albania 29, 30, 384

Alberta (province, Canada) 394

Aldean, Jason (American musician) 280–81

Aldrin, Buzz (American astronaut) 22

Algeria 384

Alice's Adventures in Wonderland (book by Lewis Carroll) 287

Al Qaeda (Muslim terrorist group) 42, 43, 45, 46, 51

Alternative energy sources 108–9, 283

Amber 133

American Museum of Natural History (New York City) 86

Ammonites (ancient mollusks), *picture* 132

Anaheim Ducks (hockey team) 183–85

Anderson, Clayton (American astronaut) 28, 38

Andorra 384

Angel Network 68

Angola 384

Animal behavior 76–83

Animals *see also* Birds; Dogs; Fish; Insects; Mammals; Pets
colossal squid 20, *picture* 20
feet and hands 339–44
fossils 132, 133, 136
mythical animals 86–91
names that describe animals 92–93
play 76–83
spider web, enormous 35, *picture* 35
stamps and coins depicting 159, 168, 169

Animation 264–65

Annan, Kofi (secretary-general of the United Nations) 18

Anniversaries
Carroll, Lewis, 175th anniversary of his birth 287
Circus Smirkus, 20th anniversary of 250
Diana, princess of Wales, 10th anniversary of death of 73
Earhart, Amelia, 75th anniversary of transatlantic flight of 208
European Union, 50th anniversary of 18
Fulton's steamboat, 200th anniversary of 112
Jamestown, 400th anniversary of founding of 27, 152, 156, 169, 197, 198–203, *pictures* 196–97, 198, 200
Little Rock desegregation, 50th anniversary of 169
Robinson, Jackie, 60th anniversary of his breaking of baseball's color barrier 192
Roosevelt, Franklin D., 125th birthday of 222
Scouting movement, 100th anniversary of 157–58, 169
"smiley face" emoticon, 25th anniversary of 34
Space Age, 50th anniversary of 139, 169
Stauffenberg, Claus von, 100th anniversary of birth of 290
Thayendanegea (Joseph Brant), 200th anniversary of death of 169
Vietnam Veterans Memorial, 25th anniversary of 284

Antarctica 136

Antelope 76

Antigua and Barbuda 384

Antonioni, Michelangelo (Italian movie director) 378

Apes, giant 88

Aqualung (music group) 278

Arabian Nights 304

Arborists 238–39

Arcade Fire (music group) 278, *picture* 278

Archaeology
Blackbeard's ship 226, 229
Chichén Itzá 214
Earhart, Amelia, search for her plane 209
Herod's tomb, *picture* 26
hugging skeletons 21, *picture* 21
Kidd, William, ship 40
Jamestown (Virginia) 201
Machu Picchu 215
Petra (Jordan) 213

Archambault. Lee (American astronaut) 28
Architecture
    Grand Canyon Skywalk, *picture* 22
    green roofs 234
    New Seven Wonders of the World 212–15
    Phare Tower 283
Arcimboldo, Giuseppe (Italian artist) 285
Arctic Monkeys (music group) 278
Are You Smarter Than a 5th Grader?
    (television program) 287
Argentina 36, 135, 384
Arizona, *picture* 22
Arkansas 169, *picture* 230–31
Armenia 384
Arthur, Chester A. (21st president of the
    United States) 270
Art Nouveau (art movement) 270–71, 273
Arts
    Arcimboldo, Giuseppe 285
    Christ the Redeemer (statue) 215, *picture*
        215
    Monet's water-lily paintings 125
    Tiffany, Louis Comfort 156–57, 268–73
Asia-Pacific Economic Cooperation (APEC)
    summit meeting 34
Assateague Island 31
Asteroids 140
Astley, Philip (English circus performer) 252
Astor, Brooke (American philanthropist) 378
Atlantis (space shuttle) 28, 138, 140
Aung San Suu Kyi (political figure in Myanmar)
    64
Aurora borealis (Northern Lights) 140, *picture*
    142
Austen, Jane (British author) 266
Australia 34, 39, 94–97, 120, 159, 384
Australian sea slugs 93, *picture* 93
Austria 18, 383, 384
Automobiles and global warming 109
Avatars (in video games) 56
Avery, John (Long Ben) (British pirate) 228
Aviation 208–11
Awards *see* Prizes and awards
Azerbaijan 384

B

Babies, cuteness of 100, *picture* 100
Bacteria 136
Baghdad (Iraq) 48, 49, 50
Bahamas 384
Bahrain 384
Bakhit, Marouf al- (prime minister of Jordan) 39
Bald eagles, *picture* 98
Baldwin, Alec (American actor), *picture* 275
Banderas, Antonio (Spanish actor) 262
Bangladesh 38, 229, 384
Ban Ki-moon (secretary-general of the United
    Nations) 18
Barbados 384
Bareilles, Sara (American musician) 276
Barnum, P. T. (American showman) 90, 252
Barroso, José Manuel (EU Commission
    President), *picture* 29

Barrymore, Drew (American actress) 266
Baseball 172–74
    Little League 175
    Rizzuto, Phil, death of 382
    Robinson, Jackie 192
    Wagner, Honus 195
Baseball cards 195
Basketball 176–78
Batista, Fulgencio (Cuban dictator) 59
Bats (animals) 80
Bay of Pigs Invasion (Cuba) 59
Beanie Babies 220, *picture* 220
Bears 80, 81, 83, 109, *picturea* 81, 99, 109
Beckett, Josh (American athlete) 172, 173
Beckham, David (British athlete) 190–91,
        picture 191
Becoming Jane (movie) 266, *picture* 266
Bee Movie (movie) 264
Bees 84–85
Beetles 92, 125–26, *picture* 92
Belarus 384
Belgium 159, 384
Belize 384
Benin 384
Beowulf (movie) 264–65
Berdymukhamedov, Kurbanguly (president of
    Turkmenistan) 20
Berger Perdomo, Oscar (president of
    Guatemala) 39
Bergman, Ingmar (Swedish movie director) 378
Berlin (Germany) 366–69
Bermuda 169
Beyoncé (American singer), *picture* 261
Bhutan 384
Bhutto, Benazir (prime minister of Pakistan) 44
Bigfoot (legendary ape-man) 88
Bindi: The Jungle Girl (TV program) 244
BioSuit 141
Birdhouses 146, 147–48, *pictures* 147, 148
Birds
    backyard bird watching 146–51
    bald eagles. *picture* 98
    cassowaries 93, *picture* 93
    coins depicting 169
    dinosaurs, relation to 135
    jacanas nest on lily pads 124
    mythical birds 90
    penguins 324–28, *picture* 100
    play 76, 78, 83
    seabirds killed by oil spills 39
Bishop, Joey (American comedian) 378
Blackbeard (British pirate) 226, 228–29, *picture*
        227
Blackwater USA 51
Blair, Tony (British prime minister) 28, 70,
        pictures 29, 70
Blige, Mary J. (American singer) 279
Blogs (Web logs) (computer journals) 54–55
Blonsky, Nikki (American actress) 266, *picture*
        266
Bloom, Orlando (British actor) 262
Bluebirds 147, *picture* 147
Blunt, James (British singer) 277
Boats and boating *see* Steamboats
Bolivia 384
Bolton, John (United States ambassador to the
    United Nations) 24

Bombings
Iraq War 49
London (England) terrorism attempt 30
"Plot Against Hitler, The" (story) 290–301
Bonds, Barry (American athlete) 173
Bon Jovi (music group) 281
Bon Jovi, Jon (American musician), *picture* 277
Books *see* Literature; Young people's literature
Bosnia and Herzegovina 384
Boston Legal (television program), *picture* 275
Boston Red Sox (baseball team) 172–73
Botanists 232
Botswana 384
Bourne Ultimatum, The (movie) 263, *picture* 263
Brady, Tom (American athlete), *picture* 180
Brant, Joseph (Native American) 169
Braun, Ryan (American athlete) 173
Brazil 22, 190, 191, 215, 229, 384, *picture* 215
Bread, superstitions about 206–7
Breslin, Abigail (American actress) 267, *picture* 245
Brewer, Corey (American athlete) 178
Bridge collapse (Minnesota) 32, *picture* 32
Bridge Over a Pool of Water Lilies (painting by Claude Monet) 125, *picture* 125
Bridge to Terabithia (movie) 263
Bright-light therapy 129, *picture* 129
British Columbia (province, Canada) 394
Broadband systems 52–53, 56
Brodeur, Martin (Canadian athlete) 185
Brown, Chris (American singer) 279
Brown, Gordon (British prime minister) 28, 50, 70, *picture* 70
Brown, James (American singer) 378, *picture* 378
Browne, Roscoe Lee (American actor) 378–79
Brunei Darussalam 384
Bryant, Kobe (American athlete) 178
Buccaneers (pirates) 227
Buchwald, Art (American humorist) 379
Buddhism 64
Budget, national (United States) 19
Bulgaria 18, 29, 384
Bullet trains 24, *picture* 24
Burckhardt, Johann Ludwig (Swiss traveler) 213
Burkina Faso 384
Burma (Myanmar) 64, 384
Burundi 384
Bush, George W. (43rd president of the United States)
APEC summit 34
Canada and Mexico, meeting with leaders of 32
Elizabeth II's U.S. visit 27
Europe, trip to 29, *picture* 29
Florida, federal aid to 20
Iraq War 18, 48, 51
Jamestown, 400th anniversary of 203
Khalilzad, Zalmay, appointed as United Nations ambassador by 24
Kyoto Protocol 110
Latin America, trip to 22
Middle East peace conference 39, *picture* 66
minimum-wage increase 26

Mukasey, Michael, named Attorney General by 34
Peake, James, nominated Veterans Affairs secretary by 36
Schafer, Edward, nominated Agriculture secretary by 36
State of the Union address 19, *picture* 19
Bush, Laura (wife of George W. Bush) 22, 27, 203

C

Cabbage Patch Kids (dolls) 220, *picture* 220
Cabinet, United States 393
Cable News Network (CNN) 53
Caillat, Colbie (American musician) 276, *picture* 278
Caldecott Medal (children's literature) 302, 303
Calderón, Felipe (president of Mexico) 22, 32
Caldwell, Tracy (American astronaut) 32
California 38, 39, 111, 120, 234, *picture* 18
Cambodia 384
Camels 136
Cameroon 385
Camping, organized 250–51
Canada 385
coins 169
football 180
Group of Eight 29
Harper's meeting with Bush and Calderón 32
Pan American Games 190
provinces and territories 394–95
space program 32
stamps 157–58, 159
"Cap-and-trade" systems 109
Capecchi, Mario R. (American scientist) 37
Cape Verde 385
Captain John Smith Chesapeake National Historic Trail 199
Carbon dioxide 106, 109, 234
Carbon footprint, reducing 111
Carbon sequestration 109
Careers in plants 232–39
Carell, Steve (American actor) 241, *picture* 240
Carriker, Dalton (American athlete) 175, *picture* 175
Carroll, Lewis (English writer) 287, *picture* 287
Cars *see* Automobiles
Cassini (spacecraft) 142–43
Cassowaries (birds) 93, *picture* 93
Castro, Fidel (president of Cuba) 58, 59–61, *picture* 58
Castro, Raúl (acting president of Cuba) 58, 60–61, *picture* 60
Cats 23, 78–79, 82
Cell phones 53, 57
Central African Republic 385
Ceres (asteroid) 140
Chad 67, 136, 385
Chan, Jackie (Chinese actor) 241
Chang Chun-hsiung (premier of Taiwan) 27
Chang'e 1 (space probe) 140

Charles Hosmer Morse Museum of American Art (Winter Park, Florida) 272
Chaudhry, Iftikhar Muhammad (Pakistani jurist) 44
Chávez, Hugo (president of Venezuela) 63–64, *picture* 63
Cheerleading 194, *picture* 194
Cheetahs 76, 79
Chemistry, Nobel Prize in 37
Chen, Steve (American co-founder of YouTube) 53
Cheney, Dick (vice president of the United States), *pictures* 19, 27
Chicago (Illinois) 234
Chicago Bears (football team) 179–80
Chichén Itzá (Mexico) 214, *picture* 214
Chickadees, *picture* 150
Child development 28
Children *see* Youth
Chile 385
Chimera (mythical monster) 91
Chimpanzees 78, 82
China 385
    APEC summit 34
    coins 169
    dinosaur fossils 135
    dog nursing tiger cubs, *picture* 99
    global warming 110
    Great Wall 213, *picture* 213
    ice cream, history of 116
    koalas in zoo 97
    Korea, North, talks with 65
    mythical animals 87, 91
    pandas 75, *picture* 74–75
    product safety concerns 23
    space program 140, 143
    water lilies and lotuses 127
    women's World Cup 191
Chincoteague Wild Pony Swim 31
Chinese New Year, stamps and coins commemorating 158, 169
Chipmunks 78
Chirac, Jacques (president of France) 26, 71, *picture* 71
Cho Seung-Hui (Korean-born American mass shooter) 25
Christ the Redeemer (statue) 215, *picture* 215
Church, Thomas Haden (American actor) 262
Churchill, Sir Winston (British statesman), *picture* 225
Circus, history of the 252
Circus Smirkus (circus training program) 250–53
Claiborne, Liz (American fashion designer) 379, *picture* 378
Claremont (Clermont) (Fulton's steamboat) 112–15, *pictures* 104–5, 112, 115
Clarkson, Kelly (American singer) 276–77
Cleveland Cavaliers (basketball team) 176–78
Climate 34, 40, 69, 106–11, 136–37
Clinton, Bill (42nd president of the United States) 110
Clinton Climate Initiative (CCI) 110
Clooney, George (American actor) 263
Clothing and fashion
    Claiborne, Liz, death of 379

Coin collecting 168–69
Cold War (in international relations) 59, 60
Cole, Keyshia (American musician) 279
Collared peccaries 81–82
Colombia 22, 385
Colom Caballeros, Alvaro (president of Guatemala) 39
Colony collapse disorder [of honeybees] 85
Color 131
Colorado Rockies (baseball team) 172–73
Colossal squid (animals) 20, 89, *picture* 20
Colosseum (Rome) 214, *picture* 214
Columbus (space station module) 140
Columbus, Christopher (Italian explorer) 89
Comic books, stamps commemorating 157
Communication
    animals' play language 82
    World Wide Web 52–57
Communications satellites 139
Communism 58, 59, 60
Comoros 385
Compact discs (CD's) 279
Computers 34 *see also* Internet; World Wide Web
Congo (Zaire) 385
Congo Republic 385
Congress of the United States 49, 51, 390–92
    see also House of Representatives; Senate
Continental drift 137
Cook Islands 169
Cooperative Extension Service 233
Costa, Heitor da Silva (Brazilian engineer) 215
Costa Rica 385
Country music 280–81
Cox, Charlie (British actor) 264
Cracker Jack (snack food) 217, *picture* 217
Crafts *see* Arts; Hobbies, handicrafts, and projects
Crime 229 *see also* Terrorism
Crist, Charlie (governor of Florida) 20
Croatia 385
Crocker, Ryan (U.S. ambassador to Iraq) 49
Crosby, Sidney (Canadian athlete) 185, *picture* 184
Crow, Sheryl (American singer) 110
Cuba 58–61, 63, 190, 385
Cuban missile crisis 59
Cultivars (new varieties of plants) 232, 233
Cuteness 100
Cyclones 38
Cyprus 385
Cyrus, Billy Ray (American singer) 244
Cyrus, Miley (American actress and singer), *picture* 244
Czech Republic 29, 385

D

Dahabi, Nader al- (prime minister of Jordan) 39
Dale, Sir Thomas (English governor of Jamestown) 200
Dall sheep, *picture* 80

Damon, Matt (American actor) 263, *picture* 263
Dance, stamps commemorating 159
Danes, Claire (American actress) 264
Darfur (region in Sudan) 67
Darwin, Charles (British naturalist) 136
Daughtry, Chris (American singer) 278
David, Laurie (American producer) 110
Dawn (space probe) 140, *picture* 142
De la Warr, Thomas West, 3rd Baron (colonial governor of Virginia) 200
Democratic Party (of the United States) 19
Dempsey, Patrick (American actor) 266, *picture* 265
Denmark 45, 120, 385
Departed, The (movie), *picture* 260
Depp, Johnny (American actor) 262
Depression (mental state) 128–29
Depression of the 1930's 223–24
Desegregation 169
Detroit Shock (basketball team) 178
De Villepin, Dominique (premier of France) 27
Diana (Princess of Wales) 73, *picture* 73
DiCaprio, Leonardo (American actor) 110, *pictures* 110, 260
Dinosaurs 86, 91, 135, 136, 169, 282, *pictures* 282
    animatronic show 282, *pictures* 282
    coins depicting 169
    fossils 135, 136
    mythical creatures based on 86, 91
Disarmament 345–46
Disasters *see* Accidents and disasters
Discovery (ship) 198
Discovery (space shuttle) 38, 138, 139, *picture* 138
Disney characters, stamps depicting 157
District of Columbia *see* Washington (D.C.)
Djibouti 385
DJ Khaled (American disc jockey) 280
DNA (Deoxyribonucleic acid) (in body cells) 133
Dogs
    pet-food recall 23
    play 78, 82, 83, *picture* 83
    tiger cubs nursed by, *picture* 99
    Westminster Kennel Club show, *picture* 101
    Yorkshire terriers, *picture* 101
Dolls 220, *picture* 220
Dolphins 76, 78, 79–80, 83, *picture* 79
Dominica 385
Dominican Republic 385
Dragons (mythical animals) 86, 91, *pictures* 86, 91
Dreamgirls (movie) 267
Drew, Benjamin, Jr. (American astronaut) 32
Driscoll, Clara (American glassworker) 272, *picture* 272
Drnovsek, Janez (president of Slovenia) 39
Drought 36
Drug industry 237
Duff, Hilary (American singer-actress) 277
Duncan, Ryan (American athlete) 185
Duncan, Tim (American athlete) 176, 178
Dunst, Kirsten (American actress) 262
Dyes and dyeing 127

E

Eagles, *picture* 98
Earhart, Amelia (American aviator) 208–11, *pictures* 208, 209, 210
Earth (planet) 106–11
Earthquakes 32
East Timor 26, 385
Eckhart, Aaron (American actor) 267, *picture* 267
Ecology *see* Environment
Economics
    Group of Eight 29
    minimum-wage increase 26
    Nobel Prizes 37
Eco-roofs 234
Ecuador 385
Education
    Intel Science Talent Search winner, *picture* 246
    National Geographic Bee winner, *picture* 243
    National Spelling Bee winner, *picture* 247
    Oprah Winfrey's schools for girls in Africa 68
    podcasting programs 56
Efron, Zac (American actor) 266, 283, *picture* 243
Egypt 66, 329–35, 385
Egypt, ancient 126–27
Elections *see* Presidents (of the United States)
Elephants 78, 81, *picture* 80
11th Hour, The (movie) 110
Elizabeth II (queen of the United Kingdom) 27, 203, *picture* 27
Elliott, Missy (American singer) 279
El Niño (Pacific Ocean current) 20
El Salvador 385
E-mail 34
Emmy Awards 274–75
Emoticons, *picture* 34
Enchanted (movie) 265–66, *picture* 265
Endangered species
    bald eagles removed from list 98
    koalas 94, 96–97
    polar bears 109
Endeavour (space shuttle) 32, 139, *picture* 140
Endophytes 237
Energy efficiency 34, 109, 283
Engines, steam 114
England *see* United Kingdom
English language 18
English springer spaniels, *picture* 101
Environment 39, 106–11, 277
Equatorial Guinea 385
Eragon (movie) 263
Erdogan, Recep Tayyip (prime minister of Turkey) 46
Eritrea 385
Ertl, Gerhard (German scientist) 37
Eskimo Pie 121
Estonia 385
Ethiopia 385
Eucalyptus trees 94, 95, 96
Europa stamps 158
Europe 29 *see also* names of countries
European Organization for Nuclear Research (CERN) 52

European Union (EU) 18
Evans, Martin J. (British scientist) 37
Everest, Mount 192
Everett, Rupert (British actor) 262
Evolution 136
Exercise, video-game, *picture* 230–31
Extinct species 136
mammoth carcass, *picture* 30

F

Fabolous (American rapper) 280
Fabric collage, how to make, *picture* 144–45
Facebook (Web site) 56, *picture* 57
Fads 216–21
Fahlman, Scott (American professor),
picture 34
Fall Out Boy (music group) 278, *picture* 276
Fanning, Dakota (American actress),
picture 241
Farming *see* Agriculture
Fashion *see* Clothing and fashion
Fassi, Abbas el (premier of Morocco) 35
Faust, Drew Gilpin (American historian) 72,
picture 72
Favre, Brett (American athlete), *picture* 179
Favrile (iridescent glass) 270
Federer, Roger (Swiss athlete) 188, 189,
pictures 170–71, 188
Feeders (for birds) 146, 148–51, *pictures* 149,
150, 151
Feeling, The (music group) 279
Feet and hands 339–44
Feist (Canadian musician) 277
Ferdinand and Isabella (Spanish monarchs) 336
Fergie (American singer) 280
Fernández de Kirchner, Cristina (president of
Argentina) 36
Ferrera, America (American actress), *picture*
275
Fert, Albert (French scientist) 37
Fey, Tina (American actress), *picture* 275
Fiennes, Ralph (British actor) 257
Fiji 385
File sharing 279
Fillon, François (premier of France) 27
Finger crossing (superstition) 205
Finland 158, 385
Finsen, Niels R. (Danish researcher) 130
Fires 33, 38, *pictures* 33
Fireside chats (Roosevelt's radio talks) 224
First Spouse coin series 168
Fish fossil, *picture* 132
Fitch, John (American inventor) 112–13
Flooding 107
Floriculturists 238
Florida 20, 59, 61
Florida, University of 178
Florists 238
Flotsam (book by David Wiesner) 303
Flower importers 238
Flowers

gardening to attract birds 146–47
plants, careers in 233, 238
stamps commemorating 157
water lilies 122–27
Folklore 204–7
Folk tales
"Aladdin and the Wonderful Lamp" (story)
304–11
"Robin Hood and the Shooting Match" (story)
314–22
Food
Cracker Jack 217, *picture* 217
feeding birds 148–51
fruits and fruit growing 371–75
ice cream 116–21
recipes 166–67
stamps commemorating 159
word puzzles about 160–61
Food and Drug Administration, United States 23
Foo Fighters (music group) 278
Football 179–81
"Forever" stamps 156
Forrester, Patrick (American astronaut) 28
Fossett, Steve (American adventurer) 379
Fossil fuels 106–7, 108
Fossils *see* Archaeology; Paleontology
Foxworthy, Jeff (American comedian) 287
Foxx, Jamie (American actor) 267
France 385
bullet train 24, *picture* 24
government change 26–27
Group of Eight 29
leadership change 71
Monet's water-lily paintings 125
Phare Tower 283
stamps 158
Fratellis (music group) 279
Freedom Writers (movie) 267, *picture* 267
Freezers, ice-cream 118
Frisbees 216, *picture* 216
Frog, fossil, *picture* 133
Fruits and fruit growing 371–75
feeding birds 149, 150–51
word puzzles about 160–61
Fry, Jordan (American actor) 264
Fukuda, Yasuo (premier of Japan) 35, 72, *picture*
72
Fulton, Robert (American inventor) 105, 112–15
Furtado, Nelly (Canadian singer) 280

G

Gabon 385
Gambia 385
Games *see* Toys and games
Gandolfini, James (American actor), *picture* 274
Gardens 146–47, 234, 235
Garuda (mythical creature) 90
Gates, Sir Thomas (lieutenant governor of
Jamestown) 200
Gaza Strip 65, 66
Gebrselassie, Haile (Ethiopian athlete) 193,
picture 194

Gelato, *picture* 121
Genes 37
Geographic Bee, National, winner, *picture* 243
Geology *see* Earth (planet)
Georgia (republic) 385
Georgia (U.S. state) 36, *picture* 36
Gerbils 347
Germany 348–64, 385
    Berlin 366–69
    Group of Eight 29
    "Plot Against Hitler, The" (story) 290–301
    polar bear cub, *picture* 99
    terrorist plot discovery 34, 45
    women's World Cup 191
    World War II 224–25
Ghana 386
Giant magnetoresistance (GMR) 37
Gigantoraptor erlianensis 135
Gilded Age (in American history) 271
Ginobili, Manu (Argentine athlete) 176, 178
Giraffe beetles 92, *picture* 92
Glaciers 107, 108
Glass, decorative 268–73
Global Positioning System *see* GPS
Global warming 34, 37, 69, 106–11, 234, 277
Glover, Crispin (American actor) 265
Goats 81
Godspeed (ship) 198, 202
Golden Compass, The (movie) 263, *picture* 263
Golf 182
Gone Wild: An Endangered Animal Alphabet
    (book by David McLimans) 303
Gonzales, Alberto R. (United States Attorney
    General) 34
Good Humor ice cream 121
Gore, Al (American politician) 37, 69, 110, 277,
    picture 69
Gorillas 78, 82
Goulet, Robert (American entertainer) 379
Governors of the states of the United States
    393
GPS (Global Positioning System) 57
Grammy Awards 281
Grand Canyon Skywalk (Arizona), *picture* 22
Grandmaster Flash and the Furious Five
    (music group) 281
Grant, Hugh (British actor) 266
Gray, Macy (American singer) 279–80
Great Britain *see* United Kingdom
Great Wall of China 213, *picture* 213
Greece 33, 386, *pictures* 33
Greece, ancient 87, 90–91, 134
Greenhouse effect 106, 109
Green roofs 234
Grenada 386
Griffin, Merv (American talk-show host) 379,
    picture 379
Griffins (mythical creatures) 91
Grint, Rupert (British actor) 257, *pictures* 257,
    258
Grounds managers 237
Group of Eight summit meeting 29, *picture* 29
Grönberg, Peter (German scientist) 37
Guantánamo Bay (Cuba) 58, 61
Guatemala 22, 39, 386
Guinea 386

Guinea-Bissau 386
Guinea pigs 365
Gül, Abdullah (president of Turkey) 33, 46
Guns 25
Gusenbauer, Alfred (chancellor of Austria) 18
Gusmao, Kay Rala Xanana (president of East
    Timor) 26
Guyana 386
Gymnastics, *picture* 190

H

Hairspray (movie) 243, 266, *picture* 266
Haiti 386
Hamas (militant Arab group) 66
Hamsters 370
Hamwi, Ernest (inventor of the ice-cream cone)
    121
Handball 337–38
Handicrafts *see* Hobbies, handicrafts, and
    projects
Hannah Montana (TV program) 244
Hanson, Daniel (American actor) 264
Happiness 242
Harmony (space station module) 38, 139–40
Harper, Ben (American musician) 276
Harper, Stephen (prime minister of Canada) 32,
    picture 29
Harry (prince of England) 73, *picture* 73
Harry Potter and the Deathly Hallows (book by
    J. K. Rowling) 256, 259, *picture 254–55*
Harry Potter and the Order of the Phoenix
    (movie) 158, 257, 263
Harry Potter books (by J. K. Rowling) 158,
    256–59, *picture 254–55*
Harvard University 72
Hathaway, Anne (American actress) 266, *picture*
    266
Hattie Big Sky (book by Kirby Lawson) 303
Health *see* Medicine
"Heat island" effect 234
Henin, Justine (Belgian athlete) 188, 189, *picture*
    189
Henry, Marguerite (American author) 31
Herod I (the Great) (king of Judea) 26
Heroes (TV program) 245
Higher Power of Lucky, The (book by Susan
    Patron) 302
High School Musical 2 (movie) 243, 283, *picture*
    283
Hijackings *see* Terrorist attacks on the United
    States
Hill, Faith (American singer) 280
Hill, Lauryn (American singer) 279
Hip-hop music 279–80
Hippogriffs (mythical creatures) 91
Hippopotamuses 78, *picture* 82
History
    circus, history of the 252
    Cuba 58–61
    Earhart, Amelia 208–11
    Egypt 334–35
    fads 216–21

Ferdinand and Isabella 336
Fulton's steamboat 112–15, *picture* 104–5
Germany 358–64, 368–69
ice cream 116, 118, 119, 121
Iraq War 48–51
Islamic militants 42–47
Jamestown, 400th anniversary of founding of
  27, 152, 156, 197, 198–203, *pictures*
  196–97, 198, 200
New Seven Wonders of the World 212–15
pirates 226–29
"Plot Against Hitler, The" (story) 290–301
Roosevelt, Franklin D. 222–25
Schlesinger, Arthur M., Jr., death of 382
superstitions, history of 204–7
Tiffany, Louis Comfort 268–73
Hitler, Adolf (German dictator) 290–301
Ho, Don (American musician) 380
Hobaugh, Charles (American astronaut) 32
Hobbies, handicrafts, and projects
  backyard bird watching 146–51
  balloon pig 162–63
  baseball card collecting 195
  coin collecting 168–69
  cooking 166–67
  cowboy dolls 164–65
  dragonfly pins 165
  fabric collage, how to make, *picture* 144–45
  fish magnets 163–64
  paper stained glass 154–55
  racing figures 164
  stamp collecting 156–59
  word puzzles 152–53, 160–61
Hockey 183–85
Holliday, Matt (American athlete) 172
Holm, Jennifer L. (American author) 302–3
Honduras 386
Honeybees 84–85
Horses 31, 76–77, 82, *picture* 103
Horticulturists 232–33
House of Representatives, United States 69,
  391–92
Howard, John (prime minister of Australia) 34,
  39
Hudgens, Vanessa (American actress) 283
Hudson, Jennifer (American singer and
  actress) 267, *picture* 261
Hugging skeletons 21
Hu Jintao (president of China) 34
Hula-Hoops 218, *picture* 218
Hummingbirds 146–47, 151, *picture* 151
Hungary 386
Hurley, Chad (American co-founder of YouTube)
  53
Hurwicz, Leonid (American economist) 37
Hussein, Saddam (president of Iraq) 48, 51
Hutcherson, Josh (American actor) 263
Hyperion (moon of Saturn) 143

I

Ice, fossils in 133
Ice cream 116–21

Iceland 386
Ice sheets 107, 108
Ice skating 186
Idaho 168
Illegal aliens 22
Illinois 120, 257 *see also* Chicago
Immigration (to the United States) 22, 59, 60
Incas (Indians of South America) 215
Inconvenient Truth, An (movie) 37, 69, 110
India 30, 127, 212, 386, *picture* 212
Indiana 120
Indianapolis Colts (football team) 179–80
Indians, American *see* Native Americans
Indigo buntings (birds), *picture* 150
Indonesia 40, 45, 103, 229, 386
Information, Web site on 248
Infrared light 131
Insects 84–85, 92, 124, 125–26, 147, *picture* 92
Intel Science Talent Search winner, *picture*
  246
**Intergovernmental Panel on Climate Change
  (IPCC)** 37, 69, 106–10
Interior design 269–70
Interiorscaping 239
International Maritime Bureau 229
International Polar Year 108, 169
International Space Station (ISS) 28, 32, 38,
  138–40, *picture* 138
Internet 52–57, 248–49, 276, 279
Io (moon of Jupiter) 142
Iowa 120
iPod (digital music player) 56
Iran 46–47, 49, 50, 63, 386
Iraq 386
Iraq War (2003–) 18, 19, 43, 48–51
  Bush's visit to troops 34
  France 71
  United Kingdom 70
  U.S. soldier searching Baghdad home, *picture*
  12–13
Ireland 127, 159, 386
Ireland, Northern *see* Northern Ireland
Irwin, Bindi (Australian television personality),
  picture 244
Islam *see* Muslims; Taliban
Israel 28, 39, 65–66, 159, 386, *picture* 26
Italy 21, 29, 135, 214, 225, 386, *picture* 214
Ivory Coast 386

J–K

Jacanas (birds) 124
Jackson, Lauren (American athlete) 178
Jamaica 386
James, LeBron (American athlete) 177, 178
Jamestown (Virginia)
  400th anniversary of founding of 27, 152,
  156, 169, 197, 198–203, *pictures* 196–97,
  198, 200
Jane Austen Book Club, The (movie) 266
Janjaweed (Arab militia in Sudan) 67
Japan 386
  "child" robot 28

Group of Eight 29
ice-cream flavors 121
Korea, North, talks with 65
leadership change 35, 72
mythical animals 87
space program 140, 143
World War II 225
Jaundice 131
Jersey (Channel Islands, Great Britain) 158
Jerusalem (Israel) 65
Jettou, Driss (premier of Morocco) 35
Jewelry
dragonfly pins, how to make 165
Tiffany, Louis Comfort 273, *picture* 273
Jewels of the Jungle (movie) 237
Johanns, Mike (American public official) 36
Johnson, Lady Bird (American First Lady) 380,
picture 379
Johnson, Shawn (American athlete), *picture* 190
Jolie, Angelina (American actress) 265
Jones, Norah (American musician) 277
Jones, Ron (American stuntman) 241
Jordan 39, 66, 213, 386, *picture* 213
Jospin, Lionel (premier of France) 71
Joubert, Brian (French athlete), *picture* 186
Jukeboxes 218, *picture* 218
Jupiter (planet) 142
Jurassic Park (book and movie) 133
Kabbah, Ahmad Tejan (president of Sierra
Leone) 35
Kaczynski, Jaroslaw (premier of Poland) 36
Kaguya (space probe) 140
Kalam, A.P.J. Abdul (president of India) 30
Kansas 26
Katsav, Moshe (president of Israel) 28
Kazakhstan 386
Keas (parrots) 78
Kelly, R. (American singer) 280
Kelly, Scott (American astronaut) 32
Kennedy, John F. (35th president of the
United States) 59
Kentucky Derby (horse race) 27
Kenya 386
Kerr, Deborah (Scottish actress) 380, *picture*
380
Khalilzad, Zalmay (United States ambassador
to the United Nations) 24
Kidd, William (British pirate) 40, 228
Kidman, Nicole (Australian actress) 263
Kids' Choice Awards 240–41
Kim Yong Il (premier of North Korea) 24
Kingston, Sean (Jamaican musician) 276
Kirchner, Nestor (president of Argentina) 36
Kiribati 386
Kirkpatrick, Jeane (U.S. ambassador to the
United Nations) 380
Klaxons (music group) 278–79
Knievel, Evel (American motorcycle stuntman)
380–81, *picture* 380
Knightley, Keira (British actress) 262
Knocking on wood (superstition) 204
Knowles, Beyoncé (American singer) 267,
picture 261
Knut (polar bear cub), *picture* 99
Koalas 94–97, *pictures* 94, 95, 96, 97
Komodo dragons (lizards), *picture* 102

Korea, North 24, 64–65, 386
Korea, South 40, 65, 158, 386
Koroma, Ernest Bai (president of Sierra Leone)
35
Kosovo 63
Kraken (mythical animal) 88–89, *picture* 88
Kurds (a people of Iraq) 48, 49
Kuwait 386
Kyoto Protocol (on global warming) 110, 111
Kyrgyzstan 386

L

LaBeouf, Shia (American actor) 264
Labor productivity 129
Lamps, Tiffany 270, 273, *pictures* 269, 271, 272
Landowski, Paul (French sculptor) 215
Landscape architects 235–36
Landscape contractors 236–37
Landscape designers 235, 236
Language 18
Laos 386
Larson, Kirby (American author) 303
Larson, Samantha (American mountain climber)
192, *picture* 193
Latin America 22
Latvia 27, 386
Laudehr, Simone (German athlete) 191, *picture*
191
Laughter 82
Laurelton Hall (Tiffany's estate) 270
Lavigne, Avril (Canadian singer) 277
Leaf, fossil, *picture* 134
Lebanon 387
Legends *see* Myths and legends
L'Engle, Madeleine (American writer) 381
Leonardo da Vinci (Italian artist and inventor)
134
Lesotho 387
Lessing, Doris (British author) 37, *picture* 37
Liberia 67, 387
Libya 387
Lidstrom, Nicklas (Swedish athlete) 185, *picture*
184
Liechtenstein 387
Light, health effects of 128–31
Lil' Kim (American singer) 279
Lily pads 122
Lin, Maya (American architect) 284, *picture* 284
Lindbergh, Charles (American aviator) 209, 211
Linkin Park (music group) 277
Lions 79, 80, 81, *picture* 76
Literature *see also* Young people's literature
Mailer, Norman, death of 381
Nobel Prizes 37
Vonnegut, Kurt, death of 383
Lithuania 387
Litter, space 143
Little League baseball 175
Little Miss Sunshine (movie), *picture* 245
Little Red Spot (on Jupiter) 142

Little Rock (Arkansas) 169
Litvinenko, Alexander (Soviet intelligence
      agant) 62
Live Earth concerts 110, 277
Living history museums 201, *pictures* 203
Livingston, Robert R. (American merchant) 113
Lizards, *picture* 102
London (England) 30
Long, Elgen (American pilot) 209
Lopez, Jennifer (American actress and singer)
      276
Lord, Cynthia (American author) 302
Los Angeles Galaxy (soccer team) 190–91
Lötschberg Base Tunnel (Switzerland) 28
Lotuses 126–27
Louisiana Purchase Exposition (St. Louis,
      1904) 121, 273
Love 21, 159
Lowell, Mike (American athlete) 172, 173,
      picture 172
Lugovoi, Andrei (Russian businessman) 62
Luxembourg 387

M

Macaques (monkeys) 78, *picture* 78
Macedonia 387
Machu Picchu (Peru) 215, *picture* 215
Madagascar 387
Maguire, Tobey (American actor) 241, 262,
      pictures 240, 262
Mailer, Norman (American writer) 381,
      picture 381
Maine 257
Malawi 387
Malaysia 387
Maldives 387
Mali 387
Malietoa Tanumafili II (head of state of
      Samoa) 28
Malkin, Evgeni (Russian athlete) 185
Malta 387
Mammals *see also* Dogs; Rodents
      koalas 94–97
      mammoth carcass, *picture* 30
      manatees, *picture* 100
      miniature horse, *picture* 103
      night (owl) monkeys 92
      orangutans 376, *picture* 103
      pandas 75, *pictures* 74–75, 100
      play 76
      polar bear cub, *picture* 99
      tigers, *pictures* 99, 103
      wild ponies 31
Mammoths 134, *picture* 30
Man, Isle of 169
Manatees 89, *pictures* 89, 100
Manitoba (province, Canada) 394
Manning, Peyton (American athlete) 180
Marathon 193
Marine life 20
Maroon 5 (music group) 276
Mars (planet) 141

Marshall Islands 387
Mars Phoenix Lander 141–42, *picture* 142
Mars Reconnaissance Orbiter 142
Marsupials 94–97
Marvel Comics, stamps commemorating 157
Maryland 31
Maskin, Eric (American economist) 37
Masterman, Mary (American student), *picture*
      246
Mastracchio, Richard (American astronaut) 32
Mathematics, Web site on 249
Mauritania 22, 387
Mauritius 158, 387
Maya (Indians of North America) 214
McAvoy, James (British actor) 266
McCartney, Paul (British musician) 279
McGraw, Tim (American singer) 280
McGuinness, Martin (deputy first minister of
      Northern Ireland) 22
McKenna, Lori (American musician) 280
McLimans, David (American author and
      illustrator) 303
Mechanism design theory 37
Medicine
      light, uses of 128–31
      Nobel Prizes 37
      water lilies, uses of 127
      "wonder drugs" 237
Meet the Robinsons (movie) 264
Meissner, Kimmie (American athlete), *picture*
      186
Melamine 23
Melatonin 128
Melroy, Pamela (American astronaut) 38, 138
Menotti, Gian Carlo (Italian-born American
      composer) 381
Merkel, Angela (German chancellor),
      picture 29
Mermaids (mythical creatures) 89–90, *picture* 89
Mermin, Rob (American circus instructor) 250
Methane 109
Metropolitan Museum of Art (New York City)
      270
Mexico 22, 32, 214, 387, *picture* 214
M.I.A. (British rapper) 280
Mice 37, 78
Michigan 234
Michigan State University 185
Micronesia 387
Middle Ages 87, 91
Middle East 38–39, 66
Mika (British singer) 277
Military *see* Iraq War
Minimum wage 26
Minneapolis (Minnesota) 32, *picture* 32
Minnesota 32, 120, *picture* 32
Mint, United States 168
Mirren, Helen (British actress), *picture* 261
Mirrors, superstition about 204–5
Missiles, defense against 29, 30, 62–63
Mississippi River 32, *picture* 32
Misty of Chincoteague (book by Marguerite
      Henry) 31
Moisiu, Alfred (president of Albania) 30
Moldova 387
Monaco 387

Monet, Claude (French painter) 125
Money see Coin collecting
Mongolia 387
Monkeys 78, 82, 83, 92, *picture* 78, *picture* 92
Monks, Buddhist 64
Montana 135, 168
Montenegro 387
Moon 140, 141
Moore, Mandy (American singer and actress) 241
Morgan, Barbara (American astronaut) 32, 139, *picture* 140
Morgan, Henry (British pirate) 228
Morocco 35, 387
Mosaics (art form) 272
Moses: When Harriet Tubman Led Her People to Freedom (book by Carole Boston Weatherford) 303
MoSoSo (network interface) 57
Mosul (Iraq) 49
Motion capture (movie technology) 264–65
Motion pictures 262–67
    Academy Awards 260–61
    Antonioni, Michelangelo, death of 378
    Bergman, Ingmar, death of 378
    Browne, Roscoe Lee, death of 378–79
    Efron, Zac, *picture* 243
    High School Musical 2 283
    Kerr, Deborah, death of 380
    Wyman, Jane, death of 383
Motorcycles 380–81
Mountain climbing 192
Mountain goats 77–78, 82, 83, *picture* 77
Mozambique 387
Mukasey, Michael (United States Attorney General) 34, *picture* 393
Murphy, Eddie (American actor) 262
Musharraf, Pervez (president of Pakistan) 44–45, *picture* 44
Music 276–81
    Brown, James, death of 378
    concert in memory of Diana, Princess of Wales 73
    Goulet, Robert, death of 379
    Ho, Don, death of 380
    jukeboxes 218, *picture* 218
    Menotti, Gian Carlo, death of 381
    Pavarotti, Luciano, death of 381
    Rostropovich, Mstislav, death of 382
    Sills, Beverly, death of 382–83
Music and Lyrics (movie) 266
Muslims
    Iraq War 48, 49, 50
    Khalilzad, Zalmay, highest-ranking Muslim in U.S. government 24
    militants 42–47
    terrorist suspects 30, 34
Myanmar see Burma
Myers, Mike (Canadian actor) 262
Myerson, Roger (American economist) 37
MySpace (Web site) 56, 276, *picture* 57
Myths and legends
    fossils, legends about 134
    mythical animals 86–91
    "Robin Hood and the Shooting Match" 314–22

N

Nadal, Rafael (Spanish athlete) 171, 189
Naked Brothers Band, The (TV program), *picture* 247
Names (of animals) 92–93
Namibia 159, 387
Nancy Drew (movie) 263
Narwhals (whales) 87, *picture* 87
Native Americans
    fossils, legends about 134
    Grand Canyon Skywalk, *picture* 22
    Jamestown 199, 200, 201, 202, 203
    water lilies 124
Nauru 387
Nauticos (company) 209
Nectar (of flowers) 85, 124
Nelson, Kadir (American illustrator) 303
Neopets (video game) 56
Nepal 387
Nespoli, Paolo (Italian astronaut) 38
Nesting shelves (for birds) 148
Netherlands 387
Newbery Medal (children's literature) 302–3
New Brunswick (province, Canada) 394
New Deal (program of Franklin D. Roosevelt) 224
Newfoundland and Labrador (province, Canada) 394
New Horizons (spacecraft) 142
New7Wonders Foundation 212
New Seven Wonders of the World 212–15
Newton, Sir Isaac (English scientist) 131
New York 120, 223
New York City 234, 287
New York Historical Society 272
New Zealand 20, 78, 120, 169, 387
Ne-Yo (American singer and songwriter) 280
Nicaragua 387
Nicholson, Jack (American actor), *picture* 260
Nicholson, Jim (American public official) 36
Nickelodeon (television network) 56, 240–41, 247
Niedermayer, Scott (Canadian athlete) 183, 185, *picture* 183
Niger 387
Nigeria 24, 229, 388
Night monkeys 92, *picture* 92
Nine Inch Nails (music group) 278
Niyazov, Saparmurat (president of Turkmenistan) 20
Nobel Prizes 37, 69
Noonan, Frederick J. (American navigator) 210, 211, *picture* 209
No Reservations (movie) 267, *picture* 267
North America see Canada; Mexico; United States
North Carolina 36, 226, 228, 229
Northern Ireland 22, 70
Northern Lights (Aurora borealis) 140, *picture* 142
North Korea see Korea, North
Northwest Territories (Canada) 395
Norway 388

Nova Scotia (province, Canada) 394
Nowitzki, Dirk (German athlete) 178, *picture* 176
Nuclear weapons 47, 64–65
Nunavut (territory in Canada) 395
Nursery managers 235

O

Obasanjo, Olusegun (president of Nigeria) 24
Ocean 20, 107, 108, *picture* 20
Ocean's Thirteen (movie) 263
O'Connor, Sandra Day (U.S. Supreme Court Justice) 202
Octopus, *picture* 108
O'Dorney, Evan (American student), *picture* 247
Ohio, *picture* 137
Oil *see* Petroleum
Oil spills 39
Olivas, John (American astronaut) 28
Olmert, Ehud (prime minister of Israel) 39, 66, *picture* 66
Olympic Games, Winter (2010) 169
Olympic Games, Winter (2014) 195
Oman 388
Ontario (province, Canada) 394
Opechancanough (Native American chief) 201
Opera 381, 382–83
Opium poppies 43
Opportunity (space probe) 142
Oranges, cold damage to, *picture* 18
Orangutans 82, 376, *pictures* 83, 103
Oregon 120
Orioles (birds) *picture* 150
Oswalt, Patton (American actor) 264
Ottawa Senators (hockey team) 183–85
Owl monkeys 92, *picture* 92
Oxfam International 50

P

Paisley, Ian (first minister of Northern Ireland) 22
Pakistan 43–45, 388
Pak Pong Chu (premier of North Korea) 24
Palau 388
Paleontology 88, 90, 91, 132–37, *pictures* 30, 38
Palestinian Arabs 65–66
Palestinian National Authority (PNA) 39, 66
Panama 388
Pan American Games 190
Pandas 75, 82, *pictures* 74–75, 100
Panettiere, Hayden (American actress), *picture* 245
Paper stained glass, how to make 154–55
Papua New Guinea 388
Paraguay 388
Parazynski, Scott (American astronaut) 38
Paris (France) 283
Parker, Candace (American athlete) 178

Parker, Tony (American athlete) 176, 178, *picture* 176
Parrots 78
Patil, Pratibha (president of India) 30
Patron, Susan (American author) 302
Pavarotti, Luciano (Italian opera star) 381, *picture* 381
Peace
    Middle East conference 38–39, 66
    Nobel Prize in 37, 69
    stamps commemorating 159
Peake, James (American public official) 36
Peanut butter 150
Peavy, Jake (American athlete) 173
Peccaries, collared 81–82
Pedroia, Dustin (American athlete) 173
Pegasus (mythical winged horse) 90–91
Pelosi, Nancy (United States Representative) 69, *pictures* 19, 69
Penguins 324–28, *picture* 100
Pennsylvania 120, 175, 257
Penny from Heaven (book by Jennifer L. Holm) 302–3
Perdue, Sonny (governor of Georgia) 36
Peres, Shimon (president of Israel) 28
Perham, Michael (British sailor) 192–93, *picture* 193
Peru 32, 124, 215, 388, *picture* 215
Pesticides 237, 239
Petra (Jordan) 213, *picture* 213
Petraeus, David (American general) 49
Petrified fossils 132
Pet rocks 219, *picture* 219
Petroleum 63
Pets 23, 347, 365, 370
Pezak 49
Pfeiffer, Michelle (American actress) 264
Phare Tower (Paris, France) 283, *picture* 283
Phelps, Michael (American athlete) 187, *picture* 187
Philadelphia (Pennsylvania) 257
Philip (Duke of Edinburgh) 27, 203
Philippines 166, 388
Phoenix (mythical bird) 90
Phoenix Mercury (basketball team) 178
Photography, plant-related 239
Physics, Nobel Prize in 37
Physiology, Nobel Prize in 37
Pigs 81–82, 158, 169
Pigs, Bay of (Cuba) 59
Pirates 40, 226–29
Pirates of the Caribbean: At World's End (movie) 262
Plants
    careers working with 232–39
    fossils 132, 133, 136
    gardening to attract birds 146–47
    water lilies 122–27
Play (of animals) 75, 76–83, *picture* 74–75
Pluto (dwarf planet) 142
Pluto, new meaning for word 18
Pocahontas (Native American princess) 199, 201, 202, *pictures* 201, 202
Podcasts 55–56
Poetry 127, 312–13
Pokémon 221, *picture* 221

Poland 29, 36, 388
Polar bears 83, 109, *pictures* 83, 99, 109
Polar regions 108
Police (music group) 279
Poliomyelitis (Infantile paralysis) (virus disease) 223
Pollination (of plants) 124, 125–26
Pollution *see* Environment
Polo, Marco (Italian explorer) 116
Pondexter, Cappie (American athlete) 178, *picture* 178
Ponies, wild 31
Pop music 276–77
Portland (Maine) 257
Portland (Oregon) 120
Portugal 388
Potter, Beatrix (British author) 158
Potter, Harry (fictional character) 256–59, *picture* 254–55
Poverty in Africa 68
Powhatan (Native American chief) 199, 201, 202, *picture* 201
Prehistoric people, fossil of 136
Presidents (of the United States)
   coins depicting 168
   election (2008) 53, *picture* 54
Pressel, Morgan (American athlete) 182, *picture* 182
Primates 76, 78, 82
Prince (American musician) 277
Prince Edward Island (province, Canada) 394
Prinz, Birgit (German athlete) 191, *picture* 191
Prisms 131
Privacy and the World Wide Web 57
Privateers 227
Prizes and awards
   Academy Awards 260–61
   Caldecott Medal 302, 303
   Emmy Awards 274–75
   Grammy Awards 281
   Intel Science Talent Search winner, *picture* 246
   Kids' Choice Awards 240–41
   National Geographic Bee winner, *picture* 243
   National Spelling Bee winner, *picture* 247
   Newbery Medal 302–3
   Nobel Prizes 37
Prodi, Romano (premier of Italy), *picture* 29
Projects *see* Hobbies, handicrafts, and projects
Pronghorns 77
Protestantism 22
Psoriasis 131
Purple martins (birds) 148
Putin, Vladimir (president of Russia) 29, 30, 34, 40, 62–63, *pictures* 29, 62
Puzzles 152–53, 160–61, 221
Pyramids of Giza 212

Q–R

Qaeda, Al *see* Al Qaeda
Qatar 388
Quebec (province, Canada) 395

Queen Anne's Revenge (Blackbeard's ship) 226, 228, 229, *picture* 228
Questions and answers, Web site on 248
Radcliffe, Daniel (British actor) 257, *pictures* 257, 258, 259
Radio 56, 224
Radiohead (music group) 279
Railroads 24, 28, *picture* 24
Ramos-Horta, José (president of East Timor) 26
Rascal Flatts (music group) 280
Ratatouille (movie) 264, *picture* 264
Rats 78, 82
Ravens 78, 83
Reading, Web site on 249
Recalls of products 23
Recipes 119, 166–67
Record holders
   biggest fossil bug ever found, *picture* 38
   Earhart, Amelia, aviation firsts of 208, 210
   Faust, Drew Gilpin, first woman president of Harvard University 72
   first time that two women were in charge of two spacecraft at the same time 38, 138
   Fossett, Steve, death of 379
   French bullet train, fastest railed vehicle 24
   High School Musical 2, all-time most watched basic cable program 243, 283
   Honus Wagner baseball card selling price 195
   Larson, Samantha, mountain climbing records of 192
   Lötschberg Base Tunnel. longest rail tunnel on land 28
   Morgan, Barbara, first educator-astronaut in space 139
   Patil, Pratibha, first woman president of India 30
   Pelosi, Nancy, first female Speaker of the House of Representatives 69
   Perham, Michael, youngest person to sail solo across the Atlantic 192–93
   Robinson, Jackie, first African American in Major League Baseball 192
   Thumbelina, world's smallest living horse, *picture* 103
   Williams, Sunita, stayed in space longer than any other woman 28
Refugees 50, 67, *picture* 50
Reilly, James (American astronaut) 28
R.E.M. (music group) 281
Reproduction 102
Rhinoceroses 81, 136, *picture* 81
Rhythm and blues music 279–80
Richards, Dakota Blue (British actress) 263, *picture* 263
Rickman, Alan (British actor) 257
Rihanna (Barbadian singer) 279
Rio de Janeiro (Brazil) 215, *picture* 215
Ripley's Believe It or Not! Odditorium (New York City) 287
Rizzuto, Phil (American athlete) 382, *picture* 382
Robb, AnnaSophia (American actress) 263
Roberts, Bartholomew (British pirate) 228
Roberts, Emma (American actress) 263
"Robin Hood and the Shooting Match" (story) 314–22

Robins 148, 149
Robinson, Jackie (American athlete) 192, *picture* 192
Robots 28, *picture* 28
Roc (mythical bird) 90, *picture* 90
Rock and Roll Hall of Fame 281
Rock music 277–79
Rocks 132, 134, 136, 137
Rodents 347, 365, 370
Rodriguez, Alex (American athlete) 173, *picture* 173
Rolfe, John (English colonist) 200, 202
Rollins, Jimmy (American athlete) 173, *picture* 173
Roman Catholic Church 22
Romania 18, 388
Romano, Lou (American actor) 264
Rome (Italy) 214, *picture* 214
Rome, ancient 116
Romeo and Juliet (play by Shakespeare) 21
Ronettes (music group) 281
Roosevelt, Eleanor (wife of Franklin D. Roosevelt) 211, 222, 223, *picture* 223
Roosevelt, Franklin D. (32nd president of the United States) 222–25, *pictures* 222, 223, 225
Roosevelt, Theodore (26th president of the United States) 222
Rose, Anika Noni (American actress) 267, *picture* 261
Rostropovich, Mstislav (Russian musician) 382
Rowling, J. K. (British author) 255, 256, 257, *picture* 257
Roy, Brandon (American athlete) 178
Rubik's Cube 219, *picture* 219
Rudd, Kevin (prime minister of Australia) 39
Rules (book by Cynthia Lord) 302
Russia 62–63, 388 *see also* Union of Soviet Socialist Republics
    APEC summit 34
    coins 169
    frozen mammoth carcass 30
    Group of Eight 29
    Korea, North, talks with 65
    oil spill 39
    space program 138, 143
    treaty suspension 30
    Winter Olympic Games (2014) 195
    Yeltsin, Boris, death of 383
Rwanda 388

S

Sabathia, C.C. (American athlete) 173
Saddam Hussein (president of Iraq) *see* Hussein, Saddam
Safety
    cheerleading 194
    Chinese product recalls 23
    World Wide Web 57
Sailing 192–93
St. Kitts and Nevis 388
St. Lucia 388

St. Vincent and the Grenadines 388
Salt, superstition about 206
Samoa 28, 388
San Antonio Spurs (basketball team) 176–78
San Francisco (California) 234
San Marino 388
São Tomé and Príncipe 388
Sarandon, Susan (American actress) 265
Sarkozy, Nicolas (president of France) 26–27, 71, *picture* 29, *picture* 71
Saskatchewan (province, Canada) 395
Sasquatch (legendary ape-man) 88
Saturn (planet) 142–43
Saudi Arabia 45, 66, 388
Schafer, Edward (American public official) 36
Schirra, Walter (Wally), Jr. (American astronaut) 382, *picture* 382
Schlesinger, Arthur M., Jr. (American historian) 382
Schools *see* Education
School shootings 25
Schössel, Wolfgang (chancellor of Austria) 18
Schwarzenegger, Arnold (governor of California) 38
Science
    botany 232
    "child" robot 28, *picture* 28
    cool Web sites 248, 249
    fossils 132–37
    global warming 106–11
    ice cream 116–21
    Intel Science Talent Search winner, *picture* 246
    International Polar Year 108
    light and health 128–31
    Nobel prizes 37
    steamboats, invention of 112–15, *picture* 104–5
    World Wide Web 52–57
Scotland 30, 45, 127
Scouting movement, stamps and coins commemorating 157–58, 169
Sculpture *see* Christ the Redeemer
Sea cows *see* Manatees
Search engines (on the World Wide Web) 52
Sea scorpion, ancient, *picture* 38
Sea serpents (mythical animals) 89
Seasonal Affective Disorder (SAD) 128–29
Sea stars, *picture* 108
Seattle (Washington) 234
Sea urchin, fossil, *picture* 134
Sedimentary rocks 132, 137
Seeds (for feeding birds) 149, 150
Seinfeld, Jerry (American actor) 264
Selanne, Teemu (Finnish athlete) 183
Self-fertilization 102
Senate, United States 390
Senegal 388
Serbia 388
Seven Wonders of the World, New 212–15
Seychelles 388
Sezer, Ahmet Necdet (president of Turkey) 33
Shannon, Molly (American actress) 267
Sharif, Nawaz (prime minister of Pakistan) 44, 45
Sheep 81, *picture* 80
Shi'ite Muslims 46, 48, 49, 50

Ships, pirate 225–29
Shootings 25
Shrek the Third (movie) 262
Sierra Leone 35, 388
Sills, Beverly (American opera singer) 382–83, *picture* 383
Simpsons Movie, The (movie) 265, *picture* 265
Singapore 169, 388
Sirico, Tony (American actor), *picture* 274
Skating *see* Hockey; Ice skating
Skiing 186
Skyscrapers (tall buildings) 283
Sleep 129
Slovakia 388
Slovenia 39, 388
Slugs (gastropods) 93, *picture* 93
"Smiley face" emoticon, *picture* 34
Smith, John (English soldier and explorer) 199, 201, 202, *pictures* 199, 201
Smith, Patti (American musician) 281
Smithies, Oliver (British scientist) 37
Snaring, Caitlin (American student), *picture* 243
Snow, Brittany (American actress) 266
Soccer 190–91
Sochi (Russia) 195
Social-networking sites (on the World Wide Web) 56–57, *pictures* 57
Society and the World Wide Web 57
Soda fountains 119
Solar panels 140
Solomon Islands 158, 388
Somalia 229, 388
Sopranos, The (television program), *picture* 274
Soulja Boy (American rapper) 279
South Africa 68, 388
South America 127, 238 *see also* names of countries
South Carolina 36
South Korea *see* Korea, South
Soyuz (Russian spacecraft) 138
Space junk 143
Space probes 140
Space programs 138–43, 169
    missions 28, 32, 38
    Schirra, Walter (Wally), Jr., death of 382
Space shuttles *see* names of space shuttles
Space suits 141
Spader, James (American actor), *picture* 275
Spain 58, 167, 336, 388
Spanish-American War (1898) 58, 61
Spears, Britney (American singer) 277
Special effects (in motion pictures) 263
Spectrographs 246
Spectrum 131
Speleers, Edward (British actor) 263
Spelling Bee, National, winner, *picture* 247
Spider-Man 3 (movie) 262, *picture* 262
Spider web, enormous 35, *picture* 35
Spirit (space probe) 142
Spoon (music group) 277
Sports
    baseball 172–74, 192, 195
    basketball 176–78
    cheerleading safety 194
    football 179–81
    golf 182
    handball 337–38
    hockey 183–85
    ice skating 186
    Little League baseball 175
    marathon 193
    mountain climbing 192
    Olympic Games, Winter (2014) 195
    Pan American Games 190
    sailing 192–93
    skiing 186
    soccer 190–91
    swimming 187
    tennis 188–89
Springsteen, Bruce (American musician) 279
Sputnik (Soviet satellite) 139, 169
Squid (animals) 20, 89, *pictures* 20, 88
Squirrels 78, 149, *picture* 77
Sri Lanka 389
Stained glass 154–55, 268–73
Stalin, Joseph (Soviet dictator), *picture* 225
Stamp collecting 156–59
Stardust (movie) 264
Starfish *see* Sea stars
"Starving time" (in Jamestown) 200
Star Wars **movies, stamps commemorating** 156
State of the Union address 19
Stauffenberg, Claus von (German colonel) 290–301
Steamboats 112–15, *pictures* 104–5, 112, 115
Steam engines 114
Step It Up! (environmental group) 110–11
Stiller, Ben (American actor) 241
Stone, Joss (British singer) 279, *picture* 280
Streaming media 53, 56
Strobel, Gary (American biologist) 237, *picture* 237
Sturckow, Frederick (American astronaut) 28
Substorms 140
Sudan 67, 389
Sudoku (number puzzles) 221, *picture* 221
Suet (animal fat) 149, 150
Sunflowers 146
Sunlight 128, 130
Sunni Muslims 46, 48, 49, 50
Superstitions 204–7
Supreme Court, United States 393
Suriname 389
Susan Constant (ship) 198
Su Tseng-chang (premier of Taiwan) 27
Swank, Hilary (American actress) 267, *picture* 267
Swanson, Steven (American astronaut) 28
Swaziland 389
Sweden 389
Swift, Taylor (American musician) 280
Swimming 187
Switzerland 28, 389
Sydney Declaration on Climate Change 34
Syria 50, 66, 389

T

Taiwan 27, 389
Tajikistan 389
Taj Mahal 212, *picture* 212
Taliban (former ruling force in Afghanistan) 42–43
Tani, Daniel (American astronaut) 38
Tanzania 389
Tar, fossils in 133
Taxes, carbon 109
Taxol (drug) 237
Tebow, Tim (American athlete) 180–81, *picture* 181
Technology
    "child" robot 28, *picture* 28
    giant magnetoresistance (GMR) 37
    space suits 141
    steamboats, invention of 112–15, *picture* 104–5
    World Wide Web 52–57
Teddy bears 217, *picture* 217
Teenagers *see* Youth
Television
    Are You Smarter Than a 5th Grader? 287
    Bindi: The Jungle Girl 244
    Bishop, Joey, death of 378
    Browne, Roscoe Lee, death of 378–79
    Cyrus, Miley 244
    Emmy Awards 274–75
    Griffin, Merv, death of 379
    High School Musical 2, all-time most watched basic cable program 243, 283
    Kids' Choice Awards 240–41
    Naked Brothers Band, The 247
    Neopets characters 56
    Wyman, Jane, death of 383
Temperature *see* Global warming
Tennessee 36
Tennessee, University of 178
Tennis 188–89, *picture* 170–71
Terrorism *see also* Bombings; Terrorist attacks on the United States
    Germany, plot discovery in 34
    Guantánamo Bay detention center 61
    Islamic militants 42–47
    United Kingdom 30
    war on 19
Terrorist attacks on the United States (September 11, 2001, and following events) 42, 51
Texas 35, 120
Thailand 389
Thayendanegea (Native American) 169
Theater
    Browne, Roscoe Lee, death of 378–79
    Goulet, Robert, death of 379
    "Walking With Dinosaurs" show 282
THEMIS mission 140, *picture* 142
Thicke, Robin (American singer) 279
30 Rock (television program), *picture* 275
Thousand and One Nights 304

Thrashers (birds), *picture* 151
Through the Looking-Glass (book by Lewis Carroll) 287
Thumbelina (miniature horse), *picture* 103
Tiffany, Louis Comfort (American artist and glassmaker) 156–57, 268–73
Tigers, *picture* 99, 103
TIGHAR (The International Group for Historic Aircraft Recovery) 209
Timbaland (American record producer) 280, *picture* 280
Timberlake, Justin (American singer) 241, 280, *picture* 240
Timor, East *see* East Timor
Tisdale, Ashley (American actress) 283
Titan (moon of Saturn) 143
Tobacco 200
Togo 389
Tonga 389
Topi, Bamir (president of Albania) 30
Tornadoes 20, 26
Toys and games 216–21
T-Pain (American singer) 279
Trade, international 18, 115
Trains *see* Railroads
Transformers, The (movie) 264
Transportation *see also* Automobiles; Aviation; Railroads
    steamboats 112–15, *picture* 104–5
Travolta, John (American actor) 266, *picture* 266
Treaty on Conventional Armed Forces in Europe 30
Trees 109, 146, 238–39
Trilobites (ancient animals) 136
Trinidad & Tobago 389
Tubman, Harriet (American abolitionist leader) 303
Tuiatua Tupua Tamasese Efi (head of state of Samoa) 28
Tunisia 389
Tunnels 28
Türk, Danilo (president of Slovenia) 39
Turkey 33, 46, 49, 389
Turkmenistan 20, 389
Tusk, Donald (premier of Poland) 36
Tuvalu 169, 389
Twain, Mark (American writer) 269
Tyrannosaurus rex 135

U–V

Uganda 389
Ugly Betty (television program), *picture* 275
Ukraine 39, 389
Ultraviolet light 130, 131
Underwood, Carrie (American singer) 280, *picture* 281
Unicorns (mythical animals) 87–88, *picture* 87
Union of Soviet Socialist Republics (1921–1991) 59, 60, 139 *see also* Russia
United Arab Emirates 389
United Kingdom 389
    coins 169

Diana, princess of Wales, 10th anniversary of death of 73
Elizabeth II's U.S. visit 27
Group of Eight 29
Iraq War 50
Komodo dragon in zoo 102
leadership change 28, 70
Northern Ireland 22
"Robin Hood and the Shooting Match" (story) 314–22
stamps 157, 158, 159
terrorism 30, 45
United Nations
   all-woman peacekeeping force 67
   Ban Ki-moon, Secretary-General of 18
   Darfur 67
   global-warming studies 106–10
   Khalilzad, Zalmay, U.S. ambassador to 24
   Kirkpatrick, Jeane, death of 380
   North Korean sanctions 65
   Roosevelt, Franklin D. 225
   stamps 159
   Waldheim, Kurt, death of 383
United States 389
   coins 168–69
   Cuba, relations with 58–61
   government 390–93
   Group of Eight 29
   ice cream 120
   Iraq War 48–51
   Jamestown, 400th anniversary of founding of 27, 152, 156, 197, 198–203, *pictures* 196–97, 198, 200
   Johnson, Lady Bird, death of 380
   Korea, North, talks with 65
   Kyoto Protocol 110
   missile-defense plans 29, 30
   Pan American Games 190
   pirates, chasing and catching of 229
   Roosevelt, Franklin D. 222–25
   space program 28, 32, 38, 138–43
   stamps 156–57, 159
   State of the Union address 19
   terrorism, war on 42, 43, 44, 47
   terrorist attacks on *see* Terrorist attacks on the United States
Unity (space station module) 139
Uruguay 22, 389
Utah 168
Uzbekistan 389
Vall, Ely Ould Mohamed (president of Mauritania) 22
Vancouver (Canada) 169
Vanderbilt, Cornelius (American industrialist) 270, 271
Van Halen (music group) 281
Vanuatu 389
Van Zandt, Steven (American actor), *picture* 274
Vases, Tiffany 273, *pictures* 271
Vatican City 389
Vaughn, Vince (American actor) 241
Vegetables, word puzzles about 160–61
Venezuela 63–64, 389
Vermont 250–51, 253, 265
Vesta (asteroid) 140

Veterans Affairs, United States Department of 36
Video games 56, *picture* 230–31
Videos 53, 55
Vietnam 158, 389
Vietnam Veterans Memorial (Washington, D.C.) 284, *picture* 284
Vigneault, Alain (Canadian hockey coach) 185
Vike-Freiberga, Vaira (president of Latvia) 27
Violence *see* Crime; Terrorism
Virginia 25, 31, 228, 229 *see also* Jamestown
Virginia Polytechnic Institute and State University 25
Virgin Islands, British 169
Vonnegut, Kurt (American novelist) 383

W

Wagner, Honus (American athlete) 195, *picture* 195
Waldheim, Kurt (Austrian diplomat and politician) 383
"Walking With Dinosaurs–The Live Experience" (show) 282
Wall of China, Great 213, *picture* 213
Washington (D.C.) 284
Washington (state) 168
Washington, George (1st president of the United States) 252
Water 36, 142, 151
Water lilies 122–27, *pictures* 122, 123, 124, 126
Watson, Emma (British actress) 257, *pictures* 257, 258, 259
Watt, James (Scottish inventor) 114
Weasels 82
Weather 20, *picture* 18
Weatherford, Carole Boston (American author) 303
Webb, Jim (United States Senator) 19
Web browsers (computer programs) 52
Weber, Bernard (Swiss businessman) 212
West, Kanye (American rapper) 280
West Bank 65, 66
Westminster Kennel Club show winner, *picture* 101
Whales 78, 87, *picture* 87
Wheelock, Douglas (American astronaut) 38
Whitaker, Forest (American actor), *picture* 261
White House (Washington, D.C.) 270
White Stripes (music group) 278
Whitson, Peggy (American astronaut) 38, 138
Whydah (pirate ship) 227
Wiesner, David (American author and illustrator) 303
Wifi (wireless networks) 53
Wikis (Web sites) 55
Wildlife *see* Animals
will.i.am (American musician) 279
William (prince of England) 73, *picture* 73
Williams, Dafydd (Canadian astronaut) 32
Williams, Lucinda (American musician) 281
Williams, Serena (American athlete) 188
Williams, Sunita (American astronaut) 28

Williams, Venus (American athlete) 189
Wilson, Gretchen (American musician) 281
Wilson, Stephanie (American astronaut) 38
Wind farms 283
Winehouse, Amy (British singer) 279
Winfrey, Oprah (American entertainer) 68,
    picture 68
Winstone, Ray (British actor) 265
Wisconsin, University of 185
Wishes, superstitions about 207
Wolff, Nat and Alex (American actors), *picture*
    247
Wolves 76, 78, 79, 82, *picture* 79
Women
    Driscoll, Clara, glassworker 272
    Earhart, Amelia, aviator 208–11
    Faust, Drew Gilpin, first woman president of
      Harvard University 72
    first time that two women were in charge of
      two spacecraft at the same time 38, 138
    Henin, Justine, tennis player 189
    Larson, Samantha, mountain climbing records
      of 192
    Pelosi, Nancy, first female Speaker of the
      House of Representatives 69
    Pressel, Morgan, golfer 182
    sports 178, 182, 185, 186, 188–89, 191
    U.N. peacekeeping force 67
    Williams, Sunita, stayed in space longer than
      any other woman 28
    Winfrey, Oprah, and girls' schools in Africa 68
"Wonder drugs" 237
Work productivity 129
World, New Seven Wonders of the 212–15
World Cup (women's soccer) 191, *picture* 191
World records *see* Record holders
World's Columbian Exposition (1893, Chicago)
    272
World Series (baseball) 172–73
    Little League 175
World's fairs 272, 273
World War II 224–25, 290–301
World Wide Web 52–57
    cool Web sites 248–49
Wrens 147–48
Writing, plant-related 239
Wyman, Jane (American actress) 383
Wyoming 168

Carroll, Lewis 287
Flotsam (book by David Wiesner) 303
*Gone Wild: An Endangered Animal
    Alphabet* (book by David McLimans) 303
Harry Potter books (by J. K. Rowling)
    256–59, *picture* 254–55
Hattie Big Sky (book by Kirby Lawson) 303
Higher Power of Lucky, The (book by Susan
    Patron) 302
L'Engle, Madeleine, death of 381
Misty of Chincoteague (book by Marguerite
    Henry) 31
*Moses: When Harriet Tubman Led Her
    People to Freedom* (book by Carole
    Boston Weatherford) 303
movies based on 263
Penny from Heaven (book by Jennifer L.
    Holm) 302–3
"Plot Against Hitler, The" (story) 290–301
    poetry 312–13
"Robin Hood and the Shooting Match" (story)
    314–22
Rules (book by Cynthia Lord) 302
Youth
    cheerleading safety 194
    "child" robot 28, *picture* 28
    Circus Smirkus 250–53
    cool Web sites 248–49
    exercising with video games, *picture* 230–31
    happiness 242
    Kids' Choice Awards 240–41
    Larson, Samantha, mountain climbing records
      of 192
    Little League baseball 175
    newsmakers, *pictures* 242–47
    Perham, Michael, youngest person to sail solo
      across the Atlantic 192–93
    Pressel, Morgan, golfer 182
    social-networking sites 56–57
YouTube (Web site) 53, *picture* 54
Yukon (territory, Canada) 395
Zambia 389
Zamka, George (American astronaut) 38
Zatlers, Valdis (president of Latvia) 27
Zellweger, Renée (American actress) 264
Zeta-Jones, Catherine (British actress) 267,
    picture 267
Zimbabwe 389
Zoos 97

Y–Z

Yar'Adua, Umaru Musa (president of Nigeria)
    24
Year of the Dog (movie) 267
Yeltsin, Boris (president of Russia) 383, *picture*
    383
Yemen 389
Yeti (legendary ape-man) 88
Yorkshire terriers, *picture* 101
Young people's literature
    "Aladdin and the Wonderful Lamp" (story)
      304–11

ILLUSTRATION CREDITS AND ACKNOWLEDGMENTS

The following list credits or acknowledges, by page, the source of illustrations and text excerpts used in this work. Illustration credits are listed illustration by illustration—left to right, top to bottom. When two or more illustrations appear on one page, their credits are separated by semicolons. When both the photographer or artist and an agency or other source are given for an illustration, they are usually separated by a slash. Excerpts from previously published works are listed by inclusive page numbers.

6   © John Cancalosi/Peter Arnold, Inc.; © Alan L. Detrick/Photo Researchers, Inc.; Bob D'Amico/© Disney Channel/Everett Collection

7   © Jupiterimages/AP Photo; © Clive Brunskill/ Getty Images; © The Gallery Collection/Corbis

12-13   © Chris Hondros/Getty Images

14   © Jonathan Hayward, CP/AP Photo; © Junko Kimura/Getty Images

15   © Khalid Mohammed/AP Photo; © Ibraheem Abu Mustafa/Reuters/Newscom

16   © RIA-Novosti, Dimitry Astakhov, Presidential Press Service/AP Photo; © Charlie Riedel/AP Photo

17   NASA; © Jason Kempin/FilmMagic/Getty Images

18   © Gary Kazanjian/AP Photo

19   © Larry Downing/AP Photo

20   © New Zealand Ministry of Fisheries/Handout/epa/Corbis; © New Zealand Ministry of Fisheries/Getty Images

21   © Archaeological Society SAP/AP Photo

22   © David Kadlubowski/Corbis

23   © Charlie Riedel/AP Photo

24   © Francois Mori/AP Photo

25   © Mario Tama/Getty Images

26   © Yaacov Sa'ar/GPO/AP Photo

27   © Tim Graham/AP Photo

28   © Koji Ueda/AP Photo

29   © Misha Japaridze/AP Photo

30   © Sergei Cherkashin/Reuters/Landov

31   © Mark Wilson/Getty Images

32   © Mandel Ngan/AFP/Getty Images

33   © John Kolesidis/Reuters/Landov; © Petros Giannakouris/AP Photo

34   © Gene J. Puskar/AP Photo

35   © Donna Garde, Texas Parks & Wildlife

36   © John Bazemore/AP Photo

37   © Juan Martin/epa/Corbis

38   © University of Bristol/AP Photo

39   © Sergei Grits/AP Photo; © The Chronicle/Reuters/Landov

40   © Jewel Samad/AFP/Getty Images

42   © Massoud Hossaini/AFP/Getty Images/Newscom

43   © Rahamt Gul/AP Photo; © David Guttenfelder/AP Photo

44   © PID/Dean Pictures/Newscom

45   © Mark Runnacles/AFP/Getty Images

46   © Burak Kara/Getty Images

47   © Sipa via AP Photo

48   © Khalid Mohammed/AP Photo

49   © Ibrahim Usta/AP Photo

50   © Wisam Sami/AP Photo

51   © Ahmad Al-Rubaye/AFP/Getty Images

52   © Jupiterimages/AP Photo

53   © Dennis MacDonald/PhotoEdit, Inc.

54   © Stan Honda/AFP/Getty Images; © David Young-Wolff/PhotoEdit, Inc.; Courtesy, http://smallbitesnutrition.blogspot.com/

55   © Joe Crocetta, The Herald-Mail/AP Photo; Courtesy, www.wookiepedia.com

56   Courtesy, www.neopets.com

57   © Colin Young-Wolff/PhotoEdit, Inc.; © Jeff Adkins, News Sentinel/AP Photo

58   © Sven Creutzmann/Mambo Photography/Getty Images

59   © Carl Mydans/Time & Life Pictures/Getty Images

60   © Joe Sohm/Visions of America/Digital Vision/Getty Images; © James L. Stanfield/National Geographic Image Collection; © Mariana Bazo/Reuters/Corbis

61   © Chip Somodevilla/Getty Images

62   © RIA-Novosti, Dimitry Astakhov, Presidential Press Service/AP Photo

63   © Francesco Spotorno/Reuters/Newscom

64   © AFP/Getty Images

65   © Xia Yu, Xinhua/AP Photo

66   © Ibraheem Abu Mustafa/Reuters/Newscom; © Susan Walsh/AP Photo

67   © Nasser Nasser/AP Photo; © Raveendran/AFP/Getty Images

68   AP Photo; © Michelly Rall/WireImage/Getty Images

69   © Chip Somodevilla/Getty Images; © Junko Kimura/Getty Images

70   © Hugo Philpott/epa/Corbis; © Andy Rain/epa/Corbis

71   © Romuald Meigneux/AFP/Getty Image; © Christian Stavel/epa/Corbis

72   © Itsuo Inouye/AP Photo; © Jodi Hilton/Getty Images

73   © Tim Graham/Corbis; © Stephen Hird/Reuters/Corbis

74-75   © Daniel A. Bedell/Animals Animals

76   © Joe McDonald/Animals Animals

77   © David Fritts/Animals Animals; © Lightwave Photography, Inc./Animals Animals

78   © Fritz Polking/Peter Arnold, Inc.

79   © Leonard Rue Enterprises/Animals Animals; © Tim Davis/Photo Researchers, Inc.

80   © Biosphoto/Ferrero J.P. & Labat J.M./Peter Arnold, Inc.; © Mark Newman/Bruce Coleman, Inc.

81   © Greg Gilman/Taxi/Getty Images; © Johnny Johnson/Animals Animals

82   © Fritz Polking/Bruce Coleman, Inc.

83   © Theo Allofs/Visuals Unlimited; © Norbert Rosing/National Geographic Image Collection

84   © E.R. Degginger/Animals Animals

85   © Gerry Broome/AP Photo; © Janet Hamlin/ AP Photo

86   © New Vision Technologies, Inc./Digital Vision/Getty Images

87   © Jacana/Photo Researchers, Inc.; © D. Fleetham/OSF/Animals Animals

88   © Mary Evans Picture Library; © Tsunemi Kubodera of the National Science Museum of Japan/AP Photo

89   The Granger Collection; © DAJ/Getty Images

90   The Granger Collection; © Joe Tucciarone/Photo Researchers, Inc.

91   The Granger Collection

92   © Nick Garbutt/npl/Minden Pictures; © Luiz C. Marigo/Peter Arnold, Inc.

93   © Art Wolfe/Photo Researchers, Inc.; © Fred Bavendam/Minden Pictures

94   © Mitsuaki Iwago/Minden Pictures

95   © Steven David Miller/Animals Animals

96   © John Cancalosi/Peter Arnold, Inc.

97   © Shin Yoshino/Minden Pictures; © photolibrary.com pty. ltd./Photo via Newscom

98   © Theo Allofs/Corbis

99   © Lu Chuanquan, Xinhua/AP Photo; © John MacDougall/AFP/Getty Images

100   © Paul Souders/Corbis; © Gene Blythe/AP Photo; © Zoe/zefa/Corbis; © Brandon D. Cole/ Corbis

101   © Jorg & Petra Wegner/Animals Animals; © Mario Tama/Getty Images

102   © Dave Thompson/AP Photo; AP Photo

103   © Brad Barket/Getty Images; © Achmad Ibrahim/AP Photo

104-05   The Granger Collection

106   © 2007 Amanda Byrd/AlaskaStock.com

107   © T. Balabaadkan - UNEP/Peter Arnold, Inc.; © Reinhard Dirscherl/Bruce Coleman, Inc.; © Jeff Haynes/AFP/Getty Images; © Frans Lanting/Corbis

108   © Elaina Jorgensen/AFP/Getty Images; © Pablo J. López, CLIMANT-ECOANTHA, 2007

109   © Jonathan Hayward, CP/AP Photo; © Steve Sack/Star Tribune

110   © Chris Polk/AP Photo

111   © George Riley/AP Photo

112   Bettmann/Corbis

113   The Granger Collection

115   The Granger Collection

116   © Westlight Stock – OZ Productions/Corbis

117   © Tom Barrett

118   The Granger Collection

119   © Charles Phillips; © John McGrail

120   © J. Barry O'Rourke/Corbis

121   © Paolo Negri/Photodisc/Getty Images

122   © Edward Kinsman/Photo Researchers, Inc.

123   © Cisca Castelijns/Foto Naura/Minden Pictures; © Gerry Ellis/Minden Pictures;

© Collection of the New York Historical Society, USA/The Bridgeman Art Library

273 © Christie's Images Ltd.

274 Craig Blackenhorn/© HBO/Everett Collection

275 Ron Tom/© ABC/Everett Collection; Mario Perez/© ABC/Everett Collection; Eric Liebowitz/© NBC/Everett Collection

276 © Sara De Boer/Retna Ltd.

277 © David Atlas/Retna Ltd.

278 © Bryan Bedder/Getty Images; © Chris Daniels/Retna Ltd.

279 Retna Ltd.

280 © Trish Tokar/Getty Images; Retna, Ltd.

281 © Kevord Djansezian/AP Photo

282 © Frank Mullen/WireImage/Getty Images

283 Fred Hayes/© Disney Channel/Everett Collection; © Unibail-Morphosis/AP Photo

284 © Global Book Publishing/The Art Archive; © Layne Kennedy/Corbis

285 © Archivo Iconografico, S.A./Corbis; © The Gallery Collection/Corbis

286 Michael Yarish/TM and Copyright © 20th Century Fox Film Corp. All rights reserved, y Everett Collection; © Mary Altaffer/AP Photo

287 The Granger Collection

288-89 © Steven Mason/Photodisc/Getty Images

290 UPI/Bettmann/Corbis

291-301 Artist, Bill Farnsworth

302 © Simon & Schuster, Inc.; Rubber duck photograph © Gary Doak/Photonica; Goldfish detail © by G.K. and Vikki Hart/Iconica from the cover of RULES by Cynthia Lord. Scholastic Inc./Scholastic Press. Used by permission.; From PENNY FROM HEAVEN by Jennifer L. Holm © 2006. Used by permission of Random House Children's Books, a division of Random House, Inc.; From HATTIE BIG SKY by Kirby Larson © 2006. Used by permission of Dela-corte Press, a division of Random House, Inc.

303 Cover from FLOTSAM by David Wiesner. Jacket illustration copyright © 2006 by David Wiesner. Reprinted by permission of Clarion Books, an imprint of Houghton Mifflin Company. All rights reserved; Reprinted by permission of Walker & Co.; From MOSES: WHEN HARRIET TUBMAN LED HER PEOPLE TO FREE-DOM by Carole Boston Weatherford. Text copyright © 2006 by Carole Boston Weatherford. Illustrations copyright © 2006 by Kadir Nelson. Reprinted by permission of Hyperion Books for Children. All rights reserved.

304-11 Artist, Laurie Jordan

312-13 Artist, Michele A. McLean

314-32 Artist, David Wenzel

324-25 © Rick Price/Corbis

324 © Tim Davis/Corbis; © Eastcott/Momatiuk/ Animals Animals

325 © Ernie Janes/NHPA; © Paul Souders/ Corbis

326 © Joseph Van Os/Riser/Getty Images; © Bill Coster/NHPA

327 © Kevin Schafer/Corbis

328 © Andres Stapff/Reuters

329 © Lee Boltin; © Fred Salaff/FPG International

330 © James R. Pearson/FPG International; © Jim Pickerell

332 © Superstock, Inc.; © Jim Pickerell

333 © Bibliotheca Alexandrina/epa/Corbis

334 © Giraudon/Art Resource

335 © Mona Sharaf/Reuters/Corbis

336 The Granger Collection

337 © U.S. Handball Association

339 © Arthur Morris/Corbis; © Julian Herbert/ Reportage/Getty Images; © David B. Fleetham/ Oxford Scientific/Jupiterimages; © GK Hart and Vikki Hart/Stone/Getty Images; © Richard Gross/Corbis; © François Savigny/naturepl.com

340 © Zina Deretsky/National Science Foundation

345 © Sam Yeh/AFP/Getty Images

347 © Bernard Castelein/naturepl.com.; © Dennie Cody/Taxi/Getty Images

348 © Richard Price/Photographer's Choice/Getty Images

349 © Margot Granitsas/Photo Researchers, Inc.; © Yavuz Arslan/Peter Arnold, Inc.; © Wolfgang Maria Weber/Peter Arnold, Inc.; © Uschi Hering/ShutterStock, Inc.

350 © Guenter Rossenbach/zefa/Corbis

351 © ullstein bild/The Granger Collection; © Herbert Spichtinger/zefa/Corbis

352 © Jose Manuel Ribeiro/Reuters; © Empics/ SportsChrome USA; © Bob Krist/Corbis

353 © Paul Freytag/zefa/Corbis

354 © Atlantide Phototravel/Corbis; © Markus Dlouhy/Peter Arnold, Inc.

356 © Rainer Stratmann/AP Photo; © Armin Weigel/dpa/Corbis

357 © Philip Lange/ShutterStock, Inc.; © age fotostock/SuperStock

358 © Torsten Krueger/Peter Arnold, Inc.

359 The Granger Collection

362 Bettmann/Corbis; The Granger Collection

363 The Granger Collection

364 © Chip Hires/Liaison Agency/Getty Images; © Fritz Reiss/AP Photo

365 © H. Reinhard/Peter Arnold, Inc.; © Myrleen Ferguson Cate/PhotoEdit, Inc.

366 © Jockel Fink/AP Photo; © Dave G. Houser/Corbis

367 © Colin Young-Wolff/PhotoEdit, Inc.

369 © Torsten Krueger/Peter Arnold, Inc.; © age fotostock/SuperStock; © Alexandra Avakian/ Woodfin Camp & Associates

370 © Robert Maier/Animals Animals; © Robert Manella/Iconica/Getty Images

371 © Stewart Cohen/FoodPix/Jupiterimages

372 © age fotostock/SuperStock; © H. Reinhard/ Peter Arnold, Inc.; © Teck Siong Ong/ ShutterStock, Inc.

373 © SuperStock

375 © Joe Cavaretta/AP Photo

376 © Kevin Schafer/Riser/Getty Images

378 © Kevord Djansezian/AP Photo; © Sean Roberts/Everett Collection

379 © Everett Collection; © Frank Wolfe, LBJ Library/AP Photo

380 © John Springer Collection/Corbis; AP Photo

381 © Serena Campanini/Reuters/Corbis; © Dennis Van Tine/Landov

382 © Jeff Zelevansky/AP Photo; © NASA/AP Photo

383 © Everett Collection; © Dmitry Lovetsky/AP Photo

393 © Brooks Craft/Corbis

416